Encyclopedia
of Prophecy

Encyclopedia
of Prophecy

Geoffrey Ashe

ABC-CLIO
Santa Barbara, California
Denver, Colorado
Oxford, England

Library of Congress Cataloging-in-Publication Data
Ashe, Geoffrey.
   Encyclopedia of prophecy / Geoffrey Ashe.
     p. cm.
Includes bibliographical references and index.
   ISBN 1-57607-079-4 (alk. paper)—ISBN 1-57607-528-1 (e-book)
1. Prophecies (Occultism)—Encyclopedias. I. Title.
BF1786 .A84 2001
133.3'03—dc21

2001001067

06 05 04 03 02 01   10 9 8 7 6 5 4 3 2 1

This book is also available on the World Wide Web as an e-book. Visit abc-clio.com for details.

ABC-CLIO, Inc.
130 Cremona Drive, P.O. Box 1911
Santa Barbara, California 93116–1911

This book is printed on acid-free paper ∞.
Manufactured in the United States of America

CONTENTS

Preface, vii
Acknowledgments, ix

Encyclopedia of Prophecy

v

CONTENTS

PREFACE

The word *prophecy* originally meant "inspired utterance." A god or goddess or spirit or, at any rate, some unseen being other than the person inspired, spoke through that person. At first, prophecy did not imply foretelling the future, but that meaning developed, especially in Greece and in ancient Israel. Largely because the Israelite prophets' predictions were preserved in the Bible and because the Bible became a sacred book for many nations, the predictive meaning of prophecy came to predominate in the Western world.

Prophecy in the predictive sense, with or without a claim to inspiration, is the subject of this encyclopedia. A distinction is needed at the outset. The encyclopedia is not about intelligent anticipation or rational forecasting, such as that attempted by political journalists, economic prognosticators, statisticians, and scientists who project what they regard as historical and current trends into the future. Activity of this type enjoyed a special vogue between about 1965 and 1975, under the name of futurology. It is not considered here or is considered only marginally. One justification for considering other sorts of prediction is that the would-be rational sort has not been conspicuously successful. A fiasco that had repercussions was the failure of rational forecasters to forecast the downfall of the Communist empire in 1991. Most of them thought it would go from strength to strength. It is fair and relevant to add that on this great issue, when nearly all the experts were wrong, an obscure

Portuguese visionary (whose story is in this book) was right.

From the experts' point of view, most of the cases surveyed here would doubtless count as irrational. People are supposed to have acquired knowledge of the future through processes that may be closer to the old concept of inspiration: through a rapport with some divine or supernatural being, through clairvoyance, through dreams, or through some paranormal technique such as astrology. In all such cases, the encyclopedia is concerned with facts. It makes no prior assumption as to whether knowledge of the future really occurs or can occur. Sometimes the facts, upon examination, may be thought to favor that possibility. Sometimes they evidently do not. There are also prophecies where the main interest lies in the way they reflect hopes or aspirations or ways of thinking, so that they have a place in the history of ideas even though the predictions may be obsolete.

There is not much in the encyclopedia about science fiction, although, of course, it often has a future setting. The volume of material is too vast to accommodate, and the best of it is rooted in rational anticipation, however fancifully extended. Writers of science fiction do not pretend to have actually had visions or to have seen ahead by divination. However, a few classics are included in which the authors are not so much making forecasts as making points. They are using future scenarios to satirize the world they live in or to fabricate myths and nightmares with a bearing on it. Their imagination is so rich and influential, even with no implied paranormal factor, that their writings deserve a place in this volume. These are listed under the authors' names. An author—H. G. Wells, for instance—may have written many other things, and, if so, the nature of this output is summarized, but the focus of the article is on a particular work. In one case, that of Olaf Stapledon, the author's mythmaking raises an interesting question about the nature of prophecy itself. That alone would be enough reason for inclusion in this book.

The first requirement for coming to terms with the topics in the encyclopedia is an open mind. If the materials are approached in that spirit, I believe enough probabilities emerge to justify a discussion of how foreknowledge may happen. That discussion appears in its place. There is certainly no easy answer, but the alternative easy answer of simply denying everything does not work.

Geoffrey Ashe

ACKNOWLEDGMENTS

A book that ranges as widely as the *Encyclopedia of Prophecy,* reflecting so much thinking and discussion over a long stretch of time, must owe obligations to more people than could ever be recalled or named individually. However, my supreme thanks are due to my wife, Patricia, who made a truly extraordinary contribution by taking on formidable tasks of copying, revision, and communication and by helping with the sometimes harder business of establishing the best text and illustrative matter. These things were done nobly and with an outpouring of effort that cannot be praised too highly.

A

ADAMS, EVANGELINE (1865–1932)

Practitioner and publicist of astrology, credited with giving it respectable status in the United States. She belonged to a prominent family in Massachusetts and was descended from John Quincy Adams, the sixth president. During convalescence from a long illness, she met Dr. J. Heber Smith, a physician who used horoscopes as a diagnostic aid. He studied hers, told her she could be an outstanding astrologer, and trained her in the art.

She took him at his word and set up as a consultant, moving in 1899 to New York City, where her warning of impending disaster for a hotel where she stayed (it was burnt the following day) was widely reported and established her reputation. She operated from a studio in Carnegie Hall, and secured the repeal of a city statute banning fortune-telling.

Her social contacts brought in rich clients and substantial fees. One of her devotees was the film star Mary Pickford. J. P. Morgan Jr. used her advice in the conduct of his banking business. In 1930 she began giving radio broadcasts, and soon afterwards she published a manual, *Astrology for Everyone*. Her fame contributed to the birth of newspaper astrology.

Though she impressed individual clients, her successful forecasts of public events were only occasional. In 1931 she predicted that the United States would be at war within eleven years—correct, and mildly interesting, since eleven is a curious number to think of, and the natural ten would not quite have extended to December 1941. About the same time she made some observations on Edward, Prince of Wales, saying he was liable to run into trouble because of an interest in married women who would not be able to share his throne when he became king. Thus it turned out five years later when, as Edward VIII, he determined to marry an American named Wallis Simpson quickly after her divorce was finalized. The British government and the royal family refused to accept her as a potential queen, and he was forced to abdicate after reigning less than a year.

Like another popular prophet, Jeane Dixon, Evangeline Adams made several fairly accurate forecasts of the death of well-known people. These included the great operatic tenor Caruso, and, apparently, herself.

See also: Dixon, Jeane

Further Reading

Wallechinsky, David, Amy Wallace, and Irving Wallace. *The Book of Predictions.* New York: William Morrow, 1980.

AGHARTI

See Shambhala

ANGELIC POPE

An ideal pope, recurrently prophesied in the Middle Ages and Renaissance.

The Angelic Pope is mentioned first in 1267 by the Franciscan polymath Roger Bacon, who refers to a revelation some unnamed person had about him. The prophecy has been current, Bacon says, for forty years. This pope will reform the Church, getting rid of corruption and internal strife, and impress the world by his goodness and justice. Thanks to his influence, the breakaway

Greek Christians will return to the Roman fold; the Jews will acknowledge Christ; and the Tartars and Saracens will cease to trouble Christendom. A brighter day will dawn, and, Bacon believes, in his own lifetime.

This glorious pontiff was adopted by the followers of Joachim of Fiore, who had already prophesied an Age of the Holy Spirit and now added the Angelic Pope to their program, as its inaugurator. In 1294 it seemed for a moment that he might have arrived. Pietro di Morrone, a humble and saintly hermit from Naples, was elected as Pope Celestine V. Public enthusiasm was tremendous, but he was unequal to the tasks of administration and soon resigned without effecting any reforms.

He became, however, a sort of prototype in Joachite imagination, and a true Angelic Pope was still hoped for. There might even be a succession of good popes, associated with another prophetic figure, the Second Charlemagne. These speculations were embodied in a series of symbolic pictures, the *Vaticinia de Summis Pontificibus* (Prophecies of the Supreme Pontiffs), culminating in the Angelic Pope.

When the Renaissance unleashed a wave of freelance preachers and prophets and the spread of printing created an enlarged audience for them, some of them spoke of fulfilling such predictions. In 1516 Fra Bonaventura, under Joachite influence, announced that he actually was the Angelic Pope and took it upon himself to excommunicate the real one, Leo X. In 1525 Pietro Galantino, an astrologer, likewise under Joachite influence, seems to have regarded himself in much the same light. The official Church tried to bring such outbreaks under control; the Fifth Lateran Council was censorious, though without denying that revelations of the future could happen and, by implication, might have happened for the Joachites. Guesswork of a more responsible kind fastened briefly on other candidates, including Leo himself, an unfortunate choice since, far from bringing harmony, he provoked the Reformation. Marcellus II, elected in 1555, may have inspired hopes, but he did not live long enough to show whether he was angelic or not.

After Marcellus, the atmosphere of the Church was unfavorable to such speculation. Nevertheless, towards the end of the sixteenth century, further prophecies became current that led up, like the *Vaticinia,* to an Angelic Pope in an indefinite future. One of them, attributed to Saint Malachy, has an interest of its own as containing—arguably—a number of fulfilled predictions.

George Eliot mentions the Angelic Pope in her historical novel *Romola.*

See also: Eliot, George; Joachim of Fiore; Malachy, Saint; Second Charlemagne

Further Reading

Ashe, Geoffrey. *The Book of Prophecy.* London: Blandford, 1999.

Reeves, Marjorie. *Joachim of Fiore and the Prophetic Future.* New York: Harper and Row, 1977.

Reeves, Marjorie, ed. *Prophetic Rome in the High Renaissance Period.* Oxford: Clarendon Press, 1992.

ANNA

See Simeon and Anna

ANTICHRIST

A future archenemy of God who figures in Christian prophecy or, rather, speculation.

He has a pre-Christian prototype, Antiochus Epiphanes, a Greek king of Syria who persecuted the Jews from 167 to 164 B.C. Antiochus installed a statue of Zeus in the Temple, stopped the sacrifices and other ceremonies, and tried to suppress Judaism entirely or at least destroy its distinctive character. Some Jews collaborated with him; others held firm and endured the first known martyrdoms for a religious cause. The biblical book Daniel denounces Anti-

A fifteenth-century fantasy of the battle with God's monstrous archenemy, who was to afflict humanity in the last days. (Ann Ronan Picture Library)

ochus and foretells his downfall. This crisis provoked a rebellion led by the Maccabee brothers, which created a Jewish kingdom that survived until the region fell under Roman dominance.

Having endured one persecution, Jews correctly expected more. They hoped for the Messiah, a future God-given champion who would bring lasting deliverance. While they were not so specific about a chief enemy, a new Antiochus, their scripture had long foreshadowed such a person in Ezekiel 38–39, which predicts that an evil northern ruler called Gog will invade the Holy Land and attack the Chosen People.

When Christian writers foretell an arch-foe of Christ, he is not at first given the natural title of Antichrist, but the New Testament does coin that word. He makes his debut in Saint Paul's second letter to the Thessalonians. Its authenticity has been questioned, but the main point is not affected, and the author may be accepted as Paul in the absence of proof to the contrary. He has heard that some of his converts are expecting Christ's Second Coming at any moment and have stopped working in the belief that everything will be different. These holy drop-outs, Paul says, should be disowned; Christians must carry on with the ordinary business of life. Not only is the time of the Lord's return unknown, something else must happen before it occurs: The "Man of Sin" or "Lawless One" must be manifested. He will set himself up as divine; he will work bogus miracles with the devil's aid and deceive many, including Christians who are not firm in the faith. After this time of testing, like the one inflicted on the Jews by Antiochus, Christ will return indeed and destroy him.

Paul suspects, perhaps, that normal life may still be disrupted by an expectation that the Lawless One will appear soon, even though Christ may not. He explains that this Antichrist has a prerequisite himself. Someone or something is acting to restrain him, and he will not be manifested until that is gone. Paul's meaning is uncertain. An early guess is that he is thinking of Roman power as a deterrent to any too-spectacular upstart. Rome, however, began to look sinister itself. When a fire devastated the city in the year 64, the emperor Nero, who was suspected of starting it, tried to shift the blame to the Christians. Many were tortured and put to death as incendiaries. This was not strictly persecution, since they were not being martyred for their religion, but the Church regarded it as such ever afterwards. In practice the distinction was hard to draw; it was their religion, which most Romans detested, that Nero was able to exploit. He became one of the archvillains of Christian tradition. After his death he was rumored to be still alive, and some Christians believed, even centuries later, that he would return and himself be the Antichrist.

The last book of the New Testament, the Revelation or Apocalypse ascribed to the apostle John, symbolizes the Roman Empire as a terrible monster, its anti-Christian character expressed in Nero and in the later emperor Domitian, who was widely regarded as, in effect, Nero over again. Revelation is not explicit about an individual Antichrist yet to come, and in two epistles also ascribed to John, the term *antichrist* is applied more generally to opponents of Christian orthodoxy. But in the writings of Fathers of the Church such as Tertullian, such minor antichrists are seen as precursors of a great one who will appear finally.

Several anticipatory notions became current. Paul's warning about Antichrist's pretense of divinity and his deceptive wonder-working caused him to be imagined as a satanic parody of the true Saviour. Owing to the Jews' supposed guilt in the death of Jesus, many thought that Antichrist would be Jewish himself. One persistent idea was that he would belong to the Israelite tribe of Dan. Genesis 49:17 makes an ominous prophecy— "Dan shall be a serpent in the way, a viper by the path"—and in Revelation 7:4–8, Dan is missing from a list of the tribes that implies divine favor towards the others. A difficulty here is that Dan was one of the northern tribes that were deported by the Assyrians and lost to view, so that it was not part of the main Jewish body. However, these Lost Tribes were still believed to exist somewhere, so a Danite might emerge from concealment and lead his fellow Israelites.

Pseudo-Sibylline writers invented a fuller Antichrist scenario. History would rise to a brief climax with a "Last Emperor" who would bring universal peace and a general Christian triumph. After him, Antichrist would appear and assail Christians with the worst persecution ever. Christ's Second Coming would follow. During the Middle Ages the Last Emperor was seriously hoped for. With or without him, there were recurrent rumors that Antichrist was near and even that he had been born already.

The witch mania of the sixteenth and seventeenth centuries, by promoting fancies of supernatural evil, made such rumors more specific. In 1599 Antichrist was reported to have been born in Babylon. In 1600 he was born near Paris to a Jewish woman impregnated by Satan. On May 1, 1623, he was allegedly born near Babylon again. Protestants contributed the theory that Antichrist was the Pope, not any particular one, but the Pope in general. A by-product of this antipapal motif was a story that Antichrist had been born long before, as the son of the legendary female pope Joan, and was biding his time in some mysterious retreat, as some had said Nero was.

Russians had ideas of their own. In Napoleon's time, many of the Orthodox clergy said the French emperor was Antichrist, a view echoed by one of Tolstoy's characters in *War and Peace.* Another Russian, the philosopher Vladimir Solovyev (1853–1900), wrote a story with touches of Dostoyevsky, presenting Antichrist as a megalomaniac reformer early in the twenty-first century. He becomes president of the United States of Europe, solves—or appears to solve—major world problems, and wins over all Christians except a remnant and practically all the Jews, who accept him as the Messiah. A few resolute Christians see through him, and so do the Jews when he declares himself "the sole true incarnation of the Supreme Deity of the universe." A Jewish-led revolt drives him to ruthless measures of repression that break the spell, and he comes to his end. A novel by Robert Hugh Benson has a theme similar to Solovyev's.

See also: Benson, Robert Hugh; Daniel; Messiah; Revelation; Sibyls and Sibylline Texts; Solovyev, Vladimir

Further Reading

Ashe, Geoffrey. *The Book of Prophecy.* London: Blandford, 1999.

Baring-Gould, S. *Antichrist and Pope Joan.* Caerfyrddin, Wales: Unicorn, 1975.

APOCALYPSE

A type of Jewish prophetic writing that professed to disclose divine secrets and unveil a spectacular future. Most of it is later than canonical Jewish Scripture.

The word *apocalypse* means "revelation." The best-known example is the last book of the New Testament, written by a Jewish Christian, but its ancestry is more than two centuries back. The apocalyptic genre has its chief prototype in Daniel, composed about 165 B.C. This has been described as a manifesto of the Hasidim, the "pious" or "saints"—Jews who stood firm under persecution at the hands of Antiochus IV (also called Epiphanes), a descendant of one of Alexander's generals who ruled over Syria and Palestine. He pursued a very un-Greek policy of religious conformity, which led to violence. The Jewish high priest Onias was murdered by Menelaus, a nominee of the king, and Menelaus's brother robbed the Temple in Jerusalem. Antiochus installed a statue of Zeus in the sacred precinct, stopped the daily sacrifice, and made it a crime to own copies of Scripture. Jews who opposed him were subjected to tortures and humiliations. A resistance group escaped into the wilderness. These were the Hasidim, and they inspired a revolt that ended the persecution.

Daniel was written during these troubles. Its central character, ostensibly the author of parts of it, is a legendary sage. The book places him, in his youth, among the Israelites deported to Babylon by Nebuchadnezzar in 597 B.C. Several episodes show the superior wisdom of the Chosen People and the divine favor they enjoy. Daniel interprets symbolic dreams and has dreams of his own, from which the main apocalyptic themes develop. By putting the story in the sixth century B.C., the author makes Daniel "foretell"

events that have already happened at the real time of composition. Some passages, however, genuinely look ahead. A repeated prophecy is that Gentile empires—Babylonian, Median, Persian, Greek—will be replaced by a "kingdom of stone" that will be everlasting. Antiochus himself is denounced and consigned to destruction. The stone kingdom is the triumphant Israelite kingdom that will arise from the debris of the rest.

In Daniel, the figure of the Messiah has not yet emerged, but the author introduces a character who foreshadows him. Daniel has a vision of the Ancient of Days—God—pronouncing doom on the Gentile powers.

And behold, with the clouds of heaven there came one like a son of man,
and he came to the Ancient of Days and was presented before him.
And to him was given dominion and glory and kingdom, that all peoples,
nations, and languages should serve him; his dominion is an everlasting dominion,
which shall not pass away, and his kingdom one that shall not be destroyed. (Daniel 7:13–14)

This being, human yet more than human, probably personifies Israel. The fall of the empires and the rise of the stone kingdom to supremacy are acts in a God-directed drama leading towards the end of the present age. The author gives a new prominence to angels and, for the first time in Jewish Scripture, speaks of a resurrection of the dead (Daniel 12:2–3).

After Daniel, several Jewish writers produced books on similar lines, in which the apocalyptic element grew more fanciful. They took up hints from authentic Scripture and unfolded what were supposed to be secret meanings. Much of this literature was "pseudepigraphic": to give their books a spurious dignity, in the same manner as with Daniel, the authors ascribed them to revered figures in the past. Apocalyptic matter occurs in books alleged to be written by Ezra, by the ancient patriarch Enoch, and even by

Adam—an extreme of seniority. Such productions were not admitted to the Bible, yet the fictitious visions they contained did not part company altogether with recognized tradition.

The effects of the Antiochus ordeal lasted far beyond the ordeal itself. After it, Jews had a heightened awareness of hostile forces. The Syrian tyrant became an archetype of evil. The revolt against him had created an independent Jewish state, which survived for about 100 years but failed to realize the hoped-for glories of the "kingdom of stone" and succumbed to Roman conquest in 63 B.C. Hopes were continually being disappointed. Some apocalyptists detected the reason in a supernatural conflict that derived from Babylonian and Persian myth but had hitherto been excluded from Jewish belief. Devils were now discovered; they were made out to be fallen angels headed by Satan, previously a minor spirit and barely mentioned in Scripture, but now beginning to be presented as an adversary of God, troubling humanity and particularly the Chosen People. A dragon-monster called Beliar also made mischief. Against these powers of evil, angels were ranged, with names and relationships and political roles; Michael being the protector of Israel.

Human agency, it was implied, could not bring final peace. Apocalyptists enlarged on texts in canonical prophecy about a coming Day of the Lord. It would be terrible, but it would end in the overthrow of Israel's enemies, human and otherwise. One of these books, the *Testament of Naphtali,* declares: "God shall appear on earth to save the race of Israel, and to gather the righteous from among the Gentiles."

The victory could be expected to involve cataclysms, foreshadowed by the long-ago drowning of Pharaoh's army in the Red Sea. It could also be expected to involve the activity of a special divine champion. Some authors took up Daniel's image of the "Son of Man" and made him an individual, heading

Israel rather than personifying it. In the *Book of Enoch,* he is the Righteous Elect One, a celestial viceroy who will sit enthroned ruling all, judging all, and enlightening the Gentiles. Other speculation developed the idea of the Messiah, a more earthly figure, a prince of the House of David who would reestablish Israel's kingdom in unassailable glory. The Messiah was not identified with the Son of Man before Christianity. However, one Jewish school of thought harmonized the conceptions by saying that a Davidic kingdom would come first and an apocalyptic world-transformation later.

All such anticipations looked towards a world to come, a golden age not in the past where most mythologies placed it but in the future. After the upheavals and the defeat of evil, the sun would shine brighter, waste places would bloom, and living creatures would cease to harm each other. A stream of purifying water would flow from Mount Zion, and Jerusalem, rebuilt and resplendent, would be the world's capital. At some stage in this universal healing, the Lord would pronounce judgment on humanity, and all would receive their true deserts. As Daniel had foretold, there would be a resurrection of the dead: perhaps only of a select few, perhaps of the dead in general. If the latter, the good would dwell in an eastern paradise, Gan Eden, and the wicked in a western country of sorrow, Gehinnom.

This Jewish literature does not include any major, definitive work, but it influenced the community that produced the Dead Sea Scrolls, and it supplied motifs for Revelation, the great apocalypse at the end of the New Testament.

See also: Antichrist; Daniel; Day of the Lord; Messiah; Revelation

Further Reading

Ashe, Geoffrey. *The Land and the Book.* London: Collins, 1965.

Brown R. E., J. A. Fitzmyer, and R. E. Murphy, eds. *The New Jerome Biblical Commentary.* Englewood Cliffs, NJ: Prentice-Hall, 1990.

APOLLO

God of prophecy who, as portrayed in classical literature, is the most Greek of deities.

However, he is a composite figure, and the earliest records indicate that Apollo was first worshiped outside Greece. One of several distinctive features is that he has close links with a mysterious people called the Hyperboreans, whom different authors shift about over a wide area but who seem, in reality, to have lived in north-central Asia. Apollo spends three months of each year among them. This far-off connection, coupled with other clues, suggests that his nucleus (so to speak) may have been a god of Asian shamans who communicated with them in their self-induced ecstasy. Such a god, carried westward and southward in folk migrations, may have blended with other deities in parts of Asia closer to Greece.

Apollo, credibly a result of this fusion, is first recognizable in Asia Minor. At Troy he was worshiped together with his sister Artemis, who also had northern affiliations. A prophetic element in him, whether shamanic or otherwise, remained potent. Legend tells how he enabled the Trojan princess Cassandra to share the gift, with unhappy consequences. His inspired Sibyls were said to flourish in the same general area.

Apollo, in some form, crossed the Aegean Sea with Artemis. A new myth gave the twins a Greek birthplace on the island of Delos, linking them with Zeus's family of Olympians. In Greece, Apollo grew civilized and complex. He became the patron of healing, music, and mathematics and (though not until long afterwards) a sun god. On the whole, he stood for harmony and rationality, but the prophetic element in him never ceased to be active. He had oracular shrines at various places—Delphi was the most important—and spoke through priestesses whom he inspired, giving advice and warnings to those who consulted him, with occasional glimpses of the future, or so it was

believed. Sometimes, his messages were open to more than one interpretation, and in his oracular role, he was known as Loxias, the Ambiguous. Inquirers went on coming until the oracles ceased to function in the fourth century A.D.

A special aspect of Apollo, strengthening the case for shamanic antecedents, is his association with the number seven. One of his titles is "Commander of Sevens": the meaning is uncertain, but probably calendric. In the Delian myth, he was born on the seventh day of the month Thargelion, about May 20. His Delphic oracle could only be consulted on the seventh day of a month when he was in residence. Most of his festivals were held on seventh days. There are further sevens in his mythology. The mystique of seven does not occur in conjunction with any other Greek god. It is prominent, however, in India's Vedic hymns, in Sumer and Babylonia, and, of course, in Israel, as the Bible shows. The motif is traceable in shamanic cults of Siberia and may have originated there. Conjecturally, it was rooted in an ancient reverence for the seven-starred constellation Ursa Major, still attested by modern anthropologists; and Apollo's sister Artemis had a mythic link with that constellation.

See also: Cassandra; Delphi; Oracles; Sibyls and Sibylline Texts

Further Reading

Ashe, Geoffrey. *Dawn behind the Dawn.* New York: Henry Holt, 1992.

Graves, Robert. *The Greek Myths.* 2 vols. New York: Penguin Books, 1960.

AQUARIUS, AGE OF

An era of transformation when, it is alleged, humanity will come under the influence of a new sign of the Zodiac.

The notion that the Earth passes through astrological phases is a product of its oscillation. Because of this, the stars go through a gradual change of position in the sky, about one degree every seventy-two years. It has been asserted that history falls into equal periods, each ruled by whichever sign of the Zodiac the Sun is in at the spring equinox. A complete revolution of the heavens takes 25,920 years (360 × 72); therefore, since there are twelve signs, the Sun is in any given one at the equinox for one-twelfth of this period, that is, 2,160 years. It then passes into another sign, and it will be that one's turn to exert a dominant influence.

At present the Age of Pisces, the Fishes, is said to have lasted for more than 2,000 years. Since the fish is an ancient Christian symbol, the Age of Pisces is understood to encompass the Christian era. The Age of Pisces will presently be left behind, and Christianity with it. According to different exponents of this theory, the world is moving—or has moved—or is on the verge of moving—into the Age of Aquarius, with the Sun in that sign in spring. While it is not clear whether the shift has happened yet, it is certainly not far off.

The "dawning of the Age of Aquarius" was proclaimed by pop culture in the 1960s. By the 1980s, belief in it was a virtual orthodoxy in some quarters, and there was talk of an "Aquarian conspiracy," meaning a network of individuals absorbing and propagating the new influences and sowing the seeds of a transformation of human consciousness. The Age of Aquarius is to be a time of increasing harmony, understanding, and spiritual growth. It appears that spiritual growth will cover a vast range of "fringe" ideas and activities.

Further Reading

Campbell, Eileen, and J. H. Brennan. *The Aquarian Guide to the New Age.* Wellingborough, England: The Aquarian Press, 1990.

ARMAGEDDON

Scene of a final conflict between good and evil.

Armageddon occurs in the vista of the future portrayed by John (perhaps the apostle, perhaps someone else) in his Revelation or Apocalypse, the last book of the New Testament. The powers of evil, headed by Satan, send out demonic spirits to summon the kings of the world for battle "on the great day of God the Almighty." "And they assembled them at the place which is called in Hebrew Armageddon" (Revelation 16:16). The battle does not begin at this point in the narrative. John takes up the thread again in chapter 19, where Christ returns in majesty with "the armies of heaven" and wins the victory.

The place intended is Megiddo in north-central Palestine: "Armageddon" is har-Megiddo, or Mount Megiddo. Strategically located, Megiddo has several associations with warfare. Here the Canaanite king Jabin was defeated by the Israelites under the leadership of Deborah and Barak. Here also King Josiah fell in 609 B.C. opposing an Egyptian army, an event recalled in Jewish tradition as a bitter tragedy. However, the chief scriptural precedent for John's battle is Ezekiel 38–39, foretelling an attack on the Holy Land by the northern ruler "Gog of the land of Magog," with a huge composite host drawn from a medley of nations. Ezekiel prophesies that the Lord will destroy Gog's multitude "upon the mountains of Israel." John's addition of "mount" to "Megiddo" probably echoes this passage.

Some interpreters of Revelation, aware that the Gog prophecy has never been fulfilled, have taken it as referring to the same future battle that John refers to. They have also seen Armageddon as an immediate prelude to the end of the world. Revelation does not support either opinion. Christ's victory in chapter 19 brings the present age to a close, but the story goes on after that. An angel "binds" Satan and shuts him in a subterranean prison for 1,000 years. During the same period, Christ is to dwell on Earth, reigning over a kingdom of resurrected martyrs and other saints, seemingly in the Holy Land. A time of renewed trouble ensues (Revelation 20:7–9), and here, not earlier, we find Ezekiel's sinister names. "Satan will be loosed from his prison and will come out to deceive the nations which are in the four corners of the earth, that is, Gog and Magog, to gather them to battle; their number is like the sand of the sea. And they marched up over the broad earth and surrounded the camp of the saints and the beloved city; but fire came down from heaven and consumed them."

This does not cancel the military finality of Armageddon because no actual battle is fought. Satan's army is annihilated, he is cast into hell, and that is truly the end. There is a general resurrection of the dead, followed by the Last Judgment. The present world ceases to exist, and the blessed enter into a glorious New Jerusalem.

John's concept of Armageddon is not fully anticipated in previous writings, but the Dead Sea Scrolls foreshadow a "War of the Sons of Light against the Sons of Darkness" that will have a decisive outcome. Though waged with God's blessing, it is envisaged on a more human level than Armageddon, and the Jewish Messiah plays no part in it. Hence, it is more like a real war, and the text gives a surprising amount of military detail, some of it Roman-inspired.

Buddhism in Tibet and Mongolia speaks of a coming "War of Shambhala," which is also to be a clash of good and evil, with good triumphant. Shambhala is a legendary holy place, conjecturally concealed in the Altai Mountains, and a messianic figure is to emerge from it. During the 1920s, this hope was taken up by Mongolian nationalists. The emerging leader was identified with Gesar, an epic hero, and the prophecy became involved with hopes of Asian resurgence against imperialist powers. After this phase blew over, the War of Shambhala lost its quasi-political character and receded into an indefinite future.

See also: Revelation; Shambhala
Further Reading
Brown R. E., J. A. Fitzmyer, and R. E. Murphy, eds. *The New Jerome Biblical Commentary.* Englewood Cliffs, NJ: Prentice-Hall, 1990.

ARTHUR, KING

British monarch in a vague medieval past, who was supposed never to have died, and whose return was prophesied.

The Arthurian Legend, one of the greatest themes of romance, is rooted in the Celtic people who inhabited Britain before the arrival of the Anglo-Saxons, ancestors of the English. These Britons, after being subjects of the Roman Empire for more than three centuries, became independent around the year 410. The Anglo-Saxons from the continent seem to have entered the country first as auxiliary troops, employed by the independent Britons. More followed without authorization. Reinforced, they got out of control and gradually expanded their settlements. After an era of shifts and changes lasting several centuries, they achieved dominance over all of what is now England.

Celtic Britons remained unsubjugated in Wales and some northern areas, as well as in Brittany across the English Channel, which they had colonized. These handed down tales of the early post-Roman period when British leaders were still active, resisting the new people and winning temporary victories. The balance of probability favors the existence of a real Arthur figure among them, in the second half of the fifth century or possibly a little later. One or two of them are known to have had Roman names, showing a slight survival of imperial culture, and the name *Arthur* is a Welsh form of the Roman name *Artorius.* The Arthur of legend and romance is, of course, an immense expansion of any credible individual and may have absorbed traditions of other men, even perhaps other men called Arthur.

King Arthur, depicted as one of the Nine Worthies, heroes of medieval tradition. Reputedly he was not dead, and he would return. (Ann Ronan Picture Library)

At some unknown stage in legend-weaving, Arthur joined the select company of historical characters who have been reported alive after they were presumed to be dead. Such persons need not be popular heroes; they can be either good or bad. The list includes the Mexican peasant leader Zapata, the British military chief Lord Kitchener, and even President Kennedy; it also includes Nero and Hitler. Normally, the rumor fades out when its subject cannot possibly have survived so long. But that is not always so. A medieval German emperor, Frederick Barbarossa, was believed to be asleep in a mountain cave centuries after his death. The Portuguese king Sebastian, officially killed in battle in 1578, was reputed to be alive for many years afterwards, and the credulous hoped for his return as a national savior as late as 1807, when Napoleon Bonaparte's army overran Portugal. The undying Arthur may have begun his career as a British Sebastian.

He is first clearly documented in the early twelfth century by references to folk beliefs about him in Cornwall and Brittany. Cornwall remained predominantly Celtic long after the rest of England was English. A party of French priests, visiting the Cornish city of Bodmin in 1113, were told by one of the locals that King Arthur was alive. They laughed at him but found to their surprise that the bystanders agreed, and a fight broke out. The first known mention of the prophecy of an actual return is in 1125, when the historian William of Malmesbury says: "The tomb of Arthur is nowhere seen, whence ancient ditties fable that he is yet to come." That expectation is on record as the "Breton hope" a few years later.

There are two principal conceptions of the secret retreat where Arthur lives on. Geoffrey of Monmouth, who wrote a famous pseudo history bringing him in, says that after his last battle, he was "carried off to the Isle of Avalon for his wounds to be attended to." According to some romancers, he is still in that enchanted place (not originally equated with Glastonbury in Somerset). The other principal story is that he is asleep in a cave. The cave legend is found in Wales, in western and northern England, and in Scotland. It has at least fifteen locations, including Cadbury Castle, an ancient Somerset hill-fort, which was refortified in the

"Arthur" period and is thought to be the prototype of Camelot so far as anything is. John Masefield's poem *Midsummer Night* is based on the Cadbury tradition. In most cases, the cave is not a real one that can be explored in the normal way. It is magically hidden and only revealed to the occasional visitor, sometimes by a mysterious stranger who may be Merlin himself. Arthur might voyage back from Avalon, or he might emerge from his cave.

In either scenario he would have been pictured first as a Celtic warrior-messiah, leading the Welsh and others against the English. During the Middle Ages, however, when Arthurian romances became popular throughout Christendom, he was transformed into a king of England as well as other lands, the lord of a past golden age, a sort of chivalric Utopia. Plantagenet sovereigns such as Edward I took him seriously as an illustrious forebear, and his prophesied return became more of a national motif. If he came back, perhaps in an hour of special need, his glory would revive.

Sir Thomas Malory, in his famous version of the legend, mentions the prophecy, though he is noncommittal himself. "Some men say in many parts of England that King Arthur is not dead, but had by the will of Our Lord Jesu into another place; and men say that he shall come again. . . . Many men say that there is written upon his tomb this verse: 'HIC JACET ARTHURUS, REX QUONDAM REXQUE FUTURUS.'" The Latin line, "Here lies Arthur, king that was and king that shall be," suggested the title of T. H. White's four-part novel *The Once and Future King*. Since Malory asserts that it was written on a tomb, it is not clear in what sense Arthur could be future.

Malory's book was published in 1485. That year marks a transition, when Arthur's return began to be symbolic rather than literal. Henry Tudor defeated Richard III at Bosworth and became King Henry VII. He was part Welsh, claiming a pedigree that took his ancestry far back towards Arthur, and his army flew a Red Dragon standard emblematic of Wales. Tudor publicists developed a myth that he was restoring the true "British" monarchy and bringing back harmony after centuries of usurpation and strife. Henry had his firstborn son baptized at Winchester, which Malory said was Camelot, and named him Arthur with the apparent intention that he should reign as Arthur II, sufficiently fulfilling the prophecy. Prince Arthur died young, and his brother became king as Henry VIII. He did not make so much of the notion, but he kept it alive, and John Leland, the court antiquary, hailed him in verse as "Arturius Redivivus," or "Arthur renewed."

The Tudor Myth rose to a new height with Elizabeth I. Edmund Spenser, in his allegorical poem *The Faerie Queene,* suggests that her realm was, in effect, Arthur's ideal Britain reconstituted. In his poem he imagines Merlin delivering a long prophecy about Britain's future, leading up to a climax with the Tudors. Even after the dynasty ended and the Stuarts came in, the propagandist theme of Arthurian revival made further appearances and was some time dying away.

Since then, while King Arthur has inspired a vast amount of literature, his return has been a topic for poetry and fantasy rather than literal hope. However, the prophecy has an enduring psychological interest. It gives mythic expression to a definable way of looking at things and a syndrome that recurs among religious and political activists. They show a tendency to conceive a movement towards reform or revolution not as a simple step forwards, but as a revival. When this happens, they evoke a long-lost glory or promise and regard it as not permanently lost. It is still potentially "there," so to speak, as the Arthur of legend still secretly exists; it can be reinstated for a fresh start, with intervening corruption swept away, as the Arthur of legend will return in glory.

Among several historic instances, a notable one is the movement for Christian reform in the sixteenth century. Reformers, both Catholic and Protestant, agreed that the Church had grown corrupt and that radical action was required. But neither party spoke of this in terms of development or progress. Both appealed to the past. In the golden age of the apostles and early saints, Christianity was pure. The reformers aimed to abolish the corruption, restore the true gospel, recapture the pristine purity.

This kind of thinking sometimes appears compulsive. The lost-but-recoverable golden age simply has to be real, even if there is no good evidence for it. Rousseau in the eighteenth century was a major inspirer of the French Revolution, but not by preaching progress. He taught that humanity had once been free, equal, and moral in a natural state. Civilization had created tyranny and misery. The proper course was to get rid of the upholders of the evil system and create a social order that would enable natural goodness to reassert itself. Significantly, Rousseau admitted that his natural golden age might never have existed, but, he said, we need to imagine it "in order to judge well of our present state." It is a necessary myth.

The early growth of Communism supplies an even more remarkable case history. Marx and his collaborator Engels, in spite of their claims of objectivity, yielded to the same compulsion. More than thirty years after their first *Communist Manifesto* appeared, they invented a long-ago and dubious era of "primitive communism" and tacked it on at the beginning of their version of history. It was a classless golden age, an age of "simple moral grandeur" that had been subverted by "vulgar covetousness, brutal lust, sordid avarice, selfish robbery of the common wealth." Thousands of years of conflict and oppression ensued, but the Revolution would—eventually—restore the ancient classless society on a higher plane. The original *Communist Manifesto* of 1848 had not contained anything of the kind. When a new edition came out in 1888, Engels had to add this new notion as a prelude. Even in the materialistic context, the long-ago golden age had reasserted itself, and so had the prophecy of its resurrection, a "Return of Arthur."

See also: Merlin

Further Reading

Ashe, Geoffrey. *The Book of Prophecy.* London: Blandford, 1999.

———. *King Arthur: The Dream of a Golden Age.* London: Thames and Hudson, 1990.

Lacy, Norris J., ed. *The New Arthurian Encyclopedia.* New York and London: Garland, 1991.

ASTROLOGY

The art of judging the influence of planets and stars on human beings—in the past, in the present, and, by extrapolation, in the future.

India and China have had astrological systems for a long time. These are highly developed, and regarded with respect. The Western version has its ancestry in Babylonia, where astronomers were listing constellations and prominent stars in the second millennium B.C. With the passage of time, they came to distinguish seven "planets," counting the five true ones visible without telescopes plus the Sun and Moon—in other words, the seven bodies that were not fixed like stars. All seven were associated with divine beings. They were seen to travel through sections of the sky that astronomers defined by twelve constellations, the signs of the Zodiac.

In the sixth century B.C., Babylonians developed a theory that these celestial orbs influenced the world below. Greek advances in astronomy presently refined the possibilities, and the Western form of astrology took shape. Earth was located at the center of the universe, with seven transparent spheres rotating around it, one outside another, each carrying a planet. The Moon's was nearest to Earth; concentrically outside it, in order,

came the spheres carrying Mercury, Venus, the Sun, Mars, Jupiter, and Saturn. Outside Saturn's sphere was a larger one bearing the stars, and outside that was an even larger one that imparted motion inward to all the others. The planets exerted influence on the world at the center, and, in their varying relations to the Zodiac and each other, were "interpreters" of destiny. As in Babylonia, deities were associated with them. "Mercury," "Venus" and the rest are the Roman names of the divinities that were assigned to these planets by classical astrologers because they were thought to be the appropriate ones. The fifth planet's influence, for example, tended towards strength, assertiveness, and anger, so it was taken to be the planet of the war god Mars.

Astronomically, the system is no longer viable, and astrologers are quite aware of the fact. But they still tacitly assume it, in its essentials, as a kind of operating fiction, its use justified by results. In practice—supposedly—it does work. A horoscope can be drawn up on the basis of the planets' positions at someone's birth. The most important is the Sun, which is in Aries (the Ram) during part of March and part of April, then in Taurus (the Bull) during the rest of April and part of May, and so on. The date of birth determines the person's Sun-sign or birth-sign: Aries, for instance, if the Sun was in that portion of the sky at the time, Taurus if it was in the next portion, and so on. The Sun-sign is said to have a crucial bearing on the personality.

Complex calculations about the positions of the other six planets—sometimes, today, computerized—can be expressed on a birth-chart, and add further insights into the individual's character and destiny. On the basis of the inferred destiny and perhaps also of the planets' foreseeable positions at some future time, events yet to come can be predicted; or, at any rate, probabilities—the celestial bodies, to quote an astrologer, "influence but do not compel." Auspicious and inauspicious days can be identified in advance for some

An astrologer casting a client's horoscope in 1617. The progress of astronomy was beginning to raise doubts about astrology, but astrologers were still being consulted. (Ann Ronan Picture Library)

important action. The technique is not confined to individuals. It can be applied to cities, states, institutions, or whatever, preferably at the time of their foundation, the equivalent of birth. Projections into the future can be made similarly. A horoscope of the city of Liverpool, in England, is said to have shown that it will become the capital of England in the twenty-third century—an extreme case but not inconsistent with the logic of the system.

To revert to history, Romans were hesitant about embracing this production of Greek cleverness, but early in the Christian era, it was growing popular at high social levels, and the casting of a horoscope at a child's birth was becoming customary. An astrologer named Thrasyllus was an adviser to the emperor Tiberius. When some of his predictions failed, Tiberius lost patience and was about to push him off a cliff, but he managed to make a good one just in time.

After the Roman Empire became officially Christian in the fourth century, astrology began to be frowned upon. Augustine, the most influential of the Church fathers, offered rational arguments against it and argued that even when astrologers got predictions right, this was probably due to inspiration by evil spirits. For a long time, it was in disfavor. However, it began to come back in the early Middle Ages as a quasi-scientific technique. Planets could no longer be gods, but in some mysterious way, they might still play a part in earthly affairs. Scholars in the Church kept it off the list of forbidden arts, and Saint Thomas Aquinas, the leading medieval philosopher, allowed it a strictly limited validity. Its practitioners worked freely, though they stressed character reading and medical diagnosis rather then prediction. It became very popular in the sixteenth-century Renaissance. John Dee, in England, was allowed to draw up horoscopes for royalty and to set a date for Elizabeth I's coronation. Nostradamus, in France, published hundreds of prophecies, some of them remarkable, though for him, astrology seems to have been subordinate to another method of forecasting that remains obscure.

The waning of Earth-centered astronomy was naturally adverse to astrology, and it declined again, but it never expired, and eventually, it began to recover. It could be rationalized, as it still can, by the argument that it reads the heavens as they *appear* to be, and no astronomical proof of what they actually *are* can make any difference. Its Western revival had its origin in Theosophy. Helena Petrovna Blavatsky, the founder of the movement, endorsed it in her book *Isis Unveiled,* published in 1877. One of her followers, writing under the name Alan Leo, was its first popularizer and produced a handbook entitled *Astrology for All.* In England, France, and the United States, interest gradually revived. However, it was only in Germany that astrology became a serious field of study, thanks partly to another Theosophist, Hugo Vollrath. The sufferings of Germans in the great inflation of 1923–1924 and in the ensuing years of mass unemployment contributed to a longing for a doctrine that would make sense of events and perhaps foreshadow a better time ahead. An Astrological Congress in Munich was the first of a series. Germans of academic standing tried to make astrology an authentic system.

During this interwar period, astrology also enjoyed a vogue on radio and in newspapers. Exponents in English-speaking countries, such as Evangeline Adams and R. H. Naylor, made forecasts on topics of public interest. However, their occasional successes were outweighed by numerous failures. Later in the twentieth century, while astrology of a sort still flourished in the press, it was more cautious and largely confined to minihoroscopes for the day (or week or month) giving vague advice to readers born under each sign and avoiding specific detail about the future. In 1967, a well-informed writer on astrology, Ellic Howe, pronounced, in the light of his own negative findings, that prediction was its "Achilles' heel."

The astrology of a more responsible kind that continues to be practiced is concerned chiefly with character and destiny. Howe's adverse verdict on prediction might be allowed to stand if it were not for an exceptional case history, that of Germany under the Nazi regime, from 1933 on. Seemingly, the activities of Vollrath and other enthusiasts showed predictive results that cannot be dismissed. Someone had cast the horoscope of the German republic on the basis of the date of its proclamation in 1918, and several attempts had been made to cast Hitler's. There is evidence—some of it indisputable, some of it circumstantial but good—for correct long-range forecasts of Hitler's career and the fortunes of Germany in World War II and its aftermath. Hitler, it was foretold, would be triumphant at first, and Germany would be victorious for two years, but in 1941, the tide would begin to turn. There would be major disasters in 1943 and a cataclysmic end, including the Führer's downfall, in 1945, though a recovery would be under way after three years of peace. All of this was right. Hitler did not believe in astrology, but his awareness of its prediction for 1941 as a threat to morale was shown by a clampdown on astrologers in June of that year.

The German successes raise a problem. Can astrology predict after all? If so, how to make sense of these facts? Whatever astrologers may say in defense of their art, it remains the case that the universe is not what it looks like from below. They have done their best to fit in the three planets added to the traditional seven, but much more is involved than that. The crystal spheres and their resident deities have gone. Mercury, Venus, Mars, Jupiter, and Saturn, together with the three latecomers, are barren globes moving through a void at vast distances from Earth and from each other. Medieval astronomy recognized greater distances than is commonly thought, but came nowhere near the remoteness of the stars, which are not only remote but in spatial relationships to each other that have nothing to do with the Zodiac: its constellations would disappear for an observer from a different vantage point.

An astrologer today might speak of correlations or synchronisms rather than influences. If such a claim were borne out by results, it would deserve to be investigated, but results are lacking. The German phenomenon may be thought to hint at some quite separate factor. The same could be said of the rare but documented triumphs of character reading by horoscope (or ostensibly by horoscope), such as one recorded at the University of Freiburg, where an astrologer named Walter Boer diagnosed the problems of a juvenile delinquent unknown to him in virtually the same way as a team of psychologists. Ellic Howe, who draws attention to this case, takes the view that such successes are not really produced by the subject's birth-chart as such but by a kind of intuition making use of it, which few would-be astrologers are capable of. Jung, as is well known, took an interest in astrology, but he used patients' horoscopes chiefly as therapeutic aids rather than sources of information.

One quasi-astrological finding has stood up to scrutiny, often very hostile. In 1955, a French statistician, Michel Gauquelin, proved that a significant number of people with certain abilities were born when certain planets were either just clearing the horizon or at the apex of their passage across the sky. Many outstanding athletes, for instance, were born when Mars was either rising or "culminating." Jupiter seemed to be connected with famous actors in the same way. The ironic fact is that Gauquelin's correlations are totally unrelated to traditional astrology, for which he found no support whatever.

See also: Adams, Evangeline; Hanussen, Erik Jan; Krafft, Karl Ernst; Nazi Germany; Newspaper Astrology; Theosophy

Further Reading

Ashe, Geoffrey. *The Book of Prophecy.* London: Blandford, 1999.

———. *Dawn behind the Dawn.* New York: Henry Holt, 1992.

Campion, Nicholas, and Steve Eddy. *The New Astrology.* London: Bloomsbury, 1999.

Cavendish, Richard, ed. *Man, Myth and Magic.* London: BPC Publishing, 1970–1972. Article "Astrology."

Howe, Ellic. *Urania's Children.* London: William Kimber, 1967.

ATLANTIS

Island-continent that is reputed to have sunk beneath the Atlantic Ocean and that some expect to reappear.

Atlantis is widely assumed to have been real, but almost everything said about it derives ultimately from one author, the Greek philosopher Plato (c. 428–348 B.C.), who was not a historian. He cites an alleged Egyptian tradition handed down for 9,000 years. Atlantis was a landmass occupying a large part of the ocean west of Gibraltar. Its rulers were descended from gods, and it was a realm of great splendor, where justice and wisdom flourished. The Atlanteans had

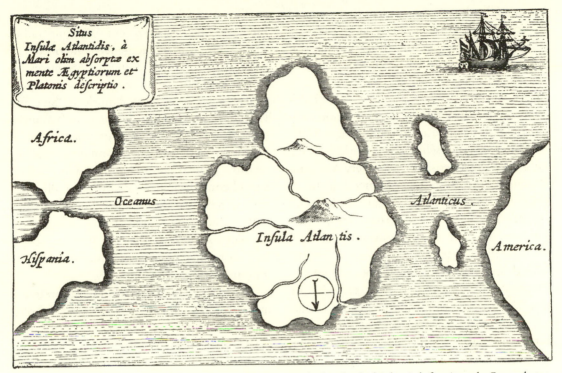

A map by Athanasius Kircher (1678) conjecturally showing the lost land of Atlantis before it sank. Somewhat confusingly, north is at the bottom. (Ann Ronan Picture Library)

colonies in Europe and Africa and in a continent on the far side of the ocean (it is tempting to see a reference to America here, but that idea must be treated with extreme caution). Eventually, the divine element in the rulers decayed, and they embarked on wars of conquest. Their conduct brought retribution from Zeus, the chief god. The free men of Athens drove back their army, and Atlantis vanished in a single day and night of earthquake and flood.

As it stands, Plato's story is impossibly dated and geologically incredible. His main purpose was probably to create a myth showing the superiority of small, well-ordered states over aggressive empires. However, his fertile imagination carried the conception too far: he said too much about Atlantis, and made it too interesting. Though few in classical times took it literally, attempts were made in the Age of Discovery to relate it to America. Authors in the nineteenth and

twentieth centuries tried to prove that it was real and more or less as described.

The first such study was by Ignatius Donnelly in his book *Atlantis: the Antediluvian World,* published in 1882. Others have followed. The favorite line of argument is that cultural similarities on both sides of the Atlantic imply a common source between them. Thus, Mexico has pyramids and Egypt has pyramids, so there must have been Atlantean pyramid builders who traveled in both directions founding ancient civilizations. But independent invention is perfectly possible, and Mexico and Egypt are too far apart in time to have had a common origin. "Proofs" based on parallels in myth and religion are no more effective.

It has been argued that although Plato was writing fiction, he used traditions of real ancient civilizations and natural disasters, somewhere else altogether—in the Aegean area, maybe. It has also been argued that he did know of land across the Atlantic, discovered by unrecorded voyagers: nothing on the scale of his mythic conception but real as far as it went. A serious case has been made out for the West Indies.

Whatever may be thought of Plato's sources, the idea that his Atlantis not only existed but may rise again is due chiefly to its inclusion in the schema of world history taught by the Theosophical Society. Madame Blavatsky, the founder, produced a book called *Isis Unveiled* in 1877. In this, she mentioned Atlantis and was perhaps the first to hit on the argument from cultural and mythological parallels between the Old World and the New, though it was left to Donnelly to develop it. In 1888, she brought out *The Secret Doctrine*. Donnelly's book had appeared in the interval, and she cited him with approval but laid more stress on her own claims to knowledge drawn from occult revelations and mysterious manuscripts. She expounded a panorama of history covering millions of years and tracing humanity's evolution through a series of "root-races." Atlantis was the home of the fourth root-race, very tall and highly civilized. As Donnelly had conjectured, they were the founders of several civilizations known to ordinary history. Atlantis, however, sank. After Madame Blavatsky's death an "astral clairvoyant," William Scott-Elliot, pursued the story of Atlantis and also that of Lemuria, another Theosophical sunken land.

For enthusiasts, Atlantis is apt to be a kind of Utopia with golden-age qualities, the home of an advanced society with knowledge and powers of magic that have been lost. One legacy of Theosophy, whether recognized or not, is a belief in huge changes of the earth's surface over geologically short periods of time, allowing an expectation that the process will continue and lost lands will resurface. Fantasies of this sort have encouraged notions of the future reappearance of Atlantis itself, a hope akin to the return of King Arthur and similar prophetic motifs.

This may take the modified form of a rebirth of Atlantean Ancient Wisdom, rather than a physical reemergence. On occult or paranormal grounds, caches of Atlantean secrets are said to have been preserved for posterity. Edgar Cayce, the American "Sleeping Prophet," asserted on the basis of a trance-revelation that the history of Atlantis was in a hidden underground chamber or hall of records near the Sphinx in Egypt, which would come to light sooner or later. He even gave directions, though not very convincingly. Colin Amery and others enlarged on his ideas, suggesting that the hall of records had more in it than he envisaged and likewise predicting its rediscovery.

However, some visionaries have foretold a literal rebirth of Atlantis, partly or wholly. One who did so in a fairly restrained way was Cayce himself. Others have ventured further. H. C. Randall-Stevens foretold, on the authority of an "Osirian" group, that the lost land will rise above the ocean in 2014. At that time, a cache of its Ancient Wisdom will be disclosed, as Amery and the rest have indicated, but in the Great Pyramid.

See also: Cayce, Edgar; Lemuria; Sphinx; Theosophy

Further Reading

Amery, Colin. *New Atlantis: the Secret of the Sphinx.* London and New York: Regency Press, 1976.

Ashe, Geoffrey. *Atlantis: Lost Lands, Ancient Wisdom.* London: Thames and Hudson, 1992.

Bramwell, James. *Lost Atlantis.* London: Cobden-Sanderson, 1937.

Bro, Harmon Hartzell. *Edgar Cayce.* Wellingborough, England: The Aquarian Press, 1990.

Collins, Andrew. *Gateway to Atlantis.* London: Headline, 2000.

AUGUSTINE, SAINT (354–430)

Christian philosopher and theologian whose views on prophecy established certain norms of interpretation.

of his life and thought, and *The City of God,* a vast survey of history, the role of Christian revelation, and its teachings about the destiny of humanity.

In *The City of God,* like other fathers of the Church, Augustine maintains that the Old Testament foreshadows the New and only makes complete sense when read retrospectively from a Christian standpoint. In particular, many of the Old Testament prophecies were really about Christianity, even though they could not have been understood in that sense when they were written. They were divinely inspired, and their meaning has been decipherable since the coming of Christ; Augustine claims that they have been instrumental in making many converts. Other prophecies, likewise inspired, are in the New Testament itself, notably in its last book, the Revelation or Apocalypse attributed to Saint John.

But what about prophecies unrelated to Christianity, by astrologers, for instance? If they are not inspired by God, does their fulfillment, when it happens, put a query over the Christian monopoly? Augustine regards them as illusory and worse than illusory even when they are right—especially when they are right. He attacks astrology as a technique, stressing such rational objections as the difficulty raised by twins, who have the same horoscope at birth but may go on to have very different lives. However, he looks deeper than that. He acknowledges that astrologers sometimes score, but he has a reason for rejecting their claims and advising Christians to mistrust them. This reason has wider applications.

According to Augustine, successful prophecy that is not of divine origin is diabolic, the work of "demons" or evil spirits. These beings can look ahead, if in a rather hit-or-miss way: "The demons . . . have much more knowledge of the future than men can have, by their greater acquaintance with certain signs which are hidden from us; sometimes they also foretell their own intentions. It is true that they are often de-

Saint Augustine, the principal Christian author in late Roman times, who condemned astrology and was suspicious of all prophecy except by divine inspiration. (Ann Ronan Picture Library)

Augustine was born in what is now Tunisia, at that time part of the Roman Empire. He taught in Rome, studied Neoplatonic philosophy, was converted to Christianity in 386, and returned to Africa, where he became a bishop. His immense literary output molded the thinking of the Church ever afterwards. Best known of his works are the *Confessions,* an autobiographical account

ceived, while the angels are never deceived." Human foreknowledge may be simply intelligent anticipation, but when it is more than that, it may be coming from "unclean demons" who are making use of their own foreknowledge to lead others astray. In the case of astrology, they mislead mortals by creating a bogus impression of validity. "When astrologers give replies that are often surprisingly true, they are inspired, in some mysterious way, by spirits, but spirits of evil, whose concern is to instil and confirm in men's minds those false and baneful notions about 'astral destiny.' These true predictions do not come from any skill in the notation and inspection of horoscopes; that is a spurious art."

Unhallowed prophecy, which may be plausible and even correct, but is communicated by evil beings for evil ends, reappears as a theme in the witch mania of the sixteenth and seventeenth centuries. It is a prominent motif in Shakespeare's *Macbeth*.

See also: Astrology; *Macbeth;* Prophecy, Theories of; Thomas Aquinas, Saint; Witchcraft

Further Reading

Augustine, Saint. *The City of God*. Translated by Henry Bettenson. Harmondsworth, England: Penguin Classics, 1984.

BACON, FRANCIS (1561–1626)

English statesman, essayist, and writer on scientific method.

Bacon is remembered for his groundbreaking discussions of systematic experiment, observation, and induction in works such as *The Advancement of Learning.* He is also unfortunately remembered for corruption in office, leading to his dismissal from the royal service. Nevertheless, his place in the history of science remains secure.

His *Essays or Counsels, Civil and Moral* presents fifty-eight essays that cover a wide range of topics; some, such as "Friendship," being of a general kind, and others, such as "Gardens," being particular. The thirty-fifth essay is "Of Prophecies." Bacon explains that he is not talking of biblical prophecies, which are in a class by themselves. He quotes several from classical literature, such as a passage in which the dramatist Seneca foretells that the bonds of the ocean will be loosed, the whole world will be opened up, and new worlds will be discovered—a prophecy, one might think, of the discovery of America. Most of Bacon's more recent examples are concerned with royalty. He recalls the English king Henry VI as foretelling the reign of a boy who unexpectedly became Henry VII. He mentions, interestingly, the prophecy of the death of the French king Henri II from a wound sustained in a tournament, a prophecy that made Nostradamus famous, though Bacon quotes a different source.

As a child, he says, he heard the prophecy

When hempe is spun
England's done.

"Hempe" was taken to refer to the initials of five successive monarchs—Henry VIII, Edward VI, Mary, her consort Philip, and Elizabeth I. After them, it was feared, disaster would befall England. It did not happen. What did happen was that Elizabeth was succeeded by James Stuart, who united the crowns of England and Scotland, so that the realm was known as Britain, and in that sense only, England *was* done.

Bacon is thoroughly dismissive. Prophecies of the kind he is talking about "ought all to be despised." Despised, but not simply ignored, because they can do harm among the credulous, and governments should take note of them and consider censorship. What is it that gives them their undeserved credence? First, selectivity. People notice them when they are fulfilled, or seem to be, and forget any number of similar ones that are not. This covers the case of dreams that supposedly come true. Secondly, a prophecy may echo a known conjecture, and when this is eventually fulfilled—more or less—it may be seen in retrospect as more exact than it was. When Seneca wrote about new worlds beyond the ocean, Greek authors had already speculated along those lines (Plato, for instance, in his account of Atlantis), and Seneca was not really doing any more; the application of his words to America was a product of later geography. Thirdly, many alleged prophecies cannot be documented as having been made before the happenings they are alleged to predict. They were made up afterwards.

Most of this criticism is sensible. Pseudo prophecy after the event is all too familiar.

Francis Bacon, Lord Chancellor of England and writer on scientific method and other topics. He thought prophecies "ought all to be despised." (Ann Ronan Picture Library)

The concoction of bogus sayings by Merlin is notorious. Seneca perhaps deserves better than Bacon allows. The argument from selectivity is more dubious. It does not dispose, for instance, of the anticipations of the *Titanic* disaster by Morgan Robertson and others. Moreover, while a prophecy picked out as successful may be only one among many that are not successful, that one may be so accurate and specific that it makes the notion of chance difficult to sustain. In the classic case of Nostradamus, it is true that only a few of his quatrains are clearly predictive, but each contains several interlocking forecasts with unique details—even personal names—that rule out ambiguity. These quatrains, some of which compress as many as five or six connected forecasts into four lines, are too complex to explain as mere lucky hits among hundreds that are not lucky.

Bacon does not discuss astrology in this essay. Elsewhere, he describes it as "pretending to discover that correspondence or concatenation which is between the superior globe and the inferior." He is thinking of the traditional system, with Earth at the center of the universe and everything else circling around it. He admits that in his own time astrology is "full of fictions," but he suggests that it might be given a rational basis in observed physical laws. If so, it could supply foreshadowings of natural phenomena, wars, revolutions, and other great events and indicate favorable times for various undertakings.

See also: Merlin; Nostradamus; Seneca, Lucius Annaeus

BAHAIS

Adherents of a religion of nineteenth-century origin that prophesies a nonsectarian, cosmopolitan future.

The Bahai faith is based on a revelation that occurred in two stages. In 1844, Mirza Ali Mohammed, a young resident of Shiraz in the southwest of Persia (now Iran), declared himself to be a manifestation of God. He assumed the title of Bab—Arabic for "gate"—and predicted a further manifestation yet to come, when someone greater than himself would usher in a new era. This future leader would be called Baha-Ullah, Splendor of God.

"Bab" was a recognized title in the Shiite division of Islam, and this one attracted a large following, helped by his descent from the Prophet Muhammad through both parents. He opposed polygamy and the slave trade. Orthodox Muslim divines were hostile, and the movement had to endure persecution. The Bab was imprisoned, then sentenced to be executed. On July 9, 1850, being about thirty years old, he confronted a firing squad. He was suspended by ropes, and the volley of bullets only severed the ropes, so that he fell unharmed. The officer in charge refused to repeat the order, but a subordinate did so, and this time, the Bab died. His remains were later transferred to Mount Carmel, near Haifa in Israel.

The new leader whom the Bab had foretold, Baha-Ullah, duly made his appearance. Aristocratic in his family background, he was named Mirza Hussain Ali. He embraced the Bab's teachings. During a fresh wave of suppression, he was exiled to Baghdad, then in the Turkish empire, and in 1863, at the age of forty-six, he declared himself to be the prophesied Baha-Ullah. The garden where he made this announcement became a sacred place in the Bahai religion that grew from it. Trouble with the Turkish authorities led eventually to Baha-Ullah's imprisonment at Acre, where he died in 1892.

He had put his essential doctrines on record. According to the Bahai theology, God is unknowable, but he communicates with humanity through manifestations adapted to the context in which they occur. These have included the founders of several other major religions—Zoroaster, Buddha, Jesus, and Muhammad. Baha-Ullah is the manifestation for the present age.

Since the religious founders have all been manifestations of the One God, who is the

God of all humanity, there is really only one religion, which they taught in forms suitable to their time; differences have arisen through later misinterpretation. The coming of Baha-Ullah is a sign that the human race has matured to a point where social and ideological unity can be realized. This unity is confidently predicted. The outgoing Bahai mission that spread to various countries was largely the work of Baha-Ullah's son Abdul-Baha (1844–1921).

Bahais recognize that the great step forward will not simply happen. They must work for it. They aim at the abolition of all forms of prejudice, whether based on race, nationality, class, or creed. This will pave the way to the "World Order of Baha-Ullah." Men and women will be equal and there will be equal educational opportunities for all children. There will be a world currency and a universal language, both perhaps auxiliary to existing ones rather than replacing them.

The Bahai faith has no clergy. Its adherents seek to influence others by exemplary conduct. They meet in "spiritual assemblies" that are subordinated to a "Universal House of Justice" in an imposing domed building on the side of Mount Carmel, where the Bab's remains are enshrined.

Further Reading

Cavendish, Richard, ed. *Man, Myth and Magic.* London: BPC Publishing, 1970–1972. Article "Bahais."

BARTON, ELIZABETH
(1506–1534)

English nun called the "Holy Maid of Kent" whose prophecies caused trouble in the reign of Henry VIII.

She attracted notice by her response to divisive changes in England that Henry had launched. He wanted to end his marriage to the Spanish princess Catherine of Aragon, who had borne a daughter but no surviving son who could be his heir. Furthermore, he had fallen in love with someone else, Anne Boleyn. He believed that there were grounds

for annulment of the marriage, but the pope had to rule on this, and negotiations dragged on for years with no decision. At last, Henry acted independently to resolve his marital problem, going beyond it in the process: he broke away from Rome and declared himself to be the head of the Church in England. None of this was done without arousing antagonism. Meanwhile, the Reformation was advancing on the continent. Henry was never inclined toward Protestantism himself, but it was gradually making converts among his subjects, and its progress, together with economic and social factors, was adding to the public uncertainty.

This situation produced a flurry of freelance prophecy. It was apt to be hostile to the king. He would be deposed, he would die in his sins, his kingdom would be afflicted with wars and plagues. Several of the doomsayers were women. During the past century or so, women mystics and visionaries had begun to be heard more often. Elizabeth Barton was one. In 1525, when she was a domestic servant in Kent, she had a long illness and exhibited what some thought to be supernatural gifts. A monk named Edward Bocking, from a Benedictine community in Canterbury, was impressed by her and accepted her claim to be inspired by the Virgin Mary. The next year, her disease was miraculously cured, as people supposed, and she entered a convent in Canterbury under Bocking's spiritual direction.

Elizabeth had visions and went into trances, sometimes lying on the floor, thrashing about, and uttering strange things. Bocking took some of these to be revelations and wrote a book about her. Others wrote pamphlets. Her sayings, when intelligible, upheld the Church's doctrines and authority so firmly as to be, by implication, critical of the king. A belief in her sanctity and miracle working spread widely, winning friends and supporters in several religious houses, notably Syon Abbey, which had a tradition of feminine devotion. The fame of the Holy

Maid of Kent reached the court; Henry himself granted her an audience, possibly in the hope of persuading her to stay within bounds. Presently, however, she began to denounce his attempts to discard his wife. She even wrote to the pope, urging him not to cooperate, and foretold that if Henry married Anne he would reign only another month. This was a dangerous matter, but some of his critics took her seriously and made her prophecies known. Prominent men who had misgivings about his policy listened to her, including Thomas More, the lord chancellor, and John Fisher, the bishop of Rochester. After reflection, More became cautious, Fisher not so cautious, but both were impartially beheaded for refusing to accept royal supremacy in the Church.

Before that, Barton's prophetic career had come to an end. She was arrested and charged with treason. Under interrogation, she virtually recanted, asserting that she had been prompted and used by opponents of the king's proceedings. There was some truth in this, but it is likely that she was not totally fraudulent. She really had produced "inspired" sayings, which conservative elements could exploit but did not invent or put in her mouth.

On April 20, 1534, together with Bocking, she was hanged. In England this was an unusual method of execution for a woman convicted of treason. Later, it became the normal treatment for women who were found guilty of witchcraft. That, however, was not a relevant issue here; a satirist called Barton a witch, but only as a term of abuse. The contemporary seer famous as "Mother Shipton," who may have been a witch in a more serious sense, is reputed to have supported Henry and thus kept out of trouble. But in any case, Mother Shipton is very probably fictitious. There is no reliable evidence that she existed.

Further Reading

Watt, Diana. *Secretaries of God: Women Prophets in Late Medieval and Early Modern England.* Cambridge: D. S. Brewer, 1997.

BELLAMY, EDWARD (1850–1898)

American novelist, author of *Looking Backward,* a Utopia offered to the public as a serious proposal.

Looking Backward, 2000–1887—to give it its full title—was the indirect inspiration of William Morris's *News from Nowhere,* as a hostile retort by a writer of very different outlook, who reacted against it. Bellamy's book is not exactly a prophecy itself or even a prediction; it is a social program in fictional disguise. He means it. He originally put his Utopia in the year 3000, then changed the date to 2000, on a more optimistic assessment of the time that would be needed to realize it.

He presents it through an imagined character, Julian West, a Bostonian who wakes from a trance in the year 2000 and learns that the United States has been transformed by adopting a Religion of Solidarity, with sweeping practical results. The Nation is now absolute and supreme. In its economic aspect, it is a single colossal corporation that owns everything and employs everybody. Its citizens, male and female, are compulsorily enrolled to do all the work in an "industrial army" under military discipline, from which the government itself is recruited; the president, elected on a restricted franchise, is the general-in-chief.

Each year, the gross national product is added up, a surplus is calculated, and everybody receives a share of it. These shares are all equal, an arrangement that is justified by the assumption that the workers do their best, and "doing one's best" is the same for all and allows no gradations. (Those who don't are put in jail.) It follows that there are no financial incentives and no financial inequalities.

This, however, means very little because there is no money. Shopping is done by filling out a form in a "sample-store" where goods are on view and paying with a credit card on which one's national share is debited by the value of the purchase. The goods are promptly delivered from a warehouse to the purchaser's home through electric "tubes"; Bellamy has great faith in technology. The whole annual allowance must be spent. Anything left over at the end of the year is confiscated by the Nation. So there is no incentive to save, but, then, nobody wants to save when the Nation provides housing, universal education, and complete social security.

Public kitchens and laundries take care of cooking and washing, and everybody eats at communal dining houses. Cultural needs are satisfied by such measures as playing music over the telephone. West, the observer from the past, comments revealingly that this is "the limit of human felicity."

At the time, many found Bellamy's Utopia attractive, probably in reaction against the uglier aspects of unbridled capitalism. It had some influence on economic thinking, and in the United States, it inspired short-lived political initiatives. Though Bellamy was contemptuous of left-wing labor organization, some Socialists approved. After a century's experience of totalitarianism in practice, his program may be less alluring.

See also: Morris, William

Further Reading

Carey, John, ed. *The Faber Book of Utopias.* London: Faber and Faber, 1999.

BENSON, ROBERT HUGH (1871–1914)

English Catholic convert, author of two fantasies picturing two opposite futures for the Church.

Benson came from a distinguished literary family. Ordained as an Anglican clergyman, he was received into the Catholic Church in 1903 and spent the last years of his life in Rome. He wrote several novels.

Lord of the World (1907), set in the twenty-first century, is reminiscent of *A Short Story of the Antichrist* by Vladimir Solovyev. Its chief character, Julian Felsenburgh—seen only through the eyes of others—is, in fact, an Antichrist figure, though Benson never actually calls him so. An enigmatic genius, he achieves supreme power and establishes a worldwide regime of peace and welfare, or so it appears. He founds an enlightened Religion of Humanity to replace all existing ones. His success is overwhelming, but the regime's true nature gradually becomes visible. His supporters are led step by step to rationalize and support appalling actions in the name of enlightenment. Rome, with its pope, is independent; Felsenburgh alleges a conspiracy by the dwindling Catholic body and destroys the city by aerial bombardment. He is hailed as divine, whereupon nonconformity to the Religion of Humanity is made a crime, and dissenters are liquidated. In the final episode, a small surviving Catholic center is condemned to destruction and doomed, humanly speaking—though, as it turns out, Benson gives the story a final twist.

Many of Benson's readers found *Lord of the World* depressing. In 1911, he produced a companion novel, *The Dawn of All,* imagining an opposite process, with the Church growing greater and greater. Strictly speaking, this is a dream or reverie rather than a prognostication. A priest who has abandoned his faith falls into a coma and wakes up—or thinks he has woken up—to find that he is Monsignor Masterman in a Church that dominates society. His memory is gone, and he has to piece together what has happened in the inferred interval. The chronology is inconsistent, perhaps on purpose: in one passage, he is told that the year is 1973, elsewhere, he is in the twenty-first century.

He learns that the Church has triumphed because of ideological and political changes. Several sciences, notably psychology, have been seen to vindicate its teachings and have given it new respectability, so that the intelligentsia who used to be opposed are now mostly believers. Concurrently with this, a reaction against Socialism has opened the way for what amounts to a high-quality clerical regime in most countries and a revival of monarchy. Only Germany is holding out. Masterman is impressed by the popularity and competence of the new order but deeply shocked when someone is put to death for a very mild heresy. He admires the pope for his courage in facing German revolutionaries who have killed his envoys. In the end, however, even a sympathetic reader may have reservations, and Benson implies that he is raising issues rather than offering a forecast of possibilities.

See also: Solovyev, Vladimir

BESANT, ANNIE (1847–1933)

English Theosophist who caused a stir by predicting the advent of a new Messiah.

Originally Annie Wood, she married an Anglican clergyman, Frank Besant. Though soon separated from him, she continued to use her married name. She went through three major conversions, throwing herself with zeal and ability into each successive cause. First, with the freethinker Charles Bradlaugh, she campaigned for atheism and birth control. Then, she joined Bernard Shaw and others in launching the Fabian Society, a body aiming at a gradual transition to Socialism. Finally, she was won over to Theosophy by Madame Blavatsky's book *The Secret Doctrine*. In 1907, she became president of the Theosophical Society. She accepted Blavatsky's claims about mysterious "Masters" who taught her telepathically and secretly influenced the world's destinies. According to Besant, there was a whole hierarchy of superior beings who met periodically in Shambhala, a northern holy place of Buddhist mythology, with a king called the King of the World; she made astral contact with him to seek his guidance.

In spite of the strangeness of her ideas, she was a person of powerful charisma and, in some ways, unusual practical wisdom. Under her leadership, the main body of the society held together through scandals and feuds.

Deeply impressed by the affinities between Theosophical doctrines and Hinduism, she spent a long time in India developing them and played an effective though strictly constitutional part in the movement for Indian self-rule.

She was interested in the Hindu concept of avatars, incarnations of the Supreme God Vishnu. In the Bhagavad Gita, Vishnu, in the form of Krishna, says: "Whenever and wherever duty decays and unrighteousness prospers, I shall be born in successive ages to destroy evil-doers and re-establish the reign of the moral law." Thinking on similar lines, though in terms of her own ideology, Besant believed that an entity whom she called the World Teacher took human form at long intervals. He had appeared as Buddha and Christ, and he was now to appear again. At the end of 1908, she claimed to have had a revelation of this approaching event, and in the following year, she began publicly proclaiming it.

About this time, a Hindu Theosophist named Narayaniah came to live and work at the Theosophical headquarters at Adyar, near Madras. A widower, he brought four sons with him, together with other relatives. One of his sons, Jiddu Krishnamurti, was then thirteen years old. Early in 1909, several men and boys in the Adyar community used to go to the beach together and swim. They were sometimes joined by Besant's principal colleague, C. W. Leadbeater. The first time he saw Krishnamurti, who happened to be with the party that day, he singled him out as spiritually exceptional. In the ensuing months, he made surprising discoveries about the boy's past incarnations. Toward the end of the year, instructed by the invisible Hierarchy, Annie Besant accepted that Krishnamurti was the destined human vehicle of the World Teacher.

She adopted him legally, after difficulties with his father, and prepared him for messiahship. A special organization was formed, the Order of the Star in the East. Not all

Theosophists were compliant: this was the occasion of Rudolf Steiner's break with the society. In 1921, however, a Dutch supporter gave the order the use of Castle Eerde, a large house near Ommen in Holland. International Star Camps were held in the grounds, at which Krishnamurti made appearances. A vision in 1922 convinced him, for the moment, that he indeed had the messianic role that was assigned to him. He traveled giving lectures. Well-known people who showed interest in the ideas he promoted included the conductor Leopold Stokowski and the former suffragette leader Christabel Pankhurst. From December 1925, a change in Krishnamurti's voice and style during his talks convinced many of his hearers that the higher being was taking possession of him. He visited the United States with much publicity and lived for a while at Ojai in California.

During the next few years, Annie Besant was busy with political activities on behalf of India, and Krishnamurti seemed less amenable. He had grown tired of being manipulated, and he laid more and more stress on the importance of people using their own judgment and not relying on his or anyone's. At Eerde in July 1929, with notable integrity, he dissolved the order and virtually abdicated. Annie Besant never recovered. Her last prophecy, also unsuccessful, was that India would achieve self-rule before her death.

A remarkable thing in this tragicomedy was that when Leadbeater intuitively picked out a young, rather frail boy with nothing obviously special about him, his insight was—after a fashion—correct. After the abdication, Krishnamurti did go on to become a public philosopher in his own style, delivering lectures, writing books, and impressing well-known persons, Aldous Huxley among them. He mentally blocked out his Theosophical career and became unwilling to talk about it, even speaking of a kind of selective amnesia. He lived until 1986.

See also: Shambhala; Theosophy
Further Reading
Nethercot, Arthur H. *The Last Four Lives of Annie Besant.* London: Rupert Hart-Davis, 1963.

BIBLICAL PROPHECY (1)—ISRAELITE AND JEWISH

Prophecy in the Jewish Bible—the Old Testament, in Christian parlance—takes several forms and shows a unique progress. At all stages, it is attributed to Yahweh, the Lord, the God of Israel. References to techniques such as Gentile soothsayers might use are few and mostly disapproving. Joseph in Genesis is not counted as a prophet, yet even he, when he interprets dreams and foretells what will happen to the dreamers, disclaims any notion that he does it by his own wisdom: "Do not interpretations belong to God?" Other early scriptural figures are called prophets in a general way, as being divinely inspired. However, when the Israelites are established in the Promised Land, full-time prophecy appears as a vocation. The term for a prophet in this sense is *nabi,* probably meaning "someone who is called."

Most of Israel's prophets, but not all, were male. Some were freelances; others combined in groups or guilds. They wore garments of skin and played musical instruments—flutes, lyres, harps, tambourines; they might be described as Yahweh's minstrels. As such, they had a shamanic quality. They could invoke the Lord's spirit, and when it blew upon them, they danced or rolled on the ground in ecstasy and saw visions. In that condition, they might utter oracular chants, which were revered as divine messages. The ecstasy could be infectious: Israel's first king, Saul, is twice seized with it. Yahweh could even take possession of non-Israelites, as in the story of the seer Balaam, who is hired to curse the Israelites and can only bless them. Nabi prophets were respected and could live on gifts and hospitality.

Elijah, the first of the great prophets of ancient Israel, denouncing King Ahab for his apostasy and tyranny. (Ann Ronan Picture Library)

Their supposedly inspired advice was seldom unacceptable to those who consulted them, and insofar as they made predictions, these were apt to be in the encouraging manner of modern fortune-tellers. But in the account of Ahab, who ruled the northern Israelites during the ninth century B.C., a new style is beginning to emerge. There is a distinction between prophecy spoken to oblige patrons and prophecy that tells the truth, however unwelcome. Elijah denounces Ahab's flagrant injustice and his attempts, under the influence of his foreign queen Jezebel, to replace Yahweh worship with Baal worship. He foretells a long drought as a sign of God's displeasure, and it happens. Later in the reign, another prophet, Micaiah, also begins to sound a new note. Ahab plans an expedition to recapture the city of Ramoth Gilead from the Syrians. He assembles a body of nabi prophets who assure him, in chorus, that the Lord will deliver the city into his hands. But Micaiah contradicts them. He describes a vision in which the Lord authorized a "lying spirit" to enter into Ahab's prophets and lure him to destruction. Ahab refuses to listen, takes his army to Ramoth-gilead, and falls in battle.

The activities of these men—especially Elijah, who is one of the outstanding biblical figures—opened the way for a succession of prophets whose revelations were written down and became part of Scripture. The greatest of these was Isaiah, who flourished in the eighth century B.C. There is no parallel outside Israel, either to this kind of prophecy itself or to the literary power of some of its productions. A prophet was "called" when the word of the Lord came to him unbidden. He might see visions and dream dreams. But the point of his experiences was that they made sense, often with a radical message. These prophets were deeply and eloquently critical of the irresponsible luxury of the rich and the reduction of Israel's religion to official ceremonies, sometimes with pagan contaminations. Showing

nostalgia for the simpler way of earlier times, they proclaimed that justice and mercy and charity were more acceptable to the Lord than rituals and sacrifices.

A pervasive theme was that Yahweh loved his people, but they were estranged from him by their own perverseness. It was largely because of the prophets' foreshadowings of divine judgment that the word *prophecy* began to acquire its predictive meaning. One idea that developed was that the Chosen People were not an indivisible bloc, secure in God's favor. Many might fall away (the northern tribes did and were conquered and uprooted by the Assyrians); but the divine blessing could be inherited by a faithful remnant, who would never be deserted or permanently dispossessed of the Promised Land. The prophet Jeremiah foretold, correctly, that his people would be deported to Babylon, but he also foretold that after a penitential exile, the survivors who remained faithful would be allowed to go back to Zion. This happened in 539 B.C., when the Persian king Cyrus conquered the Babylonian Empire and gave the captives permission to return. They and their descendants became the Jews, a name derived from *Judahite,* applying to the principal Israelite group centered on Jerusalem and its Temple.

Prophecy was much less conspicuous in the restored community. However, it reappeared in a fresh guise as a response to persecution at the hands of the Syrian king Antiochus Epiphanes. It was now more a matter of speculation by authors who might profess to be inspired and to be continuators of biblical tradition, but had little of the spontaneity of the nabi or of prophets such as Isaiah and Jeremiah. Jewish hopes of a final deliverance and triumph were expressed in forecasts of a spectacular divine intervention and in predictions of the Messiah, a king of the line of David who would be the Jews' leader and final deliverer, reigning in Zion.

Roman conquest stimulated such hopes. They had to be abandoned for the foreseeable future when two anti-Roman revolts were crushed, the second and conclusive one in A.D. 135. Jerusalem was largely destroyed with its Temple, and the Jews were scattered through the Roman world and beyond. However, the expectation of the Messiah was never extinguished, though most rabbis discouraged guesswork about him. The prophetic hope of a return to the Promised Land was kept alive through many centuries of dispersal and suffering. Its fulfillment through modern Zionism, against all rational probability and enormous odds, has impressed many as an extraordinary case of successful prophecy, even though some Orthodox Jews opposed the Zionist movement on the ground that Israel's reconstitution was to be the work of the Messiah alone and must not be anticipated by human agency.

See also: Daniel; Ezekiel; Isaiah; Jeremiah; Jonah; Messiah; Micah; Promised Land; Second Isaiah

Further Reading

Ashe, Geoffrey. *The Land and the Book.* London: Collins, 1965.

Lindblom, J. *Prophecy in Ancient Israel.* Oxford: Basil Blackwell, 1962.

BIBLICAL PROPHECY (2)— CHRISTIAN

The Church broke away from its Jewish origins in the latter part of the first century A.D., when it was virtually defunct in Jerusalem and survived elsewhere mainly as a network of Gentile groups created by the missions of Paul and others. It was still far from having an agreed documentation. Christians, however, inherited the Jewish Bible—to be known presently as the Old Testament—and while some extremists wanted to drop it, the consensus was in favor of keeping it as sacred Scripture. After all, Christ had endorsed it and quoted from it. Christians believed, however, that he had indicated a new way of understanding it, and especially of understanding its prophecies.

Many of these, they held, should be read as foreshadowing him. With that clue in mind, they began finding fresh significance in various prophetic texts. This process can be seen in the First Gospel, which bears the name of Matthew. In support of the belief that Jesus' mother was a virgin and he had no human father, the author says the miracle is foretold in Isaiah 7:14: "Behold, a virgin shall conceive and bear a son, and his name shall be called Emmanuel." Isaiah was probably referring to the birth of a royal heir in his own time, not to anything miraculous; the Hebrew word translated "virgin" does not necessarily mean that. Yet in a context of divine inspiration, it is fair to detect a secondary sense beyond the obvious one, and the name Emmanuel (meaning "God with us") may be thought to hint at such a sense.

Matthew, or whoever the author was, asserts an Old Testament confirmation of Jesus' status in Micah 5:2, where a messianic figure is to be born in Bethlehem. He also asserts an Old Testament forecast of his entry into Jerusalem in Zechariah 9:9, about Zion's king coming to her mounted on an ass. He finds foreshadowings in texts that were not originally prophetic at all, such as Zechariah 11:13, which refers to thirty pieces of silver, the sum paid to Judas. The Fourth Gospel finds similar anticipations of the crucifixion, as in Psalm 22:18: "They divided my garments among them, and for my raiment they cast lots." This discovery of symbols or "types" in Jewish Scripture went much further, as in the *Letter to the Hebrews,* where many episodes in the history of Israel are given fresh meanings and made to point in a new direction.

According to Saint Augustine in the fifth century, such anticipations of Christ, extracted from Jewish Scripture, were effective in making converts. When the essential Christian message is once accepted, these texts may indeed be seen as corroborative, yet scarcely as predictive. No one would have taken them thus at the time of writing.

Christ riding into Jerusalem, an event seen by early Christians as fulfilling a prophecy about the Messiah. (Ann Ronan Picture Library)

Granted, they are not prophecy invented after the event, but they are prophecy *recognized* after the event, when they were fulfilled; not before. The most impressive case is the citation in the New Testament (two or three times, though with surprisingly little emphasis) of the "Servant Song" in Isaiah 52:13–53:12. In this, the prophet known as Second Isaiah tells a story that is genuinely hard to account for except in terms of Christian beliefs about Jesus, and he tells it over 500 years before Jesus lived and before those beliefs took shape.

Prophecies by the Christians themselves were concerned with the Second Coming of Christ, the overthrow of the powers of evil, and the End of the World. They were based on reputed sayings of Jesus. In the Gospels, he speaks of the Kingdom—the community of believers, in which God will reign—and its imminent manifestation and ultimate glory. He makes no commitment as to duration: he hints at an undefined future, perhaps a long one, and warns that the day and hour of the End are known only to his heavenly Father. However, some of his sayings, as presented in the Gospels, are given a context suggesting that the End is close and is, in fact, to be within the lifetime of "this generation."

Wishful thinking or textual confusion may have affected the record. It certainly appears that many Christians did expect an early return of Christ in visible majesty. The second letter of Paul to his Thessalonian converts (its authenticity has been questioned, but the point is irrelevant) reveals that some of them not only thought that the Lord would return soon but that he might even have returned already and were giving up work and the ordinary business of life in that belief: were dropping out, in fact. Paul condemns this behavior, and, in doing so, makes an important contribution to Christian prophecy. He says a diabolic arch-enemy must appear first, who will afflict and divide the Church until Christ actually does return and destroy him. This is the be-ginning of the concept of Antichrist, who acquires a settled place in the Christian scheme of things.

The New Testament has one complete and famous prophetic book, the Apocalypse or Revelation by a Jewish Christian named John, traditionally the apostle. It was written, at least in its present form, during the closing decade of the first century. John still seems to be hoping for an early End, but he has touches that imply otherwise. One is a description of the Church in the future as "a great multitude . . . from every nation," pre-supposing many years of worldwide evangelism and growth yet to come.

Revelation belongs to an established genre of Jewish apocalyptic prophecy, but it has a complexity of structure and a richness of imagery that surpass the surviving Jewish examples. At the start, Christ comes to the author in a vision and tells him that he will see "what is and what is to take place here-after." This promise has led many commentators to interpret the entire book as a pre-view of history (or at least the history of those parts of the world that the commentators think important) for many years ahead, sometimes as far as the twentieth century. Such speculation has been encouraged by what look like cryptographic clues in the text. In general, it is misguided. For instance, while chapters 8 and 9, depicting plagues and other disasters, foreshadow divine judgments on the pagan world, they are mythic rather than literal. They cannot be credibly related to anything that actually happened.

In chapters 13 and 17, however, John does symbolize recognizable realities—the anti-Christian Roman Empire, in the guise of a satanically sponsored Beast, and its world-ex-ploiting capital, in the guise of the "harlot" Babylon. He alludes to emperors living in his own time, Nero certainly, Domitian probably. Given these factual references, it is not too fanciful to probe further, and these chapters do have a predictive element and even ar-guable fulfillments. John foretells a persecution of Christians immensely more ruthless and widespread than any inflicted hitherto, with a religious aspect of its own; and such a persecution happened in the early fourth century A.D. and not before. He also foretells the ruin of "Babylon," the city of Rome, by forces generated within the empire itself; and this happened when Rome was sacked by barbarians whom the empire had tried to absorb, in the fifth century and not before.

Revelation looks beyond to the Second Coming, a final conflict, and a thousand-year reign of Christ on Earth. Some Christians took this literally, saying that the Second Coming would bring a kind of Utopia, even a Utopia of material well-being. This "millenarian" opinion failed to meet with ecclesiastical approval, and the thousand-year reign was given a symbolic meaning, but the more down-to-earth reading of John's prophecy never quite expired.

See also: Antichrist; Apocalypse; End of the World; Isaiah; Jesus Christ; John the Baptist; Micah; Revelation; Second Isaiah; Simeon and Anna

Further Reading

Ashe, Geoffrey. *The Book of Prophecy.* London: Blandford, 1999.

Brown R. E., J. A. Fitzmyer, and R. E. Murphy, eds. *The New Jerome Biblical Commentary.* Englewood Cliffs, NJ: Prentice-Hall, 1990.

Swete, Henry Barclay. *The Apocalypse of St. John.* London: Macmillan, 1907.

BLAKE, WILLIAM (1757–1827)

English poet and artist, prophet of a highly individual apocalypse.

Blake spent most of his life in London as a professional engraver and book illustrator. He was familiar with the doctrines of the scientist and visionary Emanuel Swedenborg, and his thinking owed something to several contemporary eccentrics, among them Richard Brothers, the pioneer British-Israelite, John Varley, one of the few active astrologers at that time, and Owen Pughe, a follower of Joanna Southcott—especially Pughe, who had unusual notions about British antiquity, druids, and related matters. Blake, however, ranged far beyond any of these influences. His well-known lyrical poems constitute only a fraction of his output. In a series of Prophetic Books, with which much of his artistic work is associated, he built up a complex mythology of the human condition.

He saw himself as a prophet in the biblical sense, though, for him, divinity inhered in humanity and not in a transcendent God. The exact nature of his inspiration is uncertain: he may have had visionary experiences in a "hypnagogic" state between waking and sleep and developed these afterward in writing. The finished product, however arrived at, is in unrhymed verse, which, in his later work, is barely distinguishable from prose. His "prophesying" is mainly in the old sense of inspired utterance, not prediction. However, it leads up to an apocalyptic climax that is regarded as future.

The Prophetic Books are extremely difficult. It has been said that their meaning is not so much "what they say" as "what you arrive at for yourself by a sustained effort to understand them," aided, of course, by commentators who have made the same effort and reached a degree of consensus. The central idea is that the human race was formerly united, wise, and creative. Then came a fall (not the biblical Fall), and humanity became divided, inwardly as well as outwardly, declining from its ancient heights into error, disorganization, spiritual blindness, and constriction. Hence false religions, false ideologies, wars, persecutions, and other evils. But the creative imagination, which has never ceased to manifest itself in art and literature, will eventually triumph, bringing a rebirth. Vision and unity will be recovered, all that was lost will be reinstated, the pristine integrity will return.

Blake invents a group of symbolic characters, some of whom represent aspects of

One of the engravings made by William Blake for his "Prophetic Book" Jerusalem. (Ann Ronan Picture Library)

human nature. In his vast final work, *Jerusalem* (not the short poem often called so), composed during the period from 1804 to 1820, he brings his mythology to a focus in the figure of Albion. Albion is the earliest name of Britain. Blake's Albion stands for Britain but also for humanity as a whole. This identification depends on one of the unorthodox theories current in his time—that Britain was the original fountainhead of all wisdom and culture, worldwide. Humanity, in everything that matters, derives from Britain; therefore, Britain, personified under its ancient name Albion, can stand for humanity.

In Blake's primordial past, Albion becomes self-alienated from the divine vision. He sinks into a deathlike sleep, and that is the fall. But he will wake up, and that will be the rebirth, ushering in a new era of exuberant freedom, creativity, and illumination. After the multiple obscurities of *Jerusalem*, Blake describes Albion's awakening in a passage that is unexpectedly simple and moving.

Blake is a patriot, though in a semimystical style of his own, rejecting most of the paraphernalia of conventional patriotism. His Albion is more than a literary construct. He naturally takes a deep interest in Britain's history and legends and even in Britain's topography; he mentions numerous places. His most ambitious painting, taking hints from Pughe, was called *The Ancient Britons*. This is lost, but a long accompanying note survives. In it, Blake says: "The stories of Arthur are the acts of Albion, applied to a prince of the fifth century." Arthur, the glorious king who passed away but will return, is an image in a particular time and place of the great overarching theme that Albion's life span embodies.

Blake's myth of long-lost glory, decline, and apocalyptic rebirth is his own expression of a persistent syndrome, as it may be called, that is expressed also in the glory, the passing, and the return of Arthur. The motif of reinstating a past golden age has inspired actual historical movements of reform and revolution. Thus, Christian Reformers in the sixteenth century appealed to the purity of the primitive Church and claimed to be disinterring it from corruption; French revolutionaries under Rousseau's influence theorized about a free and equal ancient society that could reassert itself when tyrannies were destroyed; Gandhi aimed to revive a long-ago ideal India of village communes and saints and sages, by ending the foreign domination that had suppressed it. The return of Arthur mythifies, in a British setting, a way of looking at things that has had profound effects. Blake universalizes this in Albion's awakening.

See also: Arthur, King; British-Israel Theory; Southcott, Joanna

Further Reading

Ashe, Geoffrey. *Camelot and the Vision of Albion.* London: Heinemann, 1971, and New York: St. Martin's Press, 1971.

Todd, Ruthven. *Tracks in the Snow.* London: The Grey Walls Press, 1946.

BLAVATSKY, HELENA PETROVNA

See Theosophy

BRAHAN SEER, THE (SIXTEENTH CENTURY)

Scottish prophet located rather indefinitely in the Highlands and the Scottish Islands. His name is given as Coinneach Odhar, in Gaelic, or as Dun Kenneth. His powers are said to have come from his scrying stone, a gift of the fairy-folk. When he first looked into this, just before a meal, it showed him that the food was poisoned.

He may be identifiable with a man of his name who was arrested for witchcraft in 1577, on the estates of the earl of Seaforth. Tradition connects the Seer's most famous prophecy and his death with the Seaforth family. When the earl was away, allegedly on business, the Seer told the countess that her husband was visiting another woman. She had him put to death: he was correct, but his knowledge must have come by unhallowed means and, in any case, he had no right to talk to her like that. He found time to retort by predicting that the last of the Seaforths would be deaf and dumb and his sons would die before him. This happened during the lifetime of Sir Walter Scott. The original prophecy may, of course, have been invented or improved retrospectively.

The same applies with greater force to other prophecies attributed to the Brahan Seer. He is supposed to have foretold the battle of Culloden in 1746, when Charles Edward Stuart (Bonnie Prince Charlie) was defeated. He is even supposed to have foretold railways.

See also: Peden, Alexander; Scrying; Thomas the Rhymer

Further Reading

Folklore, Myths and Legends of Britain. London: Readers Digest Association, 1973.

Wallechinsky, David, Amy Wallace, and Irving Wallace and others. *The Book of Predictions.* New York: William Morrow, 1980.

BRITISH-ISRAEL THEORY

A theory tracing British origins in the Bible, with implications for national status and destiny.

The British-Israel theory was the most prominent of a number of theories about the Lost Tribes. As related in the Bible, the northern kingdom of Israel, comprising ten of the tribes reputedly descended from the patriarch Jacob, was destroyed by Assyrian deportations in the eighth century B.C. The deportees were transferred eastward and probably assimilated. However, the prophet Ezekiel (Ezekiel 37:21–24) assumes that their descendants still have a corporate identity and will someday be reunited in the Holy Land with descendants of their southern kin-

folk, namely, the Jews. In this passage, God promises that "my servant David" will be king over the whole community. A belief in a large body of ethnic Israelites surviving in some remote land is attested much later by the Jewish historian Josephus. Their existence has continued to be a tenet of Orthodox Judaism.

Some Christians have not been content to leave the matter indefinite. They have tried to locate and identify the lost Israelites, who, it must be presumed, wandered beyond the bounds of the Assyrian Empire. The underlying idea is that God's covenant was with all twelve tribes, and since his promises cannot be canceled, the northerners must exist somewhere. They have been found, with the aid of tenuous linguistic and historical clues, in Afghanistan and Japan and even America.

The British-Israel theory pressed such scriptural arguments further. It was foreshadowed by Richard Brothers (1757–1824), but the main development came long after his time. Exponents drew attention to prophecies of the Chosen People enjoying visible divine favor, power, and greatness. That could not be said of the Jews, who, when the theory was taking shape, did not even have a homeland. God's promises must therefore have been fulfilled in the other branch of the Chosen People. These promises fitted Britain when its empire was flourishing, so the British had to be the long-lost northern Israelites.

To confirm the equation, ingenious speculations traced the Lost Tribes, by various routes, to northwestern Europe and the British Isles. For instance, Assyrian inscriptions called the northern Israelites the people of Omri, after one of their best-known kings. The name could have been modified into "Khumri," and this could have been the origin of "Cimmerian" (applied in antiquity to a nation in southern Russia, doubtless Israel on the march) and "Cymry" (applied to the Welsh, doubtless part of Israel in its new country). A more direct argument was that the word *British* sounded like the Hebrew *b'rit ish,* meaning "covenant man." Legendary genealogies were invoked to link British royalty with King David. British-Israel theory was strongly Protestant and stressed, as proof of the British people's "chosen" character, their break with the pope, their translation of the Bible, and their distribution of it through their overseas possessions.

For a time, in spite of so much that was fanciful, the prophecies seemed to be working and pointing to a glorious future. One result of World War I was that Britain took over Palestine and sponsored the Zionist program of Jewish settlement. The two branches of the Chosen People were being brought together in the Holy Land, just as Ezekiel had foretold. The heyday of the British-Israel theory was in the 1920s and 1930s. Early in 1936, the accession of King Edward VIII, known to his intimates as David, fulfilled the word of God about "my servant David." Soon, perhaps, Ezekiel's next chapter would also be fulfilled. This predicted an invasion of the Holy Land by the evil northern ruler "Gog of the land of Magog, the chief prince of Meshech and Tubal"—surely a reference to Soviet Russia, Gog being Stalin, Meshech and Tubal being Moscow and Tobolsk. Some British-Israel advocates, with support from Pyramidology, expected an event of crucial importance in September 1936. Nothing particular happened. Shortly afterward, King Edward abdicated. Soviet Russia became otherwise engaged. In the next few decades, British rule in Palestine ended, and so did the empire itself. Everything had fallen apart, and the prophetic texts that supposedly established Britain's Israelite character were no longer relevant.

See also: Ezekiel; Pyramidology

Further Reading

Ashe, Geoffrey. *Mythology of the British Isles.* London: Methuen, 1990.

Cavendish, Richard, ed. *Man, Myth and Magic.* London: BPC Publishing, 1970–1972. Article "Lost Tribes of Israel."

Sargent, H. N. *The Marvels of Bible Prophecy.* London: Covenant Publishing, 1938.

Todd, Ruthven. *Tracks in the Snow.* London: The Grey Walls Press, 1946.

CAMISARDS

French religious nonconformists claiming prophetic inspiration.

Through most of the seventeenth century, France's Protestant minority, the Huguenots, lived in peace under the terms of an agreement, the Edict of Nantes. In 1685, however, Louis XIV revoked the edict and tried, often with cruelty, to enforce religious conformity. The anger of the Huguenots was intense, both against the authorities and against the members of their own community who professed Catholicism under pressure. Many of their pastors went into exile in Switzerland and Holland and hoped the crisis would pass.

One of the most distinguished of them, Pierre Jurieu, unwisely wrote a commentary on Revelation. He foretold that the Catholic Church in France would collapse in 1690. His book was not well received by his coreligionists in general, but it gave an impulse to apocalyptic extremism. A Huguenot named du Serre, who owned a glass factory, assembled fifteen children from the peasantry of the Monts du Vivarais in southeast France and taught them (it is not clear how) to "prophesy" and preach, with physical symptoms of inspiration. Their example was infectious. Enthusiasts would go into shivering fits and foam at the mouth. Preachers, including adult ones, had convulsions and sometimes induced convulsions in their hearers. More children followed the first wave, making successful efforts to win back Huguenots who had defected to Catholi-

cism. Soon, the phenomenon was no longer confined to children.

The Camisard movement, as it was called in allusion to the shirts worn by peasants, was accompanied by reports of miracles. Sometimes, they involved imperviousness to injury; Camisard prophets fell from heights without being hurt and stabbed themselves with knives leaving no mark. It also produced what seemed to be paranormal knowledge, together with glossolalia, the "gift of tongues," though one of the best-attested instances is less than convincing: a so-called judgment on enemies was verbalized as "Tring trang swing swang hing hang," at least in an English transcript of a later date.

Camisard prophets of both sexes disturbed the more responsible Huguenots, who tried to discredit them by insinuating immoral conduct and publicizing prophecies that had not been fulfilled. During 1689–90 there were clashes between Camisards and government troops in the Vivarais. Jurieu's fateful year ended with no collapse of the Church. But despite the failure, cataclysmic events were still expected, and major trouble was brewing. Beginning in 1702, a Camisard uprising in the Cévennes brought widespread destruction of churches and large-scale massacres of Catholics, supposedly on direct orders from God. Mainstream Huguenots were appalled: this was not legitimate resistance to persecution, it was fanaticism that played into the hands of the persecutors. The French government, struggling against external enemies in the War of the Spanish Succession, struck back at the internal revolt with the utmost ruthlessness. Jean Cavalier, the ablest Camisard leader, maintained a skillful guerrilla warfare for two years but made peace with the royal commander, the Duc de Villars, in 1704.

He had obtained some concessions, but diehards accused him of betrayal and af-

A French propagandist picture attributing outrages to the religious rebels called Camisards, who were forcibly suppressed in the early eighteenth century. (Bibliotheque Nationale/Photo Larousse)

flicted the region with futile and dwindling hostilities for six years longer. More important was a dispersal of Camisards to other countries, many of the prophets among them. Some went to Germany and may have influenced the birth of the sect known as the Moravian Brethren and thence, indirectly, Methodism. Others, including Cavalier, found their way to England—at first to London, where they were initially welcomed as victims of the French king whom the English were fighting. It was not a general welcome. The Huguenot body already in the capital disowned them; and Cavalier himself did not help by virtually deserting them. Still, Camisard activity attracted attention, even though the prophets seemed to regard the Anglican Church as little better than the Catholic and made wild predictions of the destruction of the city and the end of the world. They acquired a chapel of their own and gained a few converts, such as John Lacy, who claimed that he could talk Latin without knowing any. More surprising was the case of the scientist Fatio de Duillier, a friend of Newton, who acted as the prophets' secretary and recorded their utterances. He was suspected of manipulating the movement to spread ideas of his own.

Camisard propaganda reached its height in 1707 and was noisy enough to provoke rebuttals and prosecutions. Several of the leaders were punished by being stood in the pillory, where Fatio loyally joined them. Public ridicule grew. The Camisards' inspired frenzies and contortions were parodied by comedians. They overreached themselves by predicting that a certain Dr. Emes, then on his deathbed, would rise from the grave five months after burial. On the appointed day, a crowd gathered at Bunhill Fields cemetery. Nothing happened. The prophets attributed the corpse's lack of cooperation to their not being present themselves, owing to the danger of mob violence. After the London fiasco, some of them wandered away to Oxford and other cities, without much impact.

In Manchester, however, a group under their influence remained in being for several decades and eventually attracted a young woman named Ann Lee: she emigrated to the United States and founded the sect of Shakers, which survived into the twentieth century.

Further Reading

Cavendish, Richard, ed. *Man, Myth and Magic*. London: BPC Publishing, 1970–1972. Articles "Camisards," "Shakers."

Knox, Ronald Arbuthnott. *Enthusiasm; A Chapter in the History of Religion, with Special Reference to the XVII and XVIII Centuries*. New York: Oxford University Press, 1950.

Manuel, Frank E. *A Portrait of Isaac Newton*. Cambridge, MA: Harvard University Press, 1968.

CASSANDRA

In Greek mythology, a daughter of Priam, king of Troy. She received the gift of foreknowledge from Apollo, the god of prophecy. There are two accounts of the way in which this happened. According to one, when she was a child, a birthday feast was held for her and her brother Helenus in a sanctuary of the god. The children fell asleep in a corner, and the sacred serpents licked their ears, giving them both prophetic powers.

The other version says that Cassandra's sleep in the sanctuary occurred after she was grown up. Apollo desired her and promised her the prophetic gift if she would comply. She accepted it but then had second thoughts about her own side of the bargain. Apollo spat in her open mouth, with the result (implied also in the alternative story) that while she could foretell the future, no one would believe her.

Cassandra uttered her pronouncements in fits of frenzy suggesting insanity. Their ominous tone made her proverbial as a voice of doom. When the Greeks besieged Troy to recover the abducted Helen, Cassandra predicted the city's fall, correctly but without ef-

Cassandra as portrayed in a woodcut by the German artist Dürer. Apollo gave her a gift of prophecy, but, when she rejected his advances, he decreed that no one would believe her. (Ann Ronan Picture Library)

fect. Shakespeare introduces her briefly in *Troilus and Cressida*. While King Priam and his sons are discussing whether to continue the war or restore Helen to her husband and end it, Cassandra enters "raving, with her hair about her ears" and prophesies disaster unless Helen is returned. Her most important brother Hector is willing to listen, but another brother, Troilus, dismisses her "brainsick raptures," and the war goes on.

The Trojans had a last chance when they maneuvered the wooden horse through their gateway, unaware that Greek warriors were hidden inside it. Cassandra warned of what would happen if it were brought into the city, and was ignored as usual. During the night, the Greeks emerged from it and opened the gates to let their comrades in.

Troy fell. The Greek commander-in-chief, Agamemnon, seized Cassandra as a prize of war and took her home with him. They were both killed by Agamemnon's estranged wife and the lover she had taken during his absence. According to the dramatist Aeschylus, Cassandra foresaw her own fate.

See also: Apollo

Further Reading

Graves, Robert. *The Greek Myths.* 2 vols. New York: Penguin Books, 1960.

CATHBAD

A Druid in Irish legend who foretells the destiny of several important characters.

Among Celtic peoples during the last centuries B.C., the Druids were the principal priests, magicians, scholars, and royal counselors. Their order was organized and powerful. It may have had a remote ancestry in shamanism; primitive elements are suggested by barbarities such as human sacrifice. The Druids opposed Rome, and in countries that Rome conquered, they were suppressed or nearly so. They survived in Ireland, chiefly as individual practitioners with less influence. Early Irish laws rank them below the nobility, among "men of art."

However, a number of tales may preserve traditions of an age when they occupied a higher rank in society. The legendary Druid Cathbad (or Cathub), reputedly active in Ulster around the beginning of the Christian era, was the chief of a band of warriors and used his prophetic gifts at the topmost social levels. When the princess Nes was sitting outside the royal house with her maidens, Cathbad passed by. She asked him, "What is the present hour lucky for?" He replied, "For begetting a king upon a queen." The child would grow up to be a very great man. No other male person was in sight, so Nes invited him in. Their son Conchobar became king of Ulster.

According to another version, Cathbad and his followers had slain some of Nes's kinfolk. She recruited a band of her own with a view to vengeance, but Cathbad trapped her, and she agreed to be his wife. When she was about to give birth, he told her that if it could be deferred until nightfall, the child would have an auspicious start by arriving at the same time as a supremely glorious being, Jesus Christ; and he would become a great ruler himself. She managed to hold back by sitting on a stone slab, and Conchobar was born at the right moment.

When he was king, Cathbad remained in his household as an adviser. Besides having eight personal disciples, he instructed large classes of royal and aristocratic pupils. He taught them druidic lore and assisted at the ceremonies when they attained warrior status and were equipped with weapons.

The most famous case was that of Cu Chulainn, Conchobar's nephew, afterwards one of the principal Irish heroes. When still a child, he heard Cathbad prophesying to his class that the life of any youth armed on that day would be short but his renown would be eternal. Cu Chulainn went to Conchobar and demanded arms at once, pretending that the Druid had given him leave. The king indulged him, but he smashed every set offered to him, fifteen in all, and was satisfied only when given Conchobar's own weapons. He rode out in the royal chariot, slew three enemies, and returned with their heads, also leading a tethered deer behind the chariot and some captive swans flying above. Seeing that he was heated with battle fury, the king's men plunged him in a vat of cold water. It burst, and they put him in another, but the water boiled. Only a third water treatment finally cooled him. Cu Chulainn grew up to perform mighty exploits. Understandably, he was remembered; Cathbad's foresight was correct.

On another occasion, Conchobar and the noblemen of Ulster were feasting at the home of Feidlimid, the king's storyteller. Feidlimid's wife waited on them, though she was advanced in pregnancy. Suddenly, the child in her womb gave a scream. Cathbad foretold the birth of Derdriu (better known to modern readers as Deirdre). She would be incredibly beautiful, and she would bring sorrow to Ulster. The way in which this tragedy happened is the theme of one of the best-known of all Irish legends.

Further Reading

Early Irish Myths and Sagas. Translated Jeffrey Gantz. Harmondsworth, England: Penguin Books, 1981.

Piggott, Stuart. *The Druids.* London: Thames and Hudson, 1985.

Rees, Alwyn, and Brinley Rees. *Celtic Heritage.* London: Thames and Hudson, 1961.

The Tain. Translated by Thomas Kinsella. Oxford: Oxford University Press, 1969.

CAYCE, EDGAR (1877–1945)

The "Sleeping Prophet." Born on a farm near Hopkinsville, Kentucky, Cayce (pronounced Casey) was primarily a healer. His first successes were with ailments of his own. His reputation spread. When a sufferer came to him for a consultation, he went into a self-induced trance. In that state, he made a diagnosis and prescribed treatment. His remedies, as a rule, were unorthodox but innocuous, sometimes based on rural folk medicine, sometimes akin to osteopathy or homeopathy. He used electrical therapy of a dubious kind and even marketed patent medicines, but a long record of cures shows that he was more than a quack. National publicity attracted so many patients that in 1927 he founded a hospital at Virginia Beach, Virginia, with a staff of assistants. This developed into a research body of wider scope.

His trance experiences extended beyond the medical realm. He had visions of far-off places and times. Many in his circle found them convincing, though their validity was called in question (to put it mildly) by eccentricities such as a dating of ancient Egypt thousands of years too early by normal reckoning. Some of his experiences seemed to imply previous lives and reincarnation. As a plain Bible Christian, he had problems with these, but he was honest enough not to reject them dogmatically and tried to come to terms with them.

The archives at Virginia Beach preserve various predictions, also made in trances: hence Cayce's nickname, the "Sleeping Prophet." In April 1929, he foretold the stock market crash six months later. While this was unexpected, it was not such a total surprise as to suggest paranormal insight on his part. At least one investment counselor, Roger Babson, also saw it approaching. Cayce made some vague forecasts about future wars, the deaths of Presidents Roosevelt and Kennedy, and the independence of India. He spoke of a major religious movement originating in Russia, certainly a remarkable notion to hit on during Stalin's reign, but as yet unfulfilled. Predictions of huge natural disasters, such as California collapsing into the sea and northern Europe doing likewise, had a time limit and have been falsified.

Cayce had visions of Atlantis, which he believed was a real country submerged under the Atlantic thousands of years ago. His account of it may have been influenced by the occult "revelations" of Theosophists, from Madame Blavatsky onward. He described Atlantean society as advanced, with aircraft, electricity, and—perhaps—atomic power. It came to an end partly through misuse of applied science.

None of this is credible history, but Cayce's Atlantis material has two features of interest. He said the lost land extended into the region of the West Indies, and he prophesied that a part of it would reappear in the Bahamas during the late 1960s. As to the first point, his geography is at odds with the legend as he might have heard it yet has a curious plausibility. Plato, the original Greek authority, located Atlantis in the ocean not far west of Europe. But the only real evidence for a large sunken territory would place it close to America and in the general region of

the West Indies, as Cayce said. The clues are in books that he is most unlikely to have known.

The second point of interest is his prediction of a reappearance in the late 1960s. Investigators impressed by his assertions began, some years after his death, to search for traces of Atlantis where he indicated. In 1968—on schedule, so to speak—divers in the Bahamas found what looked like a ruined building on the seabed near the island of Andros and what looked like a stretch of paved road near Bimini. Geologists pronounced otherwise, explaining these as entirely natural formations. Yet the prophecy had, in a way, created its own fulfillment; and Atlantean fragments that were at least arguable, however wishfully, had appeared in the right area at the right time.

Cayce also maintained that the history of Atlantis was in a sealed chamber near the Sphinx in Egypt and would some day be found. But his most solid nonmedical achievement had nothing to do with reincarnation or prophecy. He invented a card game called Pit, a forerunner of Monopoly. Unfortunately, he lacked the acumen to establish rights in it. A games company to which he submitted it took it up with great success but gave him nothing himself except a few complimentary copies. His apparent failure to foresee what the company would do may or may not be thought to have a bearing on his prophetic claims.

See also: Sphinx

Further Reading

Ashe, Geoffrey. *Atlantis: Lost Lands, Ancient Wisdom.* London: Thames and Hudson, 1992.

Bro, Harmon Hartzell. *Edgar Cayce.* Wellingborough, England: The Aquarian Press, 1990.

Campbell, Eileen, and J. H. Brennan. *The Aquarian Guide to the New Age.* Wellingborough, England: The Aquarian Press, 1990. Article "Cayce."

Cavendish, Richard, ed. *Man, Myth and Magic.* London: BPC Publishing, 1970–1972. Article "Cayce."

Collins, Andrew. *Gateway to Atlantis.* London: Headline, 2000.

CAZOTTE, JACQUES (1719–1792)

French author who foretold the Reign of Terror, the extremist phase of the French Revolution when thousands of political victims were guillotined.

As a writer, Cazotte is remembered chiefly for his supernatural fantasy *Le Diable Amoureux* (The Amorous Devil), which may have influenced a famous English Gothic romance, *The Monk,* by Matthew Gregory Lewis. Cazotte was reputed to have clairvoyant gifts. He flirted with occultism, but when the Revolution approached, he still had some Christian sympathies. In this respect, he differed from most of the French intelligentsia, who, thanks to Voltaire, had dropped Christianity and were anticipating the triumph of Reason.

The story of Cazotte's prophecy is told by Jean de La Harpe, a critic and dramatist. His account is sometimes quoted as if it were all factual and proved. If that were so, Cazotte's prophecy would be one of the most extraordinary on record. La Harpe recalls a dinner he attended in Paris early in 1788, a little over a year before the Revolution began. The many distinguished guests included the Marquis de Condorcet, a mathematician and political philosopher; Sébastien de Chamfort, a fashionable author; Félix Vicq-d'Azyr, the queen's doctor; Chrétien de Malesherbes, a holder of important official posts; and Jean Sylvain Bailly, France's leading astronomer. The most prominent socially of the ladies was the Duchesse de Gramont. Present also was Jacques Cazotte himself.

La Harpe's narrative covers several pages; the following is a summary. After dinner, many of the guests chatted about their hopes for the coming Revolution, when superstition and fanaticism would give way to true philosophy. The reign of Reason was near, and it would be glorious. Cazotte dissented, speaking with a firmness and seriousness that attracted attention. The reign of Reason was coming, yes; there would even be temples of Reason. But the result would be terrible. Dreadful things would be done in the name of philosophy and liberty.

He made specific predictions for some of the guests, all of them alarming. Condorcet would be in peril of death; he would carry poison to cheat the executioner, and he would die on the floor of a prison cell. Chamfort would slash his wrists in despair. Vicq-d'Azyr would die similarly. Malesherbes and Bailly would perish on the scaffold, and so would two other guests whom Cazotte named. The Duchesse remarked that women didn't seem to be in the same danger, but Cazotte said that women would suffer equally with men. All this would happen within six years.

La Harpe says in his account that he asked if Cazotte had any message for him. Cazotte told him that he would become a Christian believer. Since La Harpe was a convinced atheist, this sounded impossible. Cazotte, however, stood his ground. He went on to hint at

Jacques Cazotte, an author who foretold the Reign of Terror period of the French Revolution, though perhaps not in so much detail as has been claimed. (Hulton Getty)

disaster for the queen, Marie Antoinette, and even for the king, Louis XVI. The host had been prepared to treat his performance as a joke, if in poor taste, but the mention of royalty threatened to get the company into trouble. Cazotte agreed to leave, but before doing so, he foretold his own death.

The Revolution broke out in 1789. Several of the dinner guests were active supporters. Notre Dame Cathedral in Paris was converted into a Temple of Reason, with an actress impersonating the Goddess of Reason. After a hopeful early phase, the atmosphere changed, and most of Cazotte's words were precisely fulfilled. He was executed himself in September 1792 for involvement in a plot to rescue the king. Bailly was guillotined in 1793, and the others for whom Cazotte had foretold execution were guillotined the following year. Condorcet, Chamfort, and Vicq-d'Azyr died more or less as predicted. La Harpe was imprisoned. While in jail, he had a spiritual experience and became a firm supporter of Church and crown. He died in retirement in 1803. It is not known when he wrote his account of the dinner party or what, if anything, he intended to do with it. Left among his papers, it was published in 1806.

All the deaths undoubtedly happened, and so did the conversion. The question is whether Cazotte really predicted them, or whether La Harpe made the story up afterward for some purpose of his own which was not disclosed. A major objection is that it is too good in a literary sense. It is carefully crafted and dramatic and does not read like a memorandum written down when the memory was fresh. However, there are letters and memoirs attesting that La Harpe spoke of the prophecy during the years 1788 and 1792—that is, before the Terror—and that Cazotte sometimes mentioned it himself.

The Comtesse d'Adhémar, a lady in attendance at court who knew of Cazotte's psychic reputation, was present at the dinner and wrote an account of it herself that confirms the main drift of the prophecy. Henriette-Louise, Baronne d'Oberkirch, has a reference to it in her memoirs. In January 1789, she mentions "the famous prophecy of Monsieur Cazotte," citing an account written by La Harpe himself, which was passed on to her by a correspondent. An English investigator who started out as a skeptic found several people who knew of the prophecy, including Cazotte's son Scévole, and he became convinced of its authenticity when they confirmed the story independently.

The testimonies converge. However, they are phrased in general terms. The gap in the evidence is the lack of details. Cazotte's predictions to named individuals are found only in La Harpe's full written account and in materials that could have been copied from it. The irreducible fact seems to be that while La Harpe doubtless drew on his imagination as well as his memory in telling the story, Cazotte did predict the Terror. That was remarkable enough. Many people saw the Revolution approaching, but Cazotte was exceptional and perhaps unique in anticipating the frightful phase through which it would pass.

It is easy to argue that he simply foresaw, by his own natural good sense, that the Revolution would (as the phrase goes) devour its children. The explanation, however, is a product of hindsight, in the light of what happened in Russia as well as France. In 1788, the prospects were different. There had been countless wars and persecutions, but the reign of Reason was expected to end such evils, and nothing like the revolutionary slaughter had ever been known. One French skeptic argued, long afterward, that it would not have been difficult for Cazotte to foresee the Terror. But if it was not difficult, others should have foreseen it too; and no one else did. The "rational" optimism of the time is shown in a popular fantasy, Louis-Sébastien Mercier's *L'An 2440* (The Year 2440), which portrayed an almost cloudless future and went into twenty-five editions.

The difficulty of explaining Cazotte's prophecy by ordinary foresight becomes greater when his own writings are taken into account. They show no trace of the rare acumen he would have needed or the plain political awareness—far from it. *Le Diable Amoureux* is about enchantments and supernatural beings, with no pretense of realism. When the Revolution was actually under way, Cazotte wavered. At first, he was mildly hopeful. Then, he moved into opposition. His royalist outpourings were utterly unrealistic, and they were not only unrealistic, they were absurd. He expected the king's release from detention, if royalists did their duty with God's help, and said the restored Louis would surpass the glories of Solomon and be a beacon for all Europe when the present troubles were over. He even plunged into the book of Revelation, as so many cranks have, and gave parts of it wild interpretations in terms of current events.

His delusions led him to the scaffold, and he perished with dignity. They were delusions, nevertheless. If he had talked so foolishly at the dinner party, on any theme at all, the guests would have laughed and turned away, not gathered round him listening and questioning. The Cazotte whose "famous prophecy" was remembered and talked about has to have been, in effect, a different person from the Cazotte revealed in the writings. When all improbabilities are discounted, the case for some kind of inspiration, some unexplained intrusion into Cazotte's mental processes, is still arguable.

In 1845, Gérard de Nerval, another writer of fantasy, brought out a short biography of him. In this, he gives "only relative credence" to the prophecy and agrees with the view that the Terror would have been easily foreseeable. Here, the wisdom of hindsight is becoming orthodoxy. However, he also draws attention to a strange passage in *Ollivier,* a narrative poem that Cazotte wrote in earlier days. He suggests that this may be a prophetic hallucination, its imagery anticipating the prophecy by many years.

The character who tells this part of the story is a woman traveling with a companion. The sinister "fay Bagassa" lures them by magic into her palace, where they fall down a pit and a machine cuts them to pieces, yet somehow they remain alive. The narrator finds that her separated head, the conscious part of her, has been ranged with 800 other heads, all of them alive as she is herself. They are bored and quarrelsome, complain of being without limbs, and have a bitter humor but evidently see no future. Nerval remarks that in the light of the happenings long afterward, this flight of fancy is curious. It is certainly odd that Cazotte, of all people, should have imagined a vast assembly of severed heads. When he wrote *Ollivier,* the guillotine was not even known in France. Mass decapitation by this method was a purely revolutionary phenomenon.

See also: Mercier, Louis-Sébastien

Further Reading

Ashe, Geoffrey. *The Book of Prophecy.* London: Blandford, 1999.

Cazotte, Jacques. *The Devil in Love.* Translated by Stephen Sarterelli. New York: Marsilio, 1993. (Includes Nerval's biography, La Harpe's account of the prophecy, and other relevant matter.)

Décote, Georges. *L'Itinéraire de Jacques Cazotte.* Geneva: Librairie Droz, 1984.

Wallechinsky, David, Amy Wallace, and Irving Wallace. *The Book of Predictions.* New York: William Morrow, 1980.

CHANNELING

A process in which information is supposed to be transmitted through human recipients from beings on another plane of existence.

Channeling is akin to mediumship but by no means the same. A spiritualistic medium performs in a trance. Channeling may involve a trance, but not necessarily—the recipient may be awake, in a state of conscious receptivity. Also, the beings that are contacted by mediums are believed to be spirits of the dead. Some opponents have claimed that they are actually evil spirits, impersonating the dead to deceive the living. The entities allegedly contacted in channeling are neither. They are regarded as higher beings with messages for humanity.

This phenomenon was at its height during the 1970s and 1980s, afterwards declining in popularity. The best known of the entities contacted was probably "Seth," who was channeled through Jane Roberts from 1963 until her death in 1984. He communicated a mass of material to a group that gathered around her, talking about the nature of reality and human beings' relation to it. His favorite maxim was that "You create your own reality." The Seth material was published in several books.

Another channeled text was *A Course in Miracles,* communicated through Helen Schucman, a research psychologist at Columbia University in New York City. Published in 1975, this was concerned, among much else, with distinguishing truth from illusion. Other entities named in the channeling connection were "Lazaris," "Ramtha," and "Emmanuel." Lazaris transmitted psychological teachings through Jach Pursel. Ramtha appeared first in a vision to J. Z. Knight, a woman in Tacoma, Washington. This was an unusual case because when Ramtha communicated afterward, she went into a trance like a medium. Ramtha claimed to have been a warrior in Atlantis 35,000 years ago. Emmanuel spoke through Pat Rodegast, the result being a volume published in 1987 entitled *Emmanuel's Book: A Manual for Living Comfortably in the Cosmos.*

While the products of channeling are voluminous, it does not appear that they have ever been seriously predictive. It must be added in fairness that a phenomenon rather like this has been suggested as underlying some prophecies that do call for an explanation. With the channelers themselves, however, the case is different. There is no need to dispute that their outpourings have had value for some readers, even, perhaps, for many readers. But it remains a question whether higher beings have ever really seemed to be speaking through them. Channeled material lacks the literary quality that might be persuasive, and it is doubtful whether it has ever included factual information, unknown at the time, that was afterwards verified—one of the few tests that could carry weight. Channelers can probably never be proved to have done more than reprocess their own reading and reflections or other people's.

See also: Prophecy, Theories of

Further Reading

Campbell, Eileen, and J. H. Brennan. *The Aquarian Guide to the New Age.* Wellingborough, England: The Aquarian Press, 1990. Article "Channelling."

CHARLEMAGNE, SECOND

See Second Charlemagne

CHEIRO (1866–1936)

British clairvoyant, originally William John Warner. He adopted the surname of his French mother, who instructed him as a boy in palmistry and astrology, and became Louis Hamon, presently adding the title "Count," to which he had no right.

After travels in India and Egypt, he settled in London as a fortuneteller, mainly though not exclusively by palmistry, on which he became the leading authority. His professional name, Cheiro, was derived from the Greek for "hand." Socially popular, he is reputed to have read more than 6,000 palms. He made accurate predictions for well-known people and visited the United States with success.

He warned Oscar Wilde that he was risking disgrace; assured the politician Arthur James Balfour that he would become prime minister; promised Mark Twain, then in financial difficulties, that he could expect an upturn at a designated time; and told the famous dancer and spy Mata Hari that she must expect a crisis in 1917, the year in which she was convicted of espionage and shot. Royal personages consulted him, and he had pleasant messages for King Edward VII but not for Czar Nicholas II, whose dethronement he foresaw.

Some of Cheiro's predictions need not imply anything more than inside information and keen perception. Some, perhaps, do more. In June 1911, he wrote to the distinguished editor W. T. Stead, advising him not to travel by water in April of the following year. Stead ignored the advice, sailed aboard the *Titanic,* and was drowned. Cheiro told Lord Kitchener, who became the principal architect of the British war effort in 1914, that he would be in danger of death in his sixty-sixth year, not as a soldier but at sea. In 1916, Kitchener set out on a mission to Russia and perished when the ship carrying him struck a mine and sank.

Speaking as a professed psychic, Cheiro made correct forecasts of several public events, including the Russian Revolution, the Jewish resettlement of Palestine, and the independence of India. These, however, might have been made by a well-informed observer without any paranormal insight. It may be significant that when he made predictions that were not simply inferences from current trends, he was wrong, as when he said that a large part of New York City would be destroyed by an earthquake and that Russian aircraft would obliterate London. One very far-fetched prophecy, about Armageddon being fought in Palestine when it was invaded by Russia, Persia, Ethiopia, and Libya, was almost certainly not suggested either by rational anticipation or by any psychic gift. Cheiro got it from Ezekiel 38 where Gog in verse 2 has been explained (notably by proponents of the British-Israel theory) as the ruler of Russia, and verse 5 in the King James Version names Persia, Ethiopia, and Libya as his allies.

A flamboyant figure noted for sexual escapades, Cheiro is supposed to have seduced women by hypnosis like the "black magician," Aleister Crowley. He worked briefly as a war correspondent and also, allegedly, in the British Secret Service, this being the explanation of his acquaintance with Mata Hari. In 1930, he emigrated to Hollywood, where he experimented with screenwriting and went on reading palms. His clients included Erich von Stroheim, Lillian Gish, and Mary Pickford, who also cultivated the astrologer Evangeline Adams.

See also: Palmistry

Further Reading

Wallechinsky, David, Amy Wallace, and Irving Wallace. *The Book of Predictions.* New York: William Morrow, 1980.

CHESTERTON, GILBERT KEITH (1874–1936)

Journalist, critic, and poet, a prominent literary figure in England during the first part of the twentieth century. Immensely versatile and noted for his paradoxical wit. Often referred to as "G. K. C."

As a social commentator, Chesterton condemned the capitalistic economy of his day, with its glaring extremes of wealth and poverty, but he did not turn to Socialism, preferring to hope for decentralization, a rebirth of craft industry, and a radical redistribution of property. His "small is beautiful" outlook (to use a slogan invented later) begins to show in his fantastic novel *The Napoleon of Notting Hill.* This was published in 1904, soon after the Boer War, in which the British Empire conquered two small South African republics, the Transvaal and the Orange Free State. The profiteering motive was obvious; the war was conducted at first with disgraceful incompetence and later with ruthlessness toward the civilian population. Chesterton opposed it. *The Napoleon of Notting Hill* has several levels of meaning, but is a plea for small communities and local loyal-

G. K. Chesterton, a versatile English writer who made fun of the prophetic pretensions of H. G. Wells and others. (Ann Ronan Picture Library)

ties in the face of giant corporations and amoral imperialism.

The story takes place toward the end of the twentieth century. Chesterton, however, does not attempt a plausible picture of the future. He makes gentle fun of H. G. Wells and other prognosticators and exposes the fallacy, as he sees it, of predicting what is to come by extrapolating current trends. By sweeping all this aside, he sets the stage for his own quite different story. His opening chapter is a whimsical survey of "rational" prediction in general. Today, after a great deal more of the same—by science-fiction writers, "futurologists," and others—this chapter still deserves quotation at some length. Like much of Chesterton's work, it is not as flippant as it looks.

> The human race, to which so many of my readers belong, has been playing at children's games from the beginning, and will probably do it till the end. . . . One of the games to which it is most attached is "Cheat the Prophet." The players listen very carefully and respectfully to all that the clever men have to say about what is to happen in the next generation. . . . They then go and do something else. . . .
>
> In the beginning of the twentieth century the game of Cheat the Prophet was made far more difficult than it had ever been before. The reason was, that there were so many prophets and so many prophecies, that it was difficult to elude all their ingenuities. . . .
>
> The way the prophets of the twentieth century went to work was this. They took something or other that was certainly going on in their time, and then said that it would go on more and more until something extraordinary happened. And very often they added that in some odd place that extraordinary thing had happened, and that it showed the signs of the times.

(In each of the following paragraphs, the first person mentioned is a real contemporary; the successor, who goes over the edge into caricature, is fictitious.)

> For instance, there were Mr H. G. Wells and others, who thought that science would take charge of the future; and just as the motor-car was quicker than the coach, so some lovely thing would be quicker than the motor-car; and so on for ever. And there arose from their ashes Dr Quilp, who said that a man could be sent on his machine so fast round the world that he could keep up a long chatty conversation in some old-world village by saying a word of a sentence each time he came round. And it was said that the experiment had been tried on an apoplectic old major, who was sent round the world so fast that there seemed to be (to the inhabitants of some other star) a continuous band round the earth of white whiskers, red complexion and tweeds—a thing like a ring of Saturn.
>
> Then there was the opposite school. There was Mr Edward Carpenter, who thought we should in a very short time return to Nature, and live simply and slowly as the animals do. And Edward Carpenter was followed by James Pickie, D.D. (of Pocahontas College), who said

that men were immensely improved by grazing, or taking their food slowly and continuously, after the manner of cows. And he said that he had, with the most encouraging results, turned city men out on all fours in a field covered with veal cutlets. Then Tolstoy and the Humanitarians said that the world was growing more merciful, and therefore no one would ever desire to kill. And Mr Mick not only became a vegetarian, but at length declared vegetarianism doomed ("shedding," as he called it finely, "the green blood of the silent animals"), and predicted that men in a better age would live on nothing but salt. And then came the pamphlet from Oregon (where the thing was tried), the pamphlet called "Why should Salt suffer?" and there was more trouble. . . .

Mr Stead, too, was prominent, who thought that England would in the twentieth century be united to America; and his young lieutenant, Graham Podge, who included the states of France, Germany, and Russia in the American Union, the State of Russia being abbreviated to Ra.

There was Mr Sidney Webb, also, who said that the future would see a continuously increasing order and neatness in the life of the people, and his poor friend Fipps, who went mad and ran about the country with an axe, hacking branches off the trees whenever there were not the same number on both sides.

Chesterton sums up the essential point:

All these clever men were prophesying with every variety of ingenuity what would happen soon, and they all did it in the same way, by taking something they saw "going strong," as the saying is, and carrying it as far as ever their imagination could stretch. This, they said, was the true and simple way of anticipating the future . . ..

It did certainly appear that the prophets had put the people (engaged in the old game of Cheat the Prophet) in a quite unprecedented difficulty. It seemed really hard to do anything without fulfilling some of their prophecies.

Nevertheless, in the future that Chesterton imagines, the people have succeeded. They have done it by simply ignoring all the inevitable trends.

Let me no longer conceal the painful truth. The people had cheated the prophets of the twentieth century. When the curtain goes up on this story, eighty years after the present date, London is almost exactly like what it is now.

The joke about the absence of change is sustained by such details as the survival of frock coats and hansom cabs. Actually, the story (beginning, oddly, in 1984) does require a somewhat altered society, but the alteration has not been due to any of the positive trends that Chesterton makes fun of. The reason is that nothing has really happened at all. England has simply drifted, becoming duller in the process. A drearily competent bureaucracy is in total control because no one sees any point in rebellion or protest. Everything local, original, eccentric is dead. For practical purposes, everybody is much the same as everybody else. The head of state, with a few minor prerogatives, is a sovereign chosen from a list as jurors are—a safe and economical method, since officialdom is all-powerful, and as everybody *is* much alike, it makes no difference who reigns.

Then, a tiny flaw appears in the system. A new king is picked, Auberon Quin, a civil servant who has managed to retain an impish sense of humor. To restore a little fun and color, in a harmless way, he gives the London boroughs sham-medieval charters and civic rituals. He insists on their officials being called by titles like Lord High Provost and dressing up in special costumes. After a first wave of grumbling, this masquerade is tolerated, and the system absorbs it.

But when it has been an accepted part of life for a decade or two, a second and larger flaw appears. A great road is to be built through western London, a sort of freeway. Plans, negotiations, and compulsory purchase orders are pushed through by the business consortium responsible. Buildings are torn down to make way. At last, everything is ready, except that the shopkeepers in one small street in Notting Hill, a district in the path of the highway, refuse to sell out. They are backed by Notting Hill's Provost, Adam Wayne, a young fanatic who has taken the royal program seriously and proclaims his readiness to "die for the sacred mountain, even if it were ringed with all the armies of Bayswater."

Aided by a shopkeeper who plays war games with model soldiers, Wayne organizes his citizens for street fighting (a remarkable anticipation of the talk of "urban guerrillas" in the 1960s). He routs every attempt to dispossess him and wins by a stratagem involving a building that unhappily no longer exists. The heroic defense awakens a new spirit in England. Local patriotism, local customs, local imagination and independence revive. The king himself is won over and accepts that he started more than he knew.

This happy ending, however, is not the end after all. Chesterton, mindful of the Boer War, has a final warning. For twenty years, the new order flourishes, and Notting Hill is honored as the source of the revolution. But at last, its ruling council turns imperialist and tries to impose its will on other parts of London. Wayne is still Provost. He knows that this betrayal of smallness is Notting Hill's doom, but he is overruled and forced to lead a hopeless fight against three other districts, Bayswater, North Kensington, and Shepherd's Bush. Old King Auberon joins him in a last stand in a park, and both are killed.

Chesterton's wayward, flamboyant style can be off-putting, and it sometimes obscures the wisdom of what he says. His romanticization of violence, perhaps excusable at the time of writing, must be counted against him. Yet *The Napoleon of Notting Hill* has an enduring value that puts it, in its curious way, above most fantasies of the future.

See also: Wells, H. G.

Further Reading

Coren, Michael. *Gilbert: The Man Who Was G. K. Chesterton.* London: Jonathan Cape, 1989.

Ward, Maisie. *Gilbert Keith Chesterton.* London: Sheed and Ward, 1944.

CHIROMANCY

See Palmistry

DANIEL (C. 165 B.C.)

Old Testament book with apocalyptic and messianic themes, sometimes construed as foretelling the date of the death of Jesus Christ.

Daniel is a sage in Hebraic folk tradition, whom the unknown author of this book makes its protagonist and, in part, its narrator. It begins with him as a youth and tells of his being among the Israelites deported from Jerusalem to Babylon by Nebuchadnezzar in 597 B.C. He becomes a palace servant and wins favor by interpreting the king's dreams. Many years afterward, he announces the fall of Babylon in the dramatic episode of the Writing on the Wall. Much of the book is taken up with symbolic visions and explanations of them, in which Daniel "foretells" historical developments that were actually past at the time of the book's composition. The belief that it is an authentic product of the sixth century B.C., so that these passages actually are predictive, has caused considerable misunderstanding. However, the claim to prediction cannot be entirely dismissed.

Daniel is not classed as prophecy by Jews; it counts as a Sacred Writing only. It was composed—or, at any rate, put in its present form—about 165 B.C. during a crisis endured by the Jewish community in Palestine. The country was then part of a Syrian kingdom under Antiochus IV, a descendant of one of Alexander's generals. He tried to impose religious conformity. In 171, a supporter of his killed the Jewish high priest Onias. During the next few years, the Tem-ple was plundered, the daily sacrifice in it was stopped, and a statue of Zeus was set up inside it. Many Jews resisted the changes, and some were martyred. In 164, Judas Maccabeus and his brothers led a revolt, and eventually a successor of Antiochus recognized Jewish independence.

The author of Daniel (to assume, for convenience, that there was only one or only one principal author) reflects this crisis and the hope of recovery. One of his aims is to encourage the faithful to stand firm; the stories of Daniel in the earlier chapters are meant to show the superiority of his God-given wisdom. The author sketches a long historical panorama. Nebuchadnezzar dreams about a great image made of different materials. A stone "cut by no human hand" strikes its feet. It topples over and falls to pieces, and the stone expands until it fills the world. Daniel explains the different sections of the image in terms of a series of kingdoms, identifiable as the Babylonian, the Median, the Persian, and the Greek. Since the book was written long after the asserted date of the dream, when all the kingdoms had come and gone, most of this is prophecy after the event. But the stone is a genuine future image: it is the everlasting Israelite kingdom that God will found on the ruins of the others.

Later in the book, Daniel is portrayed having a dream of his own that confirms Nebuchadnezzar's. It is about four beasts corresponding to the same four monarchies. The fourth has ten horns, probably representing successors of Alexander in various parts of his empire, plus an aggressive "little horn" that uproots three of the others—Antiochus IV himself, who defeated three other rulers in the course of his wars. The dream culminates in the supremacy of "one like a son of man," the first foreshadowing of a phrase applied to Jesus. Later again, Daniel has further visions covering Alexander's con-

A famous scene in the biblical book Daniel, where writing appears on the wall at a royal feast in Babylon and Daniel explains it as a divine message of doom. (Ann Ronan Picture Library)

quest of Persia, the division of his empire, the rise and tyranny of Antiochus, and his anticipated downfall. Most of this is prophecy after the event, but there is still the prediction of Israel's deliverance and future glory. Interesting for the history of Judaism is a passage about a resurrection of the dead, a new theme in the Bible.

There is a remarkable crux in chapter 9. Here, Daniel is made to recall a prophecy by Jeremiah about the Chosen People going through seventy penitential years in Babylonian captivity. From his vantage point centuries later, the author can look back over the time that has elapsed since then. Though the Jews are reestablished in Zion, they have attained neither peace nor purification. He imagines the angel Gabriel speaking to Daniel and reinterpreting Jeremiah's words. "Seventy years" means "seventy weeks of years," that is, 490 years (70 × 7). Gabriel draws an obscure distinction between the first seven "weeks" and the subsequent sixty-two, but after a total of sixty-nine an "anointed one" is to be "cut off," in other words, killed; while the ensuing final week will bring war and chaos, with Jerusalem suffering at the hands of "the prince who is to come."

Undoubtedly, the author is thinking of current events and hoping that Antiochus's onslaught is a "darkest hour before the dawn" that closes the period and will be followed by the promised good time at last. The anointed one is the murdered high priest Onias. The trouble is, however, that it is impossible to make up 490 years between Jeremiah and Antiochus. Moreover, the author gives the passage a secondary meaning by defining the starting point of the count quite differently. The 490 years begin "from the going forth of the word to restore and build Jerusalem." Jeremiah says nothing about a rebuilding of the ruined city after the exiles return from Babylon, and although some did return after Babylon's fall, there was no serious rebuilding. The phrase,

in fact, only makes sense apart from Jeremiah. The "word to restore and build Jerusalem" can hardly be anything but a commission given by the Persian king Artaxerxes I to Nehemiah, in 445 B.C. It was Nehemiah who, with the king's authority, got the rebuilding under way at last, after nearly a century of desolation.

If we test this surprising but exact starting point, which gives an alternative timescale, and count forward 490 years, we are well into the Christian era. The sixty-ninth week is to bring the killing of the "anointed one," and on this basis, the term *anointed one* has another significance. "Anointed" is the literal meaning of the word *Messiah,* of which *Christos,* or Christ, is the Greek form; and the fatal sixty-ninth week extends from A.D. 31 to 38, within most of which time Pilate was procurator of Judea. The long count beginning from the Persian king's order scores a hit or a very near miss with Pilate's execution of Christ.

This interpretation, in essence, was formerly accepted by Christian commentators as the primary one. It still appears in Ronald Knox's notes to his translation of the Bible, published in 1955.

> **See also:** Biblical Prophecy (1)—Israelite and Jewish; Jeremiah; Messiah
>
> **Further Reading:**
> Brown R. E., J. A. Fitzmyer, and R. E. Murphy, eds. *The New Jerome Biblical Commentary.* Englewood Cliffs, NJ: Prentice-Hall, 1990.

DANTE ALIGHIERI (1265–1321)

The greatest medieval Italian poet, whose imagery sometimes seems to imply knowledge that was not available in his time.

Dante was a native of Florence but spent much of his life in exile. He composed his principal work, the *Divine Comedy* (*Divine* was not part of his own title), early in the fourteenth century. It takes the form of a first-person narrative in three sections, *Inferno, Pur-*

Dante, the greatest poet of medieval Europe, who seems to have been aware in some way of Asian myths unknown to his contemporaries. (Ann Ronan Picture Library)

gatorio, and *Paradiso*—Hell, Purgatory, and Heaven. The poet imagines himself traveling through these three realms of the afterlife, guided first by Virgil, the Roman poet who describes Aeneas's visit to the Underworld, and later by Beatrice Portinari, whom he once adored and idealized and who is now dead and glorified in Heaven.

In the course of the poem, Dante makes coded political predictions about events in Italy, which are now mainly of academic interest. He praises Joachim of Fiore but does not show how far he agrees with Joachim's visions of the future. More notable from a prophetic point of view is his handling of certain issues raised by Christian tradition.

The *Comedy* can be read in several ways—as an allegory of spiritual progress, for instance—but it has a straightforward narrative sense, though it is doubtless not meant to be taken too literally. Dante fits the three realms into the medieval framework of the universe, according to contemporary geography and pre-Copernican astronomy. Earth, as he conceives it, is a sphere (the notion that everybody before Columbus thought it was flat is quite untrue). The known continental masses—Europe, most of Asia, part of Africa—are clustered together in a land hemisphere, with Jerusalem at the center. Earth's other half is covered by sea, its only land being an island at its own center, the antipodes of Jerusalem, with an immense mountain on it. Rotating around Earth are concentric transparent spheres bearing the planets and stars. This system of subheavens, as they might be called, is millions of miles in diameter. Beyond and in no definable relationship to it, Dante imagines the true Heaven of God and the angels and saints.

At the beginning of the *Comedy,* he descends with Virgil into a huge, funnel-shaped hollow, which is Hell. After many experiences, the poets pass Earth's center and return to the surface on the opposite side. They are on the antipodean island near the foot of the mountain, which they climb.

Dante's heavenward ascent begins at the summit, in the company of Beatrice. He soars through the celestial subheavens, in each of them encountering blessed souls for whom that sphere is appropriate, though all have their eternal home in the true Heaven beyond. Finally, he enters this, and is granted a momentary vision of God.

Dante stands alone in presenting a spiritual pilgrimage in terms of a journey through the medieval cosmos. No author had done it before. However, the novelty is greater in some respects than in others. Once the poet had hit on the main idea, the logic was fairly obvious, up to a point. Traditionally, Hell was "down," so it had to be inside the Earth. Heaven was "above"; Christ ascended to it. That, however, was not the whole story. The Church recognized a transitional region, Purgatory, and Dante had little to guide him in fixing a location for this. What he actually did with it was entirely original and remains puzzling.

Purgatory was the abode of the souls of the dead who were destined for Heaven but not yet ready for it. They carried a load of sin and error and perhaps had only repented at the last moment. Therefore, they had to undergo a process of purifying before they could enter into bliss. Unofficial speculation sometimes made Purgatory virtually a department of Hell, with punishments that were different only because they would end, like a prison sentence. That notion lingers in the grim speech of the Ghost in *Hamlet,* even after the rejection of Purgatory by Protestantism.

Dante takes a brighter view. If Purgatory is a bridge between Earth and Heaven, and its occupants are on their way even through penitential suffering, it ought to be a happy place. And so he makes it. He places it on the antipodean island at the center of his sea hemisphere; it is none other than the colossal mountain that rises above the island, into the sunshine and tranquility of the upper atmosphere. The Mount is septenary, having seven terraces encircling it at different levels, with connecting stairways. Each terrace has a presiding angel and corresponds to one of the principal sins—pride, envy, and so forth. Souls bearing the stain of these sins live on the terraces assigned, where they endure cleansing pain and endure it gladly as they progress toward release. Dante and Virgil climb from level to level, conversing with the inhabitants. At the top, surprisingly, is the Earthly Paradise where Adam and Eve first dwelled—in biblical terms, the Garden of Eden. From here, Dante's ascent with Beatrice through the celestial subheavens takes him into a world of dazzling light, where the blessed souls meet him.

His Mount Purgatory is unique in literature. So is his location of the Earthly Paradise at the summit. Christians before him had speculated about it and reached no conclusion. The Bible speaks of "a garden in Eden in the east" and of "the garden of God" on "the holy mountain of God." It was agreed to be high up, partly because, according to Genesis, four great rivers flowed from it over distances of thousands of miles, but no one knew where it was: perhaps in a remote part of Asia, cut off by natural barriers. Dante's conception of it, his placing it on a mountain at the antipodes of Jerusalem, his identification of the mountain with Purgatory, and his upward celestial linkage—all this is not only original but, what is more remarkable in a committedly Christian author, antiscriptural.

The Earthly Paradise on top of the mount is not "a garden in Eden in the east." It is a woodland, and it is not in Eden because there is no Eden, no country around it. Nor is it in the east: the mount's location on the spherical Earth makes it westward as much as eastward. The rivers mentioned in Genesis could not flow from his Paradise because they could not cross the sea, and Dante does not explain how Adam and Eve could have done it either, to make their way to the Middle East and people it with their descendants.

He judges that he can express what he wants like this much better than he could by using biblical imagery, and that is fair enough. But the break with Scripture and tradition is so defiant as to hint that there may have been a prototype, something relevant and vivid thrusting its way into Dante's mind. Commentators have offered guesses about mountains that figure in Islamic legends, but none of these are adequate models, and Dante's hostility to Islam makes a Muslim influence unlikely even if he was aware of the legends.

Nevertheless, a prototype exists. The problem is not to find it, but to resolve the paradox of Dante's apparently knowing of it, when the first Europeans who did know of it lived centuries later. Although this is not exactly prophecy, it is akin. The prototype is a mountain that figures in Hindu mythology and in Buddhist derivatives. The Hindu name is Meru; the Buddhist is Sumeru.

Meru is at Earth's center: admittedly, the center of a disk-Earth, but it is central as Mount Purgatory is central. It is incalculably high. In one way or another (accounts vary), it is septenary like Mount Purgatory: it has seven faces or levels or is on an island surrounded by seven concentric rings of land and water. It has encircling terraces like Mount Purgatory, one above another, and it is paradisal like Mount Purgatory. Divine and semidivine beings frequent it, like Dante's angels. On it are "the gardens of the gods" and beautiful woods, and the summit is a dwelling place and assembly place of deities. Meru is associated with a purifying spiritual ascent, not only into a happy region on its heights but into the heavens beyond. Above, where the holiest and most perfected of humans go, the Supreme Being Vishnu has his abode, in light so intense that the gods themselves are dazzled.

So far as Meru has any geography, it is in a remote north beyond the Himalayas. A legendary king, on a final pilgrimage with his wife and brothers, comes within sight of the mountain, but they die without reaching it.

Since the real Meru or Sumeru is beyond mortal access, temple builders have made models or representations of it, focusing a little of its numinousness. The most interesting in relation to Dante, heightening the paradox of his apparent knowledge, is Borobudur in Java, a Buddhist pyramid dating from about A.D. 800.

Borobudur has terraces going all round it, one above another. The walls alongside some of these are full of sculptured reliefs, more than 1,400 in all, illustrating stories from Buddhist tradition. Those on the lower levels have themes of evil and warning. Above are scenes of greater and greater good. A complete pilgrimage is an ascent from material to spiritual being. The pilgrim walks all around, meditating on the reliefs, then climbs a stairway to the next level, and so on upward. After seven circuits, two more correspond to the mountain's summit paradise. The apex of the structure is a huge bell-shaped stupa, or shrine, representing the goal of the quest, nirvana, or liberation.

To all appearances, Dante's Mount Purgatory is a Christianization of the mythical Asian mountain, using hints from its analogue at Borobudur. He has echoes even in details. As the Indian travelers die within sight of an unreachable Meru, so, in the *Inferno*, Dante portrays Ulysses undertaking a last voyage that brings him within sight of the mount, but his ship sinks before he reaches it. The poet imagines himself not only climbing stairs from terrace to terrace but seeing bas-reliefs of biblical and legendary subjects for moral reflection. The ascent, as at Borobudur and mythically on Meru, is a spiritual progress, and it culminates in a paradisal realm at the top. The celestial region above could—if one cared to press the point—be a Christian elaboration of Vishnu's dwelling place above Meru. As the gods are dazzled by the light, so Dante is when he ascends toward his own Supreme Being.

There is no reason why Dante should not have adopted and adapted the Asian mountain and derived some of the plan of Purgatory from its model at Borobudur . . . given the knowledge. If there were a book that could have supplied him with information on these topics, modern commentators would certainly acknowledge it as a major source, the inspiration of his extraordinary break with Scripture and tradition. The difficulty is that no such book existed or could have existed. Medieval Europeans knew little of India and nothing of its mythology. The Hindu sacred texts were in Sanskrit, a language undiscovered and untranslated. Western acquaintance with the culture of India did not seriously begin until long after Dante. Travelers' tales of Java could have reached him, but Borobudur would not have figured in them. Not very long after it was built, it fell into disuse and decay and became overgrown with vegetation. The advance of Islam through Indonesia extinguished it as a Buddhist monument. It was rediscovered at last in poor condition and was not studied or restored until recent years.

Hence, while Dante is not exactly prophesying, he seems to be doing something like it. On the one hand, it looks as if he was aware of these things, even in some detail. On the other, there is no way he could have been in the normal course of events. It is *as if* some kind of transtemporal contact occurred, by which knowledge in the mind of a person centuries after him—let us say, an orientalist—entered his own. By itself, the paradox might be dismissed as a curiosity. But another great Christian poet, John Milton, breaks with Scripture and tradition more radically than Dante does and, in doing so, gives the same appearance of tapping knowledge nonexistent in Europe until centuries later.

See also: Milton, John; Prophecy, Theories of; Stapledon, Olaf

Further Reading:

Ashe, Geoffrey. *The Book of Prophecy.* London: Blandford, 1999.
Boorstin, Daniel J. *The Discoverers.* New York: Vintage Books, 1985.

Boyde, Patrick. *Dante: Philomythes and Philosopher.* Cambridge: Cambridge University Press, 1981.

Encyclopedia Britannica. Article "Borobudur."

Grabsky, Phil. *The Lost Temple of Java.* London: Orion, 1999.

Jacoff, Rachel, ed. *The Cambridge Companion to Dante.* Cambridge: Cambridge University Press, 1993.

Lewis, C. S. *The Discarded Image.* Cambridge: Cambridge University Press, 1964.

Sayers, Dorothy L. *Introductory Papers on Dante.* London: Methuen, 1954.

DAY OF THE LORD

A coming day of divine judgment in Israelite prophecy.

In ancient Israel, the day of the Lord is thought to have been originally an autumn festival that marked the turn of the agricultural year and reaffirmed the bond between the Chosen People and their God, Yahweh. He had done great things for them in the past, rescuing them from Egyptian servitude by tremendous miracles. A belief seems to have taken shape in a special day of the Lord when he would do great things again.

The need was felt for a fresh divine intervention. The twelve tribes had gone through a triumphalist phase, probably somewhere about 1000 B.C., when David and Solomon had ruled them all together. Soon afterward, however, the kingdom had split, the breakaway northern portion being confusingly called "Israel" and the southern one "Judah" after its largest tribal component. Judah had Jerusalem, the Davidic dynasty, and the Temple that Solomon had built. Jeroboam, the first ruler of the north, tried to supply a religious substitute by setting up gold-plated images of bull calves at Bethel and Dan, which were supposed to be foci for the Lord's presence—an action that condemned him and his successors in the eyes of the orthodox. The northern kingdom was richer and more powerful than Judah, but prophets such as Elijah denounced its apostasy. Over

the years, forebodings of divine judgment and military pressure from neighboring states combined to foster a sense of instability that affected Judah as well.

The day of the Lord was probably envisaged at first as a deliverance, when God would act, perhaps at the time of his autumn festival, to destroy the enemies of the Chosen People and establish them in peace throughout the territory they held. But Amos, the earliest of the literary prophets who give their names to books of the Bible, saw it differently. He was active in the north about 760 B.C. and assailed the luxury and injustice of its ruling class, with their extravagant houses and oppression of the poor. Israelites, he said, imagined that they had a divine guarantee of some kind, but a future day of the Lord might not be at all as expected. He warned the northerners especially:

Woe to you who desire the day of the Lord!
Why would you have the day of the Lord?
It is darkness, and not light. (Amos 5:18)

"On that day," says the Lord God,
"I will make the sun go down at noon,
and darken the earth in broad daylight.
I will turn your feasts into mourning,
and all your songs into lamentation"(Amos 8:9–10).

"On the day I punish Israel for his transgressions,
I will punish the altars of Bethel . . .
I will smite the winter house with the summer house;
and the houses of ivory shall perish,
and the great houses shall come to an end," says the Lord
(Amos 3:14–15).

Because you trample upon the poor,
and take from him exactions of wheat,
You have built houses of hewn stone,

but you shall not dwell in them;
You have planted pleasant vineyards,
But you shall not drink their wine
   (Amos 5:11).

Apart from his cosmic hyperbole, Amos was right. The northern kingdom was conquered and devastated by the Assyrians a few years later. The mansions were torn down, and most of the wealthier citizens were deported.

The motif of a "great and terrible day of the Lord," a fearful judgment going far beyond Amos's merely regional doom, appears at the end of the Old Testament (Malachi 4:1,5). It develops in later Jewish literature and affects the apocalyptic genre, of which Revelation, at the end of the New Testament, is the principal Christian example. For Saint Paul, the emphasis is somewhat different: the day of the Lord is the day when Christ will return in majesty, bringing joy to Christians and destruction to sinners (1 Thessalonians 5:2–3).

> See also: Biblical Prophecy (1)—Israelite and
>   Jewish; Revelation
> Further Reading:
> Brown R. E., J. A. Fitzmyer, and R. E.
>   Murphy, eds. *The New Jerome Biblical
>   Commentary.* Englewood Cliffs, NJ:
>   Prentice-Hall, 1990.

DELPHI

Site of Apollo's chief oracular shrine, largely responsible, in Greece, for prophecy acquiring a predictive meaning.

Delphi was believed to be at the center of the world, then regarded as a disk. A stone, the *omphalos,* or "navel," marked the exact spot. The oracle may once have belonged to Themis, a daughter of the Earth Goddess, and legend mentions a huge guardian serpent, but when Apollo arrived in the thirteenth century B.C., he killed the serpent and took possession.

At first, the oracle functioned on only one day of the year, Apollo's birthday, the seventh day of the month in which it occurred, about May 20. Later, it could be consulted on the seventh day of any month when he was in residence. He was not always in residence. He allegedly spent three months of each year among the Hyperboreans, a mysterious northern people with whom he had ancient ties. It was said that some Hyperboreans had come to Greece long ago and helped to establish him at Delphi. One, named Olen, had prescribed the form in which his pronouncements should be given. In historical times, such appearances were rare, if they happened at all; the Hyperboreans, whoever they were, sent offerings to Delphi but generally kept to themselves in their distant homeland, so that Apollo's regular visits took him far away. During his absence, another god, Dionysus, was in charge at Delphi but did not speak through the oracle. Apollo returned on his birthday and was welcomed with a festival.

Consulting Apollo, even on one of the approved days, was not a casual procedure. The inquirer had to be free from serious guilt and also had to pay a substantial fee. Gifts to the shrine could improve the atmosphere. Apollo communicated through a priestess, the Pythia. She underwent ritual purification in the Castalian spring nearby, and took further preparatory steps that are not certain. She may have chewed laurel leaves, or she may have burned them, or hemp or bay leaves, and inhaled the fumes. Apollo took control of her, and she became a kind of medium. The inquirer asked a question, and the priestess gave a reply, which probably made no obvious sense: a priest translated it into normal language, often in hexameter verse, and a final written version constituted the god's answer, which the inquirer could take away.

Delphi, as a kind of religious capital, was the only focus of unity among the small states into which Greece was divided. The temple complex housed an art gallery exhibiting works from all quarters, and supplied

Spartans consulting Apollo's oracle at Delphi on a question of peace or war. (Ann Ronan Picture Library)

a platform for poets and musicians. It was customary for city governments to consult the oracle on matters of policy, and some of them maintained officials called exegetes who interpreted the god's messages. The Athenians claimed him as a source for their laws; the Spartans said he had virtually dictated their constitution. When he advised or warned, he was usually temperate and constructive. He gave guidance to Greeks planning settlements overseas, and the colonists built temples for him in their new homes.

Apollo was assumed to have knowledge of the future—a belief reflected in the tragic case of Cassandra—and inquirers asked him about it, wanting to be told what would happen if they did so-and-so. In Greece, this was the main reason for prophecy sometimes having a predictive meaning, though it never became as prominent as it did for Jews and Christians under biblical influence. Apollo's

responses, if not downright evasive, could sometimes be construed in more ways than one, and even when they sounded clear-cut, they might indicate alternatives rather than give a straight answer. Apollo was nicknamed "Loxias," the Ambiguous, though that did not prevent people from applying to him.

A famous anecdote, set in the year 546 B.C., illustrates the point. Croesus, king of Lydia in western Asia Minor, planned an attack on the adjacent domain of the Persian king Cyrus. He decided to test seven oracles and sent messengers inviting their priests and priestesses to say what he was doing on a certain day. To rule out lucky guesses, he did something totally bizarre, chopping up a dead tortoise and boiling the pieces in a bronze cauldron with portions of lamb. Delphi got this right—if the story is true, one is bound to suspect a leak—so Croesus made gifts to the Delphic shrine and asked about his intended campaign. The reply was that if he proceeded with it, he would destroy an empire. He took this to mean Cyrus's empire and did proceed, but Cyrus defeated him and conquered Lydia. The empire that succumbed was his own. When he complained to Delphi, the priestess replied that he should have asked for clarification.

Later, when the Persian army of Xerxes invaded Greece, Delphi told the Spartans that either their city would be captured or one of their kings would die. Three hundred Spartans led by King Leonidas made a celebrated stand at Thermopylae, and all were killed, including Leonidas. The Persians advanced beyond but never took Sparta. It may be that Leonidas knew what the oracle had said and accepted his fate to avert the alternative.

In the Persian crisis, the Athenians also consulted Delphi and were advised, alarmingly, to abandon their city, making no attempt to resist. Unable to accept this, the envoys threatened to camp in the sanctuary until they received a better answer. They were told that the Persian army would overrun their territory but they should trust in "wooden walls," and the "divine isle" of Salamis would witness many deaths at seedtime or harvest. The Athenians took "wooden walls" to mean their fleet. While Apollo did not specify whether the dead would be Greek or Persian, they judged that to call Salamis "divine" was encouraging. They risked a naval battle nearby and won.

Whatever Apollo's priestesses really said, the predictions that the priests extracted were seldom straightforward. They might be merely general, they might be hedged, or they might be sheer riddles that would only be understood in retrospect. Delphi taught the Greeks a conception of prophecy that went beyond mere fortune-telling and soothsaying, but the actual recorded predictions hardly suggest paranormal insight or divine illumination.

Delphi petered out during the fourth century A.D. as Christianity prevailed in the Roman Empire. The Emperor Julian, a pagan revivalist, sent emissaries to find whether the oracle was still active. They got a response—apparently, there was someone there to give it—but it was a farewell.

> Tell ye the king: the carven hall is fallen
>   in decay:
> Apollo hath no chapel left, no
>   prophesying bay,
> No talking spring. The stream is dry that
>   had so much to say.

See also: Apollo; Cassandra; Oracles
Further Reading:
Hoyle, Peter. *Delphi*. London: Cassell, 1967.

DIVINATION

The art of seeking knowledge or guidance from things not logically connected with the inquiry.

Divination is essentially magical and very ancient and widespread. It is concerned with finding out secrets, reaching decisions, and predicting the future. The point is always that it is *not* logical, in the sense of relying on ordinary causal connections. There are many methods. An important one is to cast lots, with a meaning attached to each possible result; tossing a coin, heads or tails, is an elementary way. In classical Greece, omens were taken from birds: it was promising if they flew on your right, unlucky if they flew on your left. When Latin was more familiar to Europeans, the *Sortes Virgilianae* were used (*sortes* is the plural of *sors*, "lot"). You opened Virgil's *Aeneid* at random, touched a passage with your finger, and took whatever it said as a response. The same has often been done with the Bible, though, in such a large book, the chances of a text being apt to the inquirer's need are slight. There is an old joke about a man who opened it and read "Judas went out and hanged himself." He tried again and read "Go thou and do likewise." A similar method, employed in China as well as the West, is to walk outdoors and try to extract hints from the words spoken by passersby. Before the invention of the tea bag, expectations were often inferred from the distribution of loose tea leaves at the bottom of a cup.

Far more complex and philosophic is divination by the Chinese *I Ching,* or *Book of Changes.* This work is very old indeed and was known to Confucius. The system is based on sixty-four hexagrams—diagrams of six lines, made up of broken and unbroken ones in every possible combination. Each hexagram has a "judgment" associated with it. To consult this oracle on a given issue, you construct a hexagram by some random method, such as tossing coins six times to decide whether each line, in turn, should be broken or unbroken. Having built the hexagram, you look up the associated judgment. The judgments tends to be enigmatic, but Jung and others who have studied the system have been struck by the relevance and profundity of the meanings that may emerge on reflection; also, by their frequent predictive effectiveness. The *I Ching* is certainly more interesting than the crude types of divination already mentioned, though the "reflection"—the contribution of the thoughtful inquirer—may be more important than the hexagrams as such.

In several advanced forms, divination requires expert practitioners. They might object to the term *divination* being used at all, on the ground that their techniques are more sophisticated, more scientific even, than throwing dice or listening to passing pedestrians. It is not easy, however, to draw the line because the lack of logical nexus is always there. Astrology, fortune-telling by cards, palmistry, all of these may seem to work when the expert uses them. But there are no proven reasons why the movement of planets in the Zodiac or the accidental fall of cards or the lines on a hand should be linked with anyone's character or destiny. It has been argued that the undoubted successes of a few astrologers, card readers, and palmists are due to their own insights and intuitions, rather than the alleged significance of the phenomena they expound.

In ancient divination, a god or other supernatural agency was sometimes thought to underlie the event from which the answer was inferred or to inspire the person who inferred it. Divination might then verge on full-scale prophecy. At the oracle of Dodona in Greece, an inquirer received a "yes" or "no" reply according to the color of a bean taken from a jar, and this reply was from Zeus because he determined which sort of bean was taken. Roman augurers made prognostications from the entrails of sacrificed animals, and the technique involved a special gift of augury. Early Israelites used the Urim and Thummim, which are mentioned several times in the Old Testament. The exact nature of these objects is mysterious, but consulting them was a form of lot casting controlled by God and not by chance. Priests carried them in an *ephod,* probably a kind of wallet. An Israelite wanting guidance could ask a priest to put a question to the Lord through the Urim and Thummim. He might give a "yes" or "no" answer, but there was at least one other potential result—that he did not answer at all (see 1 Samuel 28:6). It is strange to find an oracular procedure quite like that of Dodona (if a little more complex, owing to the null possibility) embedded in Scriptures that refer constantly to far more exalted communication with God and culminate in the great prophetic writings of Isaiah and others. Furthermore, the Urim and Thummim take a long time fading out. They are mentioned even after the Babylonian exile (Ezra 2:63).

See also: Astrology; Oracles; Palmistry; Scrying; Tarot

Further Reading:

Brown R. E., J. A. Fitzmyer, and R. E. Murphy, eds. *The New Jerome Biblical Commentary.* Englewood Cliffs, NJ: Prentice-Hall, 1990.

Cavendish, Richard, ed. *Man, Myth and Magic*. London: BPC Publishing, 1970–1972. Articles "Divination," "I Ching"

Wilson, Colin. *The Occult*. London: Hodder and Stoughton, 1971.

DIXON, JEANE (1918–1997)

A U.S. journalist who claimed prophetic powers and, over a period of forty years, convinced many readers that she possessed them. Living in the national capital, she was sometimes dubbed "the Washington Seeress."

As a child, the daughter of German immigrants, she was told by a gypsy fortune-teller that she had a psychic gift. However, her public fame stemmed from an experience much later, in 1952. While standing before a statue of the Virgin Mary in a Washington church, she had a vision of the White House with the digits 1 9 6 0 above it and a man with blue eyes and brown hair near the door. Prompted by an inner voice, she announced that a young Democrat would be elected in 1960 and would die in office. She repeated the prediction to an interviewer and developed it. Her president would be in danger of assassination.

The election of John F. Kennedy seemed to confirm her vision, though, as a matter of fact, she had second thoughts during the campaign and expected Richard Nixon, the Republican candidate, to win. She explained this mistake by another vision, which she connected with charges of electoral fraud that followed the election: Nixon had "really" won.

During Kennedy's term of office, she reverted to her talk of assassination and spoke of it to various people—this at least is well attested. According to her, she had a dim "sighting" of the name of a possible assassin. It had two syllables and five or six letters, of which the first looked like *o* or *q* and the second was *s*. Since *s* could not follow *q*, she had got sufficiently close to "Oswald,"

the name of the official suspect. On November 22, 1963, she spoke of a profound foreboding, which was borne out by events in Dallas.

Jeane Dixon's reputation was based largely on this feat. Her admirers credited her with foretelling the deaths of other prominent persons, including Gandhi, Marilyn Monroe, and Martin Luther King Jr. But the proven and documented successes are few, and the errors numerous. Her journalistic forecasts about celebrities did not score often enough to be remarkable. On the world stage, she predicted that the Soviet Union would be the first to put an astronaut on the moon; that Nixon would be one of America's greatest presidents, indeed, "our last hope"; that germ warfare would soon cause enormous loss of life. She attached immense importance to a male child born on February 5, 1962, but seemed unable to decide whether he would be a sort of Messiah or an Antichrist figure.

Occasionally, one may suspect sources other than those alleged. Robert Ripley, the author of a popular "Believe It or Not" newspaper feature, pointed out that presidents elected every twenty years from 1840 on had died in office, so 1960 was ominous anyway for its winning candidate; and that was in print long before Jeane Dixon's prognostications. She predicted the end of the papacy in its present form, but she could have taken a hint from some account of Joachim of Fiore or from "Malachy." She predicted world war in 1999, but she could have taken a hint from Nostradamus, or rather, a much publicized misreading of him.

In her book *My Life and Prophecies*, which can now be largely checked and is not impressive, her religious and moral interests are evident and sometimes raise obvious questions of bias. Many of her pronouncements were based, like the one about Kennedy, on symbolic visions, which, she assured the public, were always right—she used phrases like "the talent the Lord has given me." Errors were due to her own misinterpretations.

Further Reading:

Dixon, Jeane. *My Life and Prophecies.* London: Frederick Muller, 1971.

Montgomery, Ruth. *A Gift of Prophecy.* New York: Bantam, 1967.

Wallechinsky, David, Amy Wallace, and Irving Wallace. *The Book of Predictions.* New York: William Morrow, 1980.

DREAMS

Most human societies have attached importance to dreams and looked for meanings in them. The explorations of Freud, Jung, and their disciples are modern instances of a very ancient activity. Psychologists, however, seldom pay much attention to one long-standing belief, that dreams can reveal the future. This has always been widespread but not in the sense that events are foreseen literally. Precognitive dreams, it is supposed, take symbolic forms and have to be interpreted.

Shakespeare's *Julius Caesar* introduces a Roman instance. On March 15, 44 B.C., Caesar was about to leave for the Capitol to preside over a meeting of the Senate. His wife, Calpurnia, urged him to stay at home. She had dreamed about a statue of him with blood spurting from it. If this dream happened as described (there are different versions), it was certainly prophetic, since Brutus, Cassius, and confederates of theirs were waiting to assassinate Caesar by stabbing him with daggers. However, there had been leaks about the plot, and it was known to others besides the conspirators. The date was already rumored, the "Ides of March" (that is, March 15), and the soothsayer Spurinna had warned Caesar to beware.

One popular notion is that dreams may go by opposites. Rome supplies an instance of that belief also. The poet Lucan imagines Caesar's rival Pompey dreaming about his own triumphal reception in the city after a victory some years earlier. Lucan offers more than one explanation but mentions the idea that dreams can be deceptive and "bode contraries"; this, in the present case, being the right answer, since Pompey's army was about to be defeated by Caesar.

The Bible gives an older and more interesting story (Genesis, chapters 40 and 41). Joseph, a great-grandson of the patriarch Abraham, is a prisoner in Egypt. Pharaoh's chief butler, the court official in charge of wine, is in the same prison, and so is the chief baker. The butler tells Joseph of a dream in which he saw a vine with three branches. Clusters of grapes grew on all three, and he squeezed the juice into a royal cup and handed it to Pharaoh. Joseph assures him that in three days, Pharaoh will restore him to his position at court, and he will again be handing his master the cup. The baker also reports a dream. He had three baskets on his head, one on top of another. The top one was full of bread and cakes; birds flew down and ate its contents. Joseph speaks again of three days but says Pharaoh will hang the baker, and birds will peck at his corpse. Both readings turn out to be correct. What is most significant in this tale is that Joseph does not pretend to have any technique. Interpretations "belong to God." The author represents him as divinely inspired, for a purpose that emerges in the next chapter.

Pharaoh himself has two dreams. In the first, seven thin cows eat seven fat ones. In the second, seven meager ears of grain swallow up seven good ones. He summons his magicians and wise men, but they cannot make sense of the dreams. The butler remembers Joseph, and Pharaoh sends for him. Joseph again disclaims any expertise of his own: the message and the interpretation are from God. Seven years of plenty will be followed by seven years of famine. Joseph advises Pharaoh to store up grain during the good years as a reserve to feed Egypt during the bad years. Pharaoh is so deeply impressed that he appoints Joseph himself to oversee the program.

Joseph, in Genesis, interprets Pharaoh's dreams. He attributes his success to divine inspiration, not to techniques such as those Pharaoh's magicians use. (Ann Ronan Picture Library)

The biblical author is showing the superiority of God-given insight over Gentile wisdom. Aside from that consideration, his point about the magicians' failure is an important one. Dream symbolism may convey information about the future, but there is no unambiguous technique for deciphering it. Shakespeare brings this out in *Julius Caesar,* where Calpurnia's dream is given a more cheerful meaning by one of the conspirators, so that Caesar will not be dissuaded from going to the Capitol.

Napoleon, in one of his few recorded dreams, was devoured by a bear. He often speculated about this without reaching a conclusion. The animal image was well established and surely clear in its implication. Four years later, his disastrous campaign in Russia was the beginning of his downfall: the bear did devour him. In retrospect, the dream's essential meaning seems obvious, whether as an actual foreshadowing or as a subconscious warning. Yet in advance, apparently, it was not.

J. W. Dunne, the author of *An Experiment with Time,* developed another view, not opposed but complementary. He claimed that if dreams are written down promptly on waking, the record may show after an interval—perhaps quite a short interval—that some feature of a real-life experience was anticipated by a dream image, more or less literally. He said that such precognitive images do not foreshadow a complete scene or event, but the image and the waking "fulfillment," however modified this may be and however different in context, are alike enough for the correspondence to be plain. With a few individuals, Dunne-type phenomena may occur fairly often. Chris Robinson, whose case was publicized on British television in 1994, had dreams that were fulfilled in a manner that enabled him to recognize precognitive ones when they happened, or at least, to recognize that they could be. He gave warnings of danger that were respected by the police and other authorities.

See also: Dunne, J. W.; Napoleon; Prophecy, Theories of; Spurinna

Further Reading:

Broughton, Richard. *Parapsychology.* New York: Ballantine, 1991.

Dunne, J. W. *An Experiment with Time.* Revised and enlarged edition. London: Faber and Faber, 1938.

DUNNE, J. W. (1875–1949)

English investigator of dreams.

By profession, John William Dunne was one of the earliest important aircraft designers. However, from childhood onward, he harbored a conviction that he had a message for humanity. When he attended a séance, the medium told him that he would be a great medium himself, the greatest the world had ever seen. He never was, but he made a major contribution to ideas of the paranormal.

In the spring of 1902, being then in South Africa, he had a vivid and distressing dream in which he stood on a mountainside where the ground was fissured and jets of vapor were spurting up. He recognized the place as an island he had dreamed of before, with a volcano on it, which he knew, in the dream, was going to explode. A nightmare sequence followed in which he was trying to save the lives of 4,000 inhabitants. He shouted at the local authorities, who were French, but was merely sent from one official to another. The mayor, "Monsieur le Maire," was going out and told Dunne to return the next day when the office would be open. Throughout, he kept saying, "Four thousand people will be killed unless . . ." When a newspaper arrived, its main item was an account of the eruption of Mont Pelée on the French island of Martinique, in the West Indies. Dunne noted a headline as saying that an estimated 4,000 had died, the number in his dream. However, he reexamined the paper some years afterward and found that it gave the number as 40,000. His dream had anticipated, not exactly the event, but his own reading of the news item about it, which dropped a zero and was at variance with later reports.

This dream was not isolated; he had others that were also interesting. He began writing his dreams down, and often noticed waking events later that corresponded with them. Friends of his agreed to try. Neither he nor the others ever foresaw complete scenes, but they had previsions of parts of them, in the form of isolated images or images differently grouped.

For instance, an artist dreamed of a lifeboat painted the customary red and blue, standing on green turf with a net over it. Next day, he saw a boat painted red and blue like a lifeboat, similarly pointed at both ends, and standing on turf. It was not a lifeboat and there was no net, but some distance off he saw another boat that did have a net over it. A cousin of Dunne's dreamed of meeting a German woman in a public garden, who wore a black-and-white striped blouse and a black skirt and had a distinctive hairstyle. Soon afterward, she stayed at a hotel and was told of another woman staying there, thought to be German. She met this guest in the hotel grounds, looking very much as in the dream, but the setting was different.

Dunne published his findings in 1927 in a book entitled *An Experiment with Time,* with his theorizing as to what happened and how it happened. The book sold well, and for some years, it was fashionable to keep a dream journal. The difficulty here is that dreams must be written down immediately on waking or they will probably fade away, and not many people have the necessary determination or stamina. However, some of the journal-keepers believed that they were having experiences of the right kind, and the popular dramatist J. B. Priestley wrote several plays exploiting the idea of irregularities in time.

In spite of his own impressive results, Dunne rejected the notion that he had a special prophetic talent. He inferred from the occasional successes of others that the thing could happen for people in general and no one was exceptional in this respect. A sustained and fairly systematic project suggested otherwise. He assembled six volunteers—students at Oxford—and they, together with himself, wrote down their dreams: theoretically, until each had completed at least fourteen records. In practice, four of the students did not get so far, but two others produced more than the required number, and so did Dunne. Altogether, eighty-eight dreams were recorded. Thirty-four showed a credible resemblance to something in waking life within two and a half months before or after, usually with some degree of distortion. The records are summarized, with a few marginal cases not finally judged to be significant, in a later edition of Dunne's book. Tabulating the thirty-four that he accepted, he counted images that related to the past as P-resemblances, images that were fulfilled in the future as F-resemblances, and he classified the resemblances under the headings "good," "moderate," and "indifferent."

In all, there were fourteen P-resemblances and twenty F-resemblances. Since the natural expectation was that P-resemblances would predominate yet the reverse was true, Dunne's belief that dreams could relate to the future seemed to be borne out. But the same did not apply to his belief that it could happen to anyone, without distinction. Dunne himself, a practiced dreamer, had five F-resemblances. The volunteers designated as B, C, and F had none; A had three, and D had two. E, however, had ten, as many as all the rest put together. Moreover, E had three "good" ones and the other five volunteers had only one among them. Dunne had one himself. The logical conclusion was that the volunteers could all be eliminated except E. Dunne resisted it; he said she had no "special faculty for precognition"; it was just that "her dreams were more clearly related to distinctive episodes of waking life." Admittedly, she did better with P-resemblances, too, but she was manifestly unusual.

Against this reading of Dunne's results may be set a study more favorable to him by Louisa E. Rhine, who claimed to have collected hundreds of precognitive experiences, mostly in dreams. However, this was published in 1955, and her criteria may have been unduly elastic. The year 1968 saw the inception of a long-term project of a fairly objective kind, which slowly accumulated data supporting the view that while such experiences do seem to happen, they happen for a minority only. Robert Nelson founded the Central Premonition Registry in New York. He allowed premonitions of any kind, including dreams that the dreamers thought revealed the future, and classified and filed them. In several thousand cases, he judged that only a very few were convincingly predictive—about one percent, and presumably even these were not all given in dreams. Such a meager result could have been dismissed altogether if it were not for the distribution being skewed. Half the good ones came from only five persons, each of whom scored several times.

Among those who attracted special interest was an English "psychic," Malcolm Bessent. During one hectic night of dreaming late in November 1969, he had what he construed as advance notice of a disaster involving a Greek tanker owned by the shipping magnate Onassis; the death of the French ex-president Charles de Gaulle; and a change of government in Britain. He even had approximate time limits. His forecasts were written down, witnessed, and filed at the Central Premonition Registry. All three were fulfilled. Bessent was invited to take part in tests at the dream laboratory of the Maimonides Medical Center in Brooklyn, New York. Several times after dreaming, he gave descriptions—not in precise detail but close enough to be interesting—of pictures that he was shown later.

Dream research became easier and more exact with the discovery of REMs, the rapid eye movements that accompany dreaming.

When these are observed, the sleeper can be awakened and asked to tape an account of the dream before memory fades. But cases continue to be noted of Dunne-type experiences on quite the old lines, happening to exceptional individuals. One such, Chris Robinson, was the subject of a British Broadcasting Corporation (BBC) television program in October 1994. He had dreams that he could recognize as anticipatory, usually of some disaster, and recorded them promptly. When these were decoded, they were borne out by events often enough to interest the police. One of them foreshadowed a terrorist attack on an Air Force base; the security officer increased the number of guards for a week, then returned to normal, and the attack followed a month later. Robinson also dreamed in advance of the murder of a photographer in Somalia and warned the photographer's mother, unhappily without effect.

Possibly, Dunne was correct, and many people have precognitive dreams but simply forget them or fail to recognize the fulfillment when it comes. It can only be said that the available evidence does not point that way. Whoever is right, the question remains. The thing apparently does happen, often or not. How does it happen?

Dunne developed a theory of his own with diagrams, scientific arguments, and philosophical deductions. As presented, it is too complicated for comfort. At the heart of it is a principle called serialism, involving much more than the explanation of dreams. Consciousness and time are regarded as "serial." What Dunne seems to be arguing is that if you try to pin them down, you get into a regress with no visible end.

Suppose an individual, X, is experiencing something quite in the ordinary way—looking out of a window, for example. X may be aware of the experience as it happens and verbalize it and reflect on it, but the X who does this is distinct from the X who is simply looking out of the window. We could speak of X1 and X2. However, awareness of the X1 + X2 situation and reflection on that brings in an X3. And so on. With time, you can say as you go along a highway, "I'm moving through space at fifty miles an hour." But how fast is the world moving through time as you do it? At the rate of an hour per . . . what? Measurement involves an additional dimension, but, again, there is a regress. Our normal time may be called T1; beyond it is the additional dimension with a time that may be called T2. And so on.

In another book, Dunne uses an analogy, the impossibility of painting a picture of a scene with yourself in it, painting. The picture must include not only yourself but your easel with the picture on it; and that smaller picture must include yourself with the easel and the picture on it . . . and so on again.

Dunne thinks the regresses reach a term in some kind of ultimate observer, a superbeing at infinity, of whom we are all parts. It is doubtful whether his application of serialism to dream prevision really has to go so far. Individual consciousness is in T1, seeming to move along it, and aware of only a brief "now" at a given moment. There is also consciousness in T2, and the T2 observer, in the additional dimension, can survey an indefinitely large part of the individual's life span in T1, including what is future for the individual. From the T2 vantage point, this is like looking down from a height on a road with someone walking along it. The T2 consciousness can take in miles of the road, ahead of the person walking as well as behind. The T1 walker, who is actually on the road, sees only the immediate neighborhood. (This image was used by Saint Thomas Aquinas in the thirteenth century to show how God could have foreknowledge.) When the individual in T1 is asleep, the T2 consciousness can get through and communicate glimpses of the sleeper's future—the road ahead—probably garbled.

As sometimes happens with puzzling phenomena, speculation diverts attention from the facts. They are interesting as far as they go. But Dunne drastically limits prophetic scope. Dream prevision, on his showing, foreshadows experiences of the dreamer. Public events cannot be foreseen objectively as such; if they seem to be, as with Bessent, the key lies in Dunne's volcano dream—the dream imagery is formed not by the future event itself but by the dreamer's future experience of reading about it in a paper or learning of it otherwise. All the cases in the Oxford experiment were, in fact, personal.

Moreover, since the consciousness on the T2 level surveys only the individual's mortal existence on the T1 level, no dream transmitted from T2 can portend anything after the individual's death. And it appears that no dream ever does, within Dunne's purview. He believed in an immortality in other dimensions, but it was not open to investigation and not relevant to what he was discussing. The precognition that he claims to define and account for is of no help at all with, say, the more remarkable prophecies of Nostradamus, which extend not merely beyond Nostradamus's lifetime but into a future centuries away. Some of these prophesies are more challenging, more pressing in the demand for an explanation, than the dreams recorded by Dunne.

All the foregoing opens up questions that were already exercising minds in the Middle Ages. If the T2 consciousness can see what is future for the individual in T1, does that mean that the future is there, so to speak, and unalterable? The normal rejection of such a view raises problems, notably the much-discussed problem of prevention. If a dreamer foresees something undesirable, like an accident (that is, with no ordinary reason for anxiety or expectation), and goes to the place where it is foreseen happening and takes action so that it doesn't, what did the dreamer see in the first place? A television critic, discussing Chris Robinson and his warnings to the police, understandably wondered. Louisa E. Rhine, in the study in which she claimed to have assembled hundreds of cases of precognition, also claimed that they included cases of prevention.

Dunne's attempt to deal with this issue is not convincing. An arguable conjecture is that the T2 consciousness doesn't see the future accident as a fact, but does see a situation in which it will be a possibility, and communicates that awareness to the individual in T1 as a dream-image of it actually happening, in the hope that the individual will take notice and forestall the possibility. But this would imply an independent purposiveness at the T2 level that *An Experiment with Time* does not provide for.

One literary point. William Morris presents his fantasy of the future, *News from Nowhere,* as a dream, if an impossibly long one. But he is following an old fictional convention (Bunyan does it, too, in *The Pilgrim's Progress*), which has nothing to do with real dreaming or Dunne-style precognition.

See also: Dreams; Morris, William; Nostradamus; Premonitions; Prophecy, Theories of; Thomas Aquinas, Saint

Further Reading:

Broughton, Richard. *Parapsychology.* New York: Ballantine, 1991.

Dunne, J. W. *An Experiment with Time.* Revised and enlarged edition. London: Faber and Faber, 1938.

Gribbin, John. *Time Warps.* London: J. M. Dent, 1979.

Wallechinsky, David, Amy Wallace, and Irving Wallace. *The Book of Predictions.* New York: William Morrow, 1980.

ELIJAH

The first great prophet of ancient Israel. His name—possibly an assumed one affirming his mission—means "the Lord is my God." Some translations of the Bible preserve the Greek form "Elias."

Elijah left nothing in writing, unless we count a letter quoted in 2 Chronicles 21:12–15, but he prepared the way for the literary prophets such as Isaiah. He denounced public wrongdoing and apostasy, even at the highest levels and in spite of personal risk. It was principally because of his warnings that the inspired utterance of Israelite prophecy began to take on its predictive aspect.

He lived in the northern Israelite kingdom during the middle ninth century B.C., when Ahab reigned. Many of the king's subjects were enjoying a period of prosperity, partly through his close association with the Phoenicians, the chief trading nation of the Mediterranean; Carthage was founded about this time as a Phoenician colony. Ahab married the Phoenician princess Jezebel, an elegant and strong-minded woman who brought a new sophistication to Samaria, his capital. She also brought the cult of the Tyrian Baal, together with a train of priests. "Baal" in the early books of the Bible is usually a general term covering a medley of local gods—nature spirits and fertility spirits whom the Israelites had encountered in the Promised Land and frequently found attractive. Jezebel's Baal was much more formidable, a major god of fertility and the storm wind, who could be set up as a rival to Yahweh, the God of Israel. With him came the goddess Asherah as his consort, together with absolutist conceptions of royal power.

Ahab was willing to allow both forms of religion. His wife was not. Her new subjects had had their prophets for many years, the seers and minstrels of the Lord, not very influential and not subversive. Nevertheless, Jezebel drove them into hiding. Few of the people were enthusiastic about her Baal, but only a small number offered serious opposition.

Elijah emerged as a prophet in a new style. According to the biblical narrative, he confronted Ahab foretelling a long drought, as a sign of the Lord's wrath at what the king was allowing; it would end only when he said. This promptly happened. The prophet insisted on a rigorous either-or proposition: the people must make up their minds—Baal or Yahweh? On Mount Carmel, the ridge close to Haifa, he staged a contest to see which god would kindle fire on an altar. Baal did not, Yahweh did. Attempted rationalizations of this miracle are not relevant here. What is interesting is that the author does not present it as a victory turning the tide. The onlookers, he says, acknowledged the true God and killed many of Baal's "prophets," but the tide did not turn, though at least the drought ended.

Jezebel threatened Elijah with death, and he escaped to Mount Horeb in Sinai where, long before, Moses had heard the voice of God. He was in despair, but God spoke to him too, not spectacularly in wind and earthquake but in a "still small voice." Seven thousand Israelites in Ahab's domains had not submitted to Baal, and in spite of all appearances, a change would come. Elijah went back to Samaria. Meanwhile, Ahab, urged on by Jezebel, was engaged in getting possession of a vineyard he coveted, belonging to

The prophet Elijah, instructed by an angel, leaves the mountain where he has taken refuge. (Ann Ronan Picture Library)

Naboth, one of his subjects. By the queen's contrivance, Naboth was condemned on a trumped-up charge and stoned to death. Ahab confiscated the vineyard. While he was inspecting his new property, Elijah came to him and denounced his un-Israelite despotism. He would have a disastrous end, his family would be destroyed, Jezebel's corpse would be food for dogs. Ahab assumed an air of penitence, but he fell in battle soon after. Jezebel was killed, violently and ignominiously, in a revolt led by Jehu, and dogs devoured her. Jehu wiped out the rest of Ahab's family, massacred the Baal devotees who were still active, and converted their temple into a latrine.

In the Bible, Elijah appoints a disciple, Elisha, as his successor. Beside the Jordan he is mysteriously whirled skyward in a fiery chariot, and no one sees him again.

Besides his uncompromising stand and his predictions, the story foreshadows an enduring prophetic theme. The 7,000 who have not bowed the knee to Baal are a remnant keeping faith. Israel's prophets come to accept that the Chosen People are not an indivisible bloc. Whole sections may fall away, but a faithful remnant will always inherit the divine promises and live on as the true Israel. This explains the position of the Jews who are descended, not from all the ancient Israelite tribes, but from a minority, mainly of the tribe of Judah, who were deported to Babylon in the sixth century B.C. A crucial number of these were allowed to return and refound Zion, while others preserved Judaism in the Diaspora.

Elijah's departure in the chariot inspired a belief that he was not dead but alive among the heavenly host. A late scriptural book, Malachi, ended with a prophecy that he would reappear, to prepare for the final Day of the Lord. Evidently, God was reserving him for some great purpose, and there were guesses as to its nature. He would return as a forerunner of the Messiah and anoint him as king (this idea figures in the New Testament in connection with John the Baptist). He would preside over the resurrection of the dead at the end of all things. In the early Christian era, rabbis speculated about his immortality. Perhaps he had never sinned and therefore never incurred the death sentence pronounced in Eden. Or perhaps he was a disguised angel, not human at all.

And perhaps he made unobtrusive visits to Earth. Jewish folklore includes many stories of Elijah descending briefly from heaven as a friend to the poor, as a rescuer from peril, and as a reconciler and settler of disputes. Two important Jewish movements, Cabalism and Hasidism, claimed that he came in person to bless their founders. At the Passover, some Orthodox families keep a chair empty for the prophet, set a glass of wine in front of it, and open the door to let him in if he wishes to enter.

Much of this legendary saga passed into Islam, in which Elijah is called Ilyas, a name probably derived from the Greek form "Elias." Though barely mentioned in the Koran, he keeps his folklore character as an immortal visitor to the human world. Muslim mystics revere him as a pattern of holiness; visions of him occur in the traditions of Sufi religious orders. However, his future role in the last days has no Muslim counterpart.

The Islamic Elijah is sometimes identified, or rather confused, with a legendary hero called al-Khadir, the "green" one, green being the sacred color. Khadir is also immortal, but his saga is largely derived from non-Islamic sources, such as the Babylonian epic of Gilgamesh and medieval romances of Alexander the Great.

See also: Biblical Prophecy (1)—Israelite and Jewish

Further Reading

Brown R. E., J. A. Fitzmyer, and R. E. Murphy, eds. *The New Jerome Biblical Commentary.* Englewood Cliffs, NJ: Prentice-Hall, 1990.
The Encyclopedia of Islam.

ELIOT, GEORGE (1819–1880)

Pen name of one of the principal English novelists of the nineteenth century whose real name was Mary Ann Evans. Her historical novel *Romola*, published in 1863, is set in Florence in the last decade of the fifteenth century, the heyday of the famous preacher and social reformer Girolamo Savonarola. Influenced by the doctrines of Joachim of Fiore, he foretold revolutionary change. Joachim, long before, had spoken in fairly general terms of a future "Age of the Holy Spirit." This was to be an era of peace and liberty and universal enlightenment. During the Middle Ages, enthusiasts expanded his prophecy by adding two semimessianic figures who were to open the way to the good times. A great ruler called the Second Charlemagne would unite Christendom, and an Angelic Pope would restore the Church to holiness. Savonarola had high hopes of the French king Charles VIII, who invaded Italy and was thought by some optimists to be the Second Charlemagne.

Eliot introduces these themes, showing historical insight ahead of contemporary historians. One character in *Romola* says: "The warning is ringing in the ears of all men; and it's no new story; for the Abbot Joachim prophesied of the coming time three hundred years ago, and now Fra Girolamo has got the message afresh. He has seen it in a vision, even as the prophets of old." In the novel, Charles VIII enters Florence with his army and is hailed as the Second Charlemagne. George Eliot also takes up the companion prophecy. She imagines a Florentine telling how he "heard simple folk talk of a Pope Angelico, who was to come by-and-by and bring in a new order of things, to purify the Church from simony, and the lives of the clergy from scandal." She remarks: "The sunlight and shadows bring their old beauty . . . and men still yearn for the reign of peace and righteousness. . . . The Pope Angelico is not come yet." *Romola* treats the prophetic hopes as il-

lusory. Charles VIII accomplishes nothing, and Savonarola is discredited.

See also: Angelic Pope; Joachim of Fiore; Savonarola, Girolamo; Second Charlemagne

Further Reading

Geoffrey Ashe, *The Book of Prophecy*. London: Blandford, 1999.

END OF THE WORLD

A belief that the world is not stable or permanent is the norm rather than the exception. Mythologies tell how it has passed through phases that are finite in duration. The Aztecs, for instance, imagine four Suns in succession, with an earthly era corresponding to each. Three cosmic destructions have occurred already, by deluge, earthquake, and hurricane. We are now in a fourth era that will also terminate, probably by fire, and that seems to be the end of everything. The Greek poet Hesiod describes a series of human races going generally downhill, with "golden" people at the beginning and "iron" people (ourselves) at the end. Like the Aztecs, he is silent as to what, if anything, comes afterward. The Hindu program is similar to the Greek. It defines four ages, or yugas, each inferior to the one preceding. The fourth will close when degeneracy is at its worst. Scandinavian mythology lacks the periodic pattern but still prophesies an End and goes into it in rare detail. It will be a cataclysm called Ragnarök, the Twilight of the Gods, when monsters of chaos will slay the principal deities, the sun will be darkened, the stars will fall, and fire and water will reduce the world to a desolate void.

In Hinduism, while the End is definitely an end, something is envisaged beyond. The Messiah Kalki, an incarnation of the Supreme God Vishnu, will restore the world—wind it up again, so to speak—for a fresh start. Scandinavian myth goes further: after Ragnarök, the world will reappear, transfigured and purified, and the sons of the gods will reign in glory. The Hindu conception seems independent of outside influence,

Picture in a thirteenth-century book of psalms, illustrating the Last Judgment: The dead are raised, and their good and bad deeds are weighed. (Ann Ronan Picture Library)

but the Scandinavian, in the form that has survived, has probably been affected by Christianity. Prophecy that not only forecasts a clear and meaningful End but looks beyond to a qualitatively different sequel—not a mere new cycle or repeat performance—is mainly Christian.

The background is in Jewish literature dating from the last century or two B.C. The biblical book Daniel prophesies that God will destroy earthly powers and set up a divine, everlasting kingdom. The world will not end exactly, but it will be transformed. The dead, or some of them, will return to life. Subsequent Jewish writers carry such hopes further.

The early Christians went further again. There will be a true End when Jesus, the Son of God, returns in power and majesty. All the dead will be raised and judged; the world will be annihilated, probably burnt, and replaced by . . . something else. Passages in the Gospels quote Jesus as foretelling these events. The last book of the New Testament, the Revelation or Apocalypse ascribed to the apostle John, unfolds the prospect with a wealth of symbolic imagery.

Jesus warned his disciples against guesswork about the time of the End. Only his Heavenly Father knew the day and the hour. For several decades, nevertheless, many Christians expected the Second Coming to occur soon. Revelation leaves the door open for this, though it hints that the truth may be otherwise. It envisages an End in two phases. Christ will return and reign with the resurrected saints for a thousand years. The general resurrection and the Last Judgment will follow. The existing universe will vanish, and there will be "a new heaven and a new earth," with a glorious New Jerusalem as the abode of the blessed. The word *millennium* originally stood for the thousand-year reign of Christ. The Church preferred not to take this literally, but the motif inspired attempts to impose thousand-year divisions on the world's entire history and infer its likely duration.

As the hope of an early End receded, the future came to be pictured in a longer perspective. Christ's warning against a rash exactitude seems to have been taken to heart for many years. A few Christians indulged in fantasies about events that would lead up to the End, but no one is known to have set a date for it until 960, when a German visionary named Bernard of Thuringia said it would come on a day when the Annunciation of the Virgin coincided with Good Friday. That happened on March 25, 992. The world, however, continued.

That was an exceptional case. A persistent notion that the End was expected in the year 1000 grossly exaggerates whatever scare there was. Specific doomsday forecasts did not really begin until the religious excitements of the sixteenth century. Since then, they have attracted publicity from time to time. Some have been based on astrology, some on biblical periods, some on fancied revelations. The world's destruction may be imagined as a pure act of God, taking the form of fire or flood, or it may be given a scientific cause, such as a solar explosion or a collision with a comet. Some prophecies retain a traditional Christian scenario; others diverge.

The most committedly scriptural of all heralds of doomsday, and the most influential, was William Miller (1781–1849). A native of Massachusetts, he passed through an anti-Christian phase and then became a Baptist. He worked out a system of scriptural interpretation pointing to the End and the Second Coming about 1843. In popular lectures, he spoke of celestial trumpets sounding, the clouds parting to reveal God's throne, even "the horrid yells of the damned." By 1842, he had attracted a mass following. During that year, thirty outdoor gatherings, with attendance in thousands, were held in the eastern United States and the Midwest. Miller settled on October 22, 1844, as the last possible date. Hysteria spread. Merchants gave away their stocks; farmers left their crops to rot in the ground.

When nothing happened, Millerites called the failure "The Disappointment." Some found ways of coming to terms with it. New religious bodies grew from the wreckage, notably the Seventh-Day Adventist Church. Another consequence, though an indirect one, was the sect of Jehovah's Witnesses. Its record shows how prophetic motifs can be restated so as not to depend on a specific event or a fixed time. It originated from Charles Taze Russell, who adapted Miller's calculations. Christ had returned in 1874, but invisibly; he would be visible later. The elect dead were "resurrected" in 1878 but in Heaven, out of human sight. After Russell's death, the leader (though not all followed him) was Judge Joseph Rutherford. He shifted Christ's invisible advent to 1914 and said the Kingdom of Jehovah was in preparation. The world would be transfigured rather than physically ended. However, the changes would be fundamental, especially for its human population. Rutherford's famous slogan was "Millions now living will never die."

A number of dates that have been announced for the End are given here in chronological order. In the twentieth century, the event foretold is sometimes a natural disaster or a nuclear holocaust rather than the End in the old sense. Such predictions are not included.

1524 (i)

In June 1523, a group of astrologers in London calculated that the city would be destroyed by a deluge at the beginning of the following February, and this would be the first stage of doomsday. In January, many Londoners climbed on to higher ground in neighboring counties. When there was no deluge, the astrologers shifted the date to 1624.

1524 (ii) and 1528

A well-known German astrologer, Johannes Stoeffler, also fastened on February 1524 and spoke of floods. A nobleman had an ark built on the Rhine, which was forcibly boarded by a crowd of refugees when heavy rain fell. The End, however, did not ensue, and Stoeffler tried 1528 instead, with no better success.

1533 (i)

The Anabaptists, a revolutionary sect, expected that Christ would return in 1533 and most of the world would be destroyed by fire, but their headquarters, in Strasbourg, would survive as the New Jerusalem.

1533 (ii)

A German mathematician, Michael Steifel, calculated on the basis of Revelation that the world would end on October 18, 1533. When it failed to do so, his fellow citizens in Lochau gave him a thrashing.

1665

Solomon Eccles, a Quaker, went about in London proclaiming that the Great Plague was the beginning of the End. He interrupted a church service, carrying a dish full of hot coals on his head, and called for public repentance. The terrifying mortality in the plague encouraged listeners to believe him. Finally, however, he was arrested, and the scare blew over.

1736

William Whiston, a former professor of mathematics at Cambridge University, predicted that London would be destroyed by a deluge on October 13 and the End would follow. This prophecy, like similar ones, caused a flight of refugees.

1761

When two earthquakes shook London, separated by four weeks, a soldier named William Bell predicted the End after the same interval. He drew large audiences. When the interval was safely past, he was locked away as insane.

1881, 1936, 1953

Dates computed by measurements of the Great Pyramid (see Pyramidology) and successively abandoned.

1900

The year set by a Russian sect at Kargopol called the Brothers and Sisters of Red Death. To prepare for the End, 862 of them decided to burn themselves as a sacrifice. Troops were sent to prevent the immolation, but when they arrived, more than a hundred were already dead.

1925 and 1932

A Long Island, New York, house painter named Robert Reidt, impressed by a reported message from the Archangel Gabriel to a girl in Los Angeles, invited the public to await the End with him on a hill at midnight on February 13, 1925. His companions invoked Gabriel. When midnight passed, Reidt said they must wait for midnight Pacific standard time, three hours later. Still nothing happened. He blamed press photographers. Seven years later, after studying the Bible, he tried again with no better results.

1945

In 1938, the Reverend Charles Long woke up in the night and saw a blackboard on which a ghostly hand wrote "1945." After some reflection, which narrowed down the date to September 21, he predicted that the world would be vaporized and human beings would be turned into ectoplasm. He and his son held meetings at the Pasadena Civic Auditorium, recruiting a fair-sized following who, under their leadership, prepared during the final week by giving up food, drink, and sleep. However, they were not turned into ectoplasm. The group disbanded.

1954

When a crack appeared in the Colosseum in Rome, many recalled a prophecy, mentioned by Byron, that its fall would mean the end of the world. A Vatican spokesman calmed the excitement and the building was repaired.

1962

A conjunction of several planets in Capricorn was interpreted by Indian astrologers as portending the world's destruction on February 2. Millions joined in prayers, rituals, and sacrifices. When the day went by without incident, there was widespread agreement that these measures had averted disaster.

1970

The True Light Church of Christ, in North Carolina, revived a traditional belief that the world would last 6,000 years. They reckoned from a Creation assigned to 4000 B.C. and made an adjustment for what they thought to be an error.

1999

Widespread publicity was given to an alleged prophecy by Nostradamus that the world would end on July 4. Actually, he said no such thing. The "prophecy," like some other supposed Nostradamus prophecies, was a product of misinterpretation.

Most of the doomsday prophets in modern times have been comparatively obscure figures with few converts. No lasting sects have come into existence because of them. There are, of course, purely natural possibilities for the demise of the planet or, at any rate, the life on its surface. Earth may overheat or freeze, or collide with some other body, or be sucked into a black hole. Or it may be totally sterilized by superweapons. Speculation on such contingencies is science fiction rather than prophecy as considered here.

See also: Apocalypse; Revelation

Further Reading

Wallechinsky, David, Amy Wallace, and Irving Wallace. *The Book of Predictions.* New York: William Morrow, 1980.

EZEKIEL (SIXTH CENTURY B.C.)

Putative author of an Old Testament book foretelling the return of the dispossessed Israelites to the Promised Land.

Supposedly, this author was among the people of the southern Israelite kingdom of Judah who were deported to Babylonia in 597 B.C. That deportation was followed by another, on a much larger scale. Jerusalem was destroyed, and Judah became almost depopulated. Ezekiel, it appears, continued to write prophecies, experience visions, and create some very strange imagery well into the 570s. All this is open to dispute. The book seems to be a composite, and parts may have been composed in Judah rather than Babylonia.

The chief predictive passage, whoever wrote it, occurs in chapters 37 to 39. The prophet sees a valley full of dry bones, symbolizing the uprooted and stateless Israelites—not only those in Babylonia but also the northern ones, who were carried off by the Assyrians long before. God shows the bones coming back to life and covered with flesh and skin: the Chosen People will be reconstituted. They will dwell again as one nation in the Promised Land, and God says, "My servant David shall be king over them." The reference is to a king of a dynasty founded by the original David, who lives on in his royal descendants.

This prophecy was fulfilled, in part, by the Zionist ingathering of Jews into Palestine after many centuries of dispersal. More problematic is the further prophecy in chapters 38 and 39, which foreshadows the apocalyptic writings of later times. The ultimate peace of the Lord's resettled people is to come through his destruction of their last enemy, an invader from the remote north, "Gog of the land of Magog, the chief prince of Meshech and Tubal." Several nations are named that will accompany Gog. Some of them are from as far off as the Caucasus and even the Ukraine, represented by "Gomer." Thus far, the prophet may not be too implausible, but his inclusion of Persia, Ethiopia, and Libya as allies of Gog is going to extremes. Gog and Magog reappear in apocalyptic fantasy and in Revelation itself, chapter 20.

Exponents of the British-Israel theory used to explain this passage as prophesying an invasion of Palestine by the then Soviet Union, "Meshech" being Moscow and "Tubal" being Tobolsk. Italy, which then ruled both Ethiopia and Libya, could be brought in neatly if improbably. The passage continued to be recalled as long as Soviet Russia was a menacing superpower, and it was sometimes connected with the final battle of Armageddon. Specific as it is, yet not related to any historical situation, it is a loose end in scriptural prophecy.

See also: Armageddon; British-Israel Theory
Further Reading
Brown R. E., J. A. Fitzmyer, and R. E. Murphy, eds. *The New Jerome Biblical Commentary.* Englewood Cliffs, NJ: Prentice-Hall, 1990.

FATIMA

Village in Portugal associated with apparitions of the Virgin Mary and with correct predictions of a miraculous sign and the rise and fall of Soviet Communism.

On May 13, 1917, during World War I, a girl named Lucia dos Santos was walking in the Fatima neighborhood with two cousins. She was ten years old; the cousins were younger. She had a vision of a radiant lady identified (not at once) as the Virgin Mary. In a short conversation, the lady said she would appear again on the thirteenth day of each month. The apparition was duly repeated. In the summer, rumors of these events began to attract visitors. The Portuguese government was strongly anticlerical, and the district administrator tried to make Lucia recant, but she persisted in her story with support from her cousins, who partly shared the experiences.

Up to that point, according to Lucia, the lady had said very little beyond assurances of the children's salvation and requests for prayer, especially prayer for peace. Skepticism was excusable. The story could easily be dismissed as a fantasy, even a deception, hatched by a child who had heard of the apparitions at Lourdes. Lucia's family thought it unconvincing, and her elder sister, Maria, did not believe any of it. Matters came to a head in September when the lady promised to give a sign at noon on October 13. This promise was publicized, not least in the chief antireligious paper, *O Seculo*. The paper's editor foresaw a fiasco and went to Fatima on the appointed day to witness it. About 70,000 people assembled, though the weather was dull and wet. Lucia's family accompanied her to the scene of the apparitions, terrified of mob violence if nothing happened. She had not given the slightest hint of what the sign would be. No one was watching for anything in particular.

About midday, the rain stopped, the clouds parted, and Lucia—who was seeing more visions—suddenly exclaimed, "Look at the sun!" The voice of a child, outdoors in a huge crowd, could have been heard only by the nearest bystanders, and suggestion cannot account for what followed. The sun, visible through the gap in the clouds, appeared to lose brightness, emit colored rays of light, and revolve, then to move downward in a spiral and up again to its starting-point. The phenomenon lasted for several minutes and caused a panic. Photographs show people staring up at the sky—there is no doubt that they are looking at something.

Many eyewitness testimonies are on record. One of the most impressive came from the anticlerical editor, who, denied his fiasco, was honest enough to publish an account in *O Seculo*. He had seen the solar gyration, which he described as a "macabre dance." It was seen not only on the spot but by people miles away, who had taken little notice of Fatima and were certainly not involved in a mass hallucination. The descriptions do not entirely tally, and it is possible to explain the sign—after a fashion—as an optical illusion due to freak atmospheric conditions and cloud movements. The believer may regard these as miraculously caused; the unbeliever may regard them as accidental. The point, however, is not so much that the thing happened as that it happened at the place predicted, on the day predicted, and roughly at the time predicted. No juvenile fantasy could have produced a forecast a month ahead or projected

Pilgrims at Fatima gathered around a statue of the Virgin Mary, who is believed to have appeared here and foretold the downfall of Communism in Russia. (Hulton Getty)

a rare phenomenon into the sky at the right moment.

Fatima became a venue of pilgrimage, as it is still. Nevertheless, even for believers, the sun's eccentricities raised a question. This was a sign, a powerful one, but what was it a sign *of?* What had Mary said to justify drawing attention to it with such a spectacular effect? Lucia had quoted little more than exhortations to spiritual amend-

ment, such as might have been heard from many pulpits.

But, of course, there was one additional thing that Mary had uttered. This was the prediction itself, and its fulfillment pointed to a prophetic element in her message. At the time and for years afterward, nothing more about the future was mentioned. But in 1936–1937 and 1941–1942, Lucia, who had entered a convent, added to her first account of the apparitions. She now remembered, or claimed to remember, that Mary had said more about things to come and pointed much further ahead than October 1917.

Lucia verbalized these revelations in phrases of conventional piety, making Mary speak, for instance, of her Immaculate Heart. But plain predictions came through. "If men do not cease from offending God, a new and worse war will begin in the pontificate of Pius XI." It nearly did—not quite, unless the Spanish Civil War of 1936–1939 counts as its prologue, but it did begin less than six months into the next pontificate, that of Pius XII. More interesting was a prophecy that "Russia will spread her errors through the world, arousing wars and persecutions." During the period of the apparitions, in 1917, the Russian Revolution was moving toward the ascendancy of Lenin, the formation of the Soviet Union, and the spread of international Communism under Russian direction. Mary, however, foretold—according to Lucia—that if the Church undertook certain acts of devotion and consecration, Russia would be "converted," and the spreading of Russian errors would cease.

These belated disclosures looked dubious. Even if Mary said something of the kind, could a child of ten, in rural Portugal, have absorbed such a message before the Bolshevik revolution and before Russia had even begun "spreading errors"? By the 1930s and 1940s, it was a different matter. The process had been under way for some time, and the Catholic Church was almost obsessed with it. In any event, the pope complied with Mary's reputed wishes. Prayers for the conversion of Russia began to be recited at the end of masses, and other requested acts of consecration were performed.

The final prophecy is the surprising one. The downfall of the Soviet system in 1991 was not a conversion in the religious sense, such as Lucia would have envisaged, but the sudden collapse of Communism was enough of a conversion to count, and its end as an international movement meant that the spreading of Russia's "errors" did actually cease. In the upshot, it hardly makes any difference how far Lucia's later statements truly recalled what was said at the time. Whatever the origin of the Russian prophecy, she put it on record, and it was fulfilled. Moreover, she was a better prophet than almost anyone among the sophisticated and well-informed. Hardly any "rational" commentator among the numerous journalists and other experts foresaw the Soviet collapse. Futurology, an alleged science of forecasting, made a stir between about 1965 and 1975 and then gradually declined; Nicholas Rescher, discussing the reasons in his book *Predicting the Future,* fastened on the issue that Fatima raises. "The inability of American 'intelligence' specialists to forecast the downfall of Communism in the former USSR and its satellites was another major cause for disillusionment." Under whatever inspiration, the young village seer outdid virtually all the experts.

Lucia sent a further message to Rome with a request that it should be kept secret until 1960. As that year approached, speculation abounded. The message was rumored to predict another world war. Pope John XXIII read it but decided against publishing it, as did his two successors. An ostensible text that appeared in a German paper in 1963, on "third world war" lines, was recognized to be spurious. Cardinal Ratzinger, who knew the real contents, indicated in 1996 that the message was not "apocalyptic." An announcement was finally made in May 2000 during a visit to Fatima by Pope John Paul II. It was revealed that Lucia had a further vision of the persecution of Christians by "atheistic systems." This reinforced the Russian prophecy, but with an additional feature, that she saw a white-clad bishop being shot and falling to the ground. The image was interpreted as having foreshadowed the attempted assassination of the pope in 1981.

See also: Prophecy, Theories of

Further Reading

Ashe, Geoffrey. *The Book of Prophecy.* London: Blandford, 1999.

Martindale, C. C. *The Message of Fatima.* London: Burns Oates and Washbourne, 1950.

The New Catholic Encyclopedia. Article "Fatima." Washington, DC: Catholic University of America, 1967.

FIFTH MONARCHY MEN

Adherents of an extreme Puritan sect that flourished in England during the 1650s, after the English Civil War, when Cromwell dominated the government.

The Fifth Monarchy doctrine was based on the vision of four successive kingdoms in Daniel, chapters 2 and 7, combined with the prophecy of the reign of Christ in Revelation 20:4–6. The four kingdoms were made out to have been the Assyrian, Persian, Greek, and Roman. These were all past, and a fifth, foreshadowed in Daniel after the rest, was close at hand. Some spoke of the year 1666. It would be the earthly kingdom of Christ himself, who would return and reign with his saints for a thousand years.

At first, the Fifth Monarchy preachers believed that Cromwell was preparing the way. They welcomed the parliament that he set up in 1653, and two leaders of the sect, Thomas Harrison and Robert Overton, held important posts in his regional system of government. However, his assumption of semidictatorial powers as lord protector turned many Fifth Monarchy Men against him. Harrison, Overton, and others were arrested.

In 1657, a leader who was still at large, Thomas Venner, attempted a rebellion. A maker of barrels, he had emigrated to Massachusetts, then returned to England. He issued a manifesto with a picture of a red lion lying down and the motto "Who shall rouse them up?" Since public support was negligible, it appears that Venner and his fellow plotters thought the fulfillment of prophecy could be forced: even a very minor action could precipitate the millennium. The rising was abortive, and he was imprisoned for two years in the Tower of London.

After his release, he resumed preaching. The restoration of Charles II did not put a stop to his activities, even though the king was far more popular and secure than Cromwell had ever been. He assembled fifty followers and staged a demonstration in London—it could hardly count as a revolt—in January 1661. The watchword was "King Jesus, and the heads upon the gates" (presumably the heads of decapitated enemies). The group skirmished with the city militia, withdrew to Highgate, returned, and fought the king's guards. Some were killed, some taken into custody. Venner was executed with several others.

The Fifth Monarchy prophecy with its pathetic outcome was a parallel, on a very small scale, to the messianic error in the first century A.D. that helped to inspire the Jewish revolt against Rome. That made no military sense, but extremists imagined that they could, so to speak, force God's hand: if they took action, however recklessly, he would be bound to send the promised leader.

See also: Daniel; Revelation

Further Reading

Dictionary of National Biography (British). Article "Venner."

Encyclopaedia Britannica. Article "Fifth Monarchy Men."

FORSTER, E. M. (1879–1970)

English author known chiefly for *Passage to India* and four or five other distinguished novels. *The Machine Stops* (1909) is a long short story. Its setting is in the future, but it does not pretend to be seriously predictive. Forster described it as "a reaction to one of the earlier heavens of H. G. Wells." At the beginning and the end, he calls it a "meditation."

The story begins with a middle-aged woman living in a windowless hexagonal

William Oxman, a preacher in seventeenth-century England, one of an extremist sect that expected Christ to set up a "fifth" monarchy in succession to the four in Daniel. (Ann Ronan Picture Library)

room. Her name is Vashti. The room is artificially lit, and although there is no ventilation, the air is fresh. Sounds, musical and otherwise, are piped into it. Vashti sits in an armchair with a reading desk, the room's only furniture. The chair has a motor and moves her about the room at will. Every need is met by pressing a button in a formidable array. There are buttons for food, clothing, hot and cold baths, the bed. There are buttons for telephone conversations with other individuals. Vashti not only lives in the hexagonal room, she hardly ever leaves it because there is nothing to leave it for.

It transpires that the room is underground and everybody else lives in similar rooms, likewise underground. Earth's surface is uninhabited, or assumed to be so, and has largely reverted to wilderness. The global complex of cell dwellings is organized and governed by the Machine. The geniuses who invented and built the Machine are long since dead, but it goes on functioning, and the society that it sustains is regarded by Vashti and almost everyone else as eternally stable, problem-free, and never to be questioned.

Forster, of course, is writing before the advent of computers and speculations about their dominating humanity. His Machine dominates but more subtly. It simply provides and regulates. But it provides and regulates everything and has been doing it for centuries. There is a human Committee of the Machine, but no one controls it in any fundamental way, and it is doubtful whether anyone wants to or even knows how. It is axiomatically perfect. What it delivers is, in fact, second-rate at best—artificial fruit, for instance, is not as good as the real thing—but "good enough" has long since been accepted as a guiding principle.

One result of total dependence and acquiescence in mediocrity has been deterioration. Vashti in her mechanized chair is "a swaddled lump of flesh," small, pallid, without hair, and without energy. For her and for

The English novelist E. M. Forster, whose "meditation" The Machine Stops is a fictionalized attack on hopes for a scientific Utopia. (Ann Ronan Picture Library)

most human beings, the subterranean cellular world is reality and the world outside is not, or is real only in a very subordinate sense. She talks with her son Kuno, who lives thousands of miles away, through a sort of anticipatory television. During one of their conversations, which are rare and brief, he says he would like her to come and see him. She says, "But I can see you! What more do you want?" It is hard for her to handle the notion of meeting physically, not through the medium of the Machine.

She is in contact with thousands of other cells, constituting, in effect, an Internet—another of Forster's casual anticipations. They listen to recorded music, they converse with each other, they give short lectures. Their chief mental concern is with "ideas." These are seldom derived from experience or direct observation. In fact, they may quite well be derived from other ideas with a pedigree running back through a series of authors who had similar ones. Vashti does not go even as far as that. Her only book is the Machine manual telling which buttons to press in every conceivable contingency. She spins ideas out of her own head and gives lectures.

Not wanting to accept her son's invitation to visit him, she excuses herself, saying she is not well. Kuno takes her at her word and notifies her doctor, with the result that a huge medical apparatus drops from the ceiling and subjects her to tests and treatment. Deciding to go after all, she takes an elevator to the surface and boards an airship. Flight still happens, though on a small scale. Since every place is like every other place, there is seldom any motive for travel. Vashti's home is in Sumatra. At night, her flight attendant shuts out the stars with metal blinds. In daylight, the airship passes over the Himalayas, and she asks the attendant what the white stuff is in the cracks of the mountains. The attendant doesn't recognize snow, and as the range suggests no ideas, Vashti asks for it to be shut out. Later, flying over the Caucasus, she takes a brief look, gets no ideas from those mountains either, and shuts them out also. She does the same with Greece. Her metal blind is closed for most of the flight.

When she meets Kuno in England, he shocks her by confessing to a serious interest in the outer world. People do occasionally go up from below but only to look, not to do anything or stay for long. Kuno's interest is different. It is intense and rebellious; he is in revolt against the Machine. He has flown as his mother has, but unlike her, he looked at the stars and picked out Orion. His longing to know more of the surface has led him to an unauthorized excursion and near-destruction by the Machine. He is threatened with the ultimate punishment of homelessness—expulsion from the cellular hive and permanent exile to the outer air, which, supposedly, cannot sustain Machine-conditioned life for long. Vashti thinks him mad, and they never meet again.

Years pass. The Machine's dominance increases, and it is virtually deified, even worshiped. Admittedly, it is not infallible: it can go wrong in minor ways. When that happens, however, it puts things right itself by means of a Mending Apparatus. Since the Mending Apparatus is a built-in part of it, the small disruptions do not detract from its overall flawlessness. While there is a Committee of the Mending Apparatus, this human element is strictly subsidiary.

But something goes wrong that the Mending Apparatus fails to correct. A recorded symphony that is often played by the cell dwellers is interrupted by "gasping sighs." Complaints to the committee have no effect. Perhaps the members have no idea what to do; perhaps the workings of the Machine are beyond them. It slowly becomes apparent that the Mending Apparatus has defects of its own, but since the Machine is perfect and cannot be interfered with, the Apparatus must be allowed to mend itself. With the musical difficulty, the only nonblasphemous response is to incorporate the gasping sighs and recognize them as part of the symphony. The same happens with other, more drastic developments. Synthetic fruit goes moldy, bath water stinks, and beds fail to emerge when the cell dwellers want to sleep. In each crisis, the Mending Apparatus remains ineffective.

To Vashti, via the communicating system, Kuno makes a last enigmatic remark: "The Machine is stopping." She refuses to listen, and he says no more. But things are plainly getting worse. Exhortations to trust the Machine are carrying less and less conviction. Rumors of sabotage are spreading, but no saboteurs are found. At last, suddenly, the communication system collapses. When Vashti gives one of her lectures, she hears no applause at the end, and her attempts to contact listeners individually are unsuccessful. The light is growing dim, and opening the door on to the passage outside her cell, she finds a panic-stricken crowd milling about and fighting. She shuts herself in again and presses every button, and none work. The people in the passage cease to struggle and die feebly in the dark, incapable of any action. The Machine is stopping.

Here, Forster's "meditation" ends. His interpretation of his imagined world is that humanity's denial of its own full nature, its rejection of the life of the body and senses in unison with the soul, has ended in retribution. Because of the Machine, the neglected body has been reduced to "white pap," the mind itself is empty, the spirit that once reached heavenward has expired, and when the Machine stops, its dependants have no resources of their own. Kuno, as a last disembodied voice, reveals that he has found human beings alive on the surface—banished homeless who have survived. With the Machine eliminated at last, they may be able to make a fresh start.

See also: Wells, H. G.

FREDERICK BARBAROSSA (C. 1123–1190)

Frederick I, who ruled over the Holy Roman Empire from 1152 to 1190 and was believed, in late medieval times, to be asleep in a cave like King Arthur and destined to return.

The Holy Roman Empire was the surviving part of the enormous domain of Charlemagne, who had claimed in the year 800 to be reviving the ancient empire of Rome in western Europe. By the twelfth century, the remaining portion was chiefly made up of extensive territories in Germany and Italy. Frederick, called Barbarossa or "Redbeard," added the epithet "Holy" to stress a papal sponsorship that had begun with Charlemagne himself.

The legend of the immortal emperor did not apply first to Barbarossa but to his grandson Frederick II, who ruled from 1220 to 1250. A brilliant and controversial figure, he was regarded by some as a sort of Messiah, by

Frederick I, called Barbarossa or Redbeard. According to popular legend, this medieval emperor was asleep in a cave and would awaken as a great German leader. (Ann Ronan Picture Library)

others almost as an Antichrist. Partly because of the doctrines of Joachim of Fiore, he was widely expected to bring radical changes in society. After his death, many whose hopes had been raised were reluctant to accept that he had gone. They asserted that he was living overseas or had retired from the world as a hermit; or (more fantastically) that he had descended with his knights into an underworld beneath the crater of Etna, as Arthur himself was reputed to have done in one version of his survival. Several pretenders claimed to be Frederick and attracted a following. One of them exploited the fact that he lived close to the volcano. Two others flourished briefly in Germany during the 1280s. A third, also in Germany, may have been a madman who actually thought he *was* Frederick; he held court for some time in the city of Neuss but was finally arrested and burned at the stake. Nevertheless, he was expected to rise again.

Over the years, as apocalyptic excitement receded, the image of the undying emperor grew vague and composite. At length, the motif was transferred to Frederick I, who was a more generally acceptable hero. There was a difficulty here. Whereas Arthur's end was mysterious, Barbarossa's was not: he was drowned in a river on his way to take part in the Third Crusade and buried at Antioch. Still, it had all happened a long time ago, and popular imagination surmounted the obstacle.

Barbarossa, it was said, lay sleeping in a cave in a mountain, the Kyffhäuser, in central Germany. Occasionally, outsiders found their way in. He was seated at a table, with his beard growing ever longer and encircling it. He would wake for a moment and ask the intruders if the ravens were still flying. Sooner or later he was going to wake permanently and go outside to restore the German people to their rightful glories.

During his reign, he had strengthened the German element in the empire, and in the later Middle Ages, its ruler's title was enlarged and made more national: he became the "Holy Roman Emperor of the German Nation." The Empire declined, and Napoleon abolished it, but later in the nineteenth century a new reich was proclaimed and Barbarossa became symbolic of German greatness, to be reborn after centuries of decay and eclipse. Unfortunately perhaps, the crown prince, father of the future Kaiser Wilhelm II, showed his son pictures of the medieval imperial insignia and said: "We have got to bring this back. The power of the Empire must be restored and the Imperial Crown regain its glamour. Barbarossa must be brought down again out of his mountain cave."

Hitler's Russian campaign, which was intended to put Germany in a position of impregnable strength, was called Operation Barbarossa.

See also: Arthur, King; Joachim of Fiore; Second Charlemagne

Further Reading

Ashe, Geoffrey. *Camelot and the Vision of Albion.* London: Heinemann, 1971, and New York: St. Martin's Press, 1971.

Cohn, Norman. *The Pursuit of the Millennium.* London: Paladin, 1970.

Reeves, Marjorie. *Joachim of Fiore and the Prophetic Future.* New York: Harper and Row, 1977.

GARNETT, MAYN CLEW

U.S. author of a story, written just before the *Titanic*'s maiden voyage, about a catastrophe at sea foreshadowing the one that actually happened. Reputedly inspired by a dream Garnett had aboard *Titanic*'s sister ship, the *Olympic,* the story is entitled "The White Ghost of Disaster." The enormous imaginary liner hits an iceberg and goes down, with the loss of half the people on board because there are too few lifeboats—the reason for much of the loss of life in the real disaster. The story was complete and printed early in April 1912, a few days before the *Titanic* sailed, for publication in the May issue of *Popular Magazine.*

See also: Robertson, Morgan

Further Reading

Wade, Wyn Craig. *The Titanic: End of a Dream.* New York: Penguin Books USA, 1986.

GLASTONBURY (SOMERSET, ENGLAND)

Site of a medieval abbey that was dissolved in 1539 by royal decree and largely ruined, but is destined to rise again, according to a prophecy ascribed to the last survivor of the community.

Glastonbury is a small town cradled in a cluster of hills. This was formerly encircled by water, or nearly so, and is sometimes called the Isle of Avalon—the "apple-place," a name derived from Celtic mythology. The isle has a long history and prehistory and is thought to have been a pre-Christian sanctuary, perhaps associated with goddess-worship. On the eve of the Christian era, Celtic lake-villages rose out of the water a short distance away. For a long time, it was possible for seagoing craft to reach Avalon from the Bristol Channel.

Glastonbury has a complex aura of Christian mythology, some of it truly old, some comparatively recent. A large space at the center of the present town is said to have been the home of the first Christian settlers in Britain, led, according to medieval legend, by Joseph of Arimathea, the rich convert who obtained the body of Christ after the crucifixion and laid it in the tomb. Such beliefs evolved from a fact demonstrated by carbon dating and other research techniques: that Glastonbury actually was the site of a very ancient church, its true foundation forgotten, and of an early British monastic community, existing before the Anglo-Saxons' arrival in this part of the country. Later, under the auspices of Saxon kings, this community grew gradually into a Benedictine abbey on an impressive scale.

There were associations, not only with early Christians, but with King Arthur. One legend made Glastonbury the scene of the earliest of several stories about the abduction and rescue of Guinevere. In 1191, the monks of the abbey announced that an excavation in their graveyard had revealed the remains of Arthur and his queen, which they enshrined in their church. Archaeological work has partially confirmed their account: they did indeed dig where they said they had, and they did find an early burial, although the real identity of the person or persons buried there is now irrecoverable. Since Arthur's last earthly destination was said to be Avalon, this discovery was taken as proving that the name, hitherto only doubtfully localized, meant the Glastonbury hill-

The Lady Chapel in the ruined abbey of Glastonbury, on the reputed site of the earliest church in Britain. (Courtesy of Deborah Crawford)

cluster, and that meaning has been customary ever since.

Thanks to the tradition of Joseph as the founder of the original community and thanks also to the presence of Arthur, Glastonbury became a national shrine and made a contribution to medieval Arthurian romance. It was involved, as Joseph was, with the saga of the Grail, the wonder-working vessel of Christ's Last Supper, reputedly brought to Glastonbury through Joseph's agency. Glastonbury Abbey became the greatest and wealthiest in England, or an equal-first with Westminster, and attracted numerous pilgrims and visitors. It maintained a school and one of the finest libraries in the kingdom. As receding waters left a landscape of pools and marshes, the abbey and its tenants embanked the River Brue to prevent flooding and drained the whole territory down to the sea for farming.

King Henry VIII, however, broke with the pope and reestablished the Church in England on a national basis. His program included the suppression of all monasteries and convents, and in 1539, he dissolved Glastonbury. The abbey, its valuables, and its lands were seized for the crown, and the abbot was put to death. Most of the monks were pensioned off or given posts in Henry's Anglican Church. After a period of uncertainty, the abbey came into the hands of private owners.

It is in this phase of Glastonbury's history that its prophet appears. His name is given as Austin Ringwode, and he is said to have been the last of the monks. He lived on in the neighborhood until 1587 and made a deathbed pronouncement: "The abbey will one day be repaired and rebuilt for the like worship which has ceased; and then peace and plenty will for a long time abound."

This prophecy used to be ignored or played down because of a lack of early documentation. Ringwode, it was pointed out, was nowhere on record as a monk. Yet the transmission of such a story, in a county that became strongly Protestant and not disposed to hope for a monastic revival, tells in favor of its genuineness as a local tradition. The objection that Ringwode is not on record as a monk was removed by the publication of a memoir written in 1586 but little known until modern times. The author, William Weston, writes of meeting a very old man living near Glastonbury who kept up Catholic devotional practices in private. He had been employed at the abbey in a lay capacity, as a servant or clerical worker. Weston does not name him—his religious sympathies could have got him into trouble—but careful scrutiny has indicated that this man was very probably Austin Ringwode. With the passage of time and the disappearance of all religious communities, any man attached to this community might have been spoken of vaguely as a "monk."

No similar prophecy is connected with any other abbey in England, and at Glastonbury, the notion would have seemed extremely far-fetched. In 1587, the abbey was firmly in private hands, and a long process of destruction had already begun. The various owners, over the next 300 years, were seldom interested in preservation, but they valued the ruins as a quarry for marketable stone. More and more of the fabric found its way into houses, walls, roadbeds. A few poets and antiquarians made nostalgic comments, and some of the legends were improved in retelling. But in the early years of the twentieth century, while new books on Glastonbury were appearing, only one author mentioned Ringwode's prophecy. Resurrection was simply not an issue.

Yet resurrection happened. The Church of England acquired the site from its last owner. Services began to be held again, and pilgrimage revived, Catholic as well as Anglican. Actual rebuilding was out of the question—too little was left—but repair work was done, and the process of dilapidation was halted. In time, a new shrine came into being near the abbey. This twentieth-century rebirth was not purely ecclesiastical. It included a major festival of music and drama created by the operatic composer Rutland Boughton; this came to an end in its original form, but there were several revivals in later years, and the abbey grounds became a venue for concerts and other performances, with audiences equaling the whole population of the town. A further development, gathering momentum from about 1970 on, was the growth of Glastonbury as a kind of "alternative" spiritual center, attracting mystics and seekers of many kinds and building an international reputation as such. This was accompanied by a fresh wave of mythmaking, some of it focused on the pre-Christian background. One tangible result among several was the foundation of a unique Library of Avalon.

Austin Ringwode, of course, would have meant a monastic restoration. It was the only form in which he could have pictured rebirth. A resurgent future could only have presented itself to him through that image, at least consciously. He could not have foreseen some of the modern developments, especially those of a non-Christian kind, and he would doubtless have disapproved of them if he had. Yet it is curious that he should have predicted rebirth by a circumlocution about "the like worship which has ceased," rather than by speaking of Catholic religion, even though he undoubtedly had that in mind. On his deathbed, he no longer had any reason to fear prosecution. A modern neopagan might take his words to be inspired in a way that he himself was unaware of, and to apply not only to a new beginning of Christian worship but to a new beginning of whatever preceded it.

See also: Arthur, King

Further Reading

Ashe, Geoffrey. *Avalonian Quest.* London: Methuen, 1982.

———. *The Landscape of King Arthur.* Exeter, England: Webb and Bower, 1987.

Lacy, Norris J., ed. *The New Arthurian Encyclopedia.* New York and London: Garland, 1991.

GUGLIELMA OF MILAN (D. 1282)

Founder of an Italian religious group. Her astonishing career was one of the consequences of the prophetic movement launched by Joachim of Fiore. That twelfth-century abbot and biblical scholar applied the doctrine of the Trinity to the course of history. According to his teaching, there had been an age of God the Father, corresponding roughly to the Old Testament, followed by an age of God the Son, corresponding to the New Testament and the dominance of the Church. Thus far he was not too original, but he went beyond. There would be a third age, the age of the Holy Spirit, corresponding to the Third Person of the Trinity. New religious orders untainted by power and wealth would lead the way into it, and it would be an era of peace, liberty, love, and universal enlightenment.

Joachim was not subversive himself, but after his death, his prophecy was taken up by extremists who used it against the papacy and the existing Church. It was popular with dissident Franciscans who believed that Saint Francis had been the herald of the new day and his mission had been betrayed. Joachim had indicated, unwisely, that the year 1260 would mark the transition to the Age of the Holy Spirit. Nothing obviously happened, but some saw the prophecy as being fulfilled by Guglielma Boema, a Milanese woman who went much further than the most radical Franciscans.

Records are scanty, but she is said to have begun her activities about 1262, and she was certainly attracting disciples in 1271. Some of them were people of social standing. Her circle revered her as the Holy Spirit incarnate. The theology was lucid and logical. The Son of God had become a man—Christ—to establish the second age; so the Holy Spirit had become a woman to establish the third.

The idea of the Spirit's femininity is not unknown to Christian thinking; artists have seldom committed themselves to any human image for the Third Person of the Trinity. Guglielma, however, brought speculation down to earth. Such accounts of her teaching as remain are due to a male disciple, Andreas Saramita, and a woman associated with him, Manfreda. She was probably related to the Visconti, a prominent family in Milan. The Guglielmites believed that the male papacy was finished. Through some unexplained but peaceable revolution, Manfreda was to become pope and appoint women cardinals. The feminized Church would heal religious divisions and draw Jews and Saracens into a single fold. Saramita would preside over the composition of new scriptures, embodying the new revelation.

During Guglielma's lifetime, it does not appear that there was any official condemnation of her activities. She died in 1282 and was buried in a Cistercian monastery at Chiaravalle. The group survived and held gatherings around her tomb, seemingly with a hope of her rising from the dead. It became clear that the movement would not expire of its own accord. An ecclesiastical ban fell in 1300. About thirty persons were inculpated, and Saramita, Manfreda, and another woman were put to death as heretics. Inquisitors exhumed Guglielma's bones and burned them to discourage the notion of her resurrection.

See also: Angelic Pope; Joachim of Fiore; Second Charlemagne

Further Reading

Ashe, Geoffrey. *The Book of Prophecy.* London: Blandford, 1999.

Reeves, Marjorie. *The Influence of Prophecy in the Later Middle Ages.* Notre Dame: University of Notre Dame Press, 1993.

HANUSSEN, ERIK JAN (D. 1933)

Astrologer and reputed clairvoyant associated with Nazism. He claimed to be a Danish aristocrat but was actually Austrian, his real name being Hermann Steinschneider. To a large extent, he was simply an entertainer. From 1929 onward, he was in Berlin giving lucrative exhibitions of mind reading and hypnosis. He also practiced as a "psychic" consultant. His success with clients was due in part to his use of bugging, then unfamiliar, to pick up facts about them that they supposed he must have learned paranormally.

The widespread belief in his exceptional gifts may have had a basis beyond fraud. The novelist Arthur Koestler, who was working as a journalist in the German capital, describes him in his autobiography as "a stocky, dark-haired man with quick movements, full of dynamic energy and not without charm." In 1931, Koestler and a woman colleague subjected Hanussen to a test. They took an employee of their paper, Herr Apfel, to visit him, and handed him Apfel's bunch of keys to see if he could infer anything from it (this technique is known as psychometry). Hanussen held it and made a number of statements about the owner's recent life. Apfel denied them, and Koestler dismissed the experiment as a failure. It turned out, however, that Hanussen was correct on every count but about another person in the room, the woman who accompanied Koestler; he had achieved an impressive success by some other means than psychometry.

He had Jewish antecedents but managed to conceal them. As the Nazi movement grew stronger, he became friendly with some of its leaders, including the Berlin head of the storm troopers, the party's private army. He was invited to coach Hitler in public speaking. Wishing to have a platform of his own, he tried to gain control of a newspaper and did launch an astrological weekly, which had a ready-made readership in a nation that took astrology more seriously than most.

During 1932, Hanussen was predicting Hitler's triumph, and on January 1, 1933, he cast the Führer's horoscope and foretold that he would attain power on January 30. When this prediction was fulfilled, there were rumors of inside information, and the rumors went further. Hanussen, it was believed, had foretold that Hitler would be spectacularly successful for some years but that the tide would turn and his regime would come to a cataclysmic end in the spring of 1945—as, of course, it did. An astrological forecast on these lines is known to have existed and to have been preserved in government files, whether or not it was Hanussen's or derived from his.

Such reports were ominous for him, and the secret police discovered his Jewish background. He survived only a little longer. He sometimes worked with a medium, Maria Paudler, and at one séance she went into a trance before witnesses and spoke of a great and imminent fire, recognizable as the burning of the Reichstag. The Nazi leadership had already planned to burn the building and put the blame on the Communists, as a pretext to outlaw them. Hanussen's reputation could still be of use, and on February 26, the papers carried an officially inspired account of the séance, alleging that he himself had gone into a trance and seen (conveniently) "a blood-curdling crime committed by the Communists," "blazing flames," and "a terrible firebrand lighting up the world."

The Reichstag fire duly broke out. It is impossible to be certain what Hanussen really knew in advance or what he or his medium really said. If he had been in on the plot, he would surely have kept quiet. More likely he had suspicions and hinted at them or allowed Maria Paudler to do so. One way or another, he had gone too far. A few weeks later, he was seized by a Nazi gang outside a theater where he performed and shot in woods on the outskirts of Berlin.

A German film made in 1988 (*Hanussen*) accepted that he had a real psychic gift, connecting it with a war wound in the head. It attributed his murder to his speaking too openly of Nazi responsibility for the fire.

See also: Krafft, Karl Ernst; Nazi Germany
Further Reading

Gill, Anton. *A Dance between Flames.* London: John Murray, 1993.

Koestler, Arthur. *Arrow in the Blue.* London: Collins, with Hamish Hamilton, 1952.

Toland, John. *Adolf Hitler.* 2 vols. New York: Doubleday, 1976.

HARBOU, THEA VON (1888–1954)

German novelist, author of *Metropolis,* which became a classic of the silent cinema.

In a brief preface to her book, Thea von Harbou explained that *Metropolis* was not about any particular time or place; it was a fable making a moral point. However, especially in its film version, it was inevitably seen as a dystopia of the future. The imaginary city Metropolis is in two sections, above and below. The upper part is the luxurious home of an elite, headed by a supreme governor, Fredersen. It is dependent upon but completely dominates the lower part, which is an underworld housing a complex of machines. The workers who operate the machines live in servitude, performing repetitive tasks. Their only solace comes from the help and teaching of Maria, an evangelist who lives among them. In the face of growing unrest, she counsels peace and patience while they await a "mediator."

Visiting the upper regions, she meets Fredersen's son and shows him a group of wretched proletarian children she has brought with her. Deeply disquieted, he goes down to experience working-class conditions himself and urges his father to transfer the deadlier jobs to robots. (When this novel was written, robots had just been introduced to the public by Karel Capek's play *RUR,* though, as a matter of fact, his own robots were biologically constructed androids, not mechanical humans.) Fredersen does not respond to his son's appeal, but he is aware that all may not be well below. Disturbed about Maria's influence over the workers, he takes up the idea in another way.

Rotwang, an eccentric inventor, has produced a highly sophisticated robot that he likes to think of as female and calls Parody. Fredersen employs Parody, disguised as Maria, to change her message and stir up anger among the workers. This will bring rebellion into the open, when he will be able to crush it, discrediting Maria in the process. But the situation gets uncontrollable. The workers break out in open revolt, chanting "Death to the machines," and they throw Metropolis into chaos above and below. The author's concluding plea is for mutual goodwill. A well-ordered society cannot be created by top-level expertise alone or, in Marxist style, by working-class power alone. "The heart" must mediate, and Fredersen's son, who has seen both sides, may be the mediator whom Maria spoke of.

Thea von Harbou was married to the film director Fritz Lang. His spectacular version of *Metropolis* appeared in 1926. A few years later, Hitler's propaganda chief, Goebbels, invited him to head the German film industry; *Metropolis* may have appealed to the Nazi leadership as a warning against Communist revolution. Lang, however, left Germany for the United States, where he made many

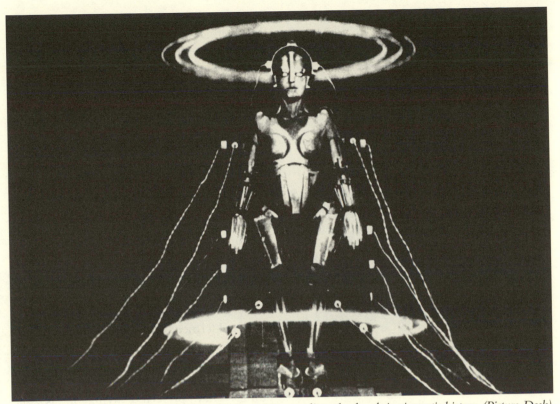

The famous robot in the film of Thea von Harbou's Metropolis, *a landmark in cinematic history. (Picture Desk)*

more films. He almost lived to see the first *Star Wars,* in which, it is said, the designer of the famous humanoid robot took a hint from Parody.

See also: Huxley, Aldous; Orwell, George; Zamyatin, Yevgeny

HERZL, THEODOR (1860–1904)
Austrian journalist who launched Zionism as a political movement and forecast a correct date for the creation of the Republic of Israel.

Herzl was a fully assimilated Jew who at first believed that all Jews could be assimilated. His belief was shaken by the Dreyfus affair in France, when a Jewish army officer was imprisoned—wrongfully, as it turned out—for espionage, and the dispute over his guilt or innocence unleashed a torrent of anti-Semitism. Though disillusioned, Herzl did not fly to the opposite extreme: there could perfectly well be "Jewish Frenchmen," as he put it, but the long-drawn-out affair, plus reports of pogroms in Russia, convinced him that anti-Semitism went deep and assimilation could never be completely successful. His reflections led him to a more drastic solution.

He did not initiate the return to the Promised Land. "Practical" Zionism, as it has been called, had begun during the 1880s with an unobtrusive Jewish resettlement in Palestine. Most of the settlers came from Russia. They judged that assimilation would never be possible under the czarist regime, and, in any case, rejected it, because the ancestral vision of the return could not be given up. Twenty-five farming communities came quietly into being. It was some time before Herzl heard of these, and when he did, he was contemptuous, saying that the

Theodor Herzl, the founder of Zionism as a political movement, who made an accurate forecast of the founding of the Republic of Israel. (Ann Ronan Picture Library)

sponsors—notably Baron Edmond de Rothschild—were virtually "paying people to go." Nothing would meet the situation but a serious movement of political nationalism. In that conviction, he wrote a manifesto, *The Jewish State,* and assembled a World Zionist Congress in Switzerland in 1897.

What followed was a remarkable illustration of the power of prophecy. Herzl conceived Zionism purely in terms of solving a problem. He could not avoid acknowledging the Palestinian hope, but he saw it only as a motive force to be harnessed. If it did open the door to the Promised Land, well and good; but if an opportunity came to found the Jewish state somewhere else—in South America, perhaps—it would be proper to divert Jewish energies in that direction. It would also be proper for prosperous Jews in

Europe and the United States to stay where they were, and, with Gentile aid, organize the haven for the less fortunate.

This version of Zionism was manipulative and, it must be admitted, patronizing. The propellant was not to be patriotism or religion or culture but the misery of the victims of anti-Semitism. Herzl, however, was a commanding personality, a powerful speaker, and an indispensable leader. After the first Zionist Congress he began going from country to country and from government to government, trying to get official support for a Jewish homeland. He tackled the German kaiser and the Turkish sultan. But in 1903, he clashed fatally with the prophetic hope. The British government actually offered him territory in Uganda, then a British colony. To his bewilderment, many of the rank-and-file Zionists were against acceptance. Moreover, the main opposition came from the Russians, the very people he thought he was rescuing. They preferred living in Russia, pogroms and all, to the abandonment of the Promised Land and the betrayal of all the generations that had cherished the vision. Recriminations followed, and Herzl died prematurely. Henceforth nearly all Zionists were agreed that Palestine was the only possible goal.

In the outcome, against every rational expectation, prophecy won. For ages it had been insisting on the return. It had foreshadowed a state of affairs, not humanly foreseeable, never approximated in more than 1,000 years, yet realized in the twentieth century. Against incredible odds, the prophecy was fulfilled with the founding of the state of Israel.

While Herzl failed to understand his own movement, he made, as its leader, one of the best political forecasts on record. In 1897, he predicted that the Jewish state would come into existence in fifty years. This was a pure inspiration. Intelligent anticipation is out of the question. He did not foresee—no one could have foreseen—the long, tortuous, and agonized process that ensued. Yet, in the end, he was vindicated. The vote of the United Nations that approved the creation of the Republic of Israel was held in 1947, fifty years almost to the month after he made the prediction. Obviously, that can be explained as a lucky guess. But extremely few such forecasts have, in practice, been equally good, and the occurrence of this one in this context has, understandably, been remarked upon.

See also: Messiah; Promised Land

Further Reading

Ashe, Geoffrey. *The Land and the Book.* London: Collins, 1965.

Stewart, Desmond. *Theodor Herzl.* London: Hamish Hamilton, 1974.

HILDEGARD OF BINGEN, SAINT (1098–1179)

German abbess, one of the most brilliant and versatile women of the Middle Ages, called by contemporaries "the Sibyl of the Rhine."

Simply as an administrator, Saint Hildegard was outstanding: she founded a large convent on unpromising ground at the Rupertsberg, above the Rhine near Bingen, and gave it a most uncommon facility, a proper supply of piped water. She wrote an encyclopedic treatise on natural history, physiology, and medicine, the earliest surviving scientific work by a woman. Her stature as a musical composer has only begun to be fully realized in recent times. She corresponded voluminously with popes, emperors, kings, and bishops, often to advocate reforms in the Church.

Hildegard had visionary experiences that have been compared to those of William Blake, and she put many of them into a major work entitled *Scivias.* In this and in some of her letters, she looked ahead, and her glances at the future give her a place in the history of prophecy. She warned of disasters threatening the Church because of its corruption. They eventually happened in the

An illustration in a twelfth-century manuscript: St. Hildegard (a very practical visionary) receives the fire of prophetic inspiration. (Erich Lessing/Art Resource)

Great Schism in the fifteenth century and the Protestant breakaway in the sixteenth. Admittedly, these were a long time coming. But her special achievement was to initiate a broadening of prophetic scope. Previously, Christians had developed a scenario of the end of the world but had said little about anything before that. After Hildegard it was beginning to be acceptable for Christian seers to foreshadow happenings in the interim, by reinterpreting Scripture or otherwise. The great medieval name here is Joachim of Fiore.

See also: Guglielma of Milan; Joachim of Fiore

Further Reading

The New Catholic Encyclopedia. Article "Hildegard of Bingen." Washington, DC: Catholic University of America, 1967.

HUXLEY, ALDOUS (1894–1963)

English novelist and essayist, author of *Brave New World* (1932).

Huxley came from a family of great distinction in science. The title of his dystopia is taken from Shakespeare. In *The Tempest,* Miranda, who has been living on the island with her father, Prospero, and lacks experience of other humans, confronts the shipwrecked Italian noblemen and exclaims:

> How many goodly creatures are there here!
> How beauteous mankind is! O brave new world,
> That has such people in't!

Prospero, who knows more about them and about the world generally, confines himself to saying, "'Tis new to thee."

While Huxley's satire and Orwell's *Nineteen Eighty-Four* have sometimes been coupled, and both owe a debt to Zamyatin's *We,* they are not really much alike. Both authors push contemporary tendencies to extremes, not forecasting that those extremes will be reached but imagining the results if they were. They are not, however, the same tendencies, and the imagined results are very different. Orwell is thinking chiefly of Communism, still aggressive and formidable in his time. Huxley is thinking of mass production, with its consequences in consumerism, and also of psychological conditioning, as developed by Pavlov and the behaviorists. The fictional 1984 is quite simply hideous: the Revolution has not delivered the goods, most of the population is worse off, and the almighty Party maintains its own power by perpetual falsification and the suppression of dissent. Huxley's Brave New World, in the twenty-sixth century, most certainly has delivered the goods. Science and technology have created peace, welfare, and stability. The goals of material progress have been achieved—but through universal shallowness. Everybody is happy because everybody has been cut down below humanity and deprived (in theory, at least) of all that is unsettling.

The essential secret is to catch human beings at their inception. The normal method of starting them has been abolished or virtually so. Marriage and all such partnerships have gone, the words *mother* and *father* have become indecent, nothing remains in that respect but promiscuous and sterile sex. Embryos are formed in state hatcheries. By varying the supply of oxygen, individuals are produced with different capacities. Each embryo is put in a jar on a conveyor. As it moves along, it is given various inoculations that have lifelong effects, so that most diseases have disappeared. After infants are "decanted," they are conditioned to like the kind of life for which the State destines them.

Society is divided into five castes defined by Greek letters, from Alphas down to Epsilons. Epsilons are semimoronic and do the simple and menial jobs, enjoying them, and are programmed to want nothing else. For instance, an Epsilon working an elevator finds all life's pleasure in going up the shaft and then going down again. There are social and functional gradations, with the Alphas at the top of the heap. These are comparatively free but still conditioned to do their allotted work and enjoy being Alphas (as Betas are conditioned to enjoy being Betas and so forth). Even moods of depression are provided for by a perfect hallucinatory drug, soma; the slogan that has been built into all its users is "One cubic centimetre cures ten gloomy sentiments." The religious impulse is satisfied by a synthetic cult of Our Ford, the deified inventor of mass production. As a result of all this, contentment of a sort is normal. The horrors of *Nineteen Eighty-Four* are not needed. Life is generally comfortable, and there is no dissent to suppress. But humanity has been reduced to fit the system. Not only such things as love and

The English novelist Aldous Huxley, a relation of eminent scientists, whose satirical vision of the future raises doubts about science. (Ann Ronan Picture Library)

parenthood but the more profound passions and all the richer manifestations of culture have vanished.

There is not much story. In the Brave New World, wild territories are allowed to exist as vacation reserves, and in one of these, a young man is discovered who was born and grew up there and has never been "processed"; he is a sort of "noble savage." Brought to England as a curiosity, he revolts against civilization and eventually commits suicide.

In a brief later discussion, *Brave New World Revisited,* Huxley expressed a fear that his vision might be closer to realization than he thought at the time of writing.

See also: Orwell, George; Zamyatin, Yevgeny

Further Reading

Carey, John, ed. *The Faber Book of Utopias.* London: Faber and Faber, 1999.

ISAIAH (FL. 742–701 B.C.)

Old Testament prophet in whose work a predictive element first becomes conspicuous and who was believed by early Christians to have foretold the Virgin Birth of Jesus.

Isaiah is the greatest of the literary prophets whose poems and prose utterances were written down, by themselves or by disciples. The book bearing his name, which has sixty-six chapters, contains nothing authentically his after the thirty-ninth. Up to that point, most of it is by him, though there has been interpolation and rehandling. The chapters that follow are attributed to a later prophet known to biblical scholars as "Deutero-Isaiah" or "Second Isaiah," a very important author who is discussed in a separate entry.

The prophet lived in Jerusalem, the capital of the southern Israelite kingdom of Judah. He was active over several decades in the latter part of the eighth century B.C. To judge from his writings, he was well educated, perhaps a professional teacher. His wife is described as a prophetess herself, and he gave their children symbolic names. God summoned him first in a visionary experience in the Temple. He remained a prominent figure and became an adviser to Hezekiah, one of Judah's more competent kings.

His prophecies show a widening of horizons that had just begun to appear in his prophetic precursors. He is aware of foreign countries such as Babylon and Assyria and has messages for them. Addressing his fellow Israelites, he continues a trend that seems to have begun with Elijah, in the reign of Ahab. The Israelite tribes had had prophets for a long time before him—soothsayers and minstrels who claimed to be divinely inspired. As a rule, they were innocuous and obliging toward those who consulted them . . . and paid them. In public life, they tended to be compliant with the establishment, assuring rulers and priests that all was well, whether it was or not. Elijah, however, defied Ahab and his Phoenician queen, Jezebel, and denounced wickedness in high places, as when Jezebel judicially murdered a subject named Naboth and enabled her husband to seize his vineyard. Since that time, two of Isaiah's forerunners, Amos and Hosea, had assailed injustice, religious corruption, and war, unlike the complacent pseudo prophets who still flourished. Isaiah himself was uncompromising in affirming the Lord's will against a backsliding people, engrossed in materialism and superstition. According to legend, he aroused so much resentment that he was put to death.

His religious and moral stance and his consciousness of the world outside Palestine combined in prophecies foreshadowing a somber future. Again, he found hints in previous prophets, again, he went further. The people are not to imagine that God is limited or circumscribed: if they forsake his covenant and stray from his commandments, he will not only afflict them with domestic misfortune, he will bring foreign conquerors against them. Isaiah interprets current events, such as an Assyrian invasion, in the light of God's providence. These prophecies are apt to be conditional rather than absolute: *if* present trends continue, *then* something will happen. But the converse holds: *if* the trends do not continue, something else will happen. If Israel—or, at any rate, a significant remnant—lives up to its divine vocation, its en-

The prophet Isaiah, whose attributed speeches and writings raised the hopes of the Israelites in times of distress. (Ann Ronan Picture Library)

emies will fall, warfare will pass away, there will be a golden age under a glorious king of David's line. Despite much doom and denunciation, a survey of Isaiah 1–39 gives a rather hopeful impression. The prophet foresees disasters for hostile nations, and the prospective good times are never altogether lost sight of.

A prophecy of a different kind is famous because of its reappearance in the New Testament, with a Christian application. The author of the First Gospel, traditionally Matthew, begins his story with the pregnancy of Jesus' mother, Mary. It was a Christian tenet that she conceived with no sexual relationship; Jesus, as the divine Son of the heavenly Father, had no human progenitor;

Mary was a virgin, and her husband, Joseph, was a foster parent only. To confirm this miracle, Matthew (as we may call him) finds it predicted in Isaiah 7:14, which he quotes: "Behold, a virgin shall conceive and bear a son, and his name shall be called Emmanuel." Which, Matthew correctly explains, means "God with us." Isaiah says it, almost exactly, but the word translated "virgin" does not necessarily mean that. He uses a rare Hebrew noun, *'almah,* denoting simply a young woman. The few others who are called so do happen to be virgins, but virginity is not inherent. The Greek Old Testament, the Septuagint, has *parthenos,* which is generally rendered "virgin," but the meaning of the text remains imprecise, and the meaning Matthew discerns in it was never demonstrably there.

In the context, Isaiah is not looking ahead to a miracle 700 years hence; he is proclaiming a divine pledge about the normal birth of a royal heir, who will carry on the line of King David. Nevertheless, here, as in some other scriptural prophecies, there may be a sort of inspired ambiguity. The attention drawn to the unusually described "young woman," the mother, is a little curious; so is "God with us," not strictly a name but a designation, more apt to Jesus than to anyone in Isaiah's day. Christians could claim justification in detecting a second, deeper meaning, elucidated by the advent of Mary's son. The same happens in other Christian applications of older texts. These are seen as containing prophecies of Christ that are, so to speak, encoded. No one at the time would have seen them as prophetic of him—in some cases, no one would have seen them as prophetic at all—but their complete sense is held to emerge when they are read with him in mind, and therefore they are considered to be foreshadowings of him.

See also: Biblical Prophecy (1)—Israelite and Jewish; Biblical Prophecy (2)—Christian; Elijah; Second Isaiah

Further Reading

Brown R. E., J. A. Fitzmyer, and R. E. Murphy, eds. *The New Jerome Biblical Commentary.* Englewood Cliffs, NJ: Prentice-Hall, 1990.

JEREMIAH (FL. 627–587 B.C.)

Old Testament prophet who foretold the Jewish exile to Babylon and rethought the conception of the Chosen People.

Jeremiah's name is proverbial for gloom, and the word *jeremiad* is derived from the "lamentations" ascribed to him, though the biblical book called by that name was probably written by someone else under his influence. He lived in Jerusalem, still the capital of the southern Israelite kingdom of Judah, surviving feebly after the collapse of the northern kingdom. Much of the biographical matter in the book is the work of his secretary, Baruch.

Like his predecessors, Jeremiah denounced the evils around him, and he was bitter against the perversion of prophecy itself. Bogus prophets were assuring the public and their rulers that all was well and saying "peace, peace" when there was no peace. Jeremiah's horizon was broad: he was well aware of other nations, and he forecast the rise of Babylon, expecting its king, Nebuchadnezzar, to be the Lord's agent for the chastisement of Judah—the corollary being that it was futile and even wrong to resist.

Events bore Jeremiah out. Nebuchadnezzar's expansion of his empire drew Judah into his orbit. He took Jerusalem in 597 B.C. and carried off some of its chief citizens. At first, he was prepared to treat Judah as a protectorate under a puppet king, but the king rebelled, and in 587, the Babylonians besieged and captured Jerusalem with much greater ruthlessness. Its walls were demolished; its principal buildings were burned down; the Temple itself was plundered and destroyed. Large numbers of Judah's city dwellers and people of importance were deported to Babylon, and as other inhabitants trickled away over the years, the country became almost depopulated. Jeremiah himself had been imprisoned during the siege as pro-Babylonian. Nebuchadnezzar's commander set him free. He is said to have gone to Egypt and died there soon afterward.

His assessment of the situation, in the last years before the final disaster, introduces themes that carry over into subsequent Jewish history. He describes a vision of two baskets of figs, good and bad. The bad figs are the Israelite sinners and apostates, and the Lord will cast them off. The good figs stand for a remnant that will survive, meaning, essentially, the deportees. These will endure a penitential exile in Babylon; while there, says Jeremiah, they must live peaceably, on as good terms as possible with their conquerors; and the experience will make them better and wiser, worthy of divine favor. This phase and the homeland's concurrent desolation will last for seventy years (Jeremiah 25:11–12; 29:10–14). Then, Babylon will fall to enemies from the north, including the Medes, and the faithful remnant will be able to return to Zion. God will deal with them graciously. He will bring back others of the dispersed Israelite tribes to join them, and he will make a new covenant with them, writing it on their hearts.

The prophet was right about the captivity coming to an end, and he was right about Babylon falling to enemies from the north (including the Medes), with the exiles' liberation resulting. It all happened in 539. The idea of the faithful remnant, though hinted at in earlier prophecy, grows more explicit in Jeremiah. It has become clear that the Cho-

The prophet Jeremiah, who lamented over the fall of Jerusalem to the Babylonians and the captivity of its people, but foresaw deliverance for those who were worthy. (Ann Ronan Picture Library)

sen People cannot be restrained from apostasy, idolatry, and a general falling-away. But while some will be lost, there will always be others who stand firm, and these will always be the Chosen, inheriting Israel's whole legacy and bearing the glory and the burden. Eventually, the Christians, who accepted Jesus as the Messiah when most Jews rejected him, applied the conception of the remnant to themselves and explained Jeremiah's prophecy of a new covenant as fulfilled in Christianity.

The seventy years of purification and penance may have been meant symbolically rather than literally; as a human lifetime, perhaps. The actual duration of the exile was less. This prophecy, however, has a strange later history. The author of Daniel reinterprets the seventy years as meaning seventy "weeks" of years, making a total of 70 × 7, that is, 490 years. This long and precise period is exceptional in Old Testament prophecy. The period cannot be related to the Babylonian exile, and there is no sign that Jeremiah truly had such a period in mind. In Daniel, to judge from events described in the final "week," it is meant to end about the time of writing, in 165 B.C. or thereabouts. But if the count starts from Jeremiah, the dates do not work. Mysteriously, the author gives an alternative starting point, leading to a final phase that is not in his own time but in the first century A.D., and can be connected with the ministry and death of Jesus—a fact naturally observed by Christians. However this calculation should be understood, it has no real connection with Jeremiah himself.

See also: Biblical Prophecy (1)—Israelite and Jewish; Biblical Prophecy (2)—Christian; Daniel

Further Reading

Ashe, Geoffrey. *The Book of Prophecy.* London: Blandford, 1999.

Brown R. E., J. A. Fitzmyer, and R. E. Murphy, eds. *The New Jerome Biblical Commentary.* Englewood Cliffs, NJ: Prentice-Hall, 1990.

JESUS CHRIST

In Christian tradition, Jesus is said to have been foreshadowed by passages in the Old Testament that have a prophetic meaning beyond what their original readers would have perceived. He is even said to have personally expounded these passages, or some of them (Luke 24:27, 44–47). To ask whether he made any prophecies himself is to invite the skeptical retort that the question cannot be answered because the facts are undiscoverable. It is proper, however, to ask whether the Gospels at least represent him as uttering prophecies and, if so, with what implications.

He speaks of himself in the third person as the Son of Man. This phrase could carry a future reference. Jewish speculation, originating in Daniel (7:13–14), included a "Son of Man" as a kind of heavenly viceroy who would appear on Earth. Speaking of oneself in the third person can suggest status, authority, royalty. When questioned by Pilate, Jesus acknowledges that he is royal in some sense, but his kingdom is not of this world, it is "the kingdom of God" or "the kingdom of heaven." He is portrayed as talking of apocalyptic events to come, when he will return as a king in truth. There will be a resurrection of the dead and a Last Judgment, over which he, the Son of Man, will preside; the world as we know it—the present age—will end, and a new world will come into being with eternal life for the blessed.

These colossal claims cannot be discussed as predictions when there is no telling what literal events they predict. Modern readers may accept them and make sense of them in whatever way they judge fitting; or reinterpret them as symbol or allegory; or dismiss them as fantasies, woven into the story by apocalypse-minded mythmakers. Gospel passages where Jesus foretells his own death and resurrection, in the near future, are clearer. Yet an ambiguity remains, and these sayings cannot really be debated either. For the traditional believer, they are authentic and were fulfilled. For the unbeliever, they could have

Christ enthroned in majesty: A mosaic in Santa Sophia Cathedral. (Ann Ronan Picture Library)

been invented or "remembered" later, to prove that his death was part of a divine plan, and that this included his rising from the dead afterward.

It is chiefly with reference to the "kingdom" that the nature of his prophetic sayings can be examined. There is apt to be an impression that the kingdom means the messianic regime that will appear at his Second Coming and will be sudden and tremendous and *different*. Actually, he is not often quoted as speaking of it thus. But he does make a prediction that some early Christians probably took in that sense and judged important, because it is recorded three times, with slight variations.

Addressing a group of hearers, he says, "Truly I tell you, there are some standing here who will not taste death before they see the kingdom of God has come with power"(Mark 9:1). Does this mean that the kingdom is going to appear visibly and vividly, making a sweeping difference in the world, and that it is going to appear soon or fairly soon, within the lifetime of some of the listeners? Albert Schweitzer, who could see no fulfillment in the lifetime of anyone who was present, came to the momentous conclusion that Jesus could be wrong. Some early Christians seem to have avoided that conclusion by postulating a miracle. At least one of Christ's disciples, one of those spoken of as "standing here," was going to live on until the Second Coming, whenever that might be. John 21:20–23 mentions a rumor that the "beloved disciple," the putative author of the gospel, was the disciple in question, though the rumor is not endorsed. It certainly looks like an attempt to cope with the fact that the prophecy had not been fulfilled in the way some Christians assumed that it must be.

Something that can be read in a similar sense is embedded in a confusing passage where Jesus foretells the destruction of the Jerusalem Temple by the Romans, which happened in A.D. 70 when the Jews rebelled. Very likely he did, and he would not have been alone in foreseeing that militant nationalism would lead to disaster. The trouble is that in this passage (three Gospels have versions of it) he speaks of upheavals prior to the End of the World, of the End itself, and of his Second Coming, and he is quoted as saying, "This generation will not pass away till all these things take place." It looks like another form of the "some standing here" prophecy. Almost certainly, those words were meant to apply only to Jerusalem's ordeal, when many of his contemporaries would still be alive. But the writers have interwoven them so closely with the rest that they seem to apply to everything and to predict the End only a few decades away, coincident with the Temple's fall or soon after it. The confusion doubtless occurs because the writers are still clinging to the hope of an early Second Coming and failing to make the distinctions that they should make.

The question of prophecy by Jesus must turn finally on what he meant by the kingdom and its manifestation. If the manifestation was to happen only at the End of the World, the "some standing here" prophecy is quite simply wrong. But a careful reading of the Gospels indicates that he meant something else. Early in his ministry, he speaks of the kingdom as imminent, "at hand," and to judge from some of the parables, it is already in active preparation. As it exists on Earth, it is the community of believers who confess Jesus as Lord. When he says the kingdom is at hand, it is not because the world is about to end but because the community is about to start taking shape, in however humble and embryonic a form; the way to salvation is opening.

After this he allows, perhaps even implies, a development of unspecified length. In a parable about wheat and weeds in the same field (Matthew 13:24–30, 37–43), an unknown time elapses between the sowing of the wheat, which means the founding of the kingdom, and the removal of the weeds alongside, which means its purification at "the close of the age." The parable shows Jesus' awareness that the Christian commu-

nity in the world will not be an assemblage of saints. It will exist for an unspecified time and be contaminated by evil, with the bad elements beside the good, although it will finally be perfected. In another parable, the kingdom is a fishing net gathering good and bad fish. The fishermen catch the fish while on the water, then come ashore to sort them out. The earthly kingdom will endure for an unknown stretch of time, drawing in members of very various quality, and will be purified only at the last, by divine action.

How far away is that "last"? Jesus warns against speculation—a warning that many misguided interpreters of prophecy should have taken to heart: "Of that day and hour no one knows"—except his heavenly Father. But there is one clue, and it could hint at whole millennia: "This gospel of the kingdom will be preached throughout the whole world, as a testimony to all nations; and then the end will come."

The "some standing here" prophecy need not refer to that end. It is given privately to a group of disciples. The promised advent "with power" means a public manifestation that will begin to happen within a finite space of time, perhaps soon, and will continue. This prophecy is placed in the Gospels shortly after Peter has acknowledged Jesus as the Christ; he assents but tells his disciples not to make it known. The first intimations of his death follow closely, and the kingdom's predicted visibility can be understood as the sequel, when the Church, inspired by his resurrection, will be publicly in existence, will proclaim him to all as the risen Lord, and will spread with its Good News.

The Christians' tradition of that dawn is embodied in the early chapters of Acts. The risen Christ, before his final departure, tells the apostles that they will receive power—here is the "power" of Mark—when the Holy Spirit descends upon them, and the word *power* is significantly repeated later. Peter addresses a crowd in Jerusalem, and many are baptized; the apostles begin to work miracles of healing. This is quite sufficient. The manifested kingdom does not have to be spectacular from the start. Jesus forestalls such a misconception when he compares the kingdom to a grain of mustard seed, a small thing, yet one that will grow into a tree. In the later chapters of Acts, the Church is spreading its branches beyond its mustard-seed origin, with Christ ever present, as shown in the conversion of Paul.

Consideration of Jesus as a prophet in a verifiable, predictive sense can be confined to three topics. His forecast of the destruction of the Temple is correct. However, it need not imply anything more than the perceptiveness of an opponent of Jewish militancy, convinced of the disaster to come. In the parables of the wheat and the fishes, he foretells that the Christian community will be a mixed body with evil in it alongside good and with so much evil that it will need a divine cleansing. Here, he is not only correct, but more realistic in his anticipation than optimists who have fancied that a holy Utopia can exist here and now.

His "some standing here" prophecy remains. A traditional Christian can say that he speaks in the knowledge that he will die and rise again, his disciples will be galvanized by the miracle, and the Church's public manifestation and growth will follow. Is there an alternative? What did he have in mind if not that? Without his death and resurrection, or at least the disciples' belief in it, the manifestation would not have happened . . . and yet, even if the author of Acts is overly enthusiastic, it did happen.

Discussion of this prophecy and its fulfillment is hard to carry further. It must end, after all, in plain assertion, on the positive side ("I accept the Christian story, he did die and rise again, and on that miracle the Church was founded") or on the negative side ("I don't know what the truth may be, but the Christian story is incredible"). The prophecy is not a mistake; it works, if properly understood, but it seems impossible to reduce to purely "rational" terms. A mystery remains.

See also: Apocalypse; Biblical Prophecy (2)—Christian; John, Saint; Messiah

Further Reading

Ashe, Geoffrey. *The Book of Prophecy.* London: Blandford, 1999.

Brown R. E., J. A. Fitzmyer, and R. E. Murphy, eds. *The New Jerome Biblical Commentary.* Englewood Cliffs, NJ: Prentice-Hall, 1990.

JOACHIM OF FIORE
(C. 1135–1202)

Italian abbot and scriptural expositor. ("Fiore" is sometimes given inaccurately as "Flora" or "Floris.") His theory of the movement of history, with the past and present leading to a foreseeable future, has been called "the most influential known to Europe until the appearance of Marxism." The prophetic part not only affected medieval thinking, it surfaced again, reinterpreted and rationalized, in later times.

Joachim was born in the south of Italy about 1135. After a pilgrimage to the Holy Land, he entered the Cistercian order and became abbot of Curazzo in Calabria. Very little is known of his life, but he built up a reputation for learning. Almost the first fact on record about him is that in 1184, Pope Lucius III asked his opinion of the "Sibylline" texts. Impressed by Joachim's response, Lucius encouraged him in a plan to study the relation between the Old and New Testaments.

Papal approval seems to have acted as a trigger, and ideas began to come in a flood. Day-to-day monastic administration interfered. Joachim left Curazzo to stay at another monastery as a guest of its head and then moved out to live by himself. However, inquirers would not leave him alone, and some became virtually disciples. At last, he got permission from Rome to form his own congregation, the community of San Giovanni in Fiore. It survived his death in 1202, but its career was undistinguished, and Joachim had no successor.

Joachim was believed to possess a gift of inspiration. This attracted the interest of public figures, among them Richard Coeur de Lion, pausing in Sicily on his way to the Third Crusade. Invited to visit and say something about the prospects, Joachim assured the king that he would achieve his objectives. They discussed the ancient prophecy of the Antichrist, agreeing (wrongly) that he would be manifested soon. Short-term prognostication, in fact, was not Joachim's strong point, and it was misguided to treat him as a fortune-teller. While he had flashes of illumination, he was not primarily a seer or visionary. His main ideas, developed in a series of books and tracts, were based on solid if controversial scholarship. Like all too many others, he tried to expound the last book of the New Testament, the Revelation or Apocalypse of Saint John, but he knew it better than most, as he knew the Bible in general. Contemporaries credited him with insight far above ordinary levels. Whatever its extent, he was extremely successful in extracting hidden meanings from Scripture.

His originality lay in a new application of the doctrine of the Trinity—Father, Son, and Holy Spirit, three equal Persons in one God. As a Catholic theologian, he accepted this. But he had the radical idea of relating the Trinity to the movement of time. He saw each Person as presiding, in turn, over a phase of history. This meant chiefly the history of people comprised in the Christian scheme of things—the biblical patriarchs, the Israelites, the Jews, and the Christians up to the Christendom that Joachim lived in, with its Church centered on Rome. This was the history that mattered, the history of the people to whom God was known, and, to be fair, everything beyond the Christian horizon was rather indefinite.

Joachim's three phases overlapped, with no sharp transitions, and he explained that there were long periods of preparation. The three can be properly called "ages" so long as the overlap is realized. First, he said, came the Age of God the Father, a time of law and fear and obedience, corresponding roughly to the Old Testament. This gave way to the Age of the Son, first clearly defined by the advent of Christ; this was the time of grace and the gospel and the Church, still going on. Twelfth-century Christians expected no further change until the end of the world. Joachim, however, took his Trinitarian logic all the way. He prophesied that after a time of tribulation, a third age would prevail, the Age of the Holy Spirit.

His ingenuity was remarkable. He drew parallels between characters in different parts of the Bible, so that they shed light on each other and on the whole pattern. He used number symbolism and diagrams. His system was not a direct challenge to the Church, which Christ, the Son, had founded; but in the third age, it would be transformed, and society would be transformed with it. The popes were the successors of Peter as they claimed to be, and the papacy would continue, but the third age would be more expressive of John, the "beloved disciple" to whom the Fourth Gospel was attributed. New religious orders, unspoiled by power and wealth, would lead the way into it. Hierarchies would be replaced by communities. Universal peace, love, and enlightenment would reign.

Critics accused Joachim of splitting up the Trinity into three gods, one for each age. This was unjust, and he was never conclusively convicted of heresy. There was talk of his canonization as a saint, and Dante puts him in Paradise among the wisest. After his death, however, seditious elements in the Church pushed his ideas to extremes he never intended, saying the papacy was obsolete and due to be overthrown. Saint Francis, who founded the Franciscan order in 1210, was regarded by some as the inaugurator of the third age, and after his death, they even placed him on a level with Christ. A dissident Franciscan party, the Spirituals, who held that the order had betrayed the founder's ideals, talked the language of revolution. They produced a book called the *Eternal Evangel* or *Everlasting Gospel* (no longer extant in its original form), which was based on Joachim's teaching but distorted it and caused trouble. He was partly to blame himself. He had conjectured that the present age would end and the great change would be visible in 1260.

While the immediate ferment slowly died down, the hope continued. Theorists who may be called "Joachites" evolved a kind of program with two prophetic characters who were to prepare the ground for the Age of the Holy Spirit. The Angelic Pope was to purify the Church, and a great emperor, the Second Charlemagne, was to unite Christendom. Several actual persons were cast in these roles but did not live up to them. A particular disappointment was the election of a saintly hermit as Pope Celestine V in 1294. After a few months of chaos, he was forced to resign; Dante blamed him for his "great refusal."

In the sixteenth century, Joachism briefly received a fresh impetus from the voyages of discovery and the missions that followed them. Columbus cited Joachim, and he and others believed that the opening-up of the world and the spreading of the Christian faith might be ushering in the third age. However, this upsurge was temporary, and the movement, in its original form, died away. A late product of its influence was a curious text known as the *Prophecies of St. Malachy*, which has a prophetic interest of its own.

Despite all vagaries, Joachim achieved one very great thing. He gave a place in Christendom for optimism about the earthly future. Christians had assumed that while there were obviously good times and bad, ours was a fallen world and could never be fundamentally better. Sooner or later, quite likely

sooner, God would end it. Joachim, by envisaging the Age of the Holy Spirit, made room for a real change and a real advance. His ideas played a part in medieval popular protest. While it would be too much to claim that he invented progress, his conception of historical changes, with a quantum leap forward and upward, reappeared in ideologies outside the Church.

Several German philosophers—Lessing, Hegel, Schelling—took it up in various ways. Lessing, writing in 1780, expressed a renewed hope for a good time coming. He acknowledged his source and spread a new awareness of Joachim or, at least, of the movement his prophecies had inspired. Hegel applied the triple pattern to the history of Germany. Schelling reinvented Joachim's three ages—independently as he thought, though the abbot's ideas may have reached him indirectly—and he was excited when someone spelt them out to him.

Followers of Saint-Simon, the French pioneer of Socialism, adapted the three ages to their own theories and spoke of a "new Christianity" as the spiritual basis for a future Utopia. Possibly because of an early association with Saint-Simon, Auguste Comte, the founder of sociology, likewise detected three phases in history or, more precisely, in human mentality. A "religious" phase and a "metaphysical" phase were leading up to a "positive" phase, when science would reign. While Comte's three phases were not Joachim's, he knew of the abbot and acknowledged his importance. The English novelist George Eliot, who absorbed some of his thought, brought Joachim's prophecies into her historical novel *Romola*.

Though Karl Marx rejected religious thinking, he was deeply influenced by Hegel and by Hegel's touches of Joachim. Marx too expounded historical phases. He lost the triadic pattern, eventually having five. But he kept the final quantum leap, when a revolution would open the way to a classless world, free from oppression and exploitation. Like

Comte, he had a famous literary disciple in England, William Morris. Morris's novel *News from Nowhere* is a wishful fantasy of society after the revolution. The happy future he imagines has been described as the Age of the Holy Spirit without the Holy Spirit.

See also: Angelic Pope; Eliot, George; Malachy, Saint; Morris, William; Second Charlemagne

Further Reading

Ashe, Geoffrey. *The Book of Prophecy.* London: Blandford, 1999.

McGinn, Bernard. *Visions of the End: Apocalyptic Traditions in the Middle Ages.* New York: Columbia University Press, 1979.

Reeves, Marjorie. *The Influence of Prophecy in the Later Middle Ages.* Notre Dame: University of Notre Dame Press, 1993.

————. *Joachim of Fiore and the Prophetic Future.* New York: Harper and Row, 1977.

Reeves, Marjorie, ed. *Prophetic Rome in the High Renaissance Period.* Oxford: Clarendon Press, 1992.

JOHANSON, ANTON (1858–1928)

A Norwegian from Finnmark in the far north who received glimpses of the future, or what he took to be so, in three ways—through intuitions, through visions seen as if from a height, and through hearing a voice that he believed to be Christ's.

Johanson was largely self-taught. His most important employment was as a surveyor. His first communications were sad ones about the deaths of relatives and neighbors, with more or less the nature of second sight. Gradually, his scope widened. He is credited with foreseeing the Martinique eruption in 1902 and the San Francisco earthquake in 1906. In a vision of a ship going down, which could apply to the *Titanic,* he picked out a member of the Astor family as lost. John Jacob Astor was, in fact, among the *Titanic* victims.

Most of Johanson's predictions of public events resulted from a single prolonged experience on the night of November 14, 1907, combining all three of his sources of information. The experience ranged over two future periods, 1914 to 1921 and 1947 to 1953. Some of the forecasts in the earlier group were published in Scandinavian papers during 1913. Johanson spoke of World War I, the military deadlock, the flu episode near the end, and Germany's victory in Russia followed by a rapid collapse and social turmoil. His second group of prophecies was far less successful. It included a Franco-Russian alliance making war on Norway and Sweden and a debacle of skyscrapers in New York. However, it also included the founding of the state of Israel, within the period specified.

Some of these prophecies can be explained by intelligent appraisal of current affairs. Some, of course, may have been improved retrospectively. Johanson's reputed bull's-eyes with Martinique and San Francisco are impressive if genuine, since, with natural disasters, no scientific techniques of forecasting existed. The oddly specific detail about an Astor perishing in a shipwreck is interesting. There was no obvious reason for Johanson to think of a faraway American family, however renowned and affluent. This touch has an air of authenticity.

See also: Titanic

Further Reading

Wallechinsky, David, Amy Wallace, and Irving Wallace. *The Book of Predictions.* New York: William Morrow, 1980.

JOHN, SAINT (FIRST CENTURY A.D.)

Disciple of Christ, whom some Christians expected to live until his Second Coming.

Questions have been raised about the person to whom this prophecy was attached. An apostle named John figures in the Gospels as the younger of the two sons of Zebedee. There is a John known as the "beloved disciple" because of his special closeness to Jesus, who, when dying, entrusts his mother to this disciple's care. Early authors think these Johns were the same. The traditional story is that John, apostle and "beloved," went to live at Ephesus in Asia Minor. During a Roman persecution he escaped, or perhaps was banished, to the Aegean island of Patmos, but when the danger passed he returned to Ephesus.

John is reputedly the author of the Fourth Gospel and three epistles, and also the Apocalypse or Revelation, which concludes the New Testament. If he wrote all these, he must have continued as an active author to a very advanced age. Much uncertainty exists, on stylistic and other grounds. The Fourth Gospel claims at the end to be giving the testimony of the "beloved disciple." It was he, regarded rightly or wrongly as the only John, who was expected by some to live until the Second Coming, on the basis of chapter 21, verses 20 to 23. Jesus has risen from the dead and appeared to some of his disciples beside the Sea of Galilee. He tells Peter to "feed his sheep"—that is, to look after the community of believers—and foretells Peter's martyrdom. Then:

> Peter turned and saw following them the disciple whom Jesus loved. . . . When Peter saw him, he said to Jesus, "Lord, what about this man?" Jesus said to him, "If it is my will that he remain until I come, what is that to you? Follow me!" The saying spread abroad among the brethren that this disciple was not to die; yet Jesus did not say that he was not to die, but, "If it is my will that he remain until I come, what is that to you?"

This report of a promise of survival may have been inspired by another enigmatic saying of Jesus', recorded elsewhere with minor variations. Addressing a group of followers, he says that "some standing here" will live to witness the advent of the Kingdom of God. Misunderstood as referring to his future return in majesty, this may have been taken as a prophecy that some of his hearers would live to see it. The supposed prophecy could have been applied to John because of the remark quoted in the Fourth Gospel and also because he was seen to be living on when all the other apostles were dead.

He too died at last, but a legend asserted that his tomb at Ephesus was empty and he had gone no one knew where. The sixth-century historian Gregory of Tours notes a still-persistent belief in his survival until the Second Coming. Perhaps, though, it was not an earthly survival. He might have been taken up bodily into Heaven. Dante, in his *Paradiso* (XXV:100–129), imagines a meeting with John in the celestial regions but dismisses the bodily assumption.

The survival motif was continued or, rather, transformed in a puzzling medieval account of a contemporary of Christ who was still living in Armenia. The name given to him, Cartaphilus, means "most beloved" and shows that the story was derived somehow from the tradition of the beloved disciple, but this immortal is not the beloved disciple. He is said to have been a door-keeper in Pilate's house. When Jesus passed, carrying the cross, he shouted, "Go on faster!" Jesus replied, "I go, but you shall wait till I come"—another echo of the gospel but in a totally different context. Cartaphilus is converted, but the legend makes his survival a punishment. In the seventeenth century, the person in this encounter is described as a Jew, and thereafter, because of the doom upon him, he is the "Wandering" Jew who can never rest, a much more famous character than Cartaphilus. Here the legend parts company finally with the gospel.

See also: Jesus Christ; Revelation; Wandering Jew

Further Reading

Brown R. E., J. A. Fitzmyer, and R. E. Murphy, eds. *The New Jerome Biblical Commentary*. Englewood Cliffs, NJ: Prentice-Hall, 1990.

Cavendish, Richard, ed. *Man, Myth and Magic.* London: BPC Publishing, 1970–1972. Article "Wandering Jew."

JOHN THE BAPTIST

Sometimes called the last of the prophets, in the sense of closing the biblical succession.

He appears in all four Gospels. According to Luke, he was the son of a Jewish priest, Zechariah, and his wife, Elizabeth, a relative of Jesus' mother, Mary. He went out to live an austere life in the Judaean wilderness near the Jordan River, preaching repentance and baptizing many people who came to him to confess their sins. Jewish messianic hopes were rising, and in the gospel narratives, there is public speculation as to whether John is the Christ himself. He replies that he is not; he is humbly preparing the way for the true one who will soon be manifested. Figuratively, he is fulfilling the prophecy of Elijah as the Messiah's forerunner. When Jesus comes to him for baptism, John hails him as the Christ he has foretold.

John continued to have a following of his own during Jesus' ministry. He never became a disciple, and the gospel writers say he began to question his own prophecy (Matthew 11:2–3). However, he had not much longer to live. Mark 6:17–28 gives the fullest version of the tradition of his death. Herod Antipas, who ruled in Galilee, had married his brother's wife, Herodias; John denounced the marriage as unlawful, and, for this reason as well as political ones, Herod imprisoned him. Herodias's daughter Salome pleased Herod with a dance, and he unwisely promised her whatever reward she asked. Prompted by her mother, she demanded John the Baptist's head on a dish; Herod had him executed, and the severed head was brought to her. The story, together with other features of John's career, is partially confirmed by the historian Josephus.

John's mode of life puts him in the same context of asceticism and messianic anticipa-tion as the community that is documented in the Dead Sea Scrolls.

> **See also:** Biblical Prophecy (1)—Israelite and Jewish; Biblical Prophecy (2)—Christian; Elijah; Messiah
>
> ***Further Reading***
> Brown R. E., J. A. Fitzmyer, and R. E. Murphy, eds. *The New Jerome Biblical Commentary.* Englewood Cliffs, NJ: Prentice-Hall, 1990.

JONAH (FL. EIGHTH CENTURY B.C.)

Old Testament prophet, the central figure in a story that raises the issue of conditional prophecy.

Jonah lived in the northern Israelite king-dom during the reign of Jeroboam II. How-ever, the small book that bears his name does not profess to be his own work. Almost cer-tainly, it is much later, and almost certainly, it is not biographical. It tells how the Lord commanded Jonah to go to Nineveh, the As-syrian capital, and denounce the wickedness of its people. This motif of a message for non-Israelites is one of the features that show the book to be written at a later time. Jonah is afraid and tries to escape, going aboard a ship bound for Tarshish, probably Tartessus in Spain.

When the ship is endangered by a storm, the crew decide that their guilty passenger is bringing bad luck, and they throw him over-board. His life is saved when the Lord causes a "great fish" to swallow him; inside it, he ut-ters a prayer of remorse and thanksgiving, and after three days, the fish vomits him onto land. Commanded again by God, he goes to Nineveh and tells its people that their city will be destroyed. The king is shaken, and, with his encouragement, the Ninevites do penance and even pray to the God of Israel. The city is not destroyed. Jonah is angry. God, however, says that, in the circumstances, he has every right to show mercy—after all, he showed mercy to Jonah himself—and the prophet should learn to practice that virtue.

John baptizing Jesus in the Jordan, an illustration from Doré's Bible (1865–1866). (Ann Ronan Picture Library)

The story is a fable, which, in inculcating its moral, brings out a point implied in older prophetic writings. A prophecy may be inspired and valid yet conditional: a warning, perhaps, rather than a prediction. If so-and-so happens, a certain consequence will follow. In this case, if the Ninevites persist in their sins, God will inflict punishment. But if

Jonah, blamed for the storm endangering the ship, is thrown into the sea where the great fish awaits him. From the medieval Bible de Souvigny. (Giraudon/Bibliothèque de Moulin/Art Resource)

the first contingency is deflected, the consequence may be also.

There is no point in speculating about the fish or asking whether Jonah could have survived inside it for three days. It is probably derived from Hebrew mythology. In the New Testament (Matthew 12:40), it is explicitly a whale, and Jonah's experience is an anticipatory symbol of Christ's entombment and resurrection.

See also: Biblical Prophecy (1)—Israelite and Jewish

Further Reading

Brown R. E., J. A. Fitzmyer, and R. E. Murphy, eds. *The New Jerome Biblical Commentary.* Englewood Cliffs, NJ: Prentice-Hall, 1990.

KALKI

Messianic manifestation of the great god Vishnu, prophesied by Hindus at the close of the present aeon.

In the system of Hinduism for which Vishnu is the Supreme Being, he is said to appear on earth at long intervals. Best known of his incarnations, or "avatars," is Krishna, who plays a crucial part in the vast sacred epic *Mahabharata*. Its central theme is the conflict between the two branches of a north Indian dynasty, the righteous Pandavas and the sinister Kauravas. Krishna aids the Pandavas and is a special friend of their chief warrior, Arjuna, becoming his spiritual mentor in the famous episode entitled the Bhagavad Gita, or "Lord's Song." Here, speaking with the voice of divinity, Krishna says: "Whenever and wherever duty decays and unrighteousness prospers, I am born in successive ages to destroy evil-doers and reestablish the reign of the moral law."

Despite his activities, however, there is a relentless movement of cosmic decline, with a logic leading toward a more fundamental intervention. The world is running down, so to speak, passing through four epochs called yugas. First came a golden age, the Krita Yuga, when all beings were wise and good and fulfilled the laws of their nature. This gave way to the shorter and inferior Treta Yuga. After that came the Dvapara Yuga, shorter again and worse again. We are now living in the Kali Yuga (nothing to do with the goddess Kali), the shortest and worst of all.

The Bhagavad Gita is silent about this doctrine, but in another part of the epic, a seer, Markandeya, expounds it. He tells his listeners that the Kali Yuga will continue to grow more evil and lawless until the cosmic running-down reaches its final point. Then, amid an apocalyptic destruction decreed by Vishnu, signs of regeneration will begin to show, and a benign planetary conjunction will herald his earthly reappearance in the form of "a brahmin by the name of Kalki," who will wind the world up again by divine power and usher in a new Krita Yuga.

Other versions point to a double manifestation of Vishnu as Kalki, first in the form of a cosmic winged horse who will carry out the destruction, then as the messianic restorer.

See also: Mahdi; Maitreya; Messiah

Further Reading

The Mahabharata. Translated by J. A. B. van Buitinen. Vol. 2. Chicago: University of Chicago Press, 1973–1978.

KRAFFT, KARL ERNST (1900–1945)

Swiss astrologer whose wartime employment in Nazi Germany inspired a myth that Hitler acted on astrological advice.

Krafft was born in Basel and studied science at its university. But séances held in an attempt to contact a dead sister gave him an interest in less orthodox matters, and he began, like some in Germany at that time, to look for a statistical basis for astrology. While his astrological interest became permanent, even obsessive, he invented related pseudo sciences with names like cosmobiology and devised a theory of sunspots. He wrote many articles and a book but made no converts of any standing; a meeting with Jung in 1934 was fruitless. However, he held a post for a time in the Globus department store, advising on personnel selection. It is not certain

THE TEN AVATARS OR INCARNATIONS OF VISHNU.

Hindu portrayals of the ten avatars or incarnations of the god Vishnu. In the tenth, under the name Kalki, Vishnu takes the form of a winged horse. (Ann Ronan Picture Library)

whether cosmobiology was of any help. It was of no help at all when he received a legacy, made investments based on his theories, and lost heavily.

During the 1930s, he began giving lectures on Nostradamus and came to know the French astrologer's work very well. Pro-German in sentiment, he settled in Germany in 1937. The following year, he attracted some attention with a prediction about a Romanian politician, and the year after that, he attracted more with a warning of an attempt to assassinate Hitler. In both cases, he was correct.

When the German invasion of Poland caused Britain to declare war in the autumn of 1939, several Germans rediscovered a book published by H. H. Kritzinger, *Mysteries of the Sun and Soul,* which was thought to be relevant to the crisis. Kritzinger quoted one of Nostradamus's prophetic quatrains, with an interpretation making out that it foretold a crisis in 1939 involving Britain and Poland. This apparent fulfillment impressed, among other readers, the wife of Joseph Goebbels, Hitler's propaganda minister. Goebbels did not believe in astrology, but it struck him that as Nostradamus evidently had a public, his prophecies might be used for the purposes of the regime. He asked Kritzinger to recommend a suitable expert, and Kritzinger suggested Krafft, who, by then, had established his credentials with his warning of the assassination attempt. Krafft agreed to cooperate in working out pro-German interpretations of Nostradamus's prophecies, and Goebbels put him on the payroll.

He succeeded for a time, noting, for instance, a quatrain (V. 94) about Belgium and part of France being absorbed into "Great Germany." In 1941, he delivered a course of lectures and published a commentary on forty of the quatrains, which appeared in French in German-occupied Belgium and was translated into Portuguese under German sponsorship.

Reports about these activities reached England and set in motion a rumor of "Hitler's astrologer," who was supposed to be advising him. The story was propagated—perhaps invented—by Louis de Wohl, an astrologer himself, who tried to convince the British government that Hitler made astrologically guided decisions. By doing so, he hoped to get a job in Intelligence, predicting, on the basis of his own expertise, what the Führer would do next. He submitted unsolicited samples with an entire lack of success but went on claiming for years that his proposal had been accepted and that he was a key factor in the war effort. The myth of Hitler's astrologer retained a life of its own.

Meanwhile, Krafft's real bosses grew to regard him with suspicion, and his work was censored. He made some good predictions of the course of the war but showed an unanticipated integrity that proved fatal. As early as the spring of 1940, at a gathering where leading Nazis were present and the expectation was that the war would not last long, he said it would go on at least until the winter of 1942–1943, and urged that it should not be allowed to continue beyond that because the outlook was grim. Arguably, he had some inkling already of the disaster at Stalingrad.

Such tactlessness could be overlooked for a while, but when the Nostradamian well ran dry, Krafft was demoted to concocting horoscopes of various world figures that could be used for propaganda. These were not always slanted as his employers wished. He produced a hostile chart for President Roosevelt but insisted that comparison of the charts for the British general Montgomery and his German opponent Rommel showed that Montgomery's was "stronger." In February 1943, very ill, he was imprisoned; he died early in 1945 on the way to the Buchenwald concentration camp. His last known prediction was that British bombs would fall on Goebbels's Propaganda Ministry in retribution. They did.

See also: Hanussen, Erik Jan; Nazi Germany
Further Reading
Howe, Ellic. *Urania's Children*. London: William Kimber, 1967.

Toland, John. *Adolf Hitler*. 2 vols. New York: Doubleday, 1976.

Wallechinsky, David, Amy Wallace, and Irving Wallace. *The Book of Predictions*. New York: William Morrow, 1980.

L

LAWRENCE, D. H. (1885–1930)

English novelist whose short story "The Rocking-Horse Winner" shows insight into the nature of precognition in cases where this has arguably occurred.

Rocking horses used to be standard equipment for the amusement of children. A painted wooden horse was mounted on rockers, on the same principle as a rocking chair. The child could sit on it and sway backward and forward, pretending to ride. In the story, a boy who is getting past the age for his rocking horse continues to ride it surreptitiously. Sometimes, he has a sense of arrival and "knows" which horses will win real-life races—a gift that naturally pays. But he does not arrive or "know" every time, and he has no notion how the knowledge comes to him when it does.

The same principle applies to the more interesting instances of real prevision. It does apparently happen, but *happen* is the word; there is no firm evidence that any technique will make it happen. It can be invited, but not produced to order. Lawrence's story makes the point, and it is not affected by an alleged case for detecting masturbatory symbolism, which, in any case, is irrelevant because the story is entirely focused on the family's money problems and the boy's growing obsession with solving them by picking winners.

See also: Prophecy, Theories of

The novelist D. H. Lawrence, who wrote a short story of precognition showing insight into its apparent nature. (Ann Ronan Picture Library)

LEMURIA

A kind of alternative Atlantis, regarded in esoteric circles as the home of a lost race and, if it reappears, of a future one.

Unlike Atlantis, Lemuria has no literary tradition. The background of the notion is scientific, though enthusiasts left science behind. A nineteenth-century geologist, Philip Sclater, thought the ancient distribution of lemurs and other animals implied a former land connection between Africa and southern Asia. He called it Lemuria and assumed that it had vanished under the Indian Ocean.

Helena Petrovna Blavatsky, the founder of Theosophy, noted this idea in *Isis Unveiled* (1877) and also mentioned a theory of a sunken continent in the Pacific, but she did not explicitly connect the two. Later, when she developed an occult pseudo history of successive human "root-races," she located the third of these in a Lemuria described as

One of the alleged sacred symbols of the lost civilization of Lemuria, or Mu. James Churchward explained it as representing a fourfold command by the Creator. (Dover Pictorial Series)

a "gigantic continent" stretching from India through Australia into the Pacific. She linked it with authentic legend—Buddhist legend—by saying that when it sank under the ocean, a few survivors took refuge in Shambhala, a sacred place in what is now the Gobi Desert. In a distant future, some of Lemuria may resurface and become the home of another "root-race."

After Madame Blavatsky's death, an amateur anthropologist, William Scott-Elliot, published an account of Lemuria based on "astral clairvoyance." Partly because of him, it shifted definitely to the Pacific. And surely a Pacific lost continent looks more plausible than Atlantis? Surely those countless islands could be the high points of a land mass that once united them and afterwards sank but not completely? On geological grounds, the answer is no. However, while the Theosophists' Lemuria faded out, an offshoot of the notion persists.

In the 1930s, James Churchward, a British army officer, set up Lemuria under another name as a rival to Atlantis. He identified it with a country called Mu that was supposed

(wrongly) to have been wrecked by volcanic action in a Mayan script. Churchward claimed to have found more about it in India, written on stone tablets in an almost forgotten language. Mu, or Lemuria, filled a large part of the Pacific and had an advanced civilization; Easter Island was the last remnant.

The Lemurian mystique acquired a local habitation through two books by Frederick Spencer Oliver, *A Dweller on Two Planets* and *An Earth Dweller's Return*. On the face of it, these are fiction, but Oliver said they were transmitted to him by "Phylos the Thibetan," largely within sight of Mount Shasta in northern California. Most of the first story is set in Atlantis, but Oliver introduces Lemuria too and associates it with an artificial chamber inside Mount Shasta.

Some readers took this seriously and believed Oliver was an inspired being with a long series of incarnations, one of them as Lemuria's emperor. A rumor grew up in the 1930s that a select group of survivors from the lost land retired into Mount Shasta's interior; their descendants were said to be still there and to come out occasionally. The underground chamber was imaginatively enlarged into a whole subterranean complex behind a great stone door in the mountainside. A further ramification was that the Pacific Coast of the United States was actually part of Lemuria, stayed above water when the rest sank, and became attached to a different continent. A Lemuria-related mystique still flourishes around Mount Shasta, though it is not clear whether this is prophetic in the sense of foretelling that the hidden people will emerge openly or that the lost land itself will reappear, as Atlantis is expected to do in some quarters.

See also: Atlantis; Shambhala; Theosophy
Further Reading

Ashe, Geoffrey. *Atlantis: Lost Lands, Ancient Wisdom*. London: Thames and Hudson, 1992.
Bramwell, James. *Lost Atlantis*. London: Cobden-Sanderson, 1937.

Cervé, W. S. *Lemuria: The Lost Continent of the Pacific.* San Jose, CA: Rosicrucian Library, 1982.

LILLY, WILLIAM (1602–1681)

English astrologer noted for his prediction of the Great Fire of London.

Born in Leicestershire, Lilly married a London widow and inherited £1,000 on her early death. This enabled him to study astrology, which, at that time, retained more prestige in England than in most countries. He made a lucrative profession of it, writing books, casting horoscopes, and teaching the art to pupils. From 1644 on, he published an annual almanac under the pseudonym Merlinus Anglicus Junior. Another of his productions was a collection of prophecies, including several ascribed to Mother Shipton, whose reputation henceforth was largely due to him.

He was involved in the politics of the day, giving Charles I advice that was ignored and then supporting Parliament in the English Civil War. His book *Monarchy or No Monarchy* (1651) repeats an earlier forecast of "sundry fires and a consuming plague" about the year 1665. The prediction of fire is accompanied by a picture of people with buckets trying to put it out, under an image of Gemini, supposedly London's astrological sign.

When the monarchy was restored in 1660, Lilly was briefly imprisoned. The Great Plague struck London in 1665; the Great Fire the following year. He was arrested again, this time on suspicion of having started the fire himself or at least of knowing about incendiaries, but he was exonerated. Samuel Pepys mentions him in his *Diary.*

Lilly seems to have claimed psychic gifts beyond anything derived from astrology. He got permission to look for hidden treasure in the cloister of Westminster Abbey and began a search using dowsing rods. However, he was stopped by a nocturnal storm that blew out his candle; he said it was the work of demons attracted to the scene by unsympa-

The seventeenth-century astrologer William Lilly, who practiced the art professionally and published annual forecasts under the pseudonym Merlinus Anglicus Junior. (Ann Ronan Picture Library)

thetic onlookers. When coal was discovered at Worplesdon in Surrey and an attempt was made to measure the depth of the seam with iron boring rods, they kept breaking and Lilly blamed "subterranean spirits." In 1670, he was consulted about an apparition near Cirencester: the mysterious being would not say whether it was a good spirit or a bad one but vanished with "a curious perfume and a most melodious twang." Lilly thought it was one of the fairy-folk.

See also: Astrology; Shipton, Mother

Further Reading

Dick, Oliver Lawson. *Aubrey's Brief Lives.* London: Secker and Warburg, 1971.

Dictionary of National Biography (British). Article "Lilly."

Folklore, Myths and Legends of Britain. London: Readers Digest Association, 1973.

Gould, Rupert T. *Oddities: A Book of Unexplained Facts.* London: Philip Allan, 1928.

MACBETH

Macbeth was an eleventh-century ruler of Scotland. According to Holinshed's *Chronicle,* before his accession he met three mysterious women—fairy-folk or "goddesses of destiny"—who told him he would be king, supplanting Duncan I, who reigned at the time. The fulfillment of this prediction led him to trust others. "Certain wizards" and "a certain witch" warned him of danger from Macduff, one of his nobles, but gave him what he took to be promises of safety. The chronicler seems to be thinking merely of soothsayers. Their promises were ambiguous and deceptive, and Macbeth was overthrown.

Shakespeare takes up the supernatural elements and transforms them. His treatment of the story reflects the demonization of witches and their predictive powers that had become normal in his time. He wrote *Macbeth* about 1606 when he belonged to the acting company called the King's Men, under the patronage of the Stuart monarch James VI of Scotland (James I of England). It was to be expected that he would write a play about Scottish royalty for performance at court. However, to complicate matters, James claimed to be an expert on witchcraft himself. Whatever Shakespeare's own beliefs, he was bound to follow the current line of thought, and the current line was that witches were agents of Satan and his infernal host.

Shakespeare ascribes all the prophesying in Macbeth's story to the same three, called the Weird Sisters. They are malignant hags, killing livestock and stirring up storms, but they are more than that. In the opening scene, the line "Fair is foul and foul is fair" marks their general commitment to evil. Meeting Macbeth and his military colleague Banquo after a victory they have won for Duncan, they salute Macbeth as thane (feudal lord) of Glamis and thane of Cawdor and say he will be king. Banquo, they add, will not be king, but his descendants will.

Macbeth is already thane of Glamis. A moment later, he hears that the thane of Cawdor has been condemned as a traitor and that Duncan has transferred the title to him. He concludes that the witches "have more in them than mortal knowledge." Banquo sees them for what they are or what, in Shakespeare's time, it must be supposed they are—diabolic agents. Macbeth, however, has already had notions of killing Duncan and claiming the crown in virtue of cousinship. Encouraged by the prophecy and urged on by his ambitious wife, he does so. Duncan's son Malcolm, on whom he pins the blame for the murder, flees to England.

The witches' pronouncements, now seemingly confirmed, give Macbeth no peace. If Banquo's descendants will rule, his own reign will be a dead end, and perhaps Banquo will plot against him. He hires assassins to dispose of Banquo and his son. When the son escapes and the father's alarming ghost appears to him, he resolves to consult the witches again. He is aware of the kind of step he is taking: "I am bent to know, By the worst means, the worst." He can now find them when he wants to; he has moved closer to their sinister world.

It is made very clear that the witches are not mere fortune-tellers but the servants of supernatural powers. When Macbeth arrives, they invite their "masters" to answer his inquiries. One of these evil beings warns him against Macduff. A second tells him that "none of woman born" will be able to harm him. A third assures him that he can never be vanquished until Birnam Wood comes to Dunsinane. These prophecies—which are adapted from the original *Chronicle* but with a profound difference of tone—give him a sense of security. The witches know this to be delusive, and they spoil his potential relief with a prevision of Banquo's royal descendants, the Stuart kings—a compliment to James.

Macduff has joined the exiled Malcolm in England. They return with an English army to support a revolt. Macbeth has become a ruthless tyrant, uninterested in earning his subjects' loyalty because he relies on the safety promised (as he imagines) by "the spirits that know all mortal consequences"—which is what the demons have convinced him they are. They have tricked him, of course. He occupies a stronghold at Dunsinane, and Birnam Wood does come there when Malcolm's troops camouflage themselves with branches. Macbeth, confronting Macduff in battle, still boasts of his invulnerability because "none of woman born" can harm him. Macduff replies that he was taken from his mother's womb in a cesarean section—therefore, not born. Macbeth curses the "juggling fiends"; he has seen through them at last, but it is too late. Macduff kills him, and Malcolm becomes king. The witches and the devils they serve have used prophecy to ruin Macbeth.

See also: Witchcraft

MAHDI

The "Rightly Guided One," a messianic figure in Muslim prophecy.

The word *Mahdi* is not found in the Koran. Early in the career of Islam, it was an honorific suggesting a special relationship with God. A man so designated was seen as divinely directed to give special leadership

Mohammed Ahmed, called the Mahdi, a Muslim leader claiming divine guidance, who ruled the Sudan from 1881 to 1885 and defeated British attempts to remove him. (Ann Ronan Picture Library)

and special benefits to the faithful. The term was applied to reforming caliphs such as Umar II. However, Islam evolved a prophecy of a greater Mahdi, a Mahdi par excellence, a Muslim conqueror and ruler destined to arise before the end of the world and destroy the powers of evil. He was associated with Isa—Jesus—who would descend from heaven to aid him.

Hopes for this supreme Mahdi in the future did not exclude other divinely directed men, to whom the title could properly be attached. In British imperial history, "the Mahdi" means a particular man, Mohammed Ahmed, who, in 1881, led a revolt against British-sponsored Egyptian rule in the Sudan. His followers, the dervishes, were nicknamed "Fuzzy-Wuzzies" by British troops because of their spectacular hair. Their reckless courage in battle drew praise from

Rudyard Kipling. They captured Khartoum and killed the British commander General Gordon. The Mahdi died soon afterward, undefeated, and the regime he had founded survived until 1898 under Abdullah el Tashi, who did not claim the title and was content to call himself the Khalifa, or successor.

A legend made Mohammed Ahmed one of the immortal heroes who lie sleeping in caves, like King Arthur; a belief allowing a messianic return and implying, perhaps, that he was *the* Mahdi all along.

Further Reading
The Encyclopedia of Islam

MAITREYA

A future Buddha with a quasi-messianic role.

A Hindu seer named Maitreya makes a brief appearance in the epic *Mahabharata*. However, the name is much more conspicuous in Buddhism. Early texts mention six Buddhas—Enlightened Ones—before Gautama, the historical founder, and one more who is yet to come. This is Maitreya, who is now what is known as a Bodhisattva.

Buddhism does not recognize gods or goddesses as such, but it does recognize beings of comparable greatness, though they are differently conceived. A Bodhisattva, in that sense, is a being who is on the way to attaining buddhahood and liberation from birth and death, who is not compelled even now to be reborn in the world, but who elects to hold back from the final goal to help other creatures, and may enter earthly existence voluntarily for that purpose.

At present, Maitreya's home is a heavenly region called Tusita. Ever compassionate, he appears to Buddhist teachers in dreams and trances, offering advice and encouragement. Humans who live rightly, are devoted to him, and pray to him, especially at the time of death, can be reborn in his heaven. He conducts them to it, and they live there happily.

Some day he will be manifested in his full glory, and his paradise dwellers will accompany him as he brings fresh wisdom to the world. The prophecy of his advent usually looks far ahead, to an age when humanity will be better prepared and riper for progress toward salvation. But he may appear sooner. Some say he will be born in Benares (now Varanasi), the holiest city of India, once an important Buddhist center. Others identify him with the great being who is to step forth from the secret kingdom of Shambhala. There is no Maitreyan orthodoxy.

See also: Shambhala
Further Reading
Cavendish, Richard, ed. *Man, Myth and Magic.* London: BPC Publishing, 1970–1972. Article "Buddhism."

MALACHY, SAINT (1094–1148)

Medieval Irish prelate whose name is attached to a series of prophecies of future popes.

Born in Armagh, he was baptized Mael Maedoc, which was converted into the biblical name Malachy. He became abbot of Bangor in 1123 and archbishop of Armagh in 1134. He was a friend of Saint Bernard of Clairvaux, one of the greatest figures in the Church at that time, and he died at Clairvaux in 1148. Malachy was the first Irishman to receive a papal canonization. Bernard, in a memoir, credits him with a gift of second sight and prevision but does not mention anything spectacular that he achieved with these gifts.

It is virtually certain that the papal *Prophecies of St. Malachy* were composed by someone else long afterwards and falsely attributed to him, though the motive for choosing that particular pseudo author remains obscure. There are no known references to them until 1595, when they are cited by Arnold Wion, a Benedictine historian. He puts them in a context of anticipation inspired by the radical theologian Joachim of Fiore. During the Middle Ages, indirectly under Joachim's influence, fanciful lists of fu-

Maitreya, the Buddha who is yet to come. At present he lives in a heaven of his own, and some day he will appear on earth bringing fresh enlightenment. (Hulton Getty)

ture popes were circulating. Several new ones appeared toward the end of the sixteenth century, looking ahead hopefully to an Angelic Pope who would purify the Church and bring universal peace.

These lists were purportedly composed earlier. Their authors gave them a faked credibility by starting with pseudo prophecies of popes who had already reigned and could thus be convincingly described. The *Prophecies of St. Malachy* belong to the same genre, but are interesting in another way. They were probably written in 1590. One of the prophecies may have been contrived with a view to influencing a papal election in that year. But the real predictions of popes after 1590, as distinct from the bogus predictions that precede, are not quite negligible.

It is rather misleading to call these productions "prophecies." The text consists of 111 curt Latin phrases or mottoes. These are matched to the popes in succession, beginning with Celestine II in 1143, plus several schismatic antipopes. Each phrase fits the corresponding pope in one way or another, by an allusion to his name or his birthplace or his family coat of arms, or some prominent feature of his reign. The series extends into the sixteenth century and far beyond. The author needs seventy-five mottoes for the seventy-five popes and antipopes up to 1590. After that, he gives thirty-six more. A distinctive feature is that whereas the other would-be prophecies lead up to the hoped-for Angelic Pope, that is not so with the *Prophecies of St. Malachy.* A *Pastor Angelicus* occurs in the list, but others come after him. At the end is the only piece of continuous prose, a short epilogue about the Last Judgment.

Many of the phrases applied to the popes before 1590 are very apt, as we might expect; they are prophecy after the event. The one that corresponds to the English pope Adrian IV, who reigned from 1154 to 1159, is *De rure albo,* meaning "from a white country." This works in three different ways. He was a

native of Albion, to give Britain its ancient name; he was born near Saint Albans; and he became cardinal bishop of Albano. Benedict XI (r. 1303–1304) is "a preacher from Patara." He was born in Patara and joined the Dominicans, the Order of Preachers. Sixtus IV (r. 1471–1484) is "the Minorite fisherman." He was the son of a fisherman and a member of the Friars Minor. And likewise with many others.

If the *Prophecies* were really composed in 1590, as appears to be the case, we would expect a failure after that, since the thirty-six subsequent phrases must, on the face of it, be pure guesswork. They do tend to be more vague and harder to connect with the popes who correspond to them. However, the contrast is far from absolute, and the pattern is odd. Matching twenty-one of the phrases to actual popes, without any very striking fulfillments, we get to Pius VI. His successor, Pius VII, was elected in 1800. With him and the ensuing pontiffs, as far as John Paul II, the phrases begin working again, or an appreciable number do. Nine are clearly apt and not transferable. Thus:

Aquila rapax—rapacious eagle
Pius VII (r. 1800–1823): Much of his reign was overshadowed by a struggle with the rapacious French Eagle, in the person of Napoleon.
De balneis Etruriae—from the baths of Etruria
Gregory XVI (r. 1831–1846): This pope started his religious career in the Camaldolese order, which was founded at a place called in Latin *Balneum,* in Etruria.
Crux de cruce—a cross from a cross
Pius IX (r. 1846–1878): The first cross can be symbolic of suffering; the second can be the emblem of the royal House of Savoy, which struck heavy blows at papal power in the course of unifying Italy.
Lumen in caelo—a light in the sky
Leo XIII (r. 1878–1903): His family coat of arms portrayed a comet.

Ignis ardens—burning fire
Pius X (r. 1903–1914): This pope was canonized, and the phrase could refer to the "heroic virtue" required of a saint.

Religio depopulata—religion laid waste
Benedict XV (r. 1914–1922): His pontificate covered the devastations of World War I and the Russian Revolution, which set up an antireligious regime in one-sixth of the world.

Fides intrepida—unshaken faith
Pius XI (r. 1922–1939): This pope was noted for his firmness in denouncing the totalitarian systems that were spreading through Europe.

Pastor et nauta—pastor and mariner
John XXIII (r. 1958–1963): Before he was pope, he was patriarch of Venice, a city of boats and travel by water.

Flos florum—flower of flowers
Paul VI (r. 1963–1978): The motto is fulfilled by a design of fleur-de-lis in his coat of arms.

Most of the phrases may seem indefinite, yet, in fact, they fit well, and they could not be switched around. *Religio depopulata,* for instance, which matches Benedict XV, works for him and would not work for any of the others. The Joachite phrase *Pastor Angelicus* does occur on the list; it comes between *Fides intrepida* and *Pastor et nauta* and corresponds to Pius XII (r. 1939–1958). Opinions notoriously differ as to his character and policies. The interesting point is that the phrase comes here, not at the end, with no implication of his bringing in a new age as the Angelic Pope was expected to do. The author may have given up on the prophetic hope. He simply goes on to the next.

Flos florum is followed by *De medietate lunae,* "of the half moon," which corresponds to John Paul I (r. 1978) and looks as if it ought to refer to his short pontificate, although he survived for a full month. John Paul II (from 1978) has *De labore solis,* "from the toil of the sun" or, according to one in-terpretation, "of the eclipse of the sun." Next and last is *Gloria olivae,* "the glory of the olive." It suggests peacemaking, or it might apply to a pope from the branch of the Benedictines called Olivetans.

Then comes the epilogue. "In the final persecution of the Holy Roman Church there will reign Peter the Roman, who will feed his flock among many tribulations, after which the seven-hilled city will be destroyed and the dreadful Judge will judge the people."

This passage is quite unlike the rest, and there is nothing to show whether Peter the Roman (the only pope actually named throughout) does or does not directly follow the last designated pontiff. It is curious that the list ends somewhere about the year 2000. The author had no way of knowing that thirty-six papal reigns after 1590 would extend to that significant-looking date. In fact, this has happened only because the average pontificate since 1590 has been much longer than those before, a difference that, on the face of it, he could not have foreseen.

See also: Angelic Pope; Joachim of Fiore
Further Reading
Bander, Peter. *The Prophecies of St. Malachy.* Rockford, IL: Tan Books, 1973.
Reeves, Marjorie. *The Influence of Prophecy in the Later Middle Ages.* Notre Dame: University of Notre Dame Press, 1993.
———. *Joachim of Fiore and the Prophetic Future.* New York: Harper and Row, 1977.
Wallechinsky, David, Amy Wallace, and Irving Wallace. *The Book of Predictions.* New York: William Morrow, 1980.

MAYA

The Mayan civilization of Central America began in the early Christian era and, despite many vicissitudes, survived until after the Spanish conquest of Mexico. One of its characteristics was a deep interest in time. Among other achievements, the Maya invented a long-range calendar that avoided cumulative error over the centuries, as effectively as the

Gregorian calendar in use today—even slightly more so.

Attempts have been made to relate their ideas about successive cycles and ages to actual prehistory and to infer their expectations about the future. *The Mayan Prophecies,* by Adrian G. Gilbert and Maurice M. Cotterell (published by Element Books in 1995), is a mélange bringing in not only the Maya but Atlantis, Egypt, the "Sleeping Prophet" Edgar Cayce, astrology, and sunspots to conclude that the present age will come to a cataclysmic end in the year 2012.

See also: Cayce, Edgar

Further Reading

Burland, C. A. *The Ancient Maya.* London: Weidenfeld and Nicolson, 1967.

Gribbin, John. *Time Warps.* London: J. M. Dent, 1979.

MERCIER, LOUIS-SÉBASTIEN (1740–1814)

Mercier was a Frenchman and a disciple of Jean-Jacques Rousseau, one of the most influential precursors of the French Revolution. Rousseau denounced civilization as largely corrupt and urged a fresh start in keeping with what he regarded as "natural" living and political organization. The Revolution, beginning in 1789, carried some of his ideas to extremes. Mercier supported it for a time but fell out of favor with the more radical elements for being too moderate.

His romance *L'An 2440* ("The Year 2440") has the distinction of being first in the line of imaginary Utopias located in the future. The genre became familiar and popular with works like *News from Nowhere* by William Morris and various fantasies by H. G. Wells. These, however, and their many successors came much later. Mercier was a pioneer far ahead of everyone else and all the more interesting because of that. His book, first published in 1771, was widely read by the great number of people in France who saw the Revolution approaching and had

high hopes for it. *L'An 2440* went through twenty-five editions.

It belongs to a tradition of "dream" literature many centuries old. The narrator—who may be identified with the author, though the book appeared first anonymously—falls asleep and finds himself in a strange and beautiful city with broad streets and fine architecture. It is Paris, but a barely recognizable Paris. A citizen with whom he makes friends tells him that the date is A.D. 2440, so that he has traveled more than 600 years into the future. In the story that follows, this citizen acts as his guide.

For a while, there is altogether too much to take in. The narrator can do little but walk about, staring and wondering. He notices that the Bastille has disappeared, and so have the slums of his own lifetime. The buildings are well spaced, and many have roof gardens. Fountains at the street corners play continually, supplying drinking water for passersby and sluicing the gutters to prevent any accumulation of refuse. All vehicles keep to the right, ensuring a smooth flow of traffic. Parisians are dressed in loose, comfortable-looking clothes. The eighteenth-century custom of carrying a sword seems to be defunct; the atmosphere, in fact, is pacific, with no visible soldiers and few policemen.

Plainly, a wonderful change has happened, and the narrator naturally wants to know how. His guide gives him a sketch of France's history. Considering the time that has elapsed, there is curiously little to tell. France is still a monarchy but no longer an absolute one. Her renewal was effected by one king, a philosophic ruler who put his kingdom to rights by a wave of the constitutional wand. He decentralized government and arranged for the States General (France's equivalent of Parliament or Congress) to meet every two years. He abandoned the great royal palace of Versailles, where previous kings had lived at a distance from their subjects, and made himself always accessible in Paris. Versailles in

The author of L'An 2440, *a hopeful fantasy of the future, Louis-Sébastien Mercier inspired many readers with optimism in the years preceding the French Revolution. (Ann Ronan Picture Library)*

2440 is a vast ruin, inhabited only by adders and the ghost of its builder, Louis XIV.

That is the whole history. In a changed atmosphere, the French apparently became good and stayed that way. The same happened in other countries. Europe's rulers, all as enlightened as their French colleague, settled their differences long ago and established perpetual peace on the basis of natural geographic frontiers, such as rivers and mountain ranges. England, which became constitutional before France did, has gone on very much as before; it does not seem to occur to Mercier that having a limited monarchy and a parliament has not been a cure-all on the other side of the English Channel. The Scots and Irish have given up nationalism so thoroughly that they prefer to call themselves English (surely one of the least credible touches). Thanks to the abolition of war, populations have grown but not explosively. London is three times the size it was in the eighteenth century. Russia has 45 million inhabitants.

One of the sights of Paris is a monument to humanity, on which several figures representing the principal nations are in attitudes of imploring forgiveness for their past sins. The sins are very past indeed, and in 2440, one would think them unintelligible for most Parisians. France is repenting the massacre of Saint Bartholomew in 1572; England is repenting "fanaticism," presumably the Puritan kind; Spain is repenting misrule in America. The nations' repentance seems to be genuine. There are no colonies; France found them expensive luxuries and could dispense with chocolate and pineapples obtained by exploitation. In any case, imperialism has been abolished—at least, over a large part of its former territory—in the only major upheaval that Mercier mentions. The whole of America has been liberated and restored to its native peoples by a black leader known as the Avenger of the New World.

This, then, is the setting of Mercier's latter-day society. What does he tell his readers about it?

On one outstanding issue, he shows his hand near the beginning. Unexpectedly, in view of what is often taken for granted in later speculations, there has been no movement toward sexual equality. On the contrary, women in 2440 have been restored to what Mercier regards as their proper station in life. He means that they attend to their homes, their families, their spinning wheels. They don't use cosmetics; they don't work in paid jobs; and they don't, generally, go in for higher education. The absence of one kind of equality may be partly compensated by the presence of another. Anyone can marry anyone else. Neither birth nor money can stand in the way, and the family is founded (or supposed to be founded) on love alone. This reverence for homely things extends through all society but in a very masculine form. Three accomplishments, the narrator's guide tells him, are considered honorable— to become a father, to cultivate a field, and to build a house. Rich and poor still exist, but the rich have a sense of responsibility, and craftsmen and laborers enjoy their work, which is not allowed to be too heavy.

Extraordinarily little is said about the economics of the new order. Mercier seems to assume that if all people pulled their weight and none were held back by unnecessary restrictions, France would be prosperous at once. A modern reader might want to know more. Take, for instance, the ownership of land. One result of the real French Revolution was the division of great estates into numerous peasant holdings. Has this happened in 2440, or has it not? Are most of the farmers proprietors or tenants? The answers are not spelled out, and, what is more significant, Mercier hardly seems aware of the questions. The idea that economic systems have a bearing on the good life has not dawned above his horizon. In one passage, he makes the surprising statement that in 2440, nobody lends or borrows money. No such institution as credit exists. That surely raises major issues concerning finance and capital. But all Mercier thinks of is that traders can no longer be swindled.

In this future kingdom, virtue prevails. According to Mercier, virtue means a judicious obedience to the promptings of one's natural goodness (a very eighteenth-century notion); and somehow, almost everybody's natural goodness contrives to give the same promptings. When this doesn't entirely work, coercion creeps in—coercion by orchestrated public opinion, not government. A remarkable feature of the transformed monarchy is its method of raising taxes. Nobody is compelled to pay anything, but a regularly published list reports the amounts everybody does pay, and those who contribute less than what is thought proper find themselves unpopular. To ostracize a person for unwillingness to pay taxes suggests an exalted level of public spirit, and that is an impression Mercier is anxious to convey. The revolution he would like to see is a revolution in thoughts and attitudes.

But coercion by consensus has a darker side. The guide tells the narrator that the kingdom has the benefits of a free press. But in the street, they pass a man wearing a mask, evidently not for fun. The guide explains that he has written a book judged to be "immoral," and so, in keeping with unanimous custom, he has to wear an emblem of shame. The sight of this branded deviationist is followed by disclosures about literature in general and studies in general. Every citizen—presumably, every male citizen—is required, at a certain age, to write a memoir of his life and opinions. This requirement would mean, in practice, that no one is genuinely free at all: if a citizen's compulsory memoir showed signs of dissent, the outraged public would stigmatize him as an immoral writer.

Worse is to come as the real nature of the ideological basis emerges more clearly. It turns out that France's Golden Age was inaugurated by a wholesale burning of books. Apart from a few approved classics, the contents of the libraries went up in flames as superfluous. A special government department made shortened versions of the doomed volumes, or some of them, but even these were "corrected according to the true principles of morality." In other words, they were rewritten to suit the philosophy approved by the State.

The list of important books that survived is amusing. Several authors in ancient Greece have come through, but not Herodotus, most definitely not Sappho, and not "the vile Aristophanes." England is represented by Shakespeare, Milton, Pope, Young, and Richardson, an impeccable list of eighteenth-century choices. Tasso, Corneille, Racine, and Molière still exist, but their critics don't: an author who is admitted at all is apparently perfect and exempt from criticism. Strangely perhaps, in view of Voltaire's importance in preparing the way for the real Revolution, most of his works were consigned to the flames as "shallow." Rousseau, Mercier's principal mentor, is intact.

Education is even more drastically reduced than the list might suggest. Greek and Latin studies have gone: the ancient authors whom "morality" tolerates are read only in authorized translations. Four foreign languages are taught (Italian, English, German, and Spanish), but they are not compulsory. Besides learning the proper use of their own language, students absorb a little history from approved textbooks but not very much, because historical events haven't usually happened in an edifying way. When they reach years of discretion they are "permitted" to read poetry; the inference is that they are somehow prevented from reading it before.

The gaps in the curriculum are filled by science, principally applied science. One of the chief duties of the rich and the king himself is to patronize it. Recent inventions include malleable glass, inextinguishable lamps, and "the art of liquefying stones." Behind these endeavors is a gospel of work. "For us," says the guide, "the plough, the shuttle, and the hammer are become more brilliant objects than the sceptre, the diadem, and the imperial robe." He does not speak of tractors or power looms. Technologically, very little has happened in all this time. Mercier fails to envisage anything like the Industrial Revolution, and the research he describes is concerned mostly with handicrafts and amenities. He has no solution for the social and political problems created by an industrial working class because no industrial working class has entered into his calculations.

Beyond the consensus that he makes so much of—which is, in fact, consensus by mental impoverishment—there is no supernatural mystique. However, he does not take the leap into atheism. In the Europe of his day, that is still exceptional. Some anomalies result. He loathes organized religion, and there are no churches in 2440, but he provides for a pope of sorts in Rome who spends his time perfecting a "catechism of reason" and sending out encyclicals on "the sublimity of virtue" and other forbidding topics. The ghost of religion lingers in other ways. Mercier regards God as too sublime to think about, but, since God exists, he invents a kind of confirmation ceremony for adolescents: they are made to look through a telescope and a microscope, and the vastness of the universe teaches them to believe in its Creator. This appeal to youthful emotions is not an emancipation from theology, it is simply bad theology, and it cuts both ways. Not long after Mercier's time, contemplation of the vastness of the universe began to promote atheism, as in Shelley's *Queen Mab*. Mercier imagines that sublimity is an argument. The citizens of his idealized France also believe in reincarnation, for no better reason than that this too is supposed to be sublime. A reader may wonder whether such woolly-mindedness could have endured alongside such rationality for several hundred years.

To do Mercier justice, he does allow for the kind of devotion that draws men and women into the full religious life. He diverts it. Monasteries and convents have long since been dissolved, but there is an order of volunteers sworn to public service, chiefly to help in emergencies and assist in useful projects. The State canonizes the best of them.

In this respect, as in others, Mercier bases the ethics of the future on the love of one's country and fellow citizens. He has no notion of the upheavals that will be caused in the real world by industrialization, nationalism, and other forces. It would be unreasonable to criticize him for not foreseeing what very few did foresee. A more culpable shortcoming is the utter blandness of the whole program. He simply takes it for granted that when people become moral, rational, and sensible, and have a constitutional government, everything will run smoothly forever. Not only does he fail to anticipate any difficulty in reaching that point, he fails to realize the impossibility of stopping the process of political change once it has begun. He admires Cromwell, yet he draws no lessons from the sequel of the king's execution, the instability and unpopularity of the Commonwealth, and the revulsion that destroyed it after barely more than a decade. As for France, revolutionary extremism and internal strife are not perils that occur to him, and anything like the Reign of Terror, with its thousands of guillotined victims, is beyond his ken—even though Robespierre was himself a disciple of Rousseau.

This attitude, however wishful, was typical of educated people in his era. A facile optimism about the approaching French Revolution was normal among the intelligentsia who expected it, even though many hoped for more expansiveness and excitement than *L'An 2440* foreshadowed. One reason why this book went through twenty-five editions was that it answered to a prevailing mood. The fact has a bearing on the much-debated prophecy of a contemporary of Mercier, Jacques Cazotte, who did see the Terror coming and whose uniqueness or near-uniqueness in doing so has been cited as evidence for paranormal prevision.

See also: Cazotte, Jacques; Chesterton, Gilbert Keith; Morris, William; Wells, H. G.

Further Reading
Carey, John, ed. *The Faber Book of Utopias.* London: Faber and Faber, 1999.

MERLIN
Legendary British seer and magician whose supposed prophecies in the Middle Ages enlarged European ideas about prophecy in general.

Merlin makes his literary debut in the Latin writings of Geoffrey of Monmouth, a cleric from Wales who was teaching at Oxford between 1129 and 1151. He was interested in Welsh traditions, especially some that concerned a seer known as Myrddin. "Myrddin" seems to have been a sobriquet for a man more authentically called Lailoken, who

lived toward the end of the sixth century A.D. in Cumbria, now part of northern England but then still inhabited by people akin to the Welsh. He is said to have been driven out of his mind by a vision, caused by the horrors of a battle for which he bore some of the responsibility. He wandered in Scotland as an inspired madman, gifted or cursed with second sight.

Geoffrey, at the start of his literary activities, knew very little about this northerner. But in the middle 1130s, he published a series of cryptic prognostications that he claimed were prophecies by "Merlin," which was his modification of "Myrddin." A few were from Welsh bardic tradition, the vast majority were probably invented by Geoffrey himself. Meanwhile, he was working on a highly imaginative *History of the Kings of Britain,* completed soon afterward, which became one of the most influential books of the Middle Ages chiefly, though not solely, because it established King Arthur as a quasi-historical monarch. Geoffrey brought Merlin into this as a character and incorporated the "prophecies." Later, he wrote a third book, *The Life of Merlin,* adapting further stories that he had learned in the interval.

In the *History,* Geoffrey confuses matters by blurring chronology and identifying Merlin with an earlier seer, Ambrosius, who was supposed to have lived in the first half of the fifth century, soon after Britain's separation from the Roman Empire. This may have been due to sheer ignorance, but an explanation may lie in myths of an older Myrddin who was a Celtic god of inspiration. Anyone under his influence would have been an inspired person, a Myrddin-man or -woman, or simply a Myrddin. Legend could have told of several, with the northerner Lailoken counted as one and the fifth-century Ambrosius as another, and Geoffrey, lacking the key, could have blended them into a single character. His Merlin prophesies under the influence of a controlling spirit, dimly reminiscent, perhaps, of the god.

A Victorian painting illustrating Merlin's downfall in medieval romance. Obsessed with Nimue, he foresees that his love will be fatal, yet is powerless to save himself. (Victoria & Albert Museum, London/Art Resource)

However that may be, in Geoffrey's *History*, Merlin is a composite figure living in the fifth century and based on the Welsh legend of Ambrosius, though his prophesying owes a debt to the utterances of the northerner. He comes on the scene in a crisis when a British king, Vortigern, has allowed heathen Saxons to settle in the country and they have gotten out of hand. Vortigern is trying to build a fortress in Snowdonia in northwest Wales, and the walls keep collapsing. His soothsayers tell him he must find a boy without a father, kill him, and sprinkle his blood on the foundations. Merlin is found at Carmarthen, a teenager whose mother says she was impregnated by a spiritual being, so that he has no father humanly speaking. Brought to the building site as a sacrifice, he outwits the soothsayers and survives. This is where Geoffrey inserts the "prophecies" already published, explaining that Merlin uttered them in the presence of Vortigern and under the influence of his controlling spirit.

Merlin laments the Saxon ravagings but foretells that a British leader symbolized as "the Boar of Cornwall" will put a stop to them. Here is the first announcement of Arthur, who, at this point in the *History*, is to appear fairly soon but not quite yet. Merlin goes on at considerable length, predicting many happenings that are obscure and some that are recognizable, such as a couple concerning the English king Henry I. These, of course, are prophecy after the event, since the speaker is really Geoffrey in the twelfth century, who obviously knows the facts as a matter of history. But Merlin does not stop there. He goes on for several more pages, foretelling things that are actually in the future for his author.

As a swiftly grown adult, Merlin appears further on in the *History*. He uses secret arts to transplant Stonehenge from what is said to have been its original site in Ireland. He uses other secret arts to bring about the begetting of Arthur at Tintagel, a rather scandalous episode. In the Arthurian romances that were composed later, he is the king's adviser, gets Excalibur for him, and otherwise supports his regime. But the "Prophecies of Merlin" in Geoffrey's *History* acquired a fame of their own, only tenuously related to Merlin's other activities.

One reason was that many medieval readers supposed them to be authentic. Geoffrey's account of them was taken at face value: a real Merlin had uttered them in the fifth century. Since he had mentioned (for instance) Henry I, he must have been a true and inspired seer. He had sound credentials, therefore it was to be expected that at least some of his later predictions would also be valid.

This was an inference that led to many perplexities and much wasted labor. The post-Geoffrey prophecies—that is, those that really look to the future—take up ten pages in a standard translation. They do include one that has a genuine Welsh pedigree, a forecast that the name "Britain," long eclipsed by "England," will again be the accepted one. This had a limited fulfillment in 1603 when James VI of Scotland became James I of England as well and took to calling his combined realm "Great Britain," though the name was slow to come into general use and "England" was not displaced. The other prophecies are a bizarre medley. Some are topographical and comprehensible if unlikely: the English Channel, for instance, is to become so narrow that people will converse across it. Many more are about symbolic animals, giants, and other unexplained beings. They sometimes look as if they ought to make sense rather as old-style political cartoons make sense, with their American eagles, Russian bears, and so forth, but Geoffrey supplies no key.

Here is a sample bringing together several of the animals:

> The Fox will come down from the mountains and will metamorphose itself into a Wolf. Under the pretense of holding a conference with the Boar, it will approach that animal craftily and eat it up. Then the Fox will change itself into a Boar and stand waiting for its brothers, pretending that it, too, has lost some of its members. As soon as they come it will kill them with its tusk without a moment's delay and then have itself crowned with a Lion's head.

After a great deal of this sort of thing, Merlin foretells an upheaval in the sky, with constellations and planets in confusion. Floods and storms follow, and the story breaks off abruptly with no proper conclusion.

When Geoffrey was dead and could no longer be consulted, the prophecies were circulated widely in manuscript. Merlin's admirers seem to have assumed that if they found him hard to understand, it was their own fault rather than his; the meaning was there. Scholars wrote commentaries trying to apply the prophecies to actual persons and events. They were translated into Welsh, French, Dutch, and other languages. In Italy, Merlin was ranked with the Sibyls and even with Isaiah. French and Spanish authors gave spurious prestige to prophecies of their own by pretending they were the work of Merlin.

François Rabelais was disrespectful. In his *Gargantua* (1534), when a bronze plate is dug up with riddling verses engraved on it, one of the characters claims to find a message in them, but another says: "The style is like Merlin the Prophet. You can read all the allegorical and serious meanings into it that you like, and dream on about it, you and all the world, as much as ever you will."

Nevertheless, the fascination with Merlin persisted. Attempted interpretation has survived into modern times, as in R. J. Stewart's *The Prophetic Vision of Merlin* (1986). Besides interpretation, the Merlin matter was added to. Edmund Spenser's allegorical poem *The Faerie Queene* (1590–1596) brings Merlin into the narrative foretelling events in other portions of Geoffrey's *History,* and subsequent ones. More prophecies were fathered on him; Shakespeare invents one in *King Lear* as a joke. Another concerned a rock off the Cornish coast at Mousehole, named after the prophet:

There shall land on the rock of Merlin
Those who shall burn Paul, Penzance
   and Newlyn.

This was "fulfilled" in 1595 when Spanish raiders landed at Mousehole and set fire to neighboring villages, but there is no proof that the verse was current before the raid. In the seventeenth century, two dramatists, William Rowley and Thomas Heywood, kept interest in Merlin alive and concocted more prophecies. The astrologer William Lilly (1602–1681) published predictions of his own under the pseudonym Merlinus Anglicus Junior. Another astrologer, John Partridge (1644–1715), called himself Merlinus Liberatus until he was ridiculed into silence by Jonathan Swift.

Why did Geoffrey of Monmouth go to so much trouble both to compose the prophecies and to work them into his *History?* Perhaps only because he needed to build Merlin up for his role as a magical sponsor of King Arthur. He made Merlin a unique figure, an eloquent British seer, and thus gave Arthur a flying start. There may have been no more to it than that. But his work, however contrived, however bogus, had an enduring and important impact. No one had done anything quite like it before, and it extended the range of prophecy in medieval Christendom.

First, it gave a new respectability to prophecy that had no basis in divine inspiration—that is, in a Christian sense. Saint Augustine had argued that this was dangerous because it might be a product of diabolic deception. His view now became less influential. Merlin was neither a biblical prophet nor a saint, yet he was surely acceptable, and so might others be. Secondly, the potential subject matter of prophecy was vastly enlarged. Christian prophecy, as in the Pseudo-Sibylline literature, had hitherto kept close to approved doctrine and been virtually confined to speculation about the last days and the end of the world. Geoffrey might be hard to decipher, but he was certainly not concerned with these things; he made Merlin deal, apparently, with all sorts of topics— public events, conflicts, plagues, natural upheavals—spread over an indefinite timescale and not leading up to doomsday. Given that precedent, it became permissible to predict anything at any time. Innumerable soothsayers, psychics, astrologers, and eccentrics are still doing it.

See also: Arthur, King; Augustine, Saint; Lilly, William; Partridge, John; Sibyls and Sibylline Texts

Further Reading

Ashe, Geoffrey. *The Book of Prophecy*. London: Blandford, 1999.

Geoffrey of Monmouth. *The History of the Kings of Britain*. Translated by Lewis Thorpe. Harmondsworth, England: Penguin Books, 1966.

Folklore, Myths and Legends of Britain. London: Readers Digest Association, 1973.

Loomis, Roger Sherman, ed. *Arthurian Literature in the Middle Ages*. Oxford: Clarendon Press, 1959.

MESSIAH

A supreme leader and liberator in Jewish prophecy, whom God is to send to his Chosen People.

Messiah means someone who is anointed. The word's original reference was to the anointing of an Israelite king, such as David (1 Samuel 16:13), or a high priest in the Temple. In the second portion of Isaiah (45:1), the word is used metaphorically to mean a man appointed by God for a great purpose. This is its only occurrence with such a meaning in the Old Testament, and the "Messiah" referred to here is not an Israelite but a Gentile, the Persian king Cyrus. He has been divinely called to overthrow Babylon, set free the captive Jews, and enable them to return to the Promised Land. The prophet foretells that a reestablished Israel, with its unique knowledge of the One God, will enlighten the world.

The actual sequel was anticlimactic. Many Jews did not return at all. Those who did return built a new Temple in Jerusalem, and their descendants survived under Persian rulers and then under successors of Alexander. Their peace was interrupted in 167 B.C.

when the Syrian king Antiochus began a violent persecution. A revolt led by Judas Maccabeus and his brothers ended the persecution and created a new Jewish state, which was briefly promising, but struggled on with declining fortunes and was swallowed up by Rome. Out of these vicissitudes, a new messianic concept arose.

The situation, it was felt, did not make sense. The Jews were God's Chosen, they had been promised an everlasting kingdom, they were called to proclaim his truth among the Gentiles—yet the dawn, two dawns, in fact, had turned out to be false. History was going nowhere, and the Maccabean kingdom had fizzled out. In this perplexity, new prophecies took shape foreshadowing a new Messiah, a strictly Jewish one, a prince of the house of David who would be Israel's final deliverer. More and more came to be expected of him. He would set up his kingdom in the Holy Land, he would gather the dispersed Jewish people there, he would "shatter unrighteous rulers," and he would make God's Chosen People supreme in the world. He would find the Lost Tribes of Israel deported long ago by the Assyrians, and he would regraft them, purified, on to the main Jewish stock. His reign would be a golden age, with the knowledge of the Lord propagated everywhere.

Some dissented. They argued that while the Messiah might be a ruler of unrivaled wisdom and holiness, he could hardly be a warrior too because he would have to stop fighting on the Sabbath and his opponents would take advantage of his inactivity. But in the first century A.D., popular resentment against the dominance of Rome in Judea made the militant view paramount. First and foremost, the Messiah would win national independence.

Christianity, at that time a sect within Judaism, led its converts in another direction. *Christos* is the Greek equivalent of *Messiah*. Many who saw Jesus in the prophesied role undoubtedly expected him to "restore the kingdom to Israel," and even close followers did not give up hope until the last moment

The birth of Jesus, seen as fulfilling the prophecy of the Messiah, with the Star of Bethlehem guiding the Magi. (Ann Ronan Picture Library)

(Acts 1:6). His triumphal entry into Jerusalem seemed to threaten a rebellion, and the authorities put him to death as a bogus "King of the Jews." He had said, however, that his kingdom was not of this world, and Christians learned to interpret his messiahship in a different, spiritual sense. The Church broke away from Judaism and became mainly gentile.

In the main Jewish body, the nationalistic hope persisted and led to disaster. A rising against Rome, futile on any rational calculation, was sustained, in part, by a notion that the rebels could force God's hand. If his people were in such an extremity, he would surely send the Messiah to save them. No Messiah appeared, Jerusalem endured an appalling siege, and in A.D. 70, the Romans laid it waste and destroyed the Temple. By an odd irony, the Roman commander Vespasian and his son Titus had a vague awareness of messianic prophecy. They had heard the rumor that "men coming from Judea" would rule the world, and exploited it themselves in a bid for power that led to their both becoming emperors.

With the Temple gone, Judaism was dominated by the rabbis who governed its local congregations. Sixty years after Jerusalem's fall, one of the best and wisest of them, Akiba ben Joseph, proclaimed that the Messiah had arrived at last. He was Simeon ben Koseba. Akiba invoked a prophecy spoken by Balaam in the book of Numbers (24:17): "I see him, but not now; I behold him, but not nigh; a star shall come forth out of Jacob, and a sceptre shall rise out of Israel." *Koseba* sounded like *kochba,* meaning a star, so Akiba's Messiah was the Son of a Star. Despite widespread misgivings, Akiba anointed Simeon as king in 132 to take the lead in a revolt that was already rumbling. But even with a Messiah, the second revolt was no more successful than the first. After its collapse, the emperor Hadrian rebuilt Jerusalem as a pagan town under the name Aelia Capitolina.

While Jews, now uprooted and scattered everywhere, still expected the real Messiah, a mood of caution set in, and speculation about him was discouraged. A curious theory was that he had been born centuries before, on the day when the Babylonians burned the first Temple, but God had chosen to wait before revealing him. To wait how long? There was no telling. A famous rabbi, Johanan ben Zakkai, was quoted as having said: "If you are engaged in planting and are suddenly informed that the Messiah has arrived, finish with your planting first, and then go to greet him." A renewed excitement around the year 500 produced one or two minor pretenders, but no serious disturbance occurred. Gradually, oppression and persecution inspired a belief in the "birth-pangs of the Messiah." He would come only when Jews had reached a nadir of suffering, a darkest hour before dawn.

Nevertheless, a self-styled Messiah caused a considerable stir in the seventeenth century. Sabbatai Zevi was born at Smyrna, now Ismir. Adopting predictions made by contemporary Jewish mystics, he said he would restore the Kingdom of Israel in Palestine in 1666. In several countries, he promised the Jews who lived there that the rigor of the Law would be superseded. The movement that grew around him was lighthearted, uninhibited, and extremely popular. His charisma was such that even Christians began to think he might be what he professed. In the crucial year, however, the Turkish sultan had him imprisoned and threatened him with death. To save himself, he ingloriously embraced Islam.

Though Sabbatai was discredited, his mystical rebellion against orthodoxy had a lasting effect, especially in eastern Europe. Some modern exponents of Judaism have rejected the traditional view of the Messiah as a person and made him symbolic. Messianic prophecy, they suggest, is fulfilled in the influence of Judaism through the monotheistic systems that have stemmed from it, Christianity and Islam, and in the contributions of great Jewish individuals to the world. Jewish converts to Christianity can resolve this personal-impersonal issue by their acceptance that Jesus actually was the Messiah: he lives on through his multiple impact, and no other person need be looked for.

Orthodox Jews have not abandoned the hope of a literal Messiah, though the more grandiose conception of him is no longer favored. The twentieth century brought a problem with the success of Zionism and the foundation of the state of Israel. The return of Jews to the Promised Land was an impressive fulfillment of biblical prophecy, yet some would say that the repatriation was properly a task for the Messiah. On this view, the secular and political return has been wrong, and while many Orthodox live in Israel, the more thoroughgoing cannot, strictly speaking, recognize the state.

The term *Messiah* can be applied by analogy to figures in other religions who are, in some degree, comparable: to Kalki, the tenth avatar of Vishnu; to Maitreya, the Buddha who is to come; and to the Islamic Mahdi. However, there is no true parallel.

See also: Kalki; Mahdi; Maitreya; Promised Land; Sabbatai Zevi

Further Reading

Ashe, Geoffrey. *The Land and the Book.* London: Collins, 1965.

Brown R. E., J. A. Fitzmyer, and R. E. Murphy, eds. *The New Jerome Biblical Commentary.* Englewood Cliffs, NJ: Prentice-Hall, 1990.

Jewish Encyclopaedia. Article "Messiah." New York and London: Funk & Wagnalls, 1901–1906.

MICAH (C. 742–687 B.C.?)

Old Testament prophet regarded as predicting the birthplace of Jesus.

Micah, a younger contemporary of Isaiah, is to some extent a continuator and echoes him. Micah's voice is definitely heard in the first three chapters of his book; after that, it becomes intermittent. Micah presents himself as a native of Moresheth, in the southern Israelite kingdom of Judah. Like the earlier prophet Amos, he denounces injustice and exploitation. He condemns the hollowness of the official cult with its rituals and sacrifices, insisting that these are futile without righteous conduct. But although his anticipations for the near future are ominous, he foretells an eventual good time, an era of peace. The God of Israel will be acknowledged by other nations, and Gentiles will come to Jerusalem seeking wisdom, though they will keep their own gods.

Judah's kings traced their ancestry back to David, and it was a constant belief that his line would never fail. Sooner or later, the Israelites would attain their peace under a great king descended from him. David was born at Bethlehem, and Micah conveys the Lord's pronouncement that the future king will also be born there (Micah 5:2–4):

But you, O Bethlehem Ephrathah,
who are little to be among the clans of Judah,
from you shall come forth for me
one who is to be ruler in Israel,
whose origin is from of old,
from ancient days . . .
And he shall stand and feed his flock in the strength of the Lord,
in the majesty of the name of the Lord his God,
And they shall dwell secure, for now he shall be great
to the ends of the earth.

The phrase "from of old, from ancient days" may refer to divine preordination or to the long royal line originating in David.

Micah is not quite foreshadowing the later hope of the Messiah. In the New Testament, however, we find his text being taken thus in the time of King Herod. Herod asks (Matthew 2:3–6) where the Christ—that is, the Messiah—is to be born. The priests and scribes tell him, "In Bethlehem," quoting Micah. Matthew and Luke say that Jesus was indeed born there.

John (7:41–42) gives a backhanded confirmation that Micah's prophecy really was understood in that sense. Doubters cite it *against* Jesus's messianic claims because they only know him as a Galilean: "Is the Christ to come from Galilee? Has not the scripture said that the Christ is descended from David, and comes from Bethlehem, the village where David was?"

John is the latest of the four gospels. But its author may be noting an objection to Jesus' messiahship that actually was made in his lifetime, and if so, the expectation of the Bethlehem birth was well entrenched, Micah's prophecy had indeed come to be read as messianic, and Christians could claim that the birth at Bethlehem fulfilled it and helped to establish who Jesus was. A skeptic, of course, is free to argue that the birth at Bethlehem is fictitious and was invented to fit the prophecy.

See also: Biblical Prophecy (1)—Israelite and Jewish; Biblical Prophecy (2)—Christian

Further Reading

Brown R. E., J. A. Fitzmyer, and R. E. Murphy, eds. *The New Jerome Biblical Commentary.* Englewood Cliffs, NJ: Prentice-Hall, 1990.

MILTON, JOHN (1608–1674)

English poet whose epic *Paradise Lost* seems to anticipate knowledge not yet available in his time.

Milton's ambition from an early age was to compose a major work: an epic or a poetic drama. He considered several subjects, including King Arthur. His literary career was interrupted by the English Civil War. Having Puritan sympathies, he supported Parliament against Charles I, wrote controversial pamphlets, and held a post in Oliver Cromwell's government. In 1660, the restoration of the monarchy drove him back into private life. By now, he had dropped King Arthur as a subject, perhaps partly because his unrepentant republicanism was inconsistent with a royalist theme. He decided, instead, on a topic better suited to his wide reading and religious convictions—the biblical story of Creation and the Fall of Adam and Eve through Satan's wiles. An early draft shows him still weighing the possibilities of drama, but the epic form was his final choice.

Paradise Lost expands the narrative in the first chapters of Genesis, plus later extensions of it in Jewish and Christian tradition. Though Genesis is far from being a mere rehash of pagan matter, it has an underlying myth, which is Babylonian and is to be found in a Creation Epic probably dating from the second millennium B.C. This is named from its opening words *Enuma elish,* or "When on high." Its role in the more remote origins of the biblical story and of all the elaborations, including those by Milton himself, is of crucial importance. Inscribed on clay tablets, it was lost after Babylon's decline and rested in oblivion until fragments were dug up in a number of sites and fitted together, a process that began in 1876 and was not completed for several decades.

Modern reconstruction shows that at least a part of it must still have been known in the Middle East when Hebrew mythology was taking shape, since Genesis adapts this. However, it has much more in it besides the actual account of Creation, and the rest gives rise to problems and, in Milton's work, a paradox.

Enuma elish starts before the birth of the world, introducing a vast primordial female being, a sort of dragon or water monster, called Tiamat. She has a consort, Apsu, and through their mingling, the gods are formed. Apsu takes a dislike to them and presses Tiamat to concur in a plan for destroying them. The chief god Ea, the All-Wise, strikes first and kills Apsu. He begets a son named Marduk and endows him with a "double godhead." Some gods who resent Marduk approach Tiamat, and at their instigation, being already vengeful and malignant, she generates an army of demons and prepares for war. The gods loyal to Ea decide that Marduk shall lead them, and they pledge their allegiance. He wins the victory virtually single-handedly. Riding a fearsome chariot and wielding divine weapons, he distends Tiamat with a blast of wind through her mouth and shoots an arrow into her, with fatal effect.

It is only after all this that Creation begins. Having subdued Tiamat's supporters, Marduk surveys her huge recumbent corpse, splits it with a horizontal slash, and separates the upper part from the lower. The upper part becomes the sky, and he attaches the celestial bodies to it. The lower part becomes the flat Earth. Aided by his father Ea, Marduk makes the first humans out of the blood of Tiamat's army commander. The gods hail him as "the Son, our avenger."

Genesis is almost solely concerned with the passage about Creation that follows his

John Milton, the great English poet whose biblical epic Paradise Lost *raises puzzling questions about his sources outside the Bible. (Ann Ronan Picture Library)*

victory. Saying nothing of the preliminaries and elder beings, the Hebrew author goes directly to the world-making. Marduk's creative work is now assigned to the solitary Lord God, a fundamental change of concept. Tiamat survives only impersonally, as the dark primeval waters of chaos that he brings under his domination. Like Marduk, he separates Above and Below, though these too are impersonal, Sky and Earth. Like Marduk also, he makes human beings at the end.

That is as far as the Bible goes. However, in later times, more of the Babylonian motifs creep back in Jewish and Christian mythology. While the gods cannot reappear as such, the heavenly company of angels takes their place; God remains totally supreme, but he is no longer alone. Tiamat, the enemy, returns with a change of gender as Satan, the archangel who opposes God and assembles his own angelic following. The Babylonian conflict takes a new form: there is a War in Heaven, and Satan is vanquished and expelled with his host. In the New Testament, Revelation 12:7–9 recalls this event. Here, Satan is a dragon—the original image of Tiamat is not effaced—and the archangel Michael, with the loyal angels, defeats him. The Babylonian victory of gods over demons has made its way, disguised, into Judaism and Christianity. It cannot have done so by direct influence because *Enuma elish* was buried (literally) before this added mythology took shape. Vague ancestral themes from it were doubtless drifting about in the Middle East, especially among the Persians, who played a part at some stage.

But vague ancestral themes, which would have faded out before Milton's time, cannot explain the further steps he takes on his own, when he handles this material in *Paradise Lost* as prologue to the fallen Satan's corruption of humanity. A large part of the epic is taken up with an account of the War in Heaven, its causes, and its outcome, which is given by the archangel Raphael to Adam. And here, while Milton is fully aware of Scripture and

tradition, he breaks away, radically and mysteriously. He seems to be reconstituting *Enuma elish* in unprecedented detail. Since it was unknown, this, on the face of it, would mean anticipating its rediscovery in the Middle East and its translation into English, which did not happen until more than 200 years later.

His departure from Christian norms is not confined to his poetry. He spells it out in all seriousness in *Christian Doctrine,* a prose treatise that lay forgotten in manuscript until 1823. Discussing the War in Heaven, he cites Revelation 12 and accepts that Michael was the leader of the good angels and Satan's chief antagonist. But, enlarging on the subject in his own way, he explicitly defies the Bible. Michael, he maintains, did not defeat Satan's host or expel him from Heaven. "Their respective forces were drawn up in battle array and separated after a fairly even fight." It was the Son of God, afterwards incarnate as Jesus Christ, who vanquished the enemy. In *Christian Doctrine,* Milton claims to be basing everything he says on scriptural texts, and in general, he does, but here, he emphatically does not. Revelation 12 gives no hint of a "fairly even fight" between the angelic armies, or a pause, or an intervention by God's Son. Nor does any other biblical passage. Yet Milton means it: this is precisely the story that he makes Raphael tell, in the fifth and sixth books of *Paradise Lost*.

His reason is theological. As *Christian Doctrine* shows, he has ideas of his own about the Son of God. In Christian orthodoxy, the Son is the Second Person of the Trinity, coeternal and coequal with the Father. Milton, however, thinks God the Father created him, then promoted him in a series of steps that he calls "begettings," over a long period. One of the steps, before the universe came into being, was an empowerment in Heaven that provoked Satan's rebellion. This led to the Son's overthrowing the archrebel and casting him out with all his host, after Michael and the loyal angels had failed.

Milton's new myth obviously parallels *Enuma elish*, where the defeat of Tiamat and the forces of evil is the work of Marduk—Marduk, who is actually called "the Son." The parallel might be dismissed as a coincidence, but it does not end there. Textual comparison reveals a series of places in which the Babylonian epic, inaccessible to the author of the English one, seems nevertheless to be affecting it—against all temporal logic.

Babylon's chief god Ea invests his son Marduk with full divinity, and Marduk's power is confirmed by an assembly of other gods. "From this day unchangeable shall be thy pronouncement / To raise or bring low—these shall be in thy hand."

God the Father, Raphael tells Adam, summoned the angels to a New Year's ceremony and presented his Son to them in a fresh, authoritative role. The scene is not only without precedent in orthodox Christian tradition but at odds with it.

"This day I have begot whom I declare
My onely son, and on this holy Hill
Him have anointed, whom ye now
    behold
At my right hand; your Head I him
    appoint;
And by my Self have sworn to him shall
    bow
All knees in Heav'n, and shall confess
    him Lord."

Just as some of the Babylonian gods refuse to accept Marduk in his exaltation and rebel with Tiamat, so, in Raphael's narrative, some of the angels—one-third of them—refuse to accept the exalted Son and rebel with Satan. His army battles with the angels loyal to God, led by Michael, and despite the loyalists' two-to-one advantage, the conflict remains the "fairly even fight" of the *Christian Doctrine* passage.

Now the parallelism goes farther. As Tiamat's defeat is to be the work of the Son of Ea, so Satan's is to be the work of the Son of God. Marduk's supporters prepare him for his attack on the monster and her followers with arms and exhortations:

They gave him matchless weapons to
    ward off the foes:
"Go and cut off the life of Tiamat,
May the winds bear her blood to places
    undisclosed."

God the Father arms and exhorts his Son at the corresponding point:

"Go then thou Mightiest in thy Fathers
    might,
Ascend my Chariot, guide the rapid
    Wheeles
That shake Heav'ns basis, bring forth all
    my Warr,
My Bow and Thunder, my Almightie
    Arms
Gird on, and Sword upon thy puissant
    Thigh;
Pursue these Sons of Darkness, drive
    them out
From all Heav'ns bounds into the utter
    Deep."

Marduk prepares for battle:

Bow and quiver he hung at his side,
In front of him he set the lightning,
With a blazing flame he filled his
    body . . .
He then made a net to enfold Tiamat
    therein.
The Lord raised up a flood-storm, his
    mighty weapon.
He mounted the storm-chariot
    irresistible and terrifying.
He harnessed and yoked to it a team-of-
    four,
The Killer, the Relentless, the Trampler,
    the Swift . . .
For a cloak he was wrapped in an
    armour of terror,

With his fearsome halo his head was
  turbaned.
The Lord went forth and followed his
  course,
Toward the raging Tiamat he set his
  face . . .
Then they milled about him, the gods
  milled about him.

So likewise the Son, in Milton's poem:

Forth rush'd with whirl-wind sound
The Chariot of Paternal Deitie,
Flashing thick flames, Wheele within
  Wheele undrawn,
It self instinct with Spirit, but conveyed
By four Cherubic shapes, four Faces each
Had wondrous, as with Starrs thir bodies
  all
And Wings were set with Eyes, with
  Eyes and Wheels
Of Beril, and careering Fires between . . .
Beside him hung his Bow
And Quiver with three-bolted Thunder
  stor'd . . .
Attended with ten thousand thousand
  Saints
He onward came, farr off his coming shon.

Marduk approaches Tiamat. She taunts
him, but his challenge demoralizes her:

When Tiamat heard this,
She was like one possessed, she took
  leave of her senses.
In fury Tiamat cried out aloud,
To the roots her legs shook both
  together.

Arriving on Milton's celestial battlefield,
the Son tells the loyal angels to fight no
more. He himself is the target of the rebels'
hate, and he alone will dispose of them. His
onset demoralizes them:

Hee on his impious Foes right onward
  drove,

Gloomie as Night; under his burning
  Wheeles
The stedfast Empyrean shook
  throughout,
All but the Throne it self of God. Full
  soon
Among them he arriv'd; in his right hand
Grasping ten thousand Thunders, which
  he sent
Before him, such as in thir soules infix'd
Plagues; they astonisht all resistance lost,
All courage; down thir idle weapons
  drop'd.

Marduk destroys Tiamat and casts her attendant demons into fetters. The renegade
gods who supported her try to escape, but he
captures them:

The gods, her helpers who marched at
  her side,
Trembling with terror, turned their backs
  about,
In order to save and preserve their own
  lives.
Tightly encircled, they could not escape.
He made them captives and he smashed
  their weapons.
Thrown into the net, they found
  themselves ensnared;
Placed in cells, they were filled with
  wailing;
Bearing his wrath, they were held
  imprisoned.

In *Paradise Lost,* the purpose of the Son
with the rebels is "not to destroy, but root them
out of Heav'n," which he does, casting them
into their allotted place of imprisonment.
(Satan, of course, is included; the story does not
allow him to be destroyed as Tiamat is.)

The overthrown he rais'd, and as a Heard
Of Goats or timerous flock together
  throng'd
Drove them before him Thunder-struck,
  pursu'd

With terrors and with furies to the
　　bounds
And Chrystall wall of Heav'n, which
　　op'ning wide,
Rowl'd inward, and a spacious Gap
　　disclos'd
Into the wastful Deep; the monstrous
　　sight
Strook them with horror backward, but
　　far worse
Urg'd them behind; headlong themselves
　　they threw
Down from the verge of Heav'n, Eternal
　　wrath
Burnt after them to the bottomless
　　pit . . .
Hell at last
Yawning receav'd them whole, and on
　　them clos'd,
Hell thir fit habitation fraught with fire
Unquenchable, the house of woe and
　　paine.

It must be stressed that no earlier work has
anything like this narrative. The ascription of
the victory to a militant Son of God, a
Christianized Marduk, is Milton's idea alone.
Dante refers briefly to Satan's fall with his
apostate angels, and he associates Michael
with it but does not imagine anything as
crude as a battle. Satan's expulsion at
Michael's hands is a Jewish tradition as well
as a Christian one, but it is irrelevant in both
versions, since Milton rejects it. Even in matters of detail, Christian precedents are not
easy to find. Describing the war chariot and
the beings accompanying it, Milton takes
hints from a visionary chariot in Ezekiel. But
the prophet sees this chariot in an entirely
nonmartial setting, and Jewish expositors regard its interpretation as a mystical exercise
leading to deeper knowledge of God. It
reappears in Dante and still has nothing to do
with war. Its militarization, recalling the terrible chariot of Marduk, is purely Miltonic.

If *Enuma elish* had been known in Milton's
time, there would be no problem. The paral-

lels would have been noticed years ago, and
the Babylonian epic would have been recognized as a source for this part of *Paradise Lost*.
The trouble is that it was not known and
never had been known in a language that
Milton could have understood. By his time,
the Babylonian language and script were long
since defunct; the tablets were buried and forgotten. The text would not fully reemerge or
be translated into English until the twentieth
century. Milton's use of it, if this were to be
considered as a hypothesis, would not be
prophecy exactly, but it would be something
akin, implying a similar transcendence of
time. It is *as if* the mind of the poet, who
could not have known *Enuma elish,* were in a
transtemporal rapport with the mind of
someone in the future who did. On any other
basis, it becomes difficult to explain not
merely the parallelisms but also Milton's extraordinary break with Scripture and Christian tradition that makes them possible.

See also: Dante Alighieri; Prophecy, Theories
　　of

Further Reading

Ashe, Geoffrey. *The Book of Prophecy.* London:
　　Blandford, 1999.
Milton, John. *Christian Doctrine.* Translated by
　　John Carey. In *Complete Works of John
　　Milton.* Vol. 6. New Haven, CT: Yale
　　University Press, 1973.
Pritchard, James B., ed. *Ancient Near Eastern
　　Texts Relating to the Old Testament.*
　　Princeton, NJ: Princeton University Press,
　　1955.

MONMOUTH, JAMES, DUKE OF (1649–1685)

English rebel said to have been the victim of
a prophecy resembling those that deceived
Macbeth.

He was born in Holland, an illegitimate
son of Prince Charles Stuart, afterwards King
Charles II. When his father became king, the
boy was treated with great favor, created
duke of Monmouth, and, when adult, given
official duties. From political and religious

motives, a powerful faction alleged that his parents had been secretly married, so that he was legitimate heir to the throne. Charles never admitted this and stated consistently that the heir was his own brother, also called James.

Monmouth traveled on the continent but, it is said, avoided Germany because a fortune-teller had warned him that the Rhine would be fatal to him. This prophecy figures in a tradition of his last days. On Charles's death in 1685, his brother became James II. Hoping to exploit the new monarch's unpopularity, Monmouth launched a rebellion in the West Country. He failed to win sufficient support and withdrew with his small army, poorly trained and equipped, to Westonzoyland in central Somerset. That part of the country is low-lying and requires constant drainage. The drainage ditches were called rhines, and Monmouth discovered too late that he had set up his camp by one of them, the Bussex Rhine. A royal force was on neighboring Sedgemoor. The ensuing battle became a rout; Monmouth was captured, brought to London, and executed.

The Monmouth episode seems to be glanced at in one of the more interesting verses of Nostradamus.

See also: Macbeth
Further Reading
Ashe, Geoffrey. *The Book of Prophecy.* London: Blandford, 1999.

MOORE, FRANCIS (1657–1715)

One of the last practicing English astrologers before a general downturn in the eighteenth century. In 1700, he launched an annual almanac with predictions for the coming year. This survived when few astrological publications did, and it still appears regularly as *Old Moore's Almanac.* Most of its predictions are vague, and clear fulfillments are uncommon. There have been some successes over the years with political and international happenings, but they have not been frequent enough to suggest that anything better than chance is at work.

See also: Astrology; Lilly, William; Partridge, John
Further Reading
Dictionary of National Biography (British). Article "Moore, Francis."

MORRIS, WILLIAM (1834–1896)

English poet, craftsman, publisher and Socialist; author of *News from Nowhere.*

Morris began his literary career among the Pre-Raphaelite Brotherhood of poets and painters. He wrote long narrative poems and translations, sometimes of high quality. His most lasting influence, however, was achieved, with several partners, in the sphere of design—books, furniture, textiles, and wallpaper. He significantly improved English taste.

Morris's detestation of large-scale industry and the ugliness and callousness of late-Victorian capitalism converted him to the ideology of Karl Marx. But his commitment to individual craftsmanship gave it an unusual twist, and this went with an un-Marxist romanticization of the Middle Ages, carried over from his earlier days.

The year 1888 saw the publication of Bellamy's American Utopia *Looking Backward,* a complacent picture of a future society in which a single gigantic corporation runs everything, employs (and conscripts) everybody, and delivers material comfort on the same basis for all. Morris revolted against Bellamy's ideas and wrote his own Utopia, *News from Nowhere,* which appeared in 1890. It is presented as a dream, but it was serialized in a political journal and was undoubtedly meant to be taken seriously.

The narrator wakes up one morning, or seems to wake, in his house by the Thames. Going outside, he finds everything changed. Factories have vanished, buildings are smaller, and the people he meets are colorfully

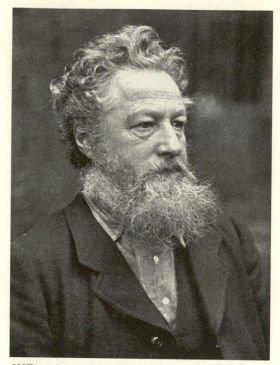

William Morris, Victorian poet, craftsman, and Socialist, author of a classic fantasy about an ideal future society. (Ann Ronan Picture Library)

dressed, good-looking, and good-humored. From a remark by one of them, he soon learns that the date is later than 2003, though he doesn't immediately find how much later. His acquaintance takes him on a horse-drawn tour of a transformed and beautiful London. Commercialism, with its repellent effects on city architecture, has long since faded away. There is, in fact, no such thing as money. People produce goods not because they are paid to but because they want to; they put them on display, shoppers take what they need, and no one takes more. Courtesy and happiness are universal or nearly so.

England has no politics or government. When collective decisions are needed, usually on local issues, they are made by small, self-regulating groups. Education is on a learn-as-you-please basis. Sexual partnerships are formed and ended by consent. Women, however, are by no means emanci-

pated. The narrator finds them attractive and flirts a little.

He explains his ignorance and curiosity by pretending to be a visitor from a distant country. However, the device wears thin, and Morris virtually gives it up when he contrives a long conversation with an old man who knows a great deal about the history of "the Change." To keep this going, the narrator has to ask the right questions, and to ask them, he has to know a great deal himself about the late nineteenth century. In this dialogue, Morris tries to outline a credible history of the future, with a working-class revolution beginning in 1952 and going on through a general strike and a two-year civil war. Since the victory of the workers and their sympathizers and the ensuing reconstruction, about 150 years have passed with no further disturbance. England has been living, to quote the book's alternative title, in "an epoch of rest."

After this episode, the narrator's friends take him on a leisurely boat trip up the Thames, rowing through an idyllic countryside to a scene of voluntary hay making. The dream dissolves at last in a church converted into a community hall (no churches are used for their original purpose).

Morris's Utopia, it must be admitted, consists largely in everyone having a sense of responsibility and being nice to everyone else. This is held to be possible because an ideally ordered society would have that result, a theory launched by Robert Owen, generally regarded as the inventor of Socialism, before Marx. The economic basis is left obscure: all the work described is craft work or agricultural work, yet the population is much the same as in Morris's time. There is no indication how such millions are supported. Machinery is just mentioned, once or twice, but not discussed, even when the narrator sees a power-driven boat. As for the activities he does describe, people work because life is arranged so that they all do work that they like doing, with diversions to prevent them from getting bored, and no further incentives are needed—another notion from a pre-Marxian Socialist, Charles Fourier.

From Marxism itself, Morris took two key ideas about the future. One was that after the revolution, there would be progress toward a society with the watchword "To each according to his needs." The other was that the state would "wither away." These would be major characteristics of a social order properly called Communist. Morris liked to imagine that it would all come about smoothly and painlessly, even quickly once the corner was turned. At the time of writing, it was still possible to hope that the revolution would have no bitter sequels and would lead more or less directly to freedom, justice, and the rest. Morris did not live to see what actually happened in Russia. He would have rejected a comparison to the medieval prophet Joachim of Fiore, yet his golden age, dawning after a clearly marked transition, is a little like Joachim's Age of the Holy Spirit.

See also: Bellamy, Edward; Joachim of Fiore

Further Reading

Carey, John, ed. *The Faber Book of Utopias.* London: Faber and Faber, 1999.

MUHAMMAD (C. 570–632)

Founder of Islam, the religion of Muslims. While it acknowledges the prophets of Israel, it exalts Muhammad himself (often spelled Mohammed) as *the* Prophet, the supreme and final messenger of divine truth, superseding all others.

He was born at Mecca in Arabia and lived the ordinary life of a merchant until he was in his thirties. Then, he began to receive what he announced as communications from Allah (his name for God), conveyed by the angel Gabriel. These were dictated to disciples, who wrote them down on leaves, bones, and other convenient objects. In due course, they were assembled and arranged to make up the Koran, Islam's sacred book. According to Muslims, its sense is bound up so closely with its phrasing and literary form that it cannot, properly speaking, be translated. The belief that Muhammad could not have composed it himself is a powerful motive for its acceptance as revelation and for his recognition as "the Prophet."

The term *prophet* is employed here in its old sense to mean simply an inspired person, not in its derivative sense to mean someone who is inspired to predict. Muhammad does not foretell anything specific that will happen after his own time. He is definite that the world will end, but he has nothing to say of future events in the interim.

Further Reading

The Encyclopedia of Islam

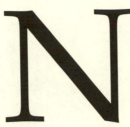

NAPOLEON (1769–1821)

Napoleon Bonaparte, emperor of France. A mystical belief in his own destiny encouraged the overconfidence that lured him into his fatal Russian campaign. He had a premonition of this that was more specific but ineffectual.

His relations with Czar Alexander I went through several phases. The czar fought against him for some years, but in 1807, they met and agreed to an alliance aimed at dominating and stabilizing Europe. The next year, they met again at Erfurt in Germany, where things did not go so smoothly. During the conference, Napoleon had what is almost his only recorded dream—an alarming one in which he was devoured by a bear. His agreement with Alexander survived for a while but eventually broke down. He invaded Russia in 1812, and "the Bear" (Russia) devoured him.

The natural explanation is that the Erfurt nightmare was due to anxiety. It was just beginning to look as if Alexander might become hostile again. However, the nightmare did not reflect any conscious concern. Napoleon was still at the height of his power, with no apprehensions of defeat, and while he often spoke of the dream afterward and tried to interpret it, he was blind to its obvious symbolism. Failing to make the Russian connection, he missed what was a sensible warning, even apart from any paranormal implication.

The dream image was like some of those that came to biblical prophets, with no meaning that they could fathom until they were given an explanation. Napoleon got no explanation. It might be thought that members of his entourage would have seen the natural one, but if any of them did, they either kept silence or were unable to convince him.

Several of the more interesting quatrains of Nostradamus can be read as applying to Napoleon.

See also: Nostradamus

Further Reading

Schom, Alan. *Napoleon Bonaparte*. New York: HarperCollins, 1997.

The French Emperor Napoleon Bonaparte, who had a dream foreshadowing a military disaster and failed to understand it. (Ann Ronan Picture Library)

NAZI GERMANY

In the years following World War I, Germany was the one major Western country where astrology was widely respected. Several of its practitioners showed insight and integrity. Hitler's ascendancy, beginning in 1933, was accompanied by predictions that were far from encouraging to him.

The wreckage of Rudolf Hess's plane, in which he flew to Britain in 1941 hoping to negotiate peace. He was influenced by astrological forecasts ominous for Germany. (Hulton-Deutsch Collection/Corbis)

As in other countries, an early impulse came from Madame Blavatsky's Theosophy. A further stimulus was the Anthroposophy taught by Rudolf Steiner, who started as a Theosophist and then moved off on his own. Like Blavatsky, he had an international following. But in Germany, additional factors were at work or were more forcefully at work than elsewhere. The interest shown by Jung gave astrology prestige. The sufferings of Germans in the war's aftermath, especially during the great inflation of 1923–1924, fostered longings for a doctrine that would make sense of life and perhaps show a better time ahead.

Astrology's chief revivalist, who had been preparing the ground for some years, was Hugo Vollrath. He was a Theosophist and also friendly with Steiner. An astrological congress at Munich in 1922 was the first of a series, and some of those who attended believed that astrology could be made an authentic science. Even as a science, it would leave room for hopes likely to be dismissed otherwise as irrational, and a number of its devotees were attracted to Nazism. As early as 1923, when Hitler made his first bid for power, an astrological writer named Rudolf von Sebottendorf was preaching the kind of nationalism he stood for. Elsbeth Ebertin, an exponent of graphology as well as astrology, was talking about a coming leader. Vollrath himself presently became an open Hitler supporter and tried to give astrology a Nazi bias.

Though Hitler was friendly with one or two of the early revivalists, he did not believe in astrology himself. A legend that he had an astrological adviser was current during World War II, but the truth is quite otherwise. Early in his dictatorship, it was already becoming clear that astrologers could be troublesome. One, Josef Schultz, foretold his eventual downfall. More specific was a horoscope of the Führer cast at about the same time by Erik Jan Hanussen, a famous if somewhat dubious clairvoyant who had been close to several leading Nazis. He was right about the date of Hitler's accession to power, but his prognostications did not stop there. He foresaw sweeping triumphs but said Hitler would be on the way out after an event described as the breaking of the "union of three." His work would vanish "in smoke and flames" in 1945.

Within a year or two of becoming chancellor, Hitler was making life difficult for astrologers. Joseph Goebbels, his propaganda chief, did not believe in astrology either, but he did employ an astrologer. He was aware that the sixteenth-century French seer Nostradamus had a substantial readership. When war broke out in September 1939, Nostradamus enthusiasts recalled one commentator's claim that he had foretold it. Goebbels saw possibilities for propaganda. He heard of a Swiss-born astrologer, Karl Ernst Krafft, who had warned of an attempt to assassinate Hitler, and put him on the payroll. Krafft's first assignment was to invent pro-German interpretations of Nostradamus's prophecies, and he gave these to the public in lectures and a new commentary. For a time, the arrangement worked, but Krafft made predictions of his own about the course of the war, and these were not slanted as his employers wished. He spoke, for instance, of a grim outlook for the winter of 1942–1943. After further indiscretions, he was imprisoned. He died on the way to a concentration camp.

Krafft's forebodings and those of Schultz and Hanussen are best seen in relation to a more elaborate prophecy that surfaces several times. It appears that on November 9, 1918,

when the kaiser abdicated and the German Republic was proclaimed, an unknown astrologer cast its horoscope and looked thirty-odd years ahead. One allusion to the contents of this horoscope is on record at the outbreak of World War II, when Georg Lucht, who saw it, was quoted as finding (appropriately) "two strong Mars directions for 1939–40." During the war, it was mentioned in conjunction with a horoscope of Hitler himself, perhaps Hanussen's or a revision of it, which was described as being in agreement.

The horoscope of Germany, supplemented by that of the Führer, seems to have been a factor in a sensational event in May 1941. Rudolf Hess, Hitler's deputy, flew to Britain without telling anyone, in the hope of negotiating peace. He had a perfectly straightforward motive: Hitler was about to launch Operation Barbarossa, the invasion of Russia, and his deputy wanted to avert a war on two fronts. But there was more. The astrological prospect led him to think that Germany had reached a zenith, and the future was liable to be downhill unless remedial action was taken. The horoscope of Hitler also suggested a peak followed by decline. Albrecht Haushofer, the son of a Nazi theorist who was one of Hess's principal mentors, said the solo mission was undertaken because Hitler's aspects were "malefic" in early May. The London *Times* alleged that Hess had actually told him so.

According to the official story, Hess had gone mad. However, the horoscope's effect on him was tacitly acknowledged. Hitler complained about Hess listening to "astrological cliques" and said "stargazers" must be silenced. On June 9, the suppression began. It was called the *Aktion Hess* and was a clampdown not only on such astrologers as were still practicing, but on a variety of occultists and spiritualists. The *Aktion Hess* betrayed a serious concern that confidence was being sapped, and rumors of a turning point during 1941 were spreading dangerously.

The astrologers were right. The turning point came early in December with the failure of Barbarossa in Russia and the involvement of the United States in the war. Furthermore, Krafft's warning about the winter of 1942–1943 was fulfilled in the disaster Germany met at Stalingrad. Hanussen's prediction about the breaking of the "union of three" could also be seen as fulfilled a few months later, when the Tripartite Alliance of Germany, Italy, and Japan was disrupted by the defection of Italy and Anglo-American forces got a foothold in Europe. His further prediction that Hitler's achievement would perish "in smoke and flames" was also moving toward fulfillment in the first months of 1945 with the aerial onslaught on German cities. This vindicated another of Krafft's unwelcome forecasts, that British bombs would hit Goebbels's Propaganda Ministry.

The long-range horoscope of Germany had been hidden away in the files of Heinrich Himmler, the chief of the SS and the Gestapo, together with the Hitler horoscope. Interpretations were filed with them. In March 1945, someone brought them to the attention of Goebbels, who may or may not have heard of them at the time of the Hess incident but had not noted or had forgotten anything subsequent. He kept a diary, and in his entry for March 29, he remarked that the horoscopes showed "some relief of our military situation" in the second half of April, followed by three bad months and an end of hostilities by mid-August. About the same time, the horoscopes were studied by other members of Hitler's entourage, including Schwerin von Krosigk, the finance minister. He, too, kept a diary. Discovered soon after the war, it says more than Goebbels's. It confirms the earlier clues to the horoscope's contents: they pointed to war in 1939, German successes until 1941, then reverses until early 1945. Von Krosigk improves the "relief" into a victory. Peace is to come in August, as Goebbels said. What is peculiarly interesting is that the German horoscope, as

summarized in this diary, went on after 1945. There were to be three difficult years, after which Germany would rise again.

A strange feature is the favorable shift during the second half of April. This, on the face of it, was a mistake. However, it was only the military interpretation that was mistaken. The shift did happen, and with profound effects. On April 13, 1945, President Roosevelt died suddenly, and Hitler hoped briefly that his death would bring the change. It did not save his regime, but it did bring the change. Roosevelt had approved a plan devised by Henry Morgenthau, his secretary of the treasury, for the postwar destruction of Germany as an industrial country. With Roosevelt's death, the presidency passed to Truman, who had a low opinion of Morgenthau. He dropped the Morgenthau plan, and German recovery became possible.

From 1945 onward, the predictions were right and in plain terms. General peace did come at mid-August, against all expectation, with the surrender of Japan. The three difficult years followed, after which the Western Allies agreed to the formation of the Federal German Republic. Its rise was rapid, and it eventually took over the eastern Communist zone.

Some of these predictions might have been improved in retrospect. However, the one about the 1941 turning point is adequately confirmed by the Hess affair and the alarmed reaction to it. The diary allusions to the last horoscope items, peace in August and German revival after three tough years, were written in spring 1945 and could not have been faked after the events. This composite performance looks like an astrological triumph. But astrologers have scored so few comparable successes that a query arises in this one case. It is out of line, an exception. It has been suggested that the astrology is a kind of camouflage for insights achieved by some other method. Such a theory would not take away from the accuracy, and it would leave the true method mysterious.

See also: Hanussen, Erik Jan; Krafft, Karl
Ernst
Further Reading
Gill, Anton. *A Dance between Flames.* London:
John Murray, 1993.
Howe, Ellic. *Urania's Children.* London:
William Kimber, 1967.
Toland, John. *Adolf Hitler.* 2 vols. New York:
Doubleday, 1976.
Trevor-Roper, Hugh. *The Last Days of Hitler.*
London: Macmillan, 1947.

NEWSPAPER ASTROLOGY

During the 1920s, astrology received a strong
impulse in the popular media from its U.S.
publicist Evangeline Adams. In August 1930,
the British *Sunday Express,* a paper aimed at
a wide public, began running astrological
items by R. H. Naylor. Like the psychic journalist Jeane Dixon, he made his name with
one good prediction, foretelling the crash of
a great airship, the R-101, that October.
From then on, he was contributing a regular
Sunday feature and was under contract to
produce weekly predictions. These were too
easily proved wrong. His record, however,
went beyond that occupational hazard and
earned him eventual immortality in print as
"the Least Successful Astrologer."

A skeptic listed some of Naylor's predictions in 1938. A few have historical interest:

General Franco will never rule Spain.
Franco, the rebel leader in the Spanish
Civil War, not only won it but remained
in power for thirty-six years.
The reunification of Ireland is imminent.
Not yet.
*A British general election on November 7 will
be won by the party in power with a small ma-
jority.*
It was not held until 1945, owing to in-
terruption by war, and it was then won by
the opposition with a large majority.
*Hitler's horoscope shows that he is not a war
maker, but he may at some point show an in-*
*terest in regaining Togoland (a small former
German colony).*
Comment seems superfluous.
War is not scheduled for 1939.
It broke out in September 1939.

In 1941, Naylor was still active: he predicted
German-Russian cooperation a few days before Germany invaded Russia.

It may or may not be fair to single Naylor
out in this way, but he was conspicuous, and
there is no evidence that other astrological
journalists did much better. They quoted a
statement of medieval origin: "The stars influence but do not compel." However, in
later years, they were less concerned with
public and verifiable facts and more concerned with individuals. They wrote
columns offering advice and forecasts for
readers born under each of the twelve signs
of the Zodiac: Aries, Taurus, and so on. Some
still do.

One effect of such minihoroscopes was
that it became more normal to know one's
sign, without necessarily caring about astrology. In the famous film *Sunset Boulevard,*
made in 1950, the middle-aged former star
asks the young man whom she entraps what
his sign is. He doesn't know. At that time, this
exchange was credible, and it made the star
look eccentric and superstitious. A few
decades later, the question would have been
ordinary, and her victim probably would
have known his sign.

See also: Adams, Evangeline; Astrology;
Dixon, Jeane
Further Reading
Pile, Stephen. *The Return of Heroic Failures.*
London: Penguin Books, 1989. (A sequel
to *The Book of Heroic Failures*)

NEWTON, ISAAC (1642–1727)

By common consent, the greatest scientist of
his time, responsible for the theory of gravita-
tion and much else besides; he is less well
known as an interpreter of biblical prophecies.

One of the greatest scientists of all time, Isaac Newton tried to interpret the biblical prophecies, sometimes applying his scientific knowledge. (Ann Ronan Picture Library)

Newton's writings in unexpected fields were not properly examined for many years after his death. He studied alchemy and worked out a new chronology of ancient history. His analysis of the prophecies was prompted, in part, by a wave of seventeenth-century interest in them. Even among scientists, a belief that the world was nearing its end, as the Bible seemed to indicate, was the rule rather than the exception. The early 1700s saw an influx into London of refugee Camisards, members of a French Protestant sect in flight from persecution; these refugees claimed direct divine inspiration and attracted some attention with apocalyptic outpourings, until their bizarre antics and utterances estranged the public. One of Newton's

few close friends, a Swiss named Fatio de Duillier, became involved with this excitement, and Newton himself took a brief interest in it.

As a prophetical interpreter, Newton follows a well-worn path by concentrating on Daniel in the Old Testament and Revelation in the New. Believing, like others, that Daniel is an authentic product of the sixth century B.C., he has no difficulty in accepting that its references to later events are predictive and divinely inspired. However, he acknowledges that in both books the authors' meaning did not become clear until after the events they foreshadowed. God's purpose in inspiring them was not that Jews and Christians should be able to foretell the future but that the fulfillments, when recognized in retrospect, should show his constant presence in history.

Newton concurs with opinions already current in the England of his day. Discussing Daniel, where great stress is laid on a dream of Nebuchadnezzar about four monarchies and on a related vision of four symbolic beasts, Newton sees this succession as supplying a basic framework for ancient history. He diverges from the author's probable intention by explaining the fourth monarchy as the Roman Empire, from which it follows that the ten horns of the corresponding beast are the barbarian kingdoms that succeeded it. An arrogant "little horn" that arises among them is identified by Newton as the Church of Rome; antipapalism is central to his version of Christianity. When Daniel introduces a mysterious period of "seventy weeks," or 490 years, he agrees with other commentators in making this lead up to Christ, as indeed it does, if the most natural method of counting is allowed.

In Revelation, considering the famous Number of the Beast, he approves the long-recognized reading "Lateinos," in which the Greek letters, given their numerical values, add up to 666. Some of his thinking is more original: it combines an ingenuity worthy of a scientific pioneer with a down-to-earth concreteness rarely found in other commentators. Chapter 9 describes a swarm of locusts (or, rather, superlocusts) with power to afflict humanity for five months. Newton is not content to make them symbolize Islamic warriors, he explains the five months by citing the life cycle of real locusts. Toward the end of Revelation, when the world has passed away and been replaced by a new heaven and a new earth, he notes that the devil and his agents are to be tormented "day and night" forever and infers that there will still be an alternation of day and night.

Newton's work on the prophecies should not be dismissed as an eccentricity. Even in scientific fields, he believed that he was not so much a discoverer as a rediscoverer, bringing truths back to light that were embodied in an "ancient wisdom." As philosophers long ago had known these things, so the Israelites, divinely taught, had learned other fundamental truths. Newton hoped to draw the traditions closer together in a unified system. While he accepted the Christian expectation of a fiery end of the world, he speculated about a comet falling into the Sun, making it so hot that Earth would burn up with all its living creatures. Science could point the same way as prophetic revelation.

See also: Camisards; Daniel; End of the World; Revelation

Further Reading

Manuel, Frank E. *A Portrait of Isaac Newton.* Cambridge, MA: Harvard University Press, 1968.

NIXON, ROBERT (?1467–1485)

The "Cheshire Prophet," said to have been born at Over Delamere in the English county of Cheshire. Reputedly, he seemed stupid, even mentally retarded, and he was very silent, but in lucid intervals he showed apparent second sight about local matters. He began his working life as a plowboy. Attracting attention by his peculiar gift, he was adopted for a time by a wealthy family, but he did not respond to attempted education and was sent back to the plow.

One day, he went into a trance in the field and spoke afterward of future historical events that had been revealed to him, beginning with the English Civil War in the 1640s. On August 22, 1485, he started shouting about a fight between Richard and Henry, which Henry won. Two days later, news was brought of the battle of Bosworth, a long way from Cheshire, which had been fought on August 22 between Richard III and Henry Tudor. Henry defeated Richard and became Henry VII.

The story goes that Henry heard about Nixon, was interested in his abilities, and employed him in the royal household. Nixon was reluctant, professing to be threatened by some mysterious doom, but he could not refuse the royal request. He obliged the king with more prophecies, including a cryptic one about an invasion by soldiers with snow on their helmets. He ate greedily and stole food from the kitchen. The infuriated cooks locked him in an empty room during Henry's absence and forgot about him. He died of starvation and dehydration.

Oral traditions about the Cheshire Prophet were handed down but seem not to have gotten into print until 1714, when John Oldmixon published a collection of them. Accounts of Cheshire's "inspired idiot" remained popular; Dickens refers to them in *The Pickwick Papers* (chapter 43).

It is odd that the events he is said to have foreseen in his trance began only in the seventeenth century. Why did he not foresee anything sooner? One theory is that he is historically misplaced and actually lived in that century; another, that he lived when he is supposed to have lived but that utterances of an unknown seventeenth-century seer were wrongly attributed to him. In any case, the absence of early documentation makes it impossible to be sure what he foretold, if anything.

Further Reading

Gould, Rupert T. *Oddities: A Book of Unexplained Facts.* London: Philip Allan, 1928.

Wallechinsky, David, Amy Wallace, and Irving Wallace. *The Book of Predictions.* New York: William Morrow, 1980.

NOSTRADAMUS (1503–1566)

French astrologer and reputed prophet, the author of numerous predictive verses for which extreme claims have often been made.

"Nostradamus" is a latinization. The seer's name was Michel de Nostredame. He was born in 1503 in a Provençal Jewish family that converted to Catholicism. A doctor by profession, he was unusually successful in caring for the sick during an outbreak of plague in southern France. However, when his wife and children succumbed to the disease, he ceased practicing for some years and wan-

The French astrologer Nostradamus, author of hundreds of cryptic predictions. Enthusiasts' claims for many of them are unjustified, but some are remarkable. (Ann Ronan Picture Library)

dered through France and Italy conferring with scholars, astrologers, and alchemists. He is said to have had a reputation for second sight or precognition, though the few anecdotes are unconvincing. In 1547, he settled at Salon in his native Provence, married again, and resumed medical practice on a part-time basis. He now had funds and leisure to pursue the studies that had come to interest him most. After issuing some not very successful astrological almanacs, he launched the much greater project that immortalized him.

He began composing rhymed quatrains making long-term predictions in cryptic language. These were grouped in sets of a hundred called Centuries (the word has nothing to do with periods of time). They were not arranged in any discernible order; he is believed to have jumbled them deliberately. They were literary productions, not spontaneous outpourings. Apparently, each one went through a rough-note stage and a Latin stage, with the rhymed four-line paraphrase in French emerging as the end product.

Nostradamus published the Centuries in installments. The first edition, comprising three Centuries and part of a fourth, came out in 1555. The second, in 1557, incorporated its predecessor and added more. He went on composing, but the final edition—ten Centuries in all, of which the seventh was incomplete—appeared only posthumously in 1568, two years after his death. There are 942 quatrains altogether.

The first edition attracted notice quickly. The quatrains were obscure, yet readers got the impression that they had a meaning if it could be worked out. Ronsard, the foremost French poet of the day, praised Nostradamus as an inspired prophet, though it was far from clear whether he had really prophesied anything. His work became known at the French court, and Queen Catherine de Medici showed interest in it. A frightful accident on June 30, 1559, tragically enhanced his fame. Despite a warning from another seer, Catherine's husband, King Henri II, insisted on riding in a tournament against a younger opponent, the Comte de Lorge, Gabriel Montgomery, captain of the Scottish Guard in the French service. Henri's visor was not securely fastened. When they clashed, Montgomery did not lower his lance enough; the wooden tip went through a little gap in Henri's visor and splintered. A large splinter pierced the king's head beside an eye. He reeled back, then slumped forward, staying on his horse until attendants lowered him down, his face covered with blood. After enduring days of agony, he died on July 12.

In the thirty-fifth quatrain of the first Century, published well before the event, Nostradamus had written the following. (The spelling here, as elsewhere, is generally modernized on the basis of the standard work on Nostradamus by Edgar Leoni.):

Le lion jeune le vieux surmontera
En champ bellique par singulier duelle:
Dans cage d'or les yeux lui crevera,
Deux classes une, puis mourir, mort
  cruelle.

The young lion will overcome the old
  one
On the field of battle in single combat:
He will put out his eyes in a cage of
  gold:
Two wounds one, then to die a cruel
  death.

Skeptics have queried the applicability of these lines to the accident. The first two are admittedly somewhat vague, and there does not seem to be any certain evidence that the visor—the "cage"—was of gold or gilded. *Classe* has to be derived, abnormally, from the Greek *klasis*, a fracture. Granted that, however, the cryptic phrase "two wounds one" is remarkable. The mortal blow of the lance caused two wounds: besides the destruction of the king's eye by the large splinter, a smaller one pierced his throat. The French court, deeply shaken, acknowledged

that Nostradamus had prophesied truly. When the news spread in Paris, he was threatened with mob violence as a sorcerer.

Passages in the Centuries show that he shared the Joachite hope for the Second Charlemagne, a great ruler who would bring universal peace, and that he may have cast Henri II in that role. After the fatal accident, he kept clear of the topic. In 1564, however, during a royal visit to Salon, he singled out a young prince who was in the party and foretold that he would be king of Navarre and then of all France. According to an early biographer, he hoped that this one would be the Second Charlemagne. The boy fulfilled his prediction by becoming Henri IV, and appropriate hopes gathered around him for a while but were extinguished by assassination.

The Centuries remained popular. New editions kept appearing, and so did commentaries and attempts to apply the quatrains to historical events. The possibilities grew with the passage of time: there was more and more history to apply them to, and apparent fulfillments in the 300 years or so after Nostradamus's death made them gradually look better. However, they are extremely puzzling. Many of them make several predictions, sometimes linked, sometimes unconnected. The French is curt and may be grammatically irregular. Traces of the previous Latin versions are occasionally embedded in them. Other languages—Greek, Provençal, Spanish—intrude. There are anagrams and near-anagrams and plain riddles.

Critics often dismiss them as being so vague, obscure, or ambiguous that it is impossible to pin down definite meanings or establish whether they have or have not been fulfilled. That is true of many but not of all. Nostradamus sometimes gives place-names and references to individuals in terms that identify them precisely. Numerous quatrains have an air of meaning something if the reader can decipher them. As a result, enthusiasts have tried to find fulfillments in hundreds of them, usually by very far-fetched interpretations. Because their researches have been spread too thinly, they have failed to focus closely enough on the quatrains that do have a respectable claim, and there are such. If the dubious or opaque majority are discarded and the interesting few are scrutinized carefully in the light of history, those few raise a serious question of prophetic foresight, however that fact should be explained.

Candidates for rejection are easily found. Here is one, the forty-eighth quatrain of the ninth Century:

La grande cité d'Océan maritime,
Environée de marais en cristal:
Dans le solstice hyemal et la prime,
Sera tentée de vent espouvantal.

The great city of the maritime Ocean,
Surrounded by a crystalline swamp:
In the winter solstice and the spring,
It will be tried by frightful wind.

One commentator has applied this to Central Park in New York City; another, to Tokyo. This disagreement might be taken as an instance of ambiguity. But the ambiguity is unreal because the lines have no evident sense at all, and neither of the invented meanings is viable. However, the text of a quatrain may be perfectly clear and still ambiguous if it has more than one application. As a hypothetical example, the prediction "a queen will be beheaded" would also have to be set aside, even though the event is uncommon: the victim might be Mary Queen of Scots or Marie Antoinette. Further identification would be required.

The irreducibly "good" quatrains may be listed as Class A. To qualify as such, a quatrain must contain at least one prediction that allows only a single interpretation; it must apply to one fact that lay in the future for Nostradamus, and only one. This bull's-eye must not be explicable by guesswork or rational foresight—not reasonably, anyhow. A famous instance of a Class A verse is found in the forty-ninth quatrain of the ninth Century:

Sénat de Londres mettront à mort leur Roi.

The Senate of London will put to death their King.

This prediction was fulfilled by the execution of Charles I in 1649, at the hands of a Parliament from which the victors in the English Civil War had excluded the moderates and royalist sympathizers. No alternative exists. The "Senate of London" has never executed another king. Ordinary foresight is out of the question; in the monarchical Europe of Nostradamus's time, such an act would have been unthinkable, and England did not even have a king when he wrote—the sovereign was either Mary or, more probably, Elizabeth I.

If a quatrain is to be admitted to Class A, different lines in it that are applicable to different future events should all "work," so that the whole of it is accounted for without loose ends. When Nostradamus scores unequivocally in one line of the four, the others may fairly be counted even if they are not quite so lucid, but they must all "work" somehow if the quatrain is to be accepted. The unique application of a Class A quatrain may arise from a single phrase, even a single word, with only one possible meaning—a meaning that is the key to the whole. Once this is recognized, the rest falls into place, quite possibly with a combined impact showing it to be equally clear and unequivocal when properly viewed. An instance is in IX.18, where the clue is very specific, a personal name.

Le lis Dauffois portera dans Nansi;
Jusqu'en Flandres Électeur de l'Empire:
Neuve obturée au grand Montmorency,
Hors lieux prouvés délivré à clere
    peyne.

The lily of the Dauphin will reach into
    Nancy;
As far as Flanders an Elector of the
    Empire:
New confinement for the great
    Montmorency,
Outside customary places delivered to
    celebrated punishment.

The third and fourth lines are the crucial ones. In 1632, one of the principal French nobles, the duc de Montmorency, was involved in a rebellion. Cardinal Richelieu, the king's chief minister, had Montmorency put in a new prison at Toulouse and beheaded, amid much publicity. Out of respect for his rank, the execution took place in a courtyard, not on the normal scaffold. No one else, not even someone else called Montmorency, would fit the prediction. The fourth line does not rhyme with the second as it should, and according to an early commentator, the irregularity is due to the fact that the executioner's name was Clerepeyne, creating a play on words that would seem beyond coincidence. This is unproved, but the statement about Montmorency is a sufficient clincher.

With that granted, the other lines can be matched to other events at no great distance in time, though the order is not quite chronological. During the decades after Nostradamus's death, the only person to have the title of dauphin and bear the French lilies in that capacity was the prince who became Louis XIII. In September 1633, he entered Nancy with an army, in the course of a campaign not relevant here. That accounts for the first line. In March 1635, the elector of Trier, in the Holy Roman Empire of Germany, was arrested by the Spanish and taken to Tervuren in Flanders. That accounts for the second line. The whole quatrain is covered.

The allusion to the execution of Charles I has the same uniqueness as the allusion to that of Montmorency. Does it open up the rest of the quatrain (IX.49)?

Gand et Bruceles marcheront contre
    Anuers;
Sénat de Londres mettront à mort leur
    Roi:
Le sel et vin lui seront à l'envers,
Pour eux avoir le regne en désarroi.

Ghent and Brussels will march against
    Antwerp;
The Senate of London will put to death
    their King:
Salt and wine will overthrow him,
Because of them to have the realm in
    confusion.

"Salt and wine" can be recognized as symbolic of taxation, a major cause of Charles's troubles with Parliament and the English Civil War, ending in his defeat and death. But what about Ghent and Brussels? Charles was beheaded in January 1649, and the previous line points to the previous year, which gives the explanation. The Spanish, who occupied these cities, had been fighting the Dutch in a sideshow of the Thirty Years' War that was devastating a large part of Europe. In 1648, as part of the peace settlement that ended it, the Spanish made concessions. One was to close the Scheldt River for the commercial benefit of Amsterdam, though this was a heavy blow to Antwerp, another of their own cities. Though not a march, it was an action by the rulers of the first two cities to the disadvantage of the third, a few months before the death of Charles; and it was the only such action ever taken in 1648 or at any other time. The first line is a military metaphor, overdramatic but well defined in its application.

In V.38 the whole quatrain refers to one individual not named but identified in the first line, after which the rest has a cumulative effect.

Ce grand monarque qu'au mort
    succédera
Donnera vie illicite et lubrique:
Par nonchalance à tous concédera,
Qu'à la parfin faudra la loi Salique.

He who will succeed that great monarch
on his death
Will lead an illicit and debauched life:
Through nonchalance he will give way
to all,
So that in the end the Salic Law will fail.

The French supplies the clincher. Only one ruler was ever called *Le Grand Monarque,* Louis XIV. Therefore, the quatrain is about his successor, Louis XV, who became king of France in 1715. His "illicit and debauched life" is notorious. The French word *nonchalance,* not-caring, is more reproachful than *nonchalance* is in English. Louis's not-caring attitude is reflected in the famous remark "Après nous le déluge" attributed to his best-known mistress, Madame de Pompadour. The consequent "giving way" is shown in such episodes as his handling of peace negotiations in 1748, after a war in which France had been successful: he was maneuvered into renouncing most of what he could have gained. The last line is a further illustration. The Salic law barred women from ruling in France, but owing to Louis's "giving way," his mistresses were able to make major decisions.

A quatrain may have a clincher that comes unexpectedly. In VII.13, Nostradamus sketches the early career of a military upstart who attains power. Three lines may appear cryptic, but the fourth is down to earth.

De la cité marine et tributaire
La tête rasé prendra la satrapie:
Chasser sordide qui puis sera contraire,
Par quatorze ans tiendra la tyrannie.

From the marine and tributary city
The shaven head will take the satrapy:
To chase the sordid one that will then be
against him,
For fourteen years he will hold the tyranny.

Napoleon Bonaparte and no one else. His personal rule—his tyranny, in the eyes of a believer in legitimate royalty like Nostradamus—

lasted from November 1799 to April 1814, fourteen years and some months. Virtually all other candidates are thus ruled out. The preceding lines can then be seen to fit the circumstances of Napoleon's rise. To sum up briefly, he began to attract national attention in 1793 by organizing the recapture of Toulon, a seaport that was under British control, hence both "marine" and "tributary." By 1796, thanks to this and other exploits, he was a popular hero, too important in the eyes of the five-man Directory that ruled France: the word *satrap,* meaning a provincial governor in ancient Persia, was used in France to mean an overmighty subject who made the government uneasy. Napoleon was at odds with the corrupt Directory, a sordid institution rather than a sordid person. He made plans to overthrow it, and the directors contemplated taking action against him but did not. Conspiring with two of them, he broke up the Directory in a coup in November 1799 and set up a consulate of three. As first consul, he held all the real authority. His fourteen-year "tyranny" had begun.

The "shaven head" is a curious touch. Many Frenchmen in the 1790s still wore wigs. Napoleon did not; he wore his hair long, in the revolutionary fashion. However, when he prepared his coup, he had it cut much shorter. The haircut was a political gesture marking a rightward shift that was a part of his accession to power. It comes a little early, but the point is made. He kept his hair short afterward.

A similar sting in the tail characterizes other quatrains. One among several others that are applicable to Napoleon is IV.75.

Prêt a combattre fera deféction,
Chef adversaire obtiendra la victoire:
L'arrière-garde fera défension,
Les defaillants morts au blanc territoire.

Ready to fight, one will desert,
The chief adversary will obtain the
victory:

The rearguard will make a defense,
The faltering ones dead in the white
  territory.

Again, the fourth line is decisive. The "white territory" where men fall and die is the snowbound landscape of Russia during the retreat from Moscow in 1812. That determines the rest. The deserter is Marshal Bernadotte, who, after fighting zealously for Napoleon, had become ruler of Sweden and made a pact with the czar, freeing Russian troops to oppose the French invasion. Russia, at this point, was Napoleon's "chief adversary" and defeated him. During the retreat, a famous rearguard action by Marshals Ney and Victor kept the enemy off while the remnant of his army escaped. But innumerable soldiers collapsed and died in the "white territory."

In IV.89, the historical allusions are closely linked.

Trente de Londres secret conjureront
Contre leur Roi, sur le pont l'entreprise:
Lui, satellites la mort dégoûteront,
Un Roi élu blond, natif de Frise.

Thirty of London will conspire secretly
Against their King, the enterprise on the
  sea:
He and his satellites will have a distaste
  for death,
A fair King elected, native of Frisia.

The first lines suggest the events of 1688, when a group plotted to remove the autocratic James II and invited William of Orange to come over from Holland and restore constitutional government. The actual invitation was signed by only seven persons, but contemporary evidence points to thirty as an acceptable number. William arrived from Holland with a fleet and army. *Pont* means "bridge" in French, but Nostradamus is probably adapting the Latin *pontus,* meaning "sea." James and his few supporters had no wish to be killed in a hopeless resistance, and he escaped abroad. Here again, the clincher comes at the end. Parliament offered William the crown, and he became William III. No other English sovereign has ever been elected, and no other has been a native of Frisia—Holland. In Nostradamus's time, the idea of a Dutchman being elected as king of England, after a conspiracy to oust the legitimate monarch, would have been as unthinkable as the beheading of Charles I, and it would never have occurred to anyone in the normal course of political reflection. (The word *blond,* meaning "fair," is perhaps a little inaccurate. William's hair in a portrait is chestnut-colored.)

So likewise in other cases. By strictly applying the criteria, it is possible to pick out twenty-six Class A quatrains from the Nostradamian jumble. Since all of them contain more than one prediction, the number of predictions is far greater. Scrutiny in the light of the record of history shows that the total is about 100, not scattered but concentrated in these twenty-six quatrains. If the twenty-six are arranged chronologically in the order of their fulfillment, thirteen fall into the period 1559 to 1793. The last of these fits events in the French Revolution. The remaining thirteen form a series that applies exclusively to France's Bonaparte rulers, Napoleon I and his nephew Napoleon III (Napoleon II, the son of the first, never reigned). From 1793 on, Nostradamus predicts Napoleonic events and no others, up to the death of Napoleon III in 1873; after that, nothing.

While the time range of the Class A quatrains is limited, their geographical distribution is limited also. With one questionable exception, they all relate to France or Britain. But a survey of the whole 942 shows that insofar as they are intelligible, most of them concern other countries or have no geographical reference. The French-British combination makes up only a minority, yet it is almost solely within that minority that Nostradamus indisputably scores. Outside it, he has hundreds of opportunities for scoring and never does, at least with the same effectiveness. The distribution of his successes is wildly skewed, far outside random probability.

If the requirements are relaxed, allowing what may be called Class B quatrains that are arguable but not clear-cut, the number of these will be, to some extent, a matter of opinion. However, there are between twenty and thirty. One is the quatrain about the French king's death in the tournament, which made Nostradamus's reputation, but is not really so very good. Others have been interpreted as applying to Mary Queen of Scots; to the fortunes of the French royal family; to floods in the west of England; to the campaigns of Oliver Cromwell; to the Great Fire of London; and to happenings in the French Revolution and its aftermath, notably the royal family's attempt to escape in 1791. The overall impression is not very different from the impression given by the Class A verses. If the Class B items are all allowed, they still cover much the same stretch of time as Class A, breaking off, in fact, earlier. They have the same biased distribution by country, not quite so plainly marked, but sufficiently to defy chance. Even when all the A and B quatrains are taken together, making fifty or so, almost everything that Nostradamus predicts is France-oriented or Britain-oriented.

Nostradamus enthusiasts would reject these conclusions. They claim to find many more quatrains that have been fulfilled; not more Class A cases—no amount of wishful thinking will produce those—but additional Class B cases, by the dozen. Some are alleged to go past the Bonapartes in time and to point to other countries besides France and Britain. Nostradamus is credited with foretelling Louis Pasteur, the Dreyfus affair, Rasputin, various episodes in both world wars, and the rise and fall of Communism. The name "Hister" in II.24, IV.68, and V.29 is equated with "Hitler"; it has been asserted

that Hitler flirted with this interpretation himself. Even if it is adopted, the three quatrains make no credible sense. "Hister" is actually a Latin name for the Danube, and in IV.68, it is bracketed with "Rhin," the Rhine. Further claims are that Nostradamus predicted the Japanese attack on Pearl Harbor and the assassinations of President Kennedy and his brother. Perhaps the wildest notion of all is that VI.5 is about an orbiting space station manned by an astronaut named Sam R. O'Brien, his name being represented in the quatrain by "Samarobrin."

This kind of speculation has harmed Nostradamus by making him appear ridiculous and by swamping his truly interesting quatrains in a mass of fantasy. One sign of its futility is that attempts to use him to forecast the future have failed. In 1999 he was reported to have foretold the end of the world on July 4, 1999. The relevant quatrain is X.72:

> L'an mil neuf cent nonante neuf sept mois,
> De ciel viendra un grand Roi deffrayeur:
> Ressusciter le rand Roi d'Angolmois,
> Avant après Mars règne par bonheur.

> The year 1999 seven months
> From the sky will come a great King of Terror:
> To bring back to life the great King of the Angolmois,
> Before and after Mars reigns by good luck.

The first line might mean the seventh month of 1999, or, with "and" understood, it could mean seven months after 1999, in the year 2000. The seventh month would be July in one possible calendar, September in another. The fourth line implies war, and since it says "after," the events in the previous lines cannot be final. They are fairly opaque. *Angolmois* implies Angoulême in southwest France, but it has been explained as an approximate anagram of *Mongolois*, the Mongols. Anyhow, there is nothing here about the end of the world.

One of these dubious interpretations had a political effect. The quatrain is III.57.

Sept fois changer verrez gent
　Britannique,
Teints en sang en deux cent nonante ans:
Franche non point appui Germanique,
Aries doute son pole Bastarnan.

Seven times will you see the British
　nation change,
Steeped in blood in 290 years:
Free not at all its support Germanic,
Aries doubts his Bastarnian pole.

Charles Nicollaud, a French commentator, explained the first two lines as referring to seven changes of government or dynasty. The "290 years" is odd; it may be linked with another quatrain, one of the better ones, in which Nostradamus gives the British Empire a life expectancy of about three centuries, though without specifying any event to mark its conclusion. Nicollaud counted the 290 years from the execution of Charles I in 1649 and arrived at 1939 for a crisis. A German commentator, identifying the ancient Bastarnae as a tribe living in Poland, predicted that the crisis would involve Poland as well as Britain. In 1939, there was no seventh change, but Germany did invade Poland and Britain did declare war in Poland's support. This extremely tenuous "prophecy" was pointed out to Joseph Goebbels, Hitler's propaganda minister. Realizing that many people took Nostradamus seriously, he employed the Swiss astrologer Karl Ernst Krafft to invent pro-German interpretations of the French seer, which could be used as propaganda.

Fancies like these are especially regrettable because the general fudging not only discredits Nostradamus but also blurs his limitations and diverts attention from them; whereas these very limitations are among the things that make him remarkable. A

prophetic gift that works for about 300 years and then peters out is more interesting than a prophetic gift going on indefinitely. A prophetic gift that is practically confined to French and British matters and fails everywhere else is more interesting than a prophetic gift wandering aimlessly all over the world. The phenomenon is not random; it has shape. Even if the good predictions were all to be dismissed as lucky hits, the distortion would remain. Since there are hundreds of quatrains and a majority concern neither France nor Britain, there ought to be a scattering of equally lucky hits for other countries. There is not.

Dismissal, however, is not really an option. An objector may say, "If you make swarms of predictions, a few will be right by chance." But the linking of the predictive lines and their concentration in a few quatrains, plus the limitations of scope, make the hypothesis of chance hard to maintain. Moreover, it is not true that in a mass of predictions a significant number will just happen to be right. The records of popular "psychics" and their kind, who make forecasts in the media, have been examined and are abysmal. Nostradamus, every so often, does much better.

He never explains how he does it, and he certainly has no technique for deliberate and sustained prediction. In an epistle to the French king that accompanies the Centuries, he offers a survey of the next few hundred years that is supposed to give them a frame, and it is utterly wrong. He is remembered as an astrologer, yet even in the most favorable view, astrology could not have supplied all the details in the better quatrains. At the beginning of the Centuries, he sketches a magical ceremony in which a "divine being" is summoned and communicates with him. His description echoes a fourth-century treatise by a late Roman mystic, Iamblichus. The procedure may involve scrying—seeing images in a bowl of water. But plenty of crystal gazers have done much the same with no comparable results.

Nostradamus keeps his secret. However, if his good quatrains are considered further in the context of other prophecies, some further light may be shed.

See also: Astrology; Krafft, Karl Ernst; Prophecy, Theories of; Psychics; Scrying; Second Charlemagne

Further Reading

Ashe, Geoffrey. *The Book of Prophecy.* London: Blandford, 1999.

Howe, Ellic. *Urania's Children.* London: William Kimber, 1967.

Leoni, Edgar. *Nostradamus and His Prophecies.* New York: Bell Publishing Company, 1982.

ORACLES

Sacred places, especially in the ancient Hellenic world, where deities could be consulted and might give messages with a predictive content.

One of the most famous was an oracle of Zeus, chief of the Olympian gods, at Dodona in northwest Greece. It was already flourishing in the second millennium B.C. Its history, to the extent that this is known, gives glimpses of a transition from simple divination to divine guidance and the beginnings—but only the beginnings—of prophecy about the future. Answers to inquirers were originally given by a large sacred oak through attendant priests called Selloi. It is not certain exactly what happened. Probably, a priest interpreted the rustling of the leaves.

Later came a procedure that involved a priestess. Those who consulted the oracle were given a thin strip of lead and told to write a question on it, in a form allowing a yes or no answer. Each strip was rolled up, with the writing on the inside for confidentiality, and marked on the outside with the inquirer's name or an identifying sign. The priestess put all the strips in a jar and took them out one by one, simultaneously drawing a lot from another container, probably a bean colored black or white: the color of the bean showed whether the god's answer to that question was yes or no.

Hundreds of these lead strips have been found on the site, and the questions can be deciphered, though sometimes the inquirer is clearly unaccustomed to writing. Most of the questions are about personal problems. Gerioton asks Zeus whether he should marry; Cleotas wonders about the advisability of sheep-farming; Lysanias wants to know whether the child with which his wife is pregnant is his own. Questions about the future do occur, including one from Leontios asking whether his son will recover from an illness. But since all questions had to allow a yes or no answer, the scope for divine prediction at Dodona was limited.

Other gods and goddesses had oracular shrines. In classical times, the responses were often given by a priest or priestess in a mediumistic trance. There were oracles of Artemis, Ares, Aphrodite, and Heracles. One of the most impressive was the oracle of Trophonius, a comparatively minor figure who was supposed to have built Apollo's temple at Delphi. He was deified after his death and could be consulted in a cave with a mazelike arrangement of spikes and railings where pilgrims supposedly passed into the infernal regions, the whole ritual being so frightening that persons who went through it were said to live thereafter in a state of settled melancholy. Outside Greece, Zeus had an oracle in Egypt, where Greeks identified him with the Egyptian god Ammon. His temple was at an oasis. Alexander the Great came here, and the priests hailed him as "Son of Ammon," assuring him of his divine descent and superiority to humans in general.

However, the most important oracle was Apollo's at Delphi, a place believed to be at the center of the world. Apollo was originally a foreigner: he reached Greece from Asia Minor together with Artemis, his sister. His worship was established at Delphi about the thirteenth century B.C. Themis, a daughter of the Earth Goddess, was said to have had an oracle there before and to have communicated in dreams with visitors who slept in the precinct. Apollo took over, with the aid, according to legend, of some Hyperboreans, people from a mysterious northern country. A remote shamanic background may be indicated. The god spoke, as elsewhere, through a priestess who was a kind of medium. Inquirers might seek advice only, but since Apollo was held to have knowledge of the future, questions about the future were sometimes asked. They might take a hypothetical form: "If I do so-and-so, what will happen?" The answer was apt to be obscure or ambiguous, yet it was mainly through Apollo and his Delphic presence that prophecy—divinely inspired utterance—began to acquire a predictive sense in Greece, though, in classical Greek, this linguistic development never went as far as it did among peoples under biblical influence.

In postclassical times, Apollo acquired two great temples in Asia Minor, at Didyma and Claros. Some cities made consultation of Claros an annual civic ceremony, with a choir singing a hymn to Apollo composed for the occasion. Inquirers admitted to the sanctuary had to walk in single file along a torch-lit subterranean passage, which went through six right-angle turns to a hall with a fountain.

With the rise of Christianity, which condemned all this as diabolic deception, the oracles gradually declined. Didyma made a stand, encouraging the emperor Diocletian to suppress the Church, but when his persecution failed, the oracle soon lapsed into silence, as did that of Delphi a little later.

See also: Apollo; Delphi; Sibyls and Sibylline Texts

Further Reading

Cavendish, Richard, ed. *Man, Myth and Magic.* London: BPC Publishing, 1970–1972. Article "Oracles."

ORWELL, GEORGE (1903–1950)
Pseudonym of Eric Blair, English novelist, journalist, and essayist.

Orwell's twice-filmed dystopia *Nineteen Eighty-Four,* published in 1949, was harmed by its title. It was assumed to be an attempt at prediction. When the fatal year passed and the world had failed to fulfill the novel, it was downgraded as erroneous, even obsolete. Actually, the exact future date was almost an afterthought in the course of composition. *Nineteen Eighty-Four* is better described as a horror story. The author attacks the totalitarian systems of his day, especially in Soviet Russia, by pushing their tendencies to extremes, and he tells the story through a character who does not understand his world and lives in a nightmare. There is an evident debt to Zamyatin's novel *We.*

The world of the fictional 1984 is dominated by three superstates, Oceania, Eurasia, and Eastasia, all ruled by monolithic regimes that are very similar. Oceania's ideology is Ingsoc, short for "English Socialism." Warfare is constant, generally on a small scale but exaggerated for purposes of propaganda. Britain, as part of Oceania, is Airstrip One and is miserably run-down after years of conflict and turmoil. The ruling Party is headed by a leader known as Big Brother, to whose wisdom everything that is good (or officially made out to be good) is attributed. The Party regards most of the population, the "proles," as virtually subhuman. London is very much as it has been since anyone can remember, only drearier. Its most conspicuous features are four huge government buildings: the Ministry of Truth, concerned with news, education, and so forth and, to a large extent, with lies; the Ministry of Peace, concerned with war; the Ministry of Plenty, concerned with economic affairs, meaning chiefly rationing; and the Ministry of Love, a windowless pyramid housing the mechanisms of social order—torture chambers, for instance.

The Party's dominance is total, thanks to its ubiquitous police, its apparatus of terror, and its controlled media telling the people how well off they are. In reality, they are not.

Party members are kept in a state of perpetual alert, partly by the supposed menace of an underground opposition, the Brotherhood, led by the archtraitor and heretic Emmanuel Goldstein. Every so often, alleged supporters of Goldstein are forced to make public confessions and branded as agents of Eurasia or Eastasia, whichever state Oceania is currently at war with.

One long-term project is the introduction of Newspeak. The Party is creating a simplified and cut-down version of English that is designed to replace the present language. Words are being abolished, changed, and redefined so as to make subversive ideas literally impossible; there will be no vocabulary to express them.

Orwell's protagonist Winston Smith is a minor Party functionary at the Ministry of Truth. His job is to rewrite newspaper files and other records so as to make it appear that Big Brother and the Party have always been right: in fact, to manipulate the past in the interests of a myth of infallibility. When at home, he is under surveillance, like all his fellow workers, through a two-way television device called a telescreen. Outwardly conscientious, he is in a constant state of repressed and bewildered anger and cherishes futile hopes of a revolt by the acquiescent proles.

He drifts into a love affair with a younger colleague, Julia, who is rebellious like himself but wears her resentment lightly and is skillful at putting on an appearance of orthodoxy. Their liaison is a grave breach of Party discipline, but they delude themselves into thinking that they are getting away with it, at least temporarily. They have furtive meetings, rent a room of their own, and finally try to contact the Brotherhood. In reality, they were being watched all along; no one *ever* gets away with it. They are arrested and taken separately to the Ministry of Love.

Winston undergoes a lengthy ordeal of brainwashing and torture, supervised by one of the Inner Party elite, O'Brien, who has taken an interest in his case for some time and arranged his entrapment. O'Brien reveals things that Winston never grasped about the Party's insane yet irrefutable philosophy, and tells him that the true aim is not public welfare or anything normally desirable but power for its own sake, expressed in tyranny, cruelty, and triumph over shattered opponents. Winston and Julia are released separately, broken in spirit. They betrayed each other. After one unhappy meeting, they part. Winston is now not merely submissive to the regime but an abject convert. He loves Big Brother.

Nineteen Eighty-Four is, fortunately, impossible. It has contradictions and inconsistencies. For instance, Newspeak is to end dangerous thoughts by making them unthinkable. But the Party's intoxication with power requires that dangerous thoughts must go on; there must always be an opposition, genuine or fabricated, to drag into the limelight and triumph over. As O'Brien puts it, "Goldstein and his heresies will live for ever. Every day, at every moment, they will be defeated, discredited, ridiculed, spat upon—and yet they will always survive." But if Newspeak takes hold and heresies cease to be even thinkable, they obviously won't survive, and there will be nothing for the Party to defeat, discredit, ridicule, and spit upon.

Nineteen Eighty-Four is an ideological nightmare, projected into a setting that, for Orwell, was future. It was not intended as a serious forecast and therefore should not be dismissed as unsuccessful.

See also: Huxley, Aldous; Zamyatin, Yevgeny
Further Reading
Carey, John, ed. *The Faber Book of Utopias.* London: Faber and Faber, 1999.

PALMISTRY

A technique for examining the hands and inferring a person's character and probable future. Palmistry is also called chiromancy.

Palmistry may have originated in India. It has been practiced for a long time in China, the Middle East, and Egypt, and, of course, in Western countries. Its association with gypsies may be due to their having brought it with them in their wanderings out of Asia.

According to palmists—or some of them—the left hand shows the basic personality, including inherited factors; the right hand shows how this is developing and what the person has done and experienced and is likely to do and experience in the future. Much more is involved than the actual palm. The shape of the hands is said to be eloquent and so are their individual features. For example, a large, straight, and well–shaped hand is said to show an expansive personality, lively and possibly aggressive. A long and slender hand indicates a fastidious and gentle personality. A hard and firm hand means that its owner is energetic and sporting, with a good memory and a potential tendency to violence. And so forth.

A thumb bent well in toward the palm shows moderation and perhaps meanness. A thumb bent unusually far out and backward is a "killer's thumb" and may be a symptom of brutality. The long–fingered person is polite, excitable, and aesthetic; the short–fingered is impatient, sensuous, and good–hearted. Even the fingernails have their place in the system. The fingers are matched to as-

trological planets, and so are the raised parts or "regions" of the palm.

The multiple significance of the palm itself lies chiefly in its creases or lines. Palmists claim that these give encoded information that they can interpret. The "life" line, starting between the thumb and forefinger and curving down toward the wrist, indicates the probable length of the person's life and, under expert scrutiny, important points in it, past, present, and to come. The "head" line, starting from the same area and running across to the other side of the palm, is a

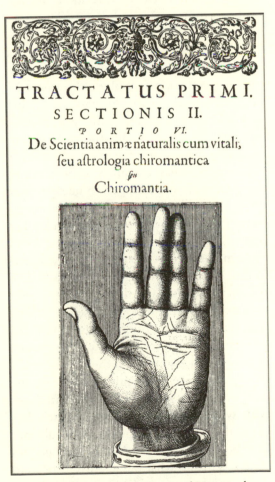

Title page of a text on palmistry, or chiromancy, by the seventeenth-century mystic Robert Fludd. (Ann Ronan Picture Library)

pointer to intellectual capacities. Alongside the "head" line is the "heart" line, expressing the sentiments. The "fate" or "destiny" line runs from the base of the middle finger down to the wrist; this is interpreted in conjunction with the "life" line, which it approaches but does not normally intersect. A short line beginning at the base of the third finger is the Apollo or "sun" line, showing artistic talent if any and also, it seems, chances of success. A line on the outside of the palm, away from the thumb, may (if it exists) reveal intuition or insight. Other, secondary lines, which are fairly numerous, need not be traced here.

Palmists explore the whole network in minute detail. Their interpretations are not confined to character and destiny. They give advice on careers and marriage, they discuss the client's past errors and how to avoid a repetition, and they predict possible illnesses.

There is no apparent physical reason why palmistry should work. As with other fortune-telling techniques, some practitioners undoubtedly do well. But the technique is not the secret, or not the essential secret. A hand reading may genuinely suggest something and may even happen to be correct in doing so. Generally, however, the successful palmist makes use of the readings as a kind of patter while the real messages take shape, and these are arrived at chiefly by psychological insight and by knowledge or observation of the client, who may shed light unconsciously by actions with the hands themselves—clasping them together, closing the fists, gesturing. The famous palmist Cheiro, who was much in demand in England and the United States during the late nineteenth century and the early twentieth, scored many publicized hits with well-known people; but, precisely because they were well known, it would not have been difficult to make informed guesses about them and what was likely to happen to them. While some of Cheiro's reputed predictions cannot be explained so simply, he did not pretend himself that it was all done

by palmistry alone. He said he had "psychic" gifts. Whether or not he had, the admission is the important thing.

See also: Astrology; Cheiro; Divination; Tarot
Further Reading
Cavendish, Richard, ed. *Man, Myth and Magic.* London: BPC Publishing, 1970–1972. Article "Palmistry," by Basil Ivan Rakoczi, whose exposition is followed here.
Cheiro. *Cheiro's Language of the Hand.* London: Corgi, 1967.

PARAPSYCHOLOGY

The professedly scientific study of extrasensory perception (ESP), telepathy, and other mental phenomena, which, if they exist, are not covered by ordinary explanations.

Experiments with precognition have consisted in setting up tests in which simple events occur in random order. A subject is asked to forecast the next occurrence. For instance, two lights, A and B, flash on and off irregularly, and the subject presses a button to indicate whether A or B is about to flash. It has been stated that the score over a test period is sometimes significantly above chance. But while a good score may be claimed as evidence for precognition, it can hardly count as prophecy. The subject does not predict an unknown event; one of the lights is definitely going to flash; the question is not "what?" but merely "which?"

Parapsychologists have tried to analyze dreams, showing whether they ever anticipate the future, but dreaming is a topic in its own right, requiring to be considered separately.

See also: Dreams; Dunne, J. W.; Prophecy, Theories of
Further Reading
Broughton, Richard. *Parapsychology.* New York: Ballantine, 1991.

PARTRIDGE, JOHN (1644–1715)

English astrologer remembered chiefly for his annihilation by Jonathan Swift.

An imaginary confrontation between the astrological charlatan John Partridge and his demolisher "Isaac Bickerstaff"—Jonathan Swift under a pseudonym. (Hulton Getty)

A shoemaker, by no means negligible as a self-taught scholar, he began bringing out an annual almanac in 1680, under the pseudonym Merlinus Liberatus. His predictions were not very impressive and were warped by religious and political bias. He shared in the intense anti-Catholic feeling of the time and in the resultant hostility to King James II, who was a convert to Catholicism and aroused fears that he aimed to restore the old religion.

That crisis passed. But Swift, in 1707, became disturbed by a vogue for fortune-telling and other forms of superstition and decided to attack it in the person of Partridge. At the end of the year, when the Merlinus Liberatus almanac came out, Swift published a forecast by "Isaac Bickerstaff" that Partridge would die on March 29 at 11 P.M. On March 30, he followed up with a detailed account of Partridge's death and confession of imposture. Partridge's protestations that he was still alive only increased the publicity and general ridicule. It was some years before he ventured to issue any more almanacs.

See also: Astrology; Lilly, William; Moore, Francis

Further Reading

Dictionary of National Biography (British). Article "Partridge, John."

PEDEN, ALEXANDER (C. 1626–1686)

Scottish preacher with a reputation for prophecy.

Born in Ayrshire, Peden studied at Glasgow and taught in a school. He became a minister in 1660 and ranged himself with the Covenanters, the uncompromising Presbyterian party. After only two years, he was expelled from his ministry as seditious, and thereafter, he wandered about addressing small groups and hiding in caves. Condemned as a rebel, he was imprisoned from 1673 to 1678 on the Bass Rock, an island in the sea east of Edinburgh.

The rural population believed that he had paranormal gifts, and this belief gave him continuing influence with them. In 1728, many stories of Peden were published in a collection by Patrick Walker. Walker was old enough to have talked with people who knew him personally, and his book names these informants, but it does not appear that he ever found much in the way of documentation. He recorded many anecdotes of Peden's second sight about individuals. Some of these are pleasant, some decidedly grim.

Peden once announced that a party of prisoners, sentenced to transportation (a form of punishment that sent prisoners to penal colonies overseas), would not actually be transported . . . and the ship's captain refused to take them. He told a man who questioned the virtue of two women martyred for religion that he would die suddenly, surprisingly . . . and the skeptic dropped dead while smoking his pipe in front of a fire. He warned a girl who laughed rudely while watching Sabbath worship that she would not laugh much longer . . . and she was blown off a cliff into the sea.

However, Peden also made some less disturbing predictions about the course of public events. During a persecution of Covenanters in the 1670s and 1680s, he foretold the death of Charles II, the dethronement and exile of Charles's successor, James II, and the fighting that ensued in Ireland when James attempted a comeback there. Peden said there would be no more Stuart kings, and this turned out to be correct. James's daughters Mary and Anne both reigned but, of course, as queens; Hanoverian monarchs followed them, and while James's son and grandson had many supporters in Scotland,

called Jacobites, neither regained the crown for the Stuart dynasty.

Peden is one of the sources for a curious prediction made by others as well: that a French army would invade Scotland. Shortly before his death, when staying with friends, he startled them by crying out in the night about impending danger from "French Monzies." "Monzie" was a Scottish colloquial form of "Monsieur" (the better-known English equivalent was "Mounseer"). The Monzies, helped by a traitorous faction in Scotland, would overrun the south and west. In versions ascribed to three other preachers, the prophecy was more elaborate. The invasion would be preceded by an end of persecution that would create a false sense of security. Then, the French would come; not immediately, but when they did they would ravage all of Scotland—maybe England and Ireland, too. Eventually, they would be driven out, and a happier time would follow.

Sir Walter Scott mentions this prophecy, which was evidently well known and remembered. Yet it was never fulfilled. After James II's departure from England, a small French force landed in Ireland to support his attempted recovery, and later, there were threats of expeditions in aid of the Jacobites, but no French army ever reached Scotland.

When Peden was dying, at Auchinleck in his native Ayrshire, he foretold that his body would not be allowed to rest where it was laid. He was buried in a churchyard, but six weeks later some soldiers dug him up and reburied him beside the gallows at Cumnock, as a suitably disgraceful spot for a rebel. The people of the neighborhood did not respond as they were meant to. They revered Peden so deeply that they abandoned their old burial ground and formed a new one around the gallows.

See also: Brahan Seer, The; Thomas the Rhymer

Further Reading

Walker, Patrick. *Six Saints of the Covenant.* Edited by D. Hay Fleming and S. R.

Crockett. Vol. 1. London: Hodder and Stoughton, 1901.

POPE AND PAPACY

See Angelic Pope; Antichrist; Guglielma of Milan; Joachim of Fiore; Malachy, Saint; Second Charlemagne

PREMONITIONS

After a catastrophe, people are apt to say "I had a feeling it was going to happen" or words to that effect. They may be sincere, they may be telling the truth, but did they express their foreboding previously to anyone else? Did they write it down? Premonitions are elusive.

An attempt to study premonitions objectively was made in 1966 by John Barker, a British psychologist. The circumstances were tragic. At the Welsh mining village of Aberfan, a mass of mine waste had slid downhill, causing 144 deaths. About 200 villagers claimed to have foreseen the disaster in one way or another; some had had anticipatory dreams about it. Barker examined sixty cases. Twenty-two of those interviewed had voiced their apprehension beforehand to others who could confirm it, sometimes to as many as four. Two more had put it in writing. Admittedly, people living on mining land might have known enough about slag heaps to see reasons for fear.

In 1968, a larger, ongoing project was launched by Robert Nelson, promotions manager of the *New York Times*. He had taken part in tests at the Dream Laboratory of the Maimonides Medical Center in Brooklyn, New York, pursuing the kind of investigation that J. W. Dunne had pioneered in *An Experiment with Time*. The results were inconclusive but interesting. Nelson launched his own Central Premonition Registry and invited the public to send in anything of the kind that they had to offer. His criteria were broad: he was willing to consider not only dreams, intuitions, and visionary experiences but conventional fortune-telling. He registered each premonition submitted and filed it under one of fourteen categories. To first-time correspondents, he sent a questionnaire designed to show whether they were psychologically unusual. His newspaper job gave him exceptional opportunities to look for fulfillments in the media.

Some of the supposed previsions of public events were grotesque or comic, such as "A new breed of dog becomes popular because of its resemblance to our new President [the recently elected Ronald Reagan]." Some that were better than that covered violent incidents and assassination attempts. In a very few cases, someone "saw" a newspaper headline that actually appeared later.

Interest in the registry built up gradually over the years. When Nelson had accumulated about 5,000 predictions of various kinds, he still put the number of real hits no higher than 50. Such a figure would mean very little except that half the hits were due to only five correspondents, each of whom scored several times. This agreed with Dunne's Oxford project, in which (though he resisted the conclusion himself) one of the student subjects did well, but only one. It appears that if such phenomena occur, they occur only for a minority, not for people in general.

Two English cases other than Dunne's give the same impression. A "psychic" who flourished during World War II, Cyril Macklin, was noted for his ability to foresee enemy air raids and always manage to be somewhere else. In more recent years, media attention was paid to Chris Robinson, whose dream premonitions and resulting warnings were good enough to gain the respect of the police.

Robinson's apparent success in averting disasters raised a question that engrossed Nelson more and more with the passage of time. Could dreams and other premonitions provide an early-warning system, so that disasters could be prevented? Louisa E. Rhine cited cases where this was allegedly done. The obvious question is: if someone foresees an undesired event and takes action so that it doesn't happen, what did that person see? To press the point is to open up a circular paradox. I dream of an accident. I go to the place where it's about to happen, and I intervene to prevent it. So the accident won't happen. So I can't have seen it in my dream. But if I didn't see it, I wouldn't have done anything to prevent it. So it will happen. So I see it and go there to intervene . . . et cetera.

The only escape, apart from total denial, is to infer that the dreamer in such a situation is getting a warning in visual form of something that *might* happen—possibly, maybe probably. Such a warning could be due to ordinary anxiety, conscious or subconscious. But if the dream warns of something unfamiliar and unexpected, anxiety is no explanation, and merely "seeing the future" is no explanation either. The problem raises the issue, in all seriousness, of helpful communication from another being—a spirit, an angel, a time traveler from the future who has glimpsed the impending danger.

See also: Dreams; Dunne, J. W.; Prophecy, Theories of

Further Reading

Ashe, Geoffrey. *The Book of Prophecy.* London: Blandford, 1999.

Broughton, Richard. *Parapsychology.* New York: Ballantine, 1991.

Wallechinsky, David, Amy Wallace, and Irving Wallace. *The Book of Predictions.* New York: William Morrow, 1980.

PROMISED LAND

The territory, roughly corresponding to Palestine, believed to have been promised by God to Abraham and the Israelite tribes descended from him: a permanent theme of Jewish prophetic hope through centuries of dispersal and exile.

The Promised Land was always central in the religion of Israel, and it remained a vital element in most versions of the Judaism that evolved from it. According to the Bible, Abraham's descendants became enslaved in Egypt. Their God—Yahweh, as he was known—appointed Moses to free them and lead them to their destined home, then called Canaan. As his Chosen People, they were to live there as he desired them to live, keeping the commandments he gave them. His gift of the Promised Land could never be canceled or withdrawn, but the Israelites came to understand that it was conditional. If they were disloyal to God, he could dispossess them, not totally and forever but for an indefinitely long time.

Canaan was not virgin territory. It was already occupied by Canaanites, who were more numerous and civilized than the Bible suggests, especially in coastal areas. The earliest Israelite settlement was chiefly on the higher ground, inland. Whatever the exact process of conquest, the Lord was uncompromising in his demands: the Canaanites must be smashed. This suppression of an indigenous people was inherent in the promise. The Land was to belong to the Israelites and to no one else. Rashi, a great medieval Jewish scholar, argued that the Bible begins with the story of Creation in Genesis to justify crushing the Canaanites. Genesis made it clear that Israel's God was supreme; he had made the world, and it was his will to form a special community in a special place; so his Chosen People had an incontrovertible right that the prior inhabitants could not appeal against.

The Israelites occupied most of the Promised Land, forming a loose tribal federation, later a monarchy. The monarchy split apart into a northern and a southern kingdom. In both, especially the north, there was a considerable falling away from the worship of Yahweh and from the simple pastoral ethics of early times. A series of prophets, inspired, as they believed, by the spirit of the

Moses, who, in the Bible, leads the Israelites to the Promised Land of Canaan, sees it from a mountain but cannot enter it himself. (Ann Ronan Picture Library)

Lord, denounced oppression and injustice as well as apostasy and proclaimed that God could and would inflict judgment on his erring people. Their foreshadowing of the future—sometimes as warning, sometimes as exhortation to reform and repent—is the main reason why the word *prophecy*, which originally referred to inspiration only, began to acquire its predictive sense.

When chastisement came, it took the form of foreign conquest: of the north by Assyria; of the south, over a century later, by Babylon. It led in both cases to wholesale deportations and the effective loss of the

Promised Land. But the prophet Jeremiah, who foretold the Babylonian conquest, also looked beyond it. The Lord would relent and a faithful remnant would return. Ezekiel, more optimistic, foresaw a general reunion in the Promised Land with even the vanished northerners reappearing.

Then, Babylon fell to the Persians, its captives were indeed allowed to return, and some did, they and their descendants being known henceforward as Jews, from the origin of most of them in the tribe of Judah. An autonomous Jewish community, centered on Jerusalem and its Temple, existed under the Persian Empire and under the Greek regime of Alexander and his successors. After various upheavals, a new kingdom came into being and survived for about 100 years. Then, however, it was conquered by Rome. Two unsuccessful revolts resulted in the destruction of Jerusalem and the Temple and the scattering of the Jewish people—those who were not scattered already—through most of the Roman world and beyond, from the second century A.D. onward.

Jews clung to their religion in spite of everything. The promise of the Land, embodied in their Scriptures, was never forgotten, nor was the prophecy of an eventual return, though all human probability was against it. This hope was associated with another prophecy, that of the Messiah, a leader sent by God who would bring the Jews' miseries to an end and restore them to their heritage.

The modern Zionist movement, prompted by anti-Semitism in czarist Russia and other countries, was only partly religious in its inspiration, and many Orthodox Jews opposed it as an attempt to bypass the Messiah. Nevertheless, the long prophetic conditioning proved to be irresistible. Theodor Herzl, the founder of the movement, simply wanted to create a homeland for oppressed Jews. His projected Jewish state might well be in Palestine, but that was not essential. He found, however, that nowhere else was acceptable.

Even the Russian Jews, who were suffering most, chose to stay where they were and go on being persecuted, rather than give up the Promised Land and betray all the generations who had cherished the prophecy of the return. Herzl's successor as leader, Chaim Weizmann, understood the issues better and initiated moves that led at last to the formation of the Republic of Israel.

> **See also:** Biblical Prophecy (1)—Israelite and Jewish; Ezekiel; Herzl, Theodor; Jeremiah; Messiah

> **Further Reading**
> Ashe, Geoffrey. *The Land and the Book.* London: Collins, 1965.
> Isserlin, B. S. J. *The Israelites.* London: Thames and Hudson, 1998.

PROPHECY, THEORIES OF

This entry touches on case histories that are discussed more fully elsewhere and are listed below under the "See also" heading. What they have in common is evidence that foreseeings, anticipations, and irregularities in the time-flow do happen and require explanation.

Happen is the right word. It may be said at once that there seems to be no technique that, in itself, reveals the future. Astrology is the front-runner, but its predictive record is not good enough to convince. Technique, astrological or otherwise, may be of help to practitioners in a catalytic way. It may increase their receptivity to whatever it is that they receive, if anything. But prophecy cannot be made to happen experimentally, under controlled and repeatable conditions. That does not dispose of it—many things that are real enough, such as falling in love and composing great music, cannot be made to happen experimentally, under controlled and repeatable conditions. But the difficulty of studying prophecy is apparent when "happen" is the right word and the phenomenon cannot be produced at will.

Various facts emerge from the case histories. Prevision seems to be confined to persons with a special gift or aptitude, and it is apt to be infrequent even with them. J. W. Dunne's Oxford "experiment with time" was supposed to prove otherwise, but, in fact, it did not: only one of the participants had a high score. Nostradamus, a rare figure who possessed the gift if anyone ever did, scores spectacularly when he does; but his "good" and "fairly good" quatrains, when extricated from the excesses of his admirers, amount at most to about five percent of the hundreds he published.

Prophecy implies transcendence of time. Insofar as it can be theorized about, the essential question that it poses is *how* time can be transcended. It originally meant inspired utterance—inspired by a divine being (such as Apollo)—and its predictive character was a development (at Delphi, for instance). It "happened" in whatever way the divine being, who could see the future, might choose. In the pagan context, this merely shifts the question from humanity: how did the divine being transcend time? Actually, Apollo's reported prognostications are too vague and equivocal to warrant serious discussion. Biblical prophecy is more challenging. The anticipations of Christ by the prophet known as Second Isaiah cannot be simply set aside. Nor can the anticipations of later history by the author of Revelation, in spite of the nonsense that misguided expositors have read into them.

The Bible supports the dismissal of techniques such as astrology. All true prophecy comes from God, and that applies where it is predictive as at any other time. It may be mediated through angelic messengers, but God is the source: he and he alone knows the future. A prophet is not someone who sees ahead by unaided insight but someone who is admitted to a share of God's knowledge. In the Judaeo-Christian tradition, an interpretation is offered. Saint Thomas Aquinas, the principal medieval philosopher, argues that God transcends time because he exists in eternity outside it. He surveys the whole course of it, including the part yet to come that is concealed from humans, as a person on high ground can look down and see the whole of a road when walkers on the road see only a small portion. He communicates something of his knowledge to prophets, including his knowledge of what, for them, is in the future.

Given the overall theology, according to which God makes many interventions in human life, this idea of special interventions accounting for prophecy cannot be faulted. The notion can even provide for the modern occurrences at Fatima; the prophecies were spoken to the young visionary by the Virgin Mary and startlingly fulfilled; but Mary may have acted as God's most exalted messenger. The difficulty is that it accounts only for prophecy that can be ascribed to a divine source and seen in terms of divine intentions. To imagine God dictating the cryptic verses of Nostradamus or the dream-trivia collected by Dunne is not consistent with Christian or Jewish ideas of him. Transcendence of time must be sought in other forms.

To take Dunne first, he claimed that dreams can anticipate in ways that are not due to normal expectation, wish fulfillment, or anxiety. He assembled evidence from dreams recorded by himself and by volunteers. However, even on his own showing, the scope is restricted. All that is ever anticipated—in a fragmentary and garbled guise—is a future experience of the dreamer, perhaps quite soon. A prevision of a public event not personally witnessed is a prevision of the dreamer's reading about it in a paper or learning of it otherwise. Dunne realized this when he considered a dream of his own, foreshadowing the eruption of Mont Pelée in Martinique. An error showed that the dream was spun out of his subsequent misreading of a newspaper account.

He fitted his findings into a theory that increased the complexity of the personality and its temporal context. In his opinion, the higher part of the personality extends into higher time dimensions beyond the visible flow, and there it can range ahead, so to speak, of the ordinary consciousness and see experiences yet to come. When that consciousness relaxes in sleep, images from the higher part of the personality that is seeing them can make their way in. Later investigators have found some support for Dunne's claims, at least as to the fact of anticipatory dreaming, though, in defiance of his own views, it seems to happen much more often for an exceptional minority than for people in general. But even if these results are accepted, they do not supply a key to prophecy in the more interesting cases. According to Dunne, dreamers cannot foresee anything outside their personal experience. Nor can they foresee anything after their own death. He believed in an immortality on his higher levels but accepted that death on this level is the end. After it, therefore, there can be no more experiences to anticipate.

Dunne's theory is irrelevant to nearly all of the "good" quatrains produced by Nostradamus, the famous French physician and seer. This is because the good quatrains refer to events that occurred after his death. Though few in number, these are impressive. The naive thing to say of his own transcendence of time is that he "saw the future." The same can be said of other prophets, such as Pseudo-Malachy and Cazotte and even, for that matter, the biblical ones, whether or not it is believed that they saw the future because God showed it to them. A natural retort is that seeing the future is impossible because it is not there to be seen. Such a dismissal is mere dogmatism; the case histories must be judged on their merits and do not favor it. The real objection to "seeing the future" as an explanation is that it doesn't explain.

In this connection, attention has been drawn to a short story by Arthur Conan Doyle (best known as the creator of Sherlock Holmes). Entitled "The Silver Mirror," it is a fantasy about seeing the past, not the future, but it happens to make the essential point all the more vividly. An accountant is working long hours on the ledgers of a businessman suspected of fraud. Near his workplace is an antique, silver-framed mirror. He begins to see it growing misty at times and then clearing. During the misty phases, gaps open in the mist and images show through. The first time, he sees a woman's face. A few days later when the same thing happens, the gap is larger, and he sees her at full length, seated in a chair. When she makes another appearance, a small man is crouching beside her. Next time, the scene expands further, and other men are visible, making threatening gestures at the one beside the woman. Finally, in a clear scene filling the mirror, they drag him away and stab him. All this has been going on in silence.

The accountant's task is finished, but he is exhausted and unwell. He describes the visions to a doctor, who infers from a brief inscription on the back of the mirror that it once belonged to Mary Queen of Scots and that it has somehow retained an impression of the murder of Rizzio, her secretary, in 1566. The accountant knew nothing of Scottish history. He saw and saw accurately, but before his talk with the doctor, the drama was meaningless. In this story, it is the past that is being seen, and at least the doctor comes in to elucidate. Anyone seeing a totally unfamiliar future, with no equivalent of the doctor available, might well be mystified even more thoroughly than the overworked accountant.

By way of illustration, how far could "seeing the future," in itself, account for the best quatrains of Nostradamus? Ten of them fit the career of Napoleon and, what is more important, nobody else's. Their interlinked lines give a total of forty-one predictions. All can be counted as fulfilled, and none are wrong. A fairly straightforward quatrain in this group (IV.75) applies (and—read as a whole—applies uniquely) to the disaster of 1812. In translation:

Ready to fight, one will desert,
The chief adversary will obtain the
   victory:
The rearguard will make a defence,
The faltering ones dead in the white
   territory.

In 1812, Napoleon's marshal Bernadotte, who had fought bravely for him but deserted his cause to become ruler of Sweden, met Czar Alexander of Russia in Finland and made a pact with him. At that point, the czar was Napoleon's chief adversary, and Bernadotte's defection helped him to defeat the French invasion. During the celebrated retreat from Moscow, Napoleon's army was overtaken by winter and dwindled away. Two marshals who remained loyal, Ney and Victor, conducted a memorable rearguard action that kept the Russians off while the remnant of Napoleon's forces escaped over the Berezina River. Meanwhile, thousands of men had collapsed and died in the snowbound landscape—the "white territory."

How much of this could Nostradamus have gathered by "seeing" it? If, in some astral flight, he eavesdropped on Bernadotte's meeting with the czar in Finland, how would he have known who they were or what they were discussing, and how would he have related it to the images that follow? If he saw Ney and Victor fighting Cossacks in an unfamiliar country a long way from Finland, how would he have known that it was a rearguard action? How could he have connected any of this with soldiers freezing to death in the snow, their presence unexplained and perhaps even their nationality unclear? Imagine Nostradamus's hypothetical sightings as a series of snapshots, without captions—how much could they have told him?

He hints himself that there is more to his prophetic experience than "seeing." At the beginning of his Centuries, he describes a magical action in which a "divine being" is manifested and—perhaps—gives him information. This awareness that seeing cannot be the whole story is made more plain in Revelation. Some of the visions of its author, John (whichever John he may be), symbolize future developments that actually happened, long after his death. He foretells a totalitarian change in the Roman Empire, which seems to be associated with a solar cult. He foretells an empirewide and ruthless persecution of Christians. He foretells the ruin of the city of Rome, at the hands of alien kings who have infiltrated the empire. Here and elsewhere, he refers repeatedly to seeing. But he could not have understood the events he symbolizes if he had merely seen them. He knows it and introduces angels who explain and comment. He is being *told* things, even though the fundamental inspiration, as the first verse of his book declares, is from God.

Manifest in both authors, however briefly in Nostradamus, is a realization that prophesying is not a solitary feat. Their transcendence of time involves, in some sense, Others. That realization appears again in authors of very different kinds. Geoffrey of Monmouth, who published the alleged prophecies of Merlin in the twelfth century, portrayed the Welsh seer as speaking under the influence of a controlling spirit. Morgan Robertson, who wrote a novel in 1898 foreshadowing the loss of the *Titanic* in remarkable detail, said he was aided by an "astral writing partner."

Such testimonies as to what prophesying is like lead toward a theory that might be described as an essay in science fiction. It owes a debt to a classic work in that genre, Olaf Stapledon's *Last and First Men*. If prophecy happens at all, it involves a transtemporal leap of some kind. But the leap in itself, "seeing the future," is plainly inadequate. It can only yield sense if there is contact with some other entity *in* the future or having knowledge that belongs to the future: an entity that communicates and enlightens and is more than Dunne's higher-level self. This is not necessarily a literal angel or a literal spirit. Nostradamus's prophecies have a peculiarity that does not suggest a supernatural mentor at all; it suggests, however weirdly, a human one. The same is true of other case histories.

The French seer has limitations. His successful prophecies run on to the end of the eighteenth century, then focus exclusively on Napoleon and his nephew who became Napoleon III, and then stop. The geographical limitation is even more marked. Practically all the "good" quatrains relate to France or Britain. Yet most of the total of 942 quatrains, insofar as they make sense, concern other countries or have no clear location. Outside the Franco-British minority, Nostradamus has hundreds of opportunities for scoring and never does. Even if his good forecasts were all to be explained away as lucky hits, the limitation would remain. There ought to be a scatter of similar lucky hits for other countries, and there are none. The distribution is wildly skewed.

Hence, Nostradamus's successes do not imply encyclopedic knowledge about the future or an omniscient informant such as an angel. If a transtemporal contact of minds can be admitted at all, a quite ordinary person would be sufficient: someone acquainted with a certain amount of French history who has also taken a mild interest in British history but has not learned more than can be gathered from general reading. Contact with such a nonspecialist browser in the future could account for all of Nostradamus's successes, for their near-confinement to matters related to France and Britain, and for the virtual blank everywhere else. In the "good" quatrains, it is *as if* he were versifying information transmitted from a human being 300 or 400 years ahead, even if it happens under the aegis of his mysterious "divine being." If the two could be brought together, we might imagine them chatting, with a few relevant books on the table. Nostradamus learns things that, for his informant, are a matter of history, but, for himself and his readers, are in the future; and

they emerge from his mental process as prophecies.

However fanciful or frivolous this may sound, the Other—the person in the future, making contact with the prophet—is evoked in deep seriousness by one of the most extraordinary passages in the Bible, Second Isaiah's detailed foreshadowing, in his chapter 53, of the early Christians' account of Christ. This cannot be explained by the cliché of "seeing the future." An Israelite in the sixth century B.C., granted a glimpse of the last days of Jesus and the immediate sequel, could not have grasped what was going on, and certainly could not have inferred what the early Church would presently make of it. Nearly all of the passage, moreover, is in the past tense; it is not a prediction but a reminiscence; we are not being told what will happen, we are being told what already has happened, from the point of view of a contemporary.

It is *as if* we were listening to a speaker who takes shape quite vividly. He is a Jew who knew Jesus before his public ministry and was not impressed. He and his friends were aware of the circumstances of Jesus' death and saw it as a divine retribution for his messianic pretensions. Later, however, the speaker met some of the disciples and heard their story of the meaning of these events and their account of the Resurrection. He was converted. In Isaiah 53:1–11, we have his personal testimony as a Christian preacher—or, more precisely, a summary that he carries in his head and expands when addressing an audience. Second Isaiah has adapted it in his own style, but the substance is unchanged.

To suppose that contact occurred across the centuries—outside time or against its flow—between the mind of such a preacher and the mind of Second Isaiah is not to reject the belief in prophecy as coming from God. The contact might have been a miracle, divinely ordained. The point is that in this profoundly serious case, the image of the Other is not merely apparent but actually more so than in speculation about Nostradamus or anyone else whose prophecies might be accounted for in some such way.

Two literary mysteries point in the same direction. Dante in the *Divine Comedy* and Milton in *Paradise Lost* both make radical departures from Scripture and Christian tradition, and in doing so, they both seem to draw on knowledge not available at the time when they wrote. They are not prophesying, but they are doing something akin. Dante portrays Purgatory as a mountain on an island in the southern ocean. It rises in a succession of tiers with connecting stairways, and it has the Earthly Paradise (otherwise known as the Garden of Eden) on top. This mountain resembles Hindu and Buddhist models. Milton takes up the legend of a War in Heaven between angels loyal to God and the rebellious followers of Satan and transforms it into something strikingly like the Babylonian epic *Enuma elish,* even in detail. But the Hindu and Buddhist mythologies and related structures were not known in Europe until orientalists discovered them in the nineteenth century, and *Enuma elish* was not known until the tablets on which it was written were dug up, deciphered, and translated in the twentieth century.

In this case it is ludicrous to invoke seeing the future. Suppose we do picture the poets making out-of-the-body journeys into a future age. Their astral selves float into libraries and look at books on mythology. Why those particular books? Why should Dante pick on India when he knew little about it and had no interest? Why should Milton explore the literature of Babylon, which, being biblically conditioned, he would have regarded as evil? And how could they have understood these books in any case? Again, the Other gleams on the horizon. It is *as if* the poets were open to minds that were future from their own standpoint, minds acquainted with future scholarship—oriental or Babylonian. And

these were drawn somehow into contact, outside time or against the flow.

A spatial analogy may serve as an aid, the "Jim and Jane" story. As applied to prediction, it runs as follows. Two drivers, Jim and Jane, are traveling along a highway in separate cars. Jim is some distance ahead of Jane, who has paused to wait for a passenger. He passes a place where a rockfall has encroached on the road. Jane's car phone is switched on; Jim can call her with a warning of the hazard. She picks up the passenger and says there's a rockfall three miles ahead. When they pass it, her awareness in advance may seem mystifying or even paranormal, if the passenger doesn't know about Jim. So it could be with prophets like Nostradamus, who have learned of future events from somebody on the other side of them and are thus able to foretell them.

With Dante and Milton, who do not actually predict, the analogy can still work. Jim, far ahead, stops and buys a newspaper that has just hit the streets. Jane is waiting for her passenger. Jim notices an article in the paper that would interest her, and he calls back to tell her about it. Where she is, the paper isn't yet available, but thanks to Jim's call, she learns the contents of the article. So might a modern scholar's knowledge of the Babylonian epic drift into the mind of Milton and shape his own.

To imagine the transcending of time in this way (strictly, of course, on an "as if" basis) is not to speculate as to how it might happen. The object is to define a transcendence that covers the phenomena, as "seeing the future" does not. As a further recommendation, the notion of the Other communicating out of the future resolves a crux raised by anticipatory dreamers, such as Chris Robinson in England. Their claims have been contested on the ground that they lead to a paradox of prevention. If a dreamer foresees an undesired event, say an accident, and takes action so that it doesn't happen, what was seen in the first place? Robinson has taken such action, and two investigators, Robert Nelson and Louisa E. Rhine, have accepted that in such a case prevention is possible. But if, as a result, the event doesn't happen, how could the dreamer have foreseen it?

The hypothesis of the Other allows the dream to be a warning and not a prevision. Suppose the dreamer sees a boat sinking in heavy seas with friends aboard. They have not mentioned an intended cruise, indeed they have not planned one yet, so this is not an anxiety dream; it has a precognitive character. The explanation could be that someone else a few weeks hence, when their plans have taken shape, is going to generate an anxiety image of their boat going down. Transtemporal contact has carried the image back to the dreamer, not as something that *will* happen but as something that *could* happen. Before the cruise gets under way, he persuades them not to run the risk. Prevention has been effected without any paradox.

Could this theory be made scientifically intelligible? Though it envisages only mental processes, it cannot avoid one of the most perilous themes of science fiction, time travel. The most that can be said at present is that dismissive talk about "time's arrow" and the single unalterable flow is inconclusive. Some scientists have argued that Einstein's equations of general relativity do not rule time travel out. Some, notably Stephen Hawking, have expressed readiness to discuss it but scented a fatal obstacle in another paradox, popularly known as "killing the grandfather." If I travel backward in time and kill my grandfather before my father's birth, I won't have been born myself, therefore my grandfather wasn't killed, therefore I *have* been born, therefore . . . and so on. The past, it seems, has to be proof against intervention. In that case, the hypothetical mentors of Nostradamus and Milton could not have instilled knowledge into minds that, for them, were past.

Stapledon, in *Last and First Men,* proposed a solution to the problem, at least as it concerns influencing past minds. Despite grandfathers, physicists have aired possibilities that may have a bearing. They have spoken, for instance, of subatomic particles called tachyons that travel faster than light. According to relativity, time would stop for a body reaching the speed of light, and for a body going faster, time would run backward. There has been speculation about tachyons being produced by cosmic rays in the upper atmosphere. There has even been speculation about their being produced by brain activity, so that thoughts might travel back in time, as the idea of the Other requires. This is still science fiction and very much so, but at least it is attached to a specific concept. One writer, Philip K. Dick, has predicted (whether seriously or not) that tachyons may be used as carriers to "alter the past with scientific information"—an approach from a different angle to the notion of the Other inspiring knowledge by going backward in time.

A concept with slightly more tangibility is the wormhole, utilized in such television programs as *Star Trek.* A wormhole is said to be created by the junction of "singularities" in space-time, bringing points together that are normally far apart in time and space. The standard analogy is provided by separate points on a sheet of paper being made to coincide by folding the paper over. H. G. Wells anticipated this in a story, " The Strange Case of Davidson's Eyes." Wormholes are alleged to occur, but only briefly. No observer has found a stable wormhole. If such a thing did exist, anyone going through would emerge in a different place and time.

In the prophetic context, all of this is fantasy. It may suggest, however, that the space-time continuum has profound strangenesses and that contact between the prophet and the Other, perhaps centuries apart, may not be a self-evident absurdity.

Dreams; Dunne, J. W.; Fatima; Merlin; Milton, John; Nostradamus; Premonitions; Revelation; Robertson, Morgan; Second Isaiah; Stapledon, Olaf

Further Reading

Ashe, Geoffrey. *The Book of Prophecy.* London: Blandford, 1999.

Broughton, Richard. *Parapsychology.* New York: Ballantine, 1991.

Gribbin, John. *Time Warps.* London: J. M. Dent, 1979.

Krauss, Lawrence M. *The Physics of Star Trek.* London: HarperCollins, 1996.

PSYCHICS

Popular "psychics" making predictions in the media, of whom Jeane Dixon was probably the best known, have sometimes built a reputation (as she did) on a few successes. It is doubtful whether any have scored often enough to impress an impartial critic. Objective studies have been rare. During the late 1970s, however, David Wallechinsky, Amy Wallace, and Irving Wallace tabulated some results over a test period and incorporated their findings in their *Book of Predictions.* To judge from samplings at other times, before and after, there is no reason to think that a similar study would ever have turned out very differently.

With ten well-known U.S. psychics, the record was as follows:

	Right Predictions	Wrong Predictions
Olof Jonsson	1	25
Clarissa Bernhardt	1	32
Florence Vaty	1	33
Page Bryant	1	35
Fredrick Davies	0	34
Kebrina Kinkade	0	34
Jack Gillen	0	36
Bill O'Hara	0	37
Shawn Robbins	0	46
Micki Dahne	0	48
Total:	4	360

Many of the predictions were about matters of ephemeral interest. However, some concerned celebrities who retained celebrity status in subsequent years, and these may be thought to have a certain maturity. As follows:

Muhammad Ali would be elected to the U.S. Congress.

Edward Kennedy would run for president.

Elizabeth Taylor would win a Best Actress Oscar for a role in an X-rated movie.

Princess Caroline of Monaco would marry, first, an African property developer and then a Wyoming rancher.

President Carter would be injured in a hang-gliding accident.

Frank Sinatra would give up show business and become manager of a minor-league baseball team in Arizona.

Pope John Paul II would visit Disney World.

Besides these personal predictions, several others had a picturesque quality:

A Miss World contest would be won by an Eskimo.

A government study would reveal that women who watch soap operas live longer than those who don't.

Men would wear miniskirts.

General Motors would introduce a "thoughtmobile" operated by the driver's thoughts.

Aliens in UFOs would contact tourists in West Palm Beach, Florida.

A point of genuine interest is that the survey refuted one objection to more successful prophets, such as Nostradamus: that if you make a great many predictions, as he does, some will be right simply by chance. Manifestly, this is not so. The truth is that while Nostradamus does not score very often, he is decidedly better than the psychics in the survey. Moreover, his quatrains are often com-

The Great Pyramid, which the astronomer Piazzi Smyth interpreted diagrammatically. Later "Pyramidologists" tried to correlate some of its measurements with world events. (Ann Ronan Picture Library)

plex, combining several interlocked forecasts in a single, four-line stanza. By contrast, two of the four "right" predictions in the survey were merely forecasts of the result of a presidential election—a simple heads-or-tails choice.

See also: Dixon, Jeane; Nostradamus
Further Reading
Wallechinsky, David, Amy Wallace, and Irving Wallace. *The Book of Predictions.* New York: William Morrow, 1980.

PYRAMIDOLOGY

A theory according to which the structure of the Pyramid of Cheops in Egypt—the Great Pyramid—was correlated in some way with the course of history, so that events yet to come could be predicted by measuring it in the right places.

This theory involved more than chronology. The Pyramid was alleged, for instance, to embody mathematical data, such as the value of pi (the ratio of a circle's circumference to its diameter). Since the Egyptians were judged to have been incapable of building it, the work must have been performed by another people under divine inspiration. Hence, it was acceptable to find links with the Bible and Christian prophecy.

Pyramidology began with John Taylor in 1859. It was developed by the Scottish Astronomer Royal Charles Piazzi Smyth, who went to Egypt to study the Pyramid firsthand and produced a book on it in 1864. He claimed to have discovered a key unit of measurement, the "pyramid inch," which was 1.001 English inches. There was no trace of it as an authentic Egyptian unit, but that fact could be cited to support the belief that the builders were not Egyptians. A lecture on Pyramidology in 1875, attended by Madame Blavatsky, prompted the foundation of the Theosophical Society.

In due course, further Pyramidologists tried to show that an inside gallery followed the course of history, with distances corresponding to years. A stretch where the roof was low matched World War I. By extending the measurement, the future could be forecast. Another low stretch presumably meant another war. There was no war, but the Depression was made to serve instead. This phase was to end in 1936 with a major event of uncertain nature, possibly the Second Coming of Christ. The British-Israelites took up Pyramidology, and some had their own expectations for 1936. However, nothing particular happened. A revised calculation pointed to 1953, and again, nothing particular happened.

As a method of prediction, Pyramidology faded out. Assertions are still made about mathematical and astronomical knowledge expressed in the Pyramid's construction. Insofar as this exists, it does not demand a paranormal explanation or imply any builders other than Egyptians.

See also: British-Israel Theory

Further Reading

Cavendish, Richard, ed. *Man, Myth and Magic.* London: BPC Publishing, 1970–1972. Article "Pyramidology."

Q

QUETZALCOATL

Aztec god who figured in a prophecy that facilitated the Spanish conquest of Mexico.

In 1519, Hernán Cortés landed on the Mexican coast with a small force. Having overcome some local resistance and recruited allies from the inhabitants, he advanced on Tenochtitlan, the capital of the Aztec Empire. The emperor, Montezuma II, did not oppose him and tried to establish friendly relations and propitiate him with gifts. The reason, according to historians of the conquest, lay in the tradition of Quetzalcoatl, the great serpent god. Long ago, he had come to Mexico in the form of a tall white man with a full beard—a strange form to assume, since the native nations of America were not white and the men had only minimal beards or none. He had taught the people wisely but had been driven out by the hostility of an-other god and departed over the sea. It was prophesied that he would come back to reclaim his rights. For calendric reasons, his return was expected in the year the Spanish arrived. Montezuma thought Cortés, a bearded white man, was the god (or could be), and so he did not resist him until it was too late.

The story has probably been improved in retrospect. But Montezuma's peculiar attitude and his reported speeches to the invaders confirm his reputed motive in principle. A similar motive paralyzed Inca resistance in Peru. The bearded god in human form is certainly not a fiction invented after the conquest. He occurs in pre-Columbian mythology over a wide area. Moreover, he seems to have a factual basis. Foreign-looking men with beards, sometimes regarded as divine, are portrayed in Central American art dating from long before any known Old World contacts. Various theories have been proposed to account for them.

Further Reading

Ashe, Geoffrey. *Land to the West*. London: Collins, and New York: Viking, 1962.

Collins, Andrew. *Gateway to Atlantis*. London: Headline, 2000.

Rally. Revelation is far from being a mere medley of hallucinations or daydreams. It is planned and structured, often by the use of numerical patterns, especially patterns of seven. One proof of its literary power is the continuing currency of expressions such as "the Four Horsemen of the Apocalypse," "the Number of the Beast," and "Armageddon" as the name of a final battle.

REVELATION

Christian apocalyptic work that looks ahead to the End of the World and may predict identifiable events before that.

Revelation is the last book of the New Testament. Written in Greek, it is the chief product of the apocalyptic genre beginning in Daniel, which it sometimes echoes. In Christian parlance, it is *the* Apocalypse, others, not included in the scriptural canon, being Jewish. The author calls himself John. Early tradition identifies him as the apostle of that name and ascribes the Fourth Gospel to him also, though the two books are very different in outlook, style, and even literacy. It is simplest to take him at his word and call him John but to assume nothing about his apostleship or his responsibility for the gospel.

He introduces himself on the island of Patmos in the Aegean Sea, where he has been banished or has taken refuge during a persecution of Christians—probably under the emperor Domitian. Irenaeus, a second-century bishop whose early life was spent in Asia Minor nearby, dates Revelation toward the end of Domitian's reign, that is, about A.D. 96. If John was the apostle, he would have been very old at that time, but not impossibly so. He addresses his book to fellow Christians in Asia Minor, inviting them to read it aloud together.

Most of it consists of a series of visionary scenes, often including exposition by angels and other beings. John says he "saw" all this, but the word need not be taken too liter-

At the start, Christ appears to John and tells him to write what he is about to see, "what is and what is to take place hereafter." Messages follow for seven Christian communities in Asia Minor. Then the visions begin with the opening of a door in Heaven, revealing God enthroned, together with beings in the heavenly court. He holds a scroll covered with writing and sealed with seven seals. Only Christ is worthy to open it. Manifested in the form of a lamb, slain yet living, he opens four of the seals. Mounted men appear on horses differently colored. These are the Four Horsemen of the Apocalypse. One is a crowned conqueror; the others are bringers of war, famine, and death. They probably stand for the pagan imperialism that has created the world in which John lives—triumphant but at a terrible price.

The Lamb opens the fifth seal, and John sees the souls of the martyrs who have already died at the hands of persecutors, chiefly Nero and Domitian. They ask how long they must wait for the end of persecution and are told that it is not yet, more will have to suffer. This might count as a prediction, if a rather obvious one, and it seems to be taken up again, more interestingly, when John speaks of a "great tribulation" to be undergone by "a great multitude which no man could number, from every nation, from all tribes and peoples and tongues": the implication being that persecution will some day be universal and will happen in a

An illustration by the French artist Gustave Doré. Toward the end of Revelation, John is shown a vision of the New Jerusalem. (Dover Pictorial Series)

world with far more Christians in it than there are at the time of writing. This is one of several hints that John's anticipations extend far ahead, even though he employs words like "soon" that, in human terms, suggest otherwise. He may fail to grasp his own implications, or, like another scriptural author, he may take the view that human time does not apply. "With the Lord one day is as a thousand years, and a thousand years as one day." The hints of a long temporal perspective do not justify "interpretations" that have made him foretell remote events, even in the twentieth century, which would have been incomprehensible and irrelevant to his readers.

When John reaches the opening of the sixth seal, his visions are definitely moving into the future, and he is watching from outside time or far ahead. But there is no coherent sequence or chronology, and there are no recognizable events. The seal unleashes an earthquake and other portents, which herald an outpouring of divine wrath on sinful humanity. Then the final seal introduces a new set of seven: seven angels with seven trumpets who sound them one after another, inflicting judgments on the earth—fire, darkness, water pollution, hordes of giant locusts, and diabolical cavalry. At some stage during all this, two "witnesses" representing the Church defy the pagan world. They are slain but return to life, and, for the first time, pagans are shaken and give glory to God. The seventh trumpet sounds and the ordeal abruptly ends. Heavenly voices chorus, "The kingdom of the world has become the kingdom of our Lord and of his Christ, and he shall reign for ever and ever."

Thus far, apart from the vague allusions to future martyrdoms, it is hard to single out anything predictive in the sense that it can be pinned down and tested against facts. The narrative is mythic rather than literal. Would-be explainers have tried to find specific fulfillments, making out, for instance, that the locusts and cavalry symbolize Arab and Turkish conquests hundreds of years after John's time, but such notions are unconvincing. With the final trumpet, the story seems to be over. However, an angel has already warned John that he must prophesy again, and in the next chapter, he enters on a fresh visionary sequence. It goes back to the beginning of Christianity and moves forward from there to Christ's triumph as before but by a different route. It is chiefly in two passages of this second sequence, chapters 13 and 17, that John evokes concrete realities, makes predictions that can be deciphered, and arguably displays foreknowledge.

In chapter 12, he describes a "great portent in heaven" (the sky, not the abode of God): "a woman clothed with the sun, with the moon under her feet, and on her head a crown of twelve stars." She is about to give birth. She is twelve-tribed Israel bringing forth the Messiah—in John's eyes, Christ—and perhaps, in a sense, his mother Mary as representing Israel at that historic moment. Then, John describes another celestial portent, a huge red Dragon with seven heads and ten horns. This is Satan, the mighty rebel angel, cast down to earth and seeking to devour the child. In that aim, he is thwarted, but he pursues the woman, who is now, by a shift of symbolism, the Church as the new Israel, continuous with the old through its Jewish origin but superseding it. Though she escapes to safety, the Dragon can still attack her offspring, the Christians.

John has in mind the situation in the first century A.D. and the onset of persecution, the first major persecutor being the emperor Nero, who executed many Christians in Rome in the year 64 on a charge of trying to burn the city. In chapter 13, the seer presents something akin to a political cartoon, a "Beast" that is a great earthly institution brought into being by the Dragon. Its linkage with him is expressed by its having seven heads and ten horns, like himself; it has other features that recall a passage in the Old Testament book Daniel, where successive beasts stand for empires, and these features in combination show that John's Beast is a superempire, evidently the Roman Empire. It appears again further on, where an evil woman, "Babylon the great," is mounted on it. "Babylon" in John's time was a code name for the city of Rome itself, and the identity is clinched by the statement that the seven heads stand for the seven hills on which Rome was situated.

They have, however, another meaning. John explains that they stand also for the seven acknowledged emperors prior to John's contemporary Domitian: Augustus, Tiberius, Caligula, Claudius, Nero, Vespasian, Titus. These personalize the imperial power. In John's words, one of the Beast's heads "seemed to have a mortal wound, but its mortal wound was healed, and the whole earth followed the Beast with wonder . . . saying 'Who is like the Beast, and who can fight against it?'" The allusion is to the death of Nero in 68 and its sequel. It touched off an imperial crisis with ephemeral pretenders fighting each other, and the empire looked as if it might be falling apart, but Vespasian pulled it together, and it seemed indestructible. The wound was healed. It was healed in a personal sense also. There was a widespread belief that Nero himself was not dead and would return. While John would hardly have shared this belief literally, he did accept the idea, not confined to Christians, that it was true figuratively: Domitian was a "second Nero," and persecution had not ended with the death or alleged death of the prototype persecutor. In chapter 17, having recalled the seven emperors, John adds that the Beast, personalized anew in Domitian, is "an eighth."

He speaks of the Beast's subjects worshiping it (13:4), a reference to the official cult of the empire and its autocrat. There were temples of the goddess Roma, and the emperor himself was already being regarded as divine—Domitian wanted to be called "Our

Master and our God." In John's time, these developments, however abhorrent to Christians, were not getting many of them into trouble as dissenters. Domitian's persecution, though it may have banished the seer to Patmos, was limited in scope. But—still in chapter 13—John begins to look further. He introduces a second Beast, also called the False Prophet, who not only organizes the worship of the first but makes it compulsory and universal, with refusal a capital crime (verse 15). Nothing like this was happening when John wrote. The vision here must refer to a future, real or imagined, to a "totalitarian" change in the empire; and it is linked with the earlier passage about a great tribulation that will make martyrs of a vast multitude of Christians, throughout the known world.

John ends this chapter with the most famous or notorious words in his entire book: "Here is wisdom. Let him who has understanding reckon the number of the Beast, for it is the number of a man; and its number is six hundred and sixty-six." To solve this riddle is evidently to learn something about the Beast or perhaps confirm what a reader may infer on other grounds. The Number of the Beast can be calculated in more ways than one, but John is probably thinking of a technique known as gematria. In Hebrew and Greek, numbers were represented by letters of the alphabet (our so-called Arabic numerals had not reached the classical world), and every letter had its number. So the numbers matching the letters of a person's name could be added together to give a total corresponding to it. A well-known instance is the calculation of a number for Jesus. Transliterated in Greek as "Iesous," with a long *e*, it gives the numerical values 10, 8, 200, 70, 400, and 200, and their total 888 is his number. The Beast, presumably, has a human manifestation with a name adding up to 666. This technique can be adapted to other languages besides Hebrew and Greek. If A = 1, B = 2, and so on or indeed if letters are assigned any logical and consistent values, gematria can be applied to names in any language that has an alphabet. Hence a medley of far-fetched theories, extending into modern times.

The serious possibilities are limited by the Beast's Roman-ness. The Number has to fit a man who is associated and in some sense identified with the empire. He has to be contemporary with it; he cannot be in some hypothetical future beyond. These requirements have not prevented fanciful explanations that can only be justified, if at all, by expanding the Beast's significance to make it a more general anti-Christian figure, so that the Number can denote a man regarded as anti-Christian himself, expressive of the Beast's evil character even when it is not present in person. With a certain amount of juggling, "Muhammad" can be made to fit, and so can "l'Empereur Napoléon." A candidate who came on the scene even later than these is one of the best examples, numerically speaking. If A = 100, B = 101, and so on, "Hitler" gives 666. But such conjectures are futile. John invites his readers to solve his riddle, and there would be no point in doing so if the solution were a name that they could not guess—the name of someone in a distant and irrelevant future, with the calculation (in such cases as Hitler) depending on an alphabet not yet in existence.

Attention returns unavoidably to the Roman Empire, and the blending of the Beast with Nero as the empire's embodiment points to a solution that has been known for some time. The reason for its not being immediately obvious is that John writes in Greek, and in that language, "Nero Caesar," *Neron Kaisar,* does not add up correctly. But it does if transliterated into the Hebrew alphabet, and this is the answer or part of it. John creates a mystification—or camouflages a dangerous message?—by using a language known to Jews but not so familiar to Greek-speaking Christians in Asia Minor.

The commentator closest to John in time, Irenaeus, is rather vague about the Beast. He is unaware of the Hebrew solution of the Number, but he notes two early suggestions that supplement the Nero identification and fit in with it. One of his candidates is LATEINOS, Greek for "the Latin" or "the Roman," which adds up as required. "Those who now reign," Irenaeus remarks, "are Latini." Nero is a Roman, a "Latin," one of "those who now reign." Irenaeus knows and is impressed by another Greek solution: TEITAN, a name of the sun and specifically its god Apollo. It is more properly "Titan," but the legitimate spelling with a short *e* makes it add up to 666.

Irenaeus is right to be impressed, though for reasons he is only dimly aware of or not at all. Nero was flattered in his lifetime as an incarnation of Apollo and as a "New Sun" illuminating the empire. Other first-century emperors were not; the solar quality of Nero is distinctive. The two supplementary solutions have found their way to Irenaeus detached from the main one. Neither would suggest Nero by itself, but, combined with the basic Hebrew solution, they may well have been early elaborations of the riddle.

From a prophetic point of view, it is TEITAN that has a special interest because it is linked with the historical reality of the great tribulation that John foresees. When Irenaeus associates the Beast with the sun god, he uses the future tense and seems to provide for a manifestation yet to come. The application to Nero need not rule out a reference to the future as well and to a time when the Beast's solar character will play a part in the empire's totalitarian change. There is, in fact, a foreshadowing here—however it should be explained—of events that did not even begin to happen until a century later; events that involved a shift of imperial focus that was quite unpredictable, by any normal means, when Revelation was written.

Septimius Severus was emperor from 193 to 211. His wife, Julia Domna, was a Syrian from Emesa, the present-day Homs, on the Orontes River. Her father was a hereditary priest of the city's sun god. By this time, classical paganism was losing its grip, and Severus turned to Julia's family god with enthusiasm. He made the "Unconquered Sun," Sol Invictus, his patron deity. The imperial couple appeared together on coins as Sol and Luna, or Sun and Moon. Severus liked the image of the emperor illuminating the empire as the sun illuminated the world and had himself portrayed with an aureole of rays.

This was a first step toward an official solar theology. Severus's sons kept the cult alive, and Julia's young great-nephew Elagabalus or Heliogabalus, who was a priest of the god of Homs and actually became emperor, tried to take it further in Rome. Irresponsible and debauched, he was soon murdered, and the next step was not taken at once; but taken it was. In 270, after a long crisis with many pretenders and external threats, the emperor Aurelian restored peace and took the step. An eastern campaign had brought him to the vicinity of Homs, and he ascribed his victory to its god. He proclaimed Sol Invictus "Lord of the Roman Empire" and built him a temple in Rome with a special college of priests. Aurelian's Unconquered Sun was much more than the original Syrian deity. He was a composite, with elements of Apollo and also of Mithras, a Persian god popular with the army. In the words of a modern historian, this Supreme Being was to be "the centre of a revived and unified paganism, and the guarantor of loyalty to the Emperor." Emperors were to be his viceroys below—earthly "suns," so to speak.

The solar mystique was soon associated with a change in the empire, as foreshadowed by John. The emperor Diocletian and his colleagues carried out sweeping reforms. At a high price in authoritarianism and taxation, the empire was virtually refounded to survive without fundamental crises for over 100 years.

But if Sol Invictus was the Supreme Being and the empire's welfare depended on him,

there was no room for a rival Supreme Being. Christianity had to go. The rulers had other motives for suppression. Despite occasional outbreaks of persecution, the Church had become a large, widespread, and formidable body, which could not be fitted into the new absolutism. In 303, Diocletian authorized a full-scale campaign of annihilation. Christian assemblies were broken up, buildings were destroyed, and sacred books were confiscated. The following year, refusal to sprinkle incense on the altar of the deified emperor became a capital crime, and thousands throughout the empire were executed for refusing. Revelation 13:15 was fulfilled. However, the Church had grown too strong, too many of its members were resolute, and public opinion, so far as it existed, was less hostile than it had been in the past. Persecution flagged.

A decisive shift came with Constantine, who started out as a worshiper of the Unconquered Sun but decided that the Supreme Being was not Sol Invictus but the God of the Christians. In 313, as ruler of part of the empire, he issued an edict of toleration, and eventually, he became sole emperor and treated the Church with favor. The "multitude which no man could number" had come through the tribulation and was victorious. It was still some time before the empire became officially Christian, and some time before heresy, popular in high places, yielded to Catholic orthodoxy, but the corner had been turned.

Some kind of precognition is a serious issue. John points ahead to a totalitarian change in the empire's character: correct. Associated with this, he points to an empirewide and exterminatory persecution: correct. He, or a disciple developing his ideas, detects an imperial sun god: also correct. When John wrote, a more oppressive regime was perhaps foreseeable, and some of his fellow Christians probably concurred in expecting a greater persecution. But a takeover of the empire by a solar mystique, originating from a Syrian deity, was far from foreseeable. Nevertheless, the takeover happened, and because of it, "Titan" enjoyed a phase of anti-Christian ascendancy in the late third century and the early fourth.

If there is a case for thinking that John looks so far ahead, is there a case for thinking that he looks further? He describes seven more plagues, an attempted recovery by the forces of evil, and preparations for a final battle at Armageddon. Though Armageddon is a real place, Megiddo in Palestine, it is hard to see any literal fulfillments.

His account of the imperial Beast, however, has an additional feature. While its seven heads are explained as emperors, it also has ten horns. These are adopted from one of Daniel's symbolic beasts, but they ought to be functional as the heads are. In chapter 17, the function is indicated. John portrays his opulent evil woman, the "great harlot" Babylon, mounted on the Beast: she represents the city of Rome itself. The chapter leads up to Babylon's fall, that is, the ruin of Rome, the city specifically. An angel expounding the vision says, "The ten horns that you saw are ten kings who have not yet received royal power, but they are to receive authority as kings for one hour together with the Beast. . . . They and the Beast will hate the harlot: they will make her desolate and naked, and devour her flesh and burn her up with fire."

One theory is that the passage refers to events expected soon. John is alleged to be echoing a rumor that Nero was still alive in the eastern country of Parthia, planning to return and take vengeance on the city that expelled him, with the support of Parthian satraps or regional governors inaccurately called kings. One of several objections is that John is most unlikely to have believed the rumor or put it in a book that is on an entirely different level from the political fantasies of the day.

His prophecy about "Babylon" is more interesting than that, and it is interesting because it is not obvious. As an anti-Roman author, he might have been expected to foretell the downfall of the great city, the fountainhead of persecution. The natural way to imagine this taking place would have been through an attack from outside, by a foreign conqueror. Yet this is precisely not what he imagines. Rome is to be smashed by forces generated within its own empire and by imperially created upstarts. It would have been difficult, in John's time, to find any past instance of such an overthrow; he is picturing a process new to the world.

It is a process, nevertheless, that did happen. It began in the fifth century when the empire was dissolving in western Europe and Africa but still cohering after a fashion. Barbarian peoples were settling within its borders and carving out territories under their own leaders, at first more or less by agreement. One such leader was Alaric, king of the Visigoths; another was Gaiseric, king of the Vandals, who formed a domain of his own in northern Africa; another, according to legend, was Hengist, who brought Saxons into Britain as auxiliary troops and made himself overlord of Kent. "Ten" is merely a round number of horns taken from Daniel, yet it is not absurd as an approximation to the actual number of barbarian kings.

These rulers pursued their interests in different ways, at first propping the empire up, later acting more and more independently. The most important and powerful of them turned against the imperial city. In 410, Alaric captured Rome and allowed his Visigoths to pillage it for six days. This unprecedented disaster was a traumatic blow felt everywhere, and it was not the last. In 455, Gaiseric sailed over from Africa with his Vandals and did likewise. This time, the sack of Rome lasted fourteen days. The city never recovered; Babylon was fallen indeed, at the hands of kings such as John had seen, correctly, arising within the empire and under its auspices. In the same chapter he speaks of the Lamb—Christ—as conquering them. Most of them were pagans or heretical Christians, Gaiseric in particular being intensely hostile to the orthodox majority; the ensuing gradual success of the Church could be seen as a conquest.

Because John's Babylon did actually fall in the fifth century, made desolate by successor rulers within the empire, it is legitimate to argue that the Beast's horns represent such rulers and that chapter 17 symbolizes fifth-century events. That is as far as John's apparent prevision extends, in the sense of pointing to a future that is verifiable in history. However, Revelation still has some way to go. After Babylon has fallen and been mourned by all who did well out of her, Christ appears in majesty. There is a conflict in which his enemies are slain, and the Beast and False Prophet are cast into a lake of fire.

John is convinced that the empire, with its hateful mystique, must perish (he gives no hint of its Christianization after the emperor Constantine), and it has filled his world so completely that he cannot conceive of history going on after its demise. He does look beyond but with narrative of a different type. In chapter 20, Satan is imprisoned, though, for some reason, only temporarily. The martyrs, with others who did not capitulate to the Beast, come to life and reign with Christ for 1,000 years. At the end of this period, Satan is released and leads a fresh onslaught, but he is thrown into the lake of fire where his creatures, the Beast and the False Prophet, already are. The rest of the dead are raised, and the Last Judgment follows. The world passes away and is replaced by a glorious New Jerusalem, the everlasting home of the blessed.

Once again, it is only in chapters 13 and 17, about the empire and the city of Rome, that John seems to be making predictions of a literal kind. In his subsequent visions, he is weaving prophetic myths of the future, rather than narratives of it, and that indeed is what he has been doing in most of his book. However, chapter 20 caused dissension in the early Church over the question whether Christ's 1,000-year reign was to be taken at face value. One school of thought believed John to be forecasting a Utopia that would flourish with an abundance of earthly delights in days to come—a reading of the text reflecting Jewish speculations about the reign of the Messiah. This opinion was called "millenarian." Its rejection by the Church delayed the admission of Revelation to the canon of Scripture. When the book's prestige and its claim to apostolic authorship compelled its acceptance, the 1,000-year reign was explained spiritually in terms of the Church's dominance. But the millenarian view never quite died, and standard dictionaries note the 1,000-year Utopia as an acceptable meaning of the word *millennium.*

See also: Antichrist; Apocalypse; Daniel; Messiah

Further Reading

Ashe, Geoffrey. *The Book of Prophecy.* London: Blandford, 1999.

Barker, Ernest. *From Alexander to Constantine.* Oxford: Clarendon Press, 1956.

Bowder, Diana. *The Age of Constantine and Julian.* London: Paul Elek, 1978.

Brown R. E., J. A. Fitzmyer, and R. E. Murphy, eds. *The New Jerome Biblical Commentary.* Englewood Cliffs, NJ: Prentice-Hall, 1990.

Grant, Michael. *Nero.* New York: Dorset Press, 1989.

Swete, Henry Barclay. *The Apocalypse of St. John.* London: Macmillan, 1907.

ROBERTSON, MORGAN (1861–1915)

A U.S. novelist who fictionally foreshadowed the sinking of the *Titanic.*

Robertson began his working life as a merchant seaman. In 1886, he gave up seafaring and became a jeweler in New York. Ten years later, his eyesight was failing, and he had to abandon the business. He started producing sea stories for magazines, making use of his own experience and knowledge of ships.

In 1897, he wrote a short novel entitled *Futility, or The Wreck of the Titan,* which was published the following year. He believed that he had the help of an unseen being, an "astral writing partner." The story is set aboard a British luxury liner named the *Titan.* She is 800 feet long, bigger than anything actually afloat at the time of writing, and is supposed to be unsinkable, with nineteen watertight compartments. She has three propellers and twenty-four lifeboats. On her maiden voyage, she strikes an iceberg at twenty-five knots and sinks with great loss of life, partly because there are too few lifeboats on board.

Robertson continued to write copiously but without much success, though his stories were praised by two novelists of greater fame, Joseph Conrad and Booth Tarkington. Some of them involved "fringe" topics such as telepathy, hypnosis, and dual personality, but it does not appear that he made any more claims about an astral partner. For a while, he was mentally unbalanced. He died suddenly of a heart attack.

On April 10, 1912, fourteen years after the *Titan* novel was published, the British luxury liner *Titanic* sailed on her maiden voyage. Even apart from her name, she was close to meeting Robertson's specifications in several respects. She was 882.5 feet long and supposed to be unsinkable, with sixteen watertight compartments. She had three propellers and twenty lifeboats. On April 15, she struck an iceberg at about twenty-three knots and sank with great loss of life, partly because there were too few lifeboats.

Robertson's novel had never been a bestseller, but after the disaster, readers who remembered it brought it to public notice. It cannot be accounted for simply as one shipwreck story among many, the one that happened to be more or less right. In its day, it was highly original, perhaps unparalleled. Few authors of fiction had the requisite professional knowledge, and nothing like the modern "disaster movie" had appeared in any medium.

See also: Garnett, Mayn Clew; Stead, W. T.

Further Reading

Ashe, Geoffrey. *The Book of Prophecy.* London: Blandford, 1999.

Wade, Wyn Craig. *The Titanic: End of a Dream.* New York: Penguin Books USA, 1986.

Wallechinsky, David, Amy Wallace, and Irving Wallace. *The Book of Predictions.* New York: William Morrow, 1980.

SABBATAI ZEVI (1626–1676)

Jewish would-be Messiah who claimed to fulfill prophecies in occult speculation.

Partly because of an influx of refugees from Spain, the late fifteenth century saw a small revival of the Jewish presence in Palestine. With this came a glimmer of renewed messianic hope, after a long period of disillusionment and caution. During the 1530s, Jacob Berab, the chief rabbi of Safed (now Zefat), proposed to prepare the Messiah's way by making the town a new center for Judaism: rabbis, he suggested, should come to Safed for ordination, and a court of appeal should be set up there to resolve disputes. This project was unsuccessful, but Safed did become a center of learning, and a young scholar, Isaac Luria, pioneered a new school of Jewish thought that turned away from the orthodox legalism of the Talmud in favor of the esoteric system known as the cabala.

One book that became popular with his disciples was the Zohar, a cryptic medieval treatise on the Unseen. Its interpreters detected clues to the messianic advent and began to form notions about the Messiah personally, using calculations and occult techniques to fix a time for his arrival. He was to be born on the Ninth of Ab in the Jewish calendar, a day in August that had seen the fall of both the Temples, the first to the Babylonians, the second to the Romans. The Ninth of Ab had been a "bad" day twice over, but the Messiah's birth would make it a "good" day. The year inferred from the Zohar for his public manifestation was 1648. Luria himself had died young, but his school was still flourishing as the time approached.

A Jew born on the Ninth of Ab would obviously have a flying start in messiahship, and Sabbatai Zevi, who was born on that day in 1626, realized as much. His home was at Smyrna in Asia Minor (now Izmir), and he grew up with advantages because his father—a Sephardic Jew of Spanish descent—became rich as the agent of an English commercial house. Sabbatai studied both the Talmud and the cabala, but he greatly preferred the latter. Drawn to Luria's teachings and learning from them that ascetic discipline could confer superhuman powers, he took cold baths regularly and abstained from sex. A group of admirers gathered around him, attracted by his peculiar charm and air of holiness. In the designated year 1648, he announced that he was the Lord's Anointed and would restore the Kingdom of Israel in the Promised Land.

Denounced by the rabbis in Smyrna, he and his clique went to Constantinople, the capital of the Ottoman Empire. Here Sabbatai made more converts, one of whom fabricated a prophecy for him. Then they moved to Salonika, where he went through a ritual "wedding" to the Torah, the fundamental Jewish Scripture. Through his father's contacts in England, he heard that a Christian sect, the Fifth Monarchy Men, were expecting a new era to start in 1666. Others noticed the coincidence. A Jewish petition to Cromwell in 1655, asking for toleration, mentions a widespread belief that the situation will soon be changed by the recovery of Palestine. Sabbatai adopted 1666 as the date for his restoration of the Kingdom of Israel.

After a period spent in Egypt, where he made some wealthy proselytes, he at last reached Jerusalem in 1663. He used his good

Many Jews believed that Sabbatai Zevi was the Messiah. He is depicted blessing his followers in his native Smyrna (now Izmir). (Ann Ronan Picture Library)

singing voice to attract audiences, whom he charmed with renditions of the Psalms and improper Spanish ballads, assuring his hearers that the ballads had inner spiritual meanings. An unexpected recruit was Sarah, a Jewish orphan from Poland who declared herself to be the Messiah's destined bride. Sabbatai agreed and married her. His movement acquired an aura of freedom and festivity. Jews under his influence gave up some of the fasts of their religion and held parties instead, since, after all, the long ages of waiting and sorrow were over.

Nathan, a visionary from Gaza, also joined the movement, claiming to be Elijah returned. He foretold that Sabbatai would go away to discover the Lost Tribes of Israel, deported by the Assyrians in biblical times, and would lead them back to the Promised Land to rejoin their brethren, riding on a lion. Orthodox rabbis threatened to excommunicate the whole sect. Sabbatai returned to his native Smyrna and was received with enthusiasm.

The year of glory, 1666, was looming close. Envoys of Sabbatai spread the word in western Europe. Some of the rabbis were won over, and in Avignon, the entire Jewish community prepared to migrate. Many Christians were willing to believe that the reinstatement of the Kingdom of Israel was near; Samuel Pepys noted the expectation in his diary.

No one knows how Sabbatai hoped to fulfill his pledge. Early in 1666, he went to Constantinople again, perhaps with an idea of making a deal with the sultan authorizing Jewish resettlement in some part of Palestine. The Turks, however, arrested him. At first, they treated him politely, housed him in comfort, and allowed him visitors. But the unchecked momentum toward the new Exodus convinced them that he was causing trouble. The palace doctor, a Jew who had turned Muslim, warned him that he would be executed unless he took the same step. He did. Granted an audience with the sultan, he removed his Jewish cap, put on a turban, and acknowledged that Muhammad was the Prophet of God.

The sultan gave him a post at court, and he made various attempts to explain his apostasy, but they were too tortuous to convince, and his movement collapsed in ignominy with disastrous effects on the Jewish communities that had believed in him. He was banished to Albania and died in 1676. A small group of followers refused to give up and tried to make out that his catastrophic conduct was part of the program. Sabbatai was fulfilling a text in the Zohar that said that the Messiah would be "good within and evil without." He had committed almost the worst sin possible for anyone subject to the Jewish Law, to show that the Law must be outgrown. He had pointed the way to a more adventurous, less guilt-ridden mode of life. Whatever might be thought of such rationalizations, he had really done so during his brief hour of triumph. In eastern Europe where his subversiveness awakened echoes, even inspiring new radical sects, Judaism grew freer and livelier. It was never quite the same again after this shake-up, and rigid legalism could never quite reestablish itself.

See also: Elijah; Fifth Monarchy Men; Messiah

Further Reading

Jewish Encyclopaedia. (where the name is spelled Shabbethai). New York and London: Funk & Wagnalls. 1901–1906.

Kastein, Joseph. *The Messiah of Ismir: Sabbatai Zevi.* Translated by Huntley Paterson. New York: Viking Press. 1931.

SAVONAROLA, GIROLAMO (1452–1498)

Dominican preacher, reformer, and self-styled prophet active in Florence.

A Puritan in spirit before Protestantism, Savonarola denounced Florentine morals and the city's preeminence in worldly culture.

Asserting a divine gift of prophecy, he predicted that Charles VIII, the king of France, would invade Italy and the French occupation would be a punishment for the people's sins. The invasion was not, in fact, difficult to foresee. Charles believed that he had a claim to the kingdom of Naples. In 1494, he crossed the Alps with an army and presently arrived in Florence on his way southward.

However, Charles became a focus for another body of prophecy that was long established and at odds with the grim pronouncements of Savonarola. The school of thought originating with Joachim of Fiore anticipated a great ruler, a Second Charlemagne, who would unite Christendom and usher in a golden age. Although the French king was less than impressive, his name at least was Charles, and enthusiasts declared that his features agreed with imaginary descriptions of the Second Charlemagne. Florence already figured in speculations about the new order, and the French expedition was hailed by some as its beginning.

Savonarola seems to have reflected on this Joachite hope. As 1494 drew toward a close, he took a less threatening tone, in keeping with the Florentines' mood. Charles's conduct toward them was not punitive at all, and he marched away peacefully to pursue his Neapolitan project. Meanwhile, Savonarola was taking up another motif from Joachite prophecy. The Second Charlemagne was to be crowned by an ecclesiastical counterpart, an Angelic Pope who would reform the Church. At that time, ironically, the pope was the Borgia Alexander VI, one of the least angelic in the whole history of the papacy. Undaunted, Savonarola began to talk of an Angelic one in the near future, after a phase of tribulation, and even suggested that Florence would become the new Rome.

Insisting on his prophetic inspiration, he tried to create a sort of theocracy. As a public demonstration of Florentine repentance, he organized a "bonfire of the vanities" in which the wealthier citizens committed all sorts of possessions to the flames—pictures, musical instruments, antiques, books, jewelry, playing cards. However, he went too far and made powerful enemies. Public opinion gradually turned against him, and Rome passed a sentence of excommunication. He held a second bonfire of vanities, but this one led to riots. In 1498, he was forced to recant and was put to death as a heretic.

See also: Angelic Pope; Eliot, George; Joachim of Fiore; Second Charlemagne

Further Reading

Reeves, Marjorie. *The Influence of Prophecy in the Later Middle Ages.* Notre Dame: University of Notre Dame Press, 1993.

———. *Joachim of Fiore and the Prophetic Future.* New York: Harper and Row, 1977.

SCRYING

Better known as crystal gazing. Quite a number of people can see images in a crystal if they fix their eyes on it for a few minutes undisturbed. These images are alleged to have meaning and, sometimes, to reveal the future. Faking by fortune-tellers does not invalidate the phenomenon. Watching the crystal induces a kind of semihypnosis in which the images project themselves from subconscious sources. They have been compared to the hypnagogic visions that flash into the mind on the verge of sleep.

The scrying instrument need not be literally a crystal. Native Americans stare into bowls of water or at polished slabs of black stone. Australian medicine men gaze at a flame or a piece of quartz. Egyptians are said to have contemplated ink, and Roman soothsayers examined sword blades. It appears that almost anything bright or shiny will do, for a person who has the gift.

Scrying was known in western Europe from the early Middle Ages. The crystal or other instrument came to be called a speculum, which means a mirror, and mirrors figure among the objects used. Whatever the method, scrying was viewed with

A magic mirror reveals secrets to the scryer: From an eighteenth-century cabalistic manuscript. (Ann Ronan Picture Library)

some disfavor by ecclesiastics, though not to the extent of getting its practitioners into trouble. An interesting passage in Hartlieb's *Book of All Forbidden Arts* (1455) condemns attempts to see angels by staring fixedly at the polished vessels of the Mass. This practice may underlie scenes in Arthurian legend where visions appear in the Holy Grail. The thirteenth-century romance *Perlesvaus* includes an episode where the author seems to be aware of the basic scrying experience and is fantasizing it into something much more elaborate and significant.

In this romance Sir Gawain is received at the castle where the Grail is housed. Several knights sit with him at dinner, and he is given to understand that he must speak when he sees the holy object in order to break an enchantment. This is a recurrent motif in Grail legend, but the testing of Gawain is exceptional.

Two maidens appeared from a chapel: in her hands one was carrying the Holy Grail, and the other held the lance with the bleeding head [a mysterious weapon sometimes associated with the Grail]. Side by side they came into the hall where the knights and Sir Gawain were eating. . . . Sir Gawain gazed at the Grail and thought he saw therein a chalice . . . and he saw the point of the lance from which the red blood flowed, and he thought he could see two angels bearing two golden candlesticks with candles burning. The maidens passed before Sir Gawain and into another chapel. Sir Gawain was deep in thought, so deep in joyful thought that he could think only of God. The knights stared at him, all downcast and grieving in their hearts.

But just then the two maidens came out of the chapel and passed once more before Sir Gawain. And he thought he saw three angels where before he had seen but two, and there in the centre of the Grail he thought he could see the shape of a child. The foremost knight cried out to Sir Gawain, but he, looking before him, saw three drops of blood drip on to the table, and was so captivated by the sight that he did not say a word. And so the maidens passed on by, leaving the knights looking at one another in dismay. . . .

The two maidens passed once more before the table, and to Sir Gawain it seemed that there were three; and looking up it appeared to him that the Grail was high up in the air. And above it he saw, he thought, a crowned king nailed to a cross with a spear thrust in his side. Sir Gawain was filled with sorrow at the sight and he could think of nothing save the pain that the king was suffering. Again the foremost knight cried out to him to speak, saying that if he delayed longer, the chance would be lost forever. But Sir Gawain remained gazing upwards in silence, hearing nothing that the knight had said. The maidens disappeared into the chapel with the Grail and the lance, the knights cleared the tables, left the feast and moved off into another chamber, and Sir Gawain was left there alone.

Gawain's silence is attributed to the semi-hypnosis recognized in real scrying. He is not, of course, seeing the future; he is undergoing a visionary experience of Christian mysteries.

To revert to actuality, the famous Elizabethan astrologer John Dee had a "shewstone" that is variously described; he may have experimented with more than one. A shew-stone of Dee's came into the hands of the eighteenth-century collector Horace Walpole and found its way to the British Museum. Dee is the first prominent person known to have used a crystal ball. Among modern clairvoyants, the most favored "crystal" is a glass globe about four inches across. They usually dispense with preparatory rituals and incantations that were prescribed in past times and simply focus on the crystal.

Apparitions may take time to manifest themselves. At first, the crystal may grow misty and opaque from within. Some say the color of the mist is itself an omen: white is good, black is bad, and so forth. When an image does clarify, it may be meaningless—an unrecognized face, an unknown landscape. But it may, supposedly, give a glimpse of some reality in another place.

And it may show things to come. The notion that it can do so is the basis for fortune-telling by this method. Claims of a responsible kind have seldom attracted much critical interest. A Victorian investigation by the Society for Psychical Research produced several cases. There was a Miss Goodrich-Freer who foresaw journeys and messages; there was a Mrs. Bickford-Smith who looked at a crystal belonging to someone else and had a prevision of a friend's death, which occurred a few days later. Such testimonies were doubtless honest, but they proved very little, and nothing more convincing from a skeptical point of view seems to have been recorded since. The use of scrying in modern times, as a guide in business decisions, for example, may not be altogether fallacious. But the successful scryer, like the successful astrologer, is very likely achieving results through knowledge of the client and the situation, with the visions taking shape under the influence of that knowledge.

See also: Brahan Seer, The

Further Reading

Cavendish, Richard, ed. *Man, Myth and Magic.* London: BPC Publishing, 1970–1972. Article "Scrying."

The High Book of the Grail (i.e., *Perlesvaus*). Translated by Nigel Bryant. Cambridge: D. S. Brewer, and Totowa, NJ: Rowman & Littlefield, 1978.

Melville, John. *Crystal Gazing.* Reprint. New York: Weiser, 1970.

SECOND CHARLEMAGNE

An ideal emperor, recurrently prophesied in the Middle Ages and Renaissance.

He appears in the speculations of followers of Joachim of Fiore. They predicted a coming Age of the Holy Spirit and a world renewal. The transition would need both spiritual and political leadership. The former would be supplied by an Angelic Pope; the latter required a great ruler acting in concert with him.

Christian yearnings had long since evolved the prophetic figure of a "Last Emperor," who would reign in peace and prosperity, unite the civilized world, repel barbarians, and raise the Church to triumphant heights, converting Jews and heathens. But he was precisely a *last* emperor, giving the human race an honorable conclusion; he would be followed at once by Antichrist and the End of the World. Joachites, who expected something more cheerful, pictured an emperor who would do much the same things but with a forward-looking orientation. Crowned by the Angelic Pope, he would usher in the Age of the Holy Spirit.

They found his historical prototype in Charlemagne, who united much of Europe on a Christian basis at the beginning of the ninth century. His domain broke up, but a

Napoleon conferring with Czar Alexander. The French Emperor claimed to be a new Charlemagne but probably did not know the Joachite prophecies of such a person. (Ann Ronan Picture Library)

large part of it survived, chiefly in Germany and Italy—the so-called Holy Roman Empire. During the First Crusade, there had been a legend that he would return to life. The Joachites may have taken a hint from such fancies but were not really concerned with them. They simply hoped for another emperor who would be like Charlemagne, only more so.

Some enthusiasts unwisely cast contemporaries in that role. Frederick of Trinacria, king of Sicily, was the first candidate. He took the prophecy seriously but, despite Joachite urging, made no attempt to act on it. Charles VIII of France, who invaded Italy in 1494 amid outpourings by the famous preacher Savonarola, was viewed similarly. A French poet, Guilloche of Bordeaux, foretold that he would go on from Italy to become

king of Greece and conquer the Turks. He did neither.

A sixteenth-century candidate was the emperor Charles V, who united Germany and Spain under the House of Hapsburg. Nostradamus favored the Second Charlemagne idea in a somewhat reduced form. He correctly forecast a splendid future for the young French prince who became Henri IV and who was hailed in his lifetime as *Carolus Magnus Redivivus,* Charlemagne Revived. But the dream was becoming less mystical and more purely political, even controversial, being attached to different sovereigns and invoked by different parties, Catholic and Protestant.

The only important person who ever actually claimed to be a new Charlemagne was Napoleon, and he illustrates the change.

When he was crowned emperor in 1804, he had appropriate emblems painted on his coach and carried what was supposed to be Charlemagne's scepter. He even wrote "I am Charlemagne" in a letter. But he probably never heard of Joachim, and he certainly had no notion of inaugurating an Age of the Holy Spirit.

See also: Angelic Pope; Eliot, George; Joachim of Fiore; Nostradamus

Further Reading

Ashe, Geoffrey. *The Book of Prophecy.* London: Blandford, 1999.

Reeves, Marjorie. *Joachim of Fiore and the Prophetic Future.* New York: Harper and Row, 1977.

Reeves, Marjorie, ed. *Prophetic Rome in the High Renaissance Period.* Oxford: Clarendon Press, 1992.

SECOND ISAIAH (FL. 539 B.C.)

Old Testament prophet whose work is attached to the original text of Isaiah and who has been widely believed to foretell Christ.

Chapters 1–39 of Isaiah are, in substance, by the prophet of that name and belong to the eighth century B.C. From chapter 40 on, the book reflects a much later situation, which would have been incomprehensible to Isaiah's audience. There is no serious doubt that the author is someone other than Isaiah himself. For want of a name, he is referred to as "Deutero-Isaiah," or Second Isaiah. It is not known how or why the texts were combined. The last chapters of the book may even have been composed by a third author, but they are not relevant here.

Second Isaiah writes in Babylon toward 539 B.C. His main theme is the imminent liberation of the Israelites who have been in captivity since Nebuchadnezzar's army destroyed Jerusalem. Their exile is now virtually over. The Persian king Cyrus has defeated the Babylonians. The prophet hails him as the anointed of the Lord and rejoices at the return to Zion, which the Persian victory will make possible. He takes a vitally important religious step: with him, the God of Israel becomes unequivocally the only God, Lord of all nations. He hopes that the deliverance of God's Chosen People and their future glories will lead all others to acknowledge God.

In four passages, somewhat detached from the rest, the prophet introduces a figure who has no exact antecedents. They are known as the "Servant of the Lord Oracles" or "Servant Songs." Earlier scriptural characters are spoken of in passing as God's "servants," but Second Isaiah has a Servant in mind whose status is more specific. He will "bring forth justice to the nations." The prophet seems to waver between treating him as an individual and treating him as a personification of Israel.

The fourth and longest Song is strikingly different from the others. It extends from the end of one chapter into the next, from 52:13 to 53:12. Here, the Servant has a role that is unprecedented and unparalleled. He undergoes terrible suffering, dies, and yet lives on and is exalted. Early Christians took this Song as a prophecy of Christ, and many since have followed them. Phrases in it are familiar from Handel's *Messiah,* and the tradition is so firmly entrenched that the pre-Christian nature of the source is not always realized.

In the Revised Standard Version of the Bible, the passage runs as follows. (The verse form is not reproduced here.) It falls into three unequal parts. At the end of chapter 52, the Lord speaks:

13. Behold, my servant shall prosper, he shall be exalted and lifted up, and shall be very high.

14. As many were astonished at him—his appearance was so marred, beyond human semblance, and his form beyond that of the sons of men—

15. so shall he startle many nations; kings shall shut their mouths because of him; for that which has not been told them they shall

see, and that which they have not heard they shall understand.

In 53:1–11a, an unidentified speaker tells the story. In a couple of places, translations differ about the tense of the verbs, but, except at the end, the passage is almost certainly narrative throughout—which is strange in a prophecy.

1. Who has believed what we have heard? And to whom has the arm of the Lord been revealed?

2. For he grew up before him like a young plant, and like a root out of dry ground; he had no form or comeliness that we should look at him, and no beauty that we should desire him.

3. He was despised and rejected by men; a man of sorrows, and acquainted with grief; and as one from whom men hide their faces he was despised, and we esteemed him not.

4. Surely he has borne our griefs and carried our sorrows; yet we esteemed him stricken, smitten by God, and afflicted.

5. But he was wounded for our transgressions, he was bruised for our iniquities; upon him was the chastisement that made us whole, and with his stripes we are healed.

6. All we like sheep have gone astray; we have turned every one to his own way; and the Lord has laid on him the iniquity of us all.

7. He was oppressed, and he was afflicted, yet he opened not his mouth; like a lamb that is led to the slaughter, and like a sheep that before its shearers is dumb, so he opened not his mouth.

8. By oppression and judgment he was taken away; and as for his generation, who considered that he was cut off out of the land of the living, stricken for the transgression of my people?

9. And they made his grave with the wicked and with a rich man in his death, although he had done no violence, and there was no deceit in his mouth.

10. Yet it was the will of the Lord to bruise him; he has put him to grief; when he makes himself an offering for sin, he shall see his offspring, he shall prolong his days; the will of the Lord shall prosper in his hand;

11a. he shall see the fruit of the travail of his soul and be satisfied.

In the rest of verse 11 and in verse 12, God speaks again and confirms what has been said.

11b. By his knowledge shall the righteous one, my servant, make many to be accounted righteous; and he shall bear their iniquities.

12. Therefore I will divide him a portion with the great, and he shall divide the spoil with the strong; because he poured out his soul to death, and was numbered with the transgressors; yet he bore the sin of many, and made intercession for the transgressors.

Jewish interpreters take this fourth Song as a sequel to the others. The Servant is Israel personified, undergoing agonies yet vindicated at last; if there is a hint at a messianic individual, it is subsidiary. But even if that is the primary meaning, the passage has a further meaning, like some other prophetic texts, and in this case, it is hard to deny that it overshadows the primary one. The further meaning has become dominant, and the passage has details that a purely "Israel" symbolism cannot accommodate.

If the Servant is simply Israel, there is a difficulty at once with the "we" at the beginning of the main passage. It would have to refer to the gentile kings in 52:15, making them recall their contempt for the Chosen People and confess that Israel's endurance and rebirth will bring salvation to the Gentiles themselves. But the prophet has just said that the kings never heard the Servant's history and that even when they do, they will be "shutting their mouths," not pouring out testimony. These objections seem to apply however the Servant is explained. The voice in chapter 53 cannot be the voice of the kings. There is a slight doubt about the reading "my people" in verse 8, but if it is correct, the story is being told by one person who speaks for others.

The Servant may be a supreme representative of Israel, but he is a person, not merely a personification. A verse in the New Testament (Acts 8:34) mentions, only to reject, a curious notion that the prophet is speaking of himself. A modern commentator has taken this up, but it is hard to see how it would work. The fact must be faced that the orthodox account of Christ's sufferings, death, and resurrection is plainly detectable here, in a loosely narrative form with backtrackings and observations. At least ten features of the New Testament's presentation of Christ are to be found in the Servant Song. Thus:

His rejection by his people (chapter 53:3);

His silence before his accusers (53:7);

His trial and condemnation (53:8);

His disfigurement by scourging and other torments (52:14, 53:5);

His crucifixion—"lifted up," cp. John 3:14, 12:32–33 (52:13);

His death in the company of criminals (53:8–9, 12);

His atonement, guiltless himself, for other's sins (53:4–6, 9–10, 12);

His burial in the tomb of the wealthy Joseph of Arimathea (53:9);

His triumph over death and after it (52:13, 53:10–11);

His creation of a community of believers, his spiritual offspring (53:10–11).

But what precisely is being foreshadowed? Not the last days of the "historical Jesus," if that phrase has any meaning; not a series of events that might have been filmed, if film had been invented. It is the Christian interpretation of these events: the story of the rejected Savior, atoning by his sufferings for the sins of the world, conquering death by his resurrection, and forming the mystical community of the Church. This was the Good News, the Christians' kerygma, as it is sometimes called, meaning their proclamation—the inwardness of the visible facts.

A skeptical view would be that the passage is not actually prophetic. It is an invention of Second Isaiah, and Christians adopted it and spun their kerygma out of it to explain what they needed to explain. This theory, however, would only create another mystery. It would leave the Servant's identity completely obscure. Moreover, the two main themes—atonement for the sins of humanity and effective life after death—were unknown to Israelites in the sixth century B.C. To account for the Song like this, it would almost be necessary to invoke inspiration anyhow, planting ideas in the prophet's mind when they were still remote. There is no evidence that the early Christians did draw their beliefs from the Servant Song. New Testament writers quote excerpts from it, as they quote excerpts from other passages, but they do it much less frequently than might be expected and only in support of their message, not as its basis.

The Servant Song is thus paradoxical: prophetic, but not in a way that can be naively explained as "seeing the future." An unidentified speaker tells a story, in the past tense, that does not fit any recorded person whom the prophet could have had in mind. It embodies themes that were unknown to Israelite belief in his time and could never, in the ordinary course of events, have occurred to him. But this speaker would be a wholly intelligible figure in the first century A.D., as a Christian talking of Jesus—not an original follower of his, perhaps even hostile, but converted afterward to the Christian view of him. Some light may be shed on the paradox by consideration of other cases that are more or less parallel; a few exist.

See also: Biblical Prophecy (2)—Christian; Dante Alighieri; Isaiah; Milton, John; Prophecy, Theories of

Further Reading

The New Catholic Encyclopedia. Article "Isaiah." Washington, DC: Catholic University of America, 1967.

North, Christopher R. *The Second Isaiah.* Oxford: Oxford University Press, 1962.

SENECA, LUCIUS ANNAEUS (C. 4 B.C.–A.D. 65)

Roman philosopher and dramatist who can be claimed as the first person to predict the discovery of America. He was Nero's boyhood tutor and wrote fulsome praise of him when he became emperor but ended as one of his victims on a charge of conspiracy.

Seneca took an interest in geography. Born in Spain, he was more conscious of the Atlantic Ocean than most Romans, and he wrote about the possibility of reaching Asia by sailing west. Greeks had long since proved that the Earth was spherical and made good estimates of its size, but how far would a ship actually have to go? One Greek author, Posidonius, had suggested a distance of 7,700 miles from Spain to India. Seneca was more optimistic and argued that they were quite close together and that, with a fair wind, the ocean could be crossed in a matter of days.

Like Posidonius, he assumed that there was nothing else in between, and his guess at the Atlantic's breadth obviously ruled out anything large. As a dramatist, however, he contradicted himself as a geographer. At that time, the limit of the known world was Thule, an island not immensely far beyond Britain, reached apparently by way of the Shetlands. Early authors make it Iceland, rightly or wrongly. "Ultima Thule" was the end of everything. But in Seneca's tragedy *Medea,* the chorus sings of voyagers venturing ever farther and builds up to a climax: "The time shall come when the vast Earth will lie open, when the sea-goddess will reveal new worlds, and Thule will not be the last of lands." This, despite the fact that in a less lyrical mood, he had left no room for "new worlds." His poetry contradicted his prose with an unexplained insight. Classical literature has no real antecedent. Plato, in his account of lost Atlantis, briefly mentions land beyond it, but this is probably pure mythmaking. No one before Seneca relates such a notion to actual future exploration or foreshadows the discovery of America.

Columbus read the lines in *Medea* and was impressed by them. He did not accept, however, that the "new worlds" to be discovered across the ocean would be literally new. After reaching America, he spent the rest of his days trying to make out that it was Asia.

See also: Atlantis; Bacon, Francis

Further Reading

Ashe, Geoffrey. *Land to the West.* London: Collins, 1962.

Grant, Michael. *Nero.* New York: Dorset Press, 1989.

SHAMANISM

An ancient technique of communion with spirits and deities, in self-induced and controlled ecstasy. The technique has been practiced widely among precivilized peoples by practitioners known generically as shamans, this actual word being of Siberian derivation.

Shamanism is found in many cultures, and long ago, may have been the substratum of more sophisticated religious systems such as druidism. Its heartland is in Siberia and Central Asia. Communist repression almost extinguished it, but not quite, and it can still be legitimately spoken of as a living thing. Anthropologists have accumulated a wealth of data here from different tribes, including rich bodies of mythology about the deities and spirits, the upper and lower worlds, the history of humanity, and the lore of animals.

Shamanism has never been a male preserve, and some anthropologists believe it originated with women. The shaman, of either gender, is a person who commands respect and is well qualified to exert influence: he or she is neither a witch doctor in the bad sense, exploiting superstition, nor yet a holy lunatic, in spite of the peculiar outfits sometimes worn and the dancing and drumming that build up the ecstasy. To attain full status

A shaman dancing and beating his drum in the course of a healing ritual. (Courtesy of John Webb)

as one in contact with superior beings, the shaman has had to pass severe initiatory tests and has come through as someone above most fellow tribespeople in wisdom and strength of character, a guide and healer for the community.

Hence, shamans' speeches when their gods communicate through them are not mere gibberish. Arguably, they may have as fair a claim to be counted as prophecy, in the old sense of "inspired utterance," as some of the sayings of early prophets in the Bible. However, it never seems to have been characteristic of shamans to take the next step and speak of things to come, as their biblical counterparts did. Surprisingly, the Greeks' prophetic god Apollo may be relevant here. He is a composite figure with an ancient background in regions far from Greece, and it is likely that a shamanic god was part of the composite, accounting for his oracular role. His messages about the future, received by priestesses at Delphi and elsewhere, may hint at a potentiality that was always present.

See also: Apollo; Delphi; Prophecy, Theories of

Further Reading

Ashe, Geoffrey. *Dawn behind the Dawn.* New York: Henry Holt, 1992.

Dodds, E. R. *The Greeks and the Irrational.* Berkeley: University of California Press, 1951.

Eliade, Mircea. *Shamanism.* Boston: Routledge and Kegan Paul, 1964.

Guthrie, W. K. C. *The Greeks and Their Gods.* New York: Methuen, 1950.

SHAMBHALA

A hidden holy place in Buddhist mythology, associated with a future Messiah.

The name means "quietude." Shambhala figures in the Lamaistic Buddhism of Tibet and Mongolia as a venue of spiritual initiation. It is the source or principal source of a system of esoteric lore called Kalachakra, the

Wheel of Time, which lays a stress unusual in Buddhism on astronomy and astrology. While Kalachakra is still taught by a surviving Lamaistic school, its reputed place of origin is elusive. Shambhala has been tracked to the north, and the same direction is implied in Tibetan legend. The most detailed account makes it a paradisal valley concealed among mountains, accessible only through a cave or narrow gorge. It may not be "there" in quite the ordinary sense! Lamas connect it with the aurora borealis and say that would-be seekers can only find it if they are summoned by its resident sages. It has a king, who lives in a tower or citadel. One of the royal line received a visit from Buddha himself and wrote down some of his teachings, which were embodied in Kalachakra; this king was an incarnation of Manjushri, the god of divine wisdom.

A Jesuit missionary, Father Stephen Casella, who died in Tibet in 1650, was told about Shambhala. It was known also to Csoma de Körös, a nineteenth-century Hungarian orientalist. Neither, however, discovered where it was. James Hilton may have had it in mind when he invented Shangri-La, but if so, his novel *Lost Horizon* reflects a theory locating it in the Himalayas, which is a modern fancy incompatible with genuine legend. To the slight extent that real geographic clues have ever emerged, they point toward the Altai range extending from Mongolia into Siberia.

Despite the name's peaceful connotations, lamas have prophesied a future War of Shambhala in which good forces will conquer evil and bring in a golden age. The messianic figure who will then step forth from the holy place is conceived in different ways. He may be a king of Shambhala called Rigden Jye-po. He may be Gesar, a Mongolian legendary hero. He may be Maitreya, the next Buddha, or a forerunner. There seems to be a remote connection with Hindu beliefs about a future world regeneration by a forthcoming avatar of Vishnu.

During the late nineteenth century, Shambhala began attracting the notice of Western esotericists and inspiring fantastic theories. Madame Blavatsky "HPB," the founder of Theosophy, mentions it in her writings and spells it with variations such as "Shambalah" and "Shamballah." She makes one assertion that has left an enduring and misleading mark—that Shambhala is in the Gobi Desert. Long ago, the desert was a vast lake, and Shambhala was an island. It became a haven for a select remnant of "Lemurians" whose homeland sank in the Pacific. It still exists in some sense, though perceptible only to occult vision. Annie Besant, who became Theosophy's chief leader and ideologue, claimed to have made astral visits to "Shamballa" and had consultations with its ruler, whom she called the King of the World. The king, she explained, was the head of an invisible hierarchy of great beings who met in Shamballa every seven years and guided humanity. In 1913, the king reassured her on the political issue that interested her most: India, he predicted, would become a self-governing member of the British Empire, like Canada or Australia.

Alice Bailey, a latecomer to Theosophy who broke away and started her own esoteric movement, echoes Annie Besant, with elaborations. "Shamballa" was founded by superior beings who came from Venus 18 million years ago. It is built of "etheric physical matter" and, as Theosophists say correctly, is the earthly home of the great spiritual Hierarchy. Bailey gives it several locations, but the Blavatsky-Besant Gobi Desert is the favorite. When the desert was a lake, the island was linked by a bridge with a city of colonists from Atlantis on the south shore. Shamballa is still invisibly present on the site of the island, a sacred city with seven gates ruled by the "Lord of the World." The Hierarchy confers there in an annual gathering called the Wesak Festival. Buddha is involved in all this, and so is Christ, who is the same person as Maitreya. Alice Bailey predicted his Second Coming before the end of the twentieth century.

Nearly all of this is Theosophical fancy evolved from a few bits of Lamaistic legend. The Gobi location is often referred to as if it were traditional, but it seems to be a product of HPB's imagination. There is somewhat more authenticity in stories of Shambhala having a sort of downward extension, a subterranean region known as Agharti or Agartha, the "inaccessible." This, it seems, has a large population and spreads a long way underground. The ruler of Shambhala rules over Agharti also. Lamas who spoke of him to travelers early in the twentieth century described him as the King of the World—there, perhaps, is the source of the phrase as used by Theosophists. He and his council have telepathic influence over persons in power outside and are secretly manipulating events: this much Annie Besant got right, after a fashion. Rene Guénon, discussing Agharti in *Le Roi du Monde,* tries to relate it to other sacred centers such as Delphi, but his interpretations are mainly a product of European comparative mythology; at least, their pretensions to being more than that are not very substantial.

The Shambhala-Agharti mythos became influential for a while after World War I and the revolution in Russia. It was picked up by Baron Roman Ungern-Sternberg, a Cossack army leader and anti-Communist fanatic. He journeyed eastward with a notion of organizing a Greater Mongolian state as a bulwark against bolshevism. In 1919, he attached himself to Grigorii Semenov, an adventurer who had seized control of part of Siberia and who welcomed his alliance in the hope of extending his own influence into Mongolia.

Ungern-Sternberg told Mongols that he was a reincarnation of Genghis Khan and would revive their past glories. He also pretended to have an understanding with the King of the World in Agharti. Those who knew him best regarded him as a megaloma-

niac, almost literally insane. His career was brief—he was killed in 1921 in one of the last flickers of anti-Soviet military action. Yet he had an impact. At Urga in Mongolia, he met Ferdinand Ossendowski, a doctor who had escaped from Siberia. Ossendowski was struck by his ideas and collected lore of Agharti and the King of the World, which he put in a book entitled *Beasts, Men and Gods,* introducing these topics to the Western public. He included related speculations about an imminent Asian upsurge, heard from the monk in charge of a temple at Narabanchi. According to this monk, the King of the World made a foray from his retreat in 1890 and visited the temple, where he uttered a long prophecy covering "the coming half century"—actually, much more than that.

As recorded by Ossendowski, the prophecy runs through a succession of horrors more or less fitting World War I, though not closely enough to be impressive. It refers to the Crescent growing dim, a possible allusion to the decline of Turkey; to the fall of kings (as happened in Germany, Austria, and Russia); to roads covered with wandering crowds—refugees, perhaps. But the fairly good predictions are almost swamped by long, vague outpourings about slaughter and earthquakes and fires and depopulation.

After these, the last part of the prophecy is more interesting, not as a forecast but as a just-possible influence in a surprising quarter. Its assessment requires a glance at the context of the early 1920s. Thanks partly to Ungern-Sternberg, the hope of a Shambhalic Messiah grew more specific and even political. The Panchen Lama, at the great monastery of Shigatse, claimed that a predecessor had received a message from the King of the World, written on golden tablets. Expelled in 1923 through a dispute with the more powerful Dalai Lama, he traveled north in the direction of Mongolia, founding colleges allegedly in touch with Shambhala. Mongols began to speak of the War of Shambhala as getting close and to favor the identification of the promised Messiah as Gesar Khan, a hero of their own epic tradition who was destined to return like King Arthur. He would form an Asian alliance against the white races.

Alexandra David-Neel, a student of Lamaism who translated the Gesar epic, saw a shrine with an image of the hero, before which a woman prayed for a son who could fight for him. She was assured several times that he was already in the world and would be manifested in fifteen years. According to her own account, the bard who dictated the epic to her gave her a flower that was a present from Gesar himself—a blue flower of a species that bloomed in July, though it was winter at the time. Another Western inquirer was the distinguished Russian artist and anthropologist Nicholas Roerich, remembered especially as Stravinsky's collaborator in devising rituals for his ballet *The Rite of Spring*. Hearing of the ferment in Central Asia, Roerich led an expedition that set off in 1923 and assembled many reports and rumors. He respected some of these as predictive but hoped for a new dawn of enlightenment rather than an outbreak of militancy. As a Shambhalic Messiah he preferred the pacific Maitreya to the martial Gesar.

Communist progress in Mongolia dampened down the excitement. However, Japanese imperialists tried to woo non-Communist Mongols by applying the Shambhala-Agharti mythos to themselves. It has been claimed—though only as part of a dubious "secret history"—that the mythos became a factor in Nazism. The story focuses on Karl Haushofer, a racial mystic who was the principal mentor of Hitler's deputy Rudolf Hess. During the 1920s, Haushofer allegedly fed information about Shambhala and Agharti to leading Nazis, separating the two places, relocating both in Tibet, and asserting that their occupants possessed occult wisdom and psychic powers that could be used against enemies. On his advice, German expeditions went to Tibet and brought back a large number of Tibetans

supposed to have secret knowledge or clairvoyant gifts. Some of them fought in the German army and were found dead in Berlin when the city fell.

Hardly any of this is well attested, though prominent Nazis such as Himmler held bizarre beliefs, and at least one expedition did go to Tibet, but to study Tibetans in the interests of racial pseudo science. Notions about subterranean peoples, derived from fantasy literature, figured in German fringe thinking, but do not seem to have been associated with Agharti. A serious possibility does exist—that Ossendowski's book, sketching the proposals of Ungern-Sternberg, was seen as offering a hint for disrupting Russia from the rear. If the Hitler elite became aware of it, the last part of the prophecy of the King of the World could certainly have been taken as relevant. Looking ahead from 1890 to the aftermath of World War I, the king speaks of the action he will take by his own mysterious power. "I shall send a people, now unknown, which shall tear out the weeds of madness and vice with a strong hand and will lead those who still remain faithful to the spirit of man in the fight against Evil. They will found a new life on the earth purified by the death of nations."

Hitler might have seen himself and his movement in this passage. Purification of the earth "by the death of nations" could apply to the extermination of Jews and other condemned breeds: the word *genocide* was coined to define this aspect of the Führer's policy when in power. The King concludes: "In the fiftieth year only three great kingdoms will appear, which shall exist happily for seventy-one years. Afterwards there will be eighteen years of war and destruction. Then the peoples of Agharti will come up from their subterranean caves to the surface of the earth."

This carries the story as far as 2029. Here, it is only the first of the time periods that is interesting. The fiftieth year from the prophetic pronouncement was 1940. In that year, Germany, Italy, and Japan, "three great kingdoms," formed the Tripartite Alliance that was intended to dominate the world. The subsequent attacks on Russia and the United States were acts of apparent lunacy, yet it could be that delusions about the king's foreknowledge and guidance of events played a part in the overriding of sanity.

There is a strange sequel. While Communist rule in Mongolia almost broke Buddhism as an organized religion, lamas were allowed to survive as individual scholars. Some of them still expounded Kalachakra and still connected it with Shambhala. In 1970, they acquired an English initiate, Stephen Jenkins, who held a teaching post in their country. He heard a tradition that toward the end of Buddha's life, a European came to him to learn the wisdom of Shambhala, and this man, the lamas believed, was a Celt. Possibly, he went back, taking what he had learned with him; at any rate, during the last centuries B.C., Shambhala was visibly manifested in Britain. Jenkins wrote that he was "considerably taken aback" to hear this, as well he might be. Can it be given any kind of rational meaning? Some tenuous evidence exists for an Asian influence on the Druids. But it is hard to see what these lamas meant and why their speculations should have fastened on Britain.

See also: Besant, Annie; Kalki; Nazi Germany; Theosophy

Further Reading

Ashe, Geoffrey. *Avalonian Quest.* London: Methuen, 1982.

―――. *Dawn behind the Dawn.* New York: Henry Holt, 1992.

Ossendowski, Ferdinand. *Beasts, Men and Gods.* London: Edward Arnold, 1922.

Roerich, Nicholas. *Altai-Himalaya.* London: Jarrolds, 1930.

SHAW, GEORGE BERNARD (1856–1950)

Irish dramatist, critic, and controversialist.

Shaw moved to England at the age of nineteen and remained there for the rest of

George Bernard Shaw, "G. B. S.," Irish author of plays dramatizing social issues, who imagined a future in which humans would be transformed by living much longer. (Ann Ronan Picture Library)

his life. He was one of the earliest and most influential members of the Fabian Society, a group that advocated the spread of Socialism through gradual reform. In his Fabian phase he was associated with Annie Besant, who, however, became a Theosophist and went her own way. He clashed ideologically with H. G. Wells. Chesterton, however, who disagreed with him more profoundly than Wells did, was a lifelong friend and wrote a book about him.

Shaw was a pioneer in the theater of ideas, exploring social themes in brilliant and popular comedies. His largest dramatic work, *Back to Methuselah* (completed 1920), is a series of five plays showing his interest in Creative Evolution, a theory expounded by the French philosopher Bergson. Shaw believed that evolution has a purposive element: a "Life Force" is at work in it, and species may evolve and mutate because they need to and, in some deep-seated sense, want to. He applied this theory to an idea of his own—that human beings will become wiser and better only when they take an evolutionary leap and live much longer. In *Back to Methuselah,* he portrays this change happening and traces the results into a remote future.

The first play of the five, "In the Beginning," opens with a scene in the Garden of Eden, introducing the Serpent as well as Adam and Eve. The Serpent tells Eve about Lilith, who, according to Jewish legend, was Adam's first wife. Here, she is described as a kind of Mother Goddess who originated birth but, finding it too difficult and painful to renew life alone, divided herself into male and female. Adam and Eve are potentially immortal, but immortality as their own limited selves is a burden and goes nowhere: life must be renewed again, and there must be development through the species. In a second scene centuries later, the couple have produced descendants. Their firstborn, Cain, is scornful of the agricultural drudgery to which Adam is reduced. He has committed murder, and he talks with relish of violence and domination. Yet perhaps what we call evil is simply an error in the experimental process by which the Life Force operates. Eve sees further than her husband, with visions of what their descendants may achieve.

The second play, "The Gospel of the Brothers Barnabas," is contemporary. Two brothers of that name have been converted to Creative Evolution and the goal of longevity by a charismatic woman (who, however, appears only in a scene that Shaw decided to drop, though he published it separately later). They are visited by two politicians—acute caricatures of David Lloyd George, the British prime minister, and Herbert Henry Asquith, a former prime minister—who form the notion that the brothers have invented an elixir and that the idea of lengthened life can be exploited electorally: "Back to Methuselah" emerges as a slogan. When they are disillusioned, it becomes clear that while such men may have the energy that the Life Force needs, they lack the vision.

The third play is entitled "The Thing Happens." It is 250 years later. Characters in the second play reappear. They actually have lived longer, in perfect health and without a hint of senility. The fourth play, "The Tragedy of an Elderly Gentleman," takes place in the year 3000. There is now a community of long-lived people in Ireland, whom short-lived people come to consult. War virtually wiped out the "pseudo-Christian civilization," yet, because short-lived people can never solve their problems, peace did not ensue. The long-lived retired to their Irish settlement. They are clearly going to be dominant. The "elderly gentleman" of the title is a short-lived person who can live in neither milieu and despairs.

The final play, "As Far as Thought Can Reach," is set in the year 31,920—that is, 30,000 years ahead. Only long-lived people exist, and apparently not many of them. They control biological processes and can take any shape they wish. They have arranged for birth from eggs to replace birth in the traditional way. The humans who are hatched are like seventeen-year-olds in our own time. They enjoy four years of "infancy" devoted to art, sport, and emotional pleasures. Then, they age rapidly. The mature figures of this world are the Ancients, living in a purely intellectual state, hairless, emotionless, with gender still, but no sex. An Ancient says to an "infant," "One moment of the ecstasy of life as we live it would strike you dead." The Ancients have a future: they will shed the body entirely and evolve into a state of pure thought.

At the end, Lilith is seen in person for the first time and delivers an epilogue. She foretells that the era of bodiless intellect will come indeed. But . . . "Of Life only is there no end; and though of its million starry mansions many are empty and many still unbuilt, and though its vast domain is as yet unbearably desert, my seed shall one day fill it and master its matter to its uttermost confines. And for what may be beyond, the eyesight of Lilith is too short. It is enough that there *is* a beyond."

Back to Methuselah had a mixed reception. In book form, with a long preface by Shaw, it sold well. It was staged—in New York, first—but it was never a commercial success. Shaw's prophetic vision is one of perpetual change, propelled by the impersonal Life Force. He acknowledged a point of contact with a gloomier author, Thomas Hardy. In his epic-drama *The Dynasts,* about the Napoleonic Wars, Hardy conceives an unconscious "Immanent Will" manipulating events. It is not, however, concerned with progress, or with anything in particular. Its role is simply . . .

To alter evermore
Things from what they were before.

Hardy closes with a vague hope that the Will may eventually become conscious and "fashion all things fair," but the hope is very vague indeed, and he later regretted even that. Shaw found the Immanent Will interesting, as Hardy's version of the Life Force. He was, of course, more cheerful himself. His own Life Force moves its puppets onward and upward, however erratically. Still, if the Ancients are to be its prize products after another 30,000 years, a reader may not feel highly encouraged. Shaw admitted that he had set himself an impossible task. As a short-liver himself, he could not really imagine long-livers.

See also: Besant, Annie; Chesterton, Gilbert Keith; Wells, H. G.

Further Reading

Holroyd, Michael. *Bernard Shaw.* Vol. 3. New York: Random House, 1991.

SHIPTON, MOTHER (?1488–1561)

English seer and reputed witch. It is by no means certain that she actually existed. No account of her is anywhere near to being contemporary, and a "biography" written much later is full of fabulous matter that makes it quite untrustworthy.

Supposedly, her name was Ursula Southiel or Sontheil. A native of Yorkshire in northern England, she was born at Knaresborough in July 1488 in a cave near the castle, which is still called Mother Shipton's Cave. According to legend, her father was a wizard or even a supernatural being, and he gave her paranormal powers. In childhood, it is said, she attracted poltergeist phenomena. As an adult, she was ugly, even slightly deformed, but very intelligent. She married a carpenter, Tobias Shipton, and was known and remembered by her married name.

She is credited with much private soothsaying for neighbors. Her public activities began with an outpouring about an invasion of France by Henry VIII, in 1513. She foreshadowed the rise and fall of Henry's great minister, Cardinal Wolsey. He ordered an investigation, and she told the fortunes of the men he sent to investigate. When he was archbishop of York, she predicted that on a journey toward the city, he would see it from a distance but not get there. Fulfillment came, after a fashion, when he was arrested for treason eight miles away, but the historical circumstances do not agree with the prophecy as reported. Probably, it was invented or "improved" by someone not very well informed about Wolsey's career.

Mother Shipton fits into a known context of prophecy during Henry VIII's reign. The visionary Elizabeth Barton, known as the Maid of Kent, made threatening pronouncements about the king's marital and religious proceedings, which annoyed him, especially when prominent figures such as Thomas More were willing to take her seriously. Mother Shipton, however, is represented as favorable to Henry and to the English Re-

Woodcut of Ursula Southiel, called Mother Shipton, who is said to have foretold the downfall of the powerful Cardinal Wolsey during the reign of Henry VIII. (Ann Ronan Picture Library)

formation that he began and to have stayed out of trouble.

The first printed account of her prophecies appeared in 1641, eighty years after the date given for her death. In 1646, the astrologer William Lilly quoted several in a book of his own. The cryptic doggerel refers to happenings in the reigns of Tudor and Stuart sovereigns, including the defeat of the Spanish Armada. Most of this is pseudo prophecy concocted after the events; at least, there is no evidence that it was current before them, as vaticination by Mother Shipton or anyone else. The only prediction with any interest refers obscurely to the Great Fire of London, which did not happen until 1666. Lilly predicted the fire himself, and he may have invented the Shipton version to reinforce his. However, public memory connected the prophecy with Mother Shipton as

well as Lilly. Pepys records in his diary that when the fire broke out, Charles II's cousin Prince Rupert, in a boat on the Thames, remarked that she was vindicated.

An implausible *Life and Death of Mother Shipton* by Richard Head appeared in 1677. A much later revival of Mother Shipton's fame was due mainly to a reprint of this, published in 1862 by a bookseller, Charles Hindley. Besides including prophecies already ascribed to her, he added a series of verses said to have been copied from a long-lost manuscript. These foretold "thoughts flying around the world," presumably by telegraph; "carriages without horses," presumably railway trains; and tunnels through hills, iron ships, and other nineteenth-century phenomena, together with the end of the world in 1881. In advance of that date, however, Hindley confessed that he had composed the verses himself. The truth never caught up with the hoax. Hindley's faked prophecies were still being quoted as authentic 100 years later, with doomsday transferred—uselessly, as it turned out—to 1991.

Mother Shipton's name is preserved by a small British moth, which has markings supposed to look like a witch's face.

See also: Witchcraft

Further Reading

Dictionary of National Biography (British). Article "Shipton."

Folklore, Myths and Legends of Britain. London: Readers Digest Association, 1973.

Gould, Rupert T. *Oddities: A Book of Unexplained Facts.* London: Phillip Allan, 1928.

Mother Shipton. Reprint of anonymous booklet. Bath, England: West Country Editions, 1976.

Wallechinsky, David, Amy Wallace, and Irving Wallace. *The Book of Predictions.* New York: William Morrow, 1980.

"SIBYL" (NORSE)

A prophetess in the Elder Edda who foretells the end of the world, with an unexpected sequel.

The Elder or "Poetic" Edda is a collection of Old Norse poems, preserved in a thirteenth-century Icelandic manuscript. They date from a period about 200 years earlier. Christian influence is present but seldom conspicuous.

One of the longer poems is the *Voluspa,* the "Sibyl's Prophecy." The Sibyl, in Norse *volva,* is an ancient and rather sinister figure, a witch. Her name is Heidi. She dies, but the chief god, Odin, temporarily restores her to life. After uttering her prophecy, she expires again. The *Voluspa* is the work of a single poet with ideas of his own, and it may not give an entirely reliable picture of Norse mythology, but it certainly embodies a large amount of it, though in a cryptic, allusive style. It is Heidi's revelation to Odin about the world's history, its destined annihilation,

and a time beyond that. Most of the characters are gods, giants, and other mythical beings. Humans are mentioned only in general terms and not often.

In the primordial void, various beings took shape, especially the giant Ymir. When the gods began to appear, Odin and two brothers of his killed Ymir and created the universe from his body. Its structure is complicated: Heidi recognizes nine distinct worlds, the abodes of different races—gods, giants, humans, and others. Odin and his divine companions "built up the lands" and regulated the movements of the Sun and Moon, which at first were at a loss where to go. The gods' own home was Asgard, a place of wealth, where they built temples, worked with metal and jewels, and played chess (or a board game sometimes interpreted as chess).

After an indefinite golden age, Odin's son Baldur, the beautiful spirit of nature, was killed by a trick at the instigation of the wicked god Loki. With the death of Baldur, woe and decline set in. Heidi foresees an age when evil and strife will be dominant on Earth, mercy will perish among humans, and brother will strike at brother. Loki's monstrous son, the cosmic wolf Fenrir (Fenris), who has been kept in bonds until now, will break loose; Ragnarök, the "fate" or "destruction" of the gods, will begin. The universe will slide into chaos, the lands will sink beneath the ocean, the sun will turn black, the sky will burst into flames, and the stars will fall.

That is the end . . . yet it is not the end. Perhaps but not definitely under Christian influence, the *Voluspa* poet depicts Heidi as seeing a new world beyond. Earth will rise out of the sea foam, fresh and green. There will be birds and fishes and flowing water. A better humanity will come into being, and the fields will bear crops without being sown. Baldur will live again, and so will some of the other deities, dwelling in glory. They will even recover the original chessboards.

See also: End of the World

Michelangelo included some of the mythical Sibyls in the Sistine Chapel because of the belief that they corroborated Christian teachings. The Erythraean was the first Sibyl in Greek tradition. (From the collection of the author)

Further Reading

Taylor, Paul B., and W. H. Auden, eds. and trans. *The Elder Edda*. London: Faber and Faber, 1969.

Turville-Petre, E. O. G. *Myths and Religion of the North*. London: Weidenfeld and Nicolson, 1964.

SIBYLS AND SIBYLLINE TEXTS

Sibyl is sometimes spelled *Sybil,* but less correctly.

Besides Apollo's oracular priestesses, the ancient Greek world had freelance prophetic women inspired by the same god. Very little is known about them historically, but they are reported in western Asia Minor, which was early Apollo country. The Trojan Cassandra is a sort of prototype Sibyl and is occasionally referred to as such. However, she makes real predictions, whereas the Sibyls seem to have gone into frenzies and poured out wild verbiage about plagues, famines, and other disasters, too vague to be interesting. The philosopher Heraclitus speaks of one of them as having a "raving mouth, uttering things without smiles or grace."

Sibyls who were greater than ordinary mortals figured in a special mythology. A senior one was reputedly Apollo's half sister.

Born before the Trojan War, she settled at Erythrae on the coast opposite the island of Chios and became known as the Erythraean Sibyl. According to legend, she lived an immensely long time, perhaps 1,000 years. Nine other long-lived Sibyls were located in various countries, including Persia and Egypt. The Erythraean, however, remained the most important and was usually *the* Sibyl unless another were specified. At Erythrae, sayings ascribed to her were preserved, written on single leaves notoriously liable to become mixed up.

Romans had special respect for the Cumaean Sibyl, who lived in a cave at Cumae near Naples, the site of an early colony of Greeks. In Virgil's *Aeneid,* the migrant Trojan prince Aeneas comes to consult her about the prospects for himself and his companions, seeking a new home in Italy after Troy's fall. The god takes possession of her, and under his inspiration, she foretells that the Trojans will establish a settlement but will have to fight for it. This is poetic legend, but there may have been a shrine here later with a succession of prophetesses, the current occupant being "the Sibyl." Robert Graves gives a fictionalized account in his novel *I, Claudius.*

Graves mentions the Sibylline Books, which were certainly real. There was a time-honored version of their origin. In the sixth century B.C., the Cumaean Sibyl (presumably the original one) brought nine books of Greek verses to the Roman king Tarquin and offered to sell them. He refused. She destroyed three and offered the remaining six at the same price. Again he refused. She destroyed three more, and he was persuaded to buy the three that were left. The Sibylline Books may have come from the collection at Erythrae. They were kept at Rome in a stone chest and consulted in times of crisis for the predictions and advice they were supposed to contain. The message was in more or less cryptographic form, and the custodians had to work it out. It was liable to call for some

special act to propitiate the gods. Material from later seers, genuine or alleged, was added to the collection. In 81 B.C., it was destroyed by fire. Priests restored what they could from memory and traveled to Erythrae and elsewhere to find more. After some weeding out by the emperor Augustus, the new collection was placed in two gilded cases under a statue of Apollo, where it remained until Christians burned it.

Virgil, in the fourth of a series of poems called *Eclogues,* declared that the Cumaean Sibyl foreshadowed an imminent golden age. He connected the change with the birth of a wonderful child, a pagan Messiah. His meaning is uncertain, and it is unlikely that the birth is a truly Sibylline motif, though the golden age may be. The child failed to materialize, but Christians later saw the poem as a prophecy of Christ and claimed that Virgil was divinely inspired, though unconsciously.

The Sibylline tradition was enlisted in another way to support beliefs alien to the Sibyls' world. In the third century B.C., a Babylonian priest, Berosus, invented a Babylonian Sibyl and produced verses she was alleged to have uttered, endorsing Babylonian religion and mythology. About 160 B.C., an unknown Jewish writer in Alexandria adapted and expanded Berosus's material to create a pseudo-Sibylline text that confirmed Jewish beliefs. Further alleged Sibylline writings in the same style proclaimed the one God and foretold the end of the present age, with Jerusalem as the capital of a divinely renewed world. Some readers accepted these effusions as authentic prophecies by a real Sibyl, testifying from outside to the truth of Judaism. They carried a certain weight in the conversion of Gentiles that was going on toward the close of the pre-Christian era.

When Christians came on the scene, they not only annexed Virgil, they improved the pseudo-Sibylline literature, giving it their own bias and adding Christian topics such as the expected advent of Antichrist. Several Church fathers believed the results to be authentic and ancient and claimed the Erythraean Sibyl as an inspired prophetess. Saint Augustine, who was to guide Christian thinking for a long time, was more cautious, but in his great work *The City of God,* completed in 427, he gives a Latin translation of a supposedly Sibylline prophecy of Christ. This Christianization explains why "the Sibyl" is cited as foretelling doomsday in the medieval hymn *Dies Irae,* familiar from Verdi's *Requiem,* and why Michelangelo portrays Sibyls in the Sistine Chapel.

Christians produced two original Sibylline works. These were speculations about the end of the world. The first was called the *Tiburtina,* after one of the classical Sibyls. The second, not explicitly "Sibylline," was an essay in the same manner; it was attributed to a fourth-century bishop, Methodius, though it was actually composed later. Both predicted a final climactic phase of history when a glorious Last Emperor will unite the world in peace and prosperity and the Church will be triumphant. When his work is done, he will abdicate in Jerusalem. Antichrist will be manifested, bringing the last and worst persecution, but Christ will return, and all will be over. These fictions were taken seriously in the Middle Ages and influenced the more imaginative followers of Joachim of Fiore.

See also: Antichrist; Apollo; Cassandra; Hildegard of Bingen, Saint; Joachim of Fiore; Virgil

Further Reading

Bate, H. N. *The Sibylline Oracles, Books III–V.* London: Society for the Promotion of Christian Knowledge, 1918.

Cavendish, Richard, ed. *Man, Myth and Magic.* London: BPC Publishing, 1970–1972. Article "Sibyls."

Cohn, Norman. *The Pursuit of the Millennium.* London: Paladin, 1970.

SIMEON AND ANNA

An aged man and woman in one of the stories of Jesus's birth and infancy (Luke 2:22–38). Both live in Jerusalem. Simeon believes he has received a divine promise that he will live to see the Christ. When Joseph and Mary bring their child to the Temple for a ceremony required by Jewish law, he declares that the promise is fulfilled and he can die in peace. With reminiscences of Scripture, he foretells Jesus' greatness but warns Mary of future grief as well as glory—"a sword shall pierce your soul."

Anna, a widow, is called a prophetess. She has been praying and worshiping in the Temple with similar hopes, and she corroborates Simeon's words. There are two points of interest in what is said about her. She is a rarity among biblical characters as a woman whose age is given—eighty-four (according to the likeliest reading), and she is the daughter of Phanuel, "of the tribe of Asher." This was one of the northern Israelite tribes deported by the Assyrians long before and not part of the Jewish nation in Palestine. The northern tribes were believed to exist in some far-off country, but to refer to an individual in Jerusalem as belonging to one of them is curious. There may be something special about this prophetess, but if so, its nature is not revealed.

See also: Biblical Prophecy (1)—Israelite and Jewish; Biblical Prophecy (2)—Christian

Further Reading

Brown R. E., J. A. Fitzmyer, and R. E. Murphy, eds. *The New Jerome Biblical Commentary.* Englewood Cliffs, NJ: Prentice-Hall, 1990.

SMITH, JOSEPH (1805–1844)

Founder of the Mormon Church (Church of Jesus Christ of Latter-Day Saints), which has a belief of its own about the Second Coming of Christ.

For members of this religious body, the founder is "the Prophet Joseph Smith." The word *prophet* is used here in its original sense, to mean an inspired person. Smith is credited with making predictions, but they

Two old people awaiting the Messiah in the Temple at Jerusalem, Simeon and Anna recognize the infant Jesus as the promised one. (Ann Ronan Picture Library)

are not central to the development of Mormon doctrine.

His youth was spent in upstate New York, an area full of competing Christian sects. He found these unsatisfactory. In 1823, an angel appeared to him and told him of a sacred text written on gold plates and concealed not far away. After some years, according to the received account, he obtained the plates with the angel's aid. Their language was "Reformed Egyptian." In 1830, he published a translation as the *Book of Mormon,* named after the ancient editor to whom the text was attributed. The book contained what was said to be a history of America in biblical and early postbiblical times, when the continent was settled by Old World migrants—Israelites and others. Religious teachings were interwoven with the story, together with material from the Bible itself, which the *Book of Mormon* professed to supplement and expand, not to supersede. To a large extent, in fact, its own style was quasi-biblical.

Joseph Smith had more revelations, and his new Scripture made converts. Several testified to the reality of the gold plates, but presently, these were seen no more. By modern standards of archaeology and history, the *Book of Mormon* is very hard to accept. At the time, however, so little was known of ancient America that the message of the gold plates did not present factual obstacles to readers who were attracted by it.

The new Church grew rapidly. Mormons founded communities in Ohio and Missouri, but the hostility of non-Mormons made their lives difficult. A more successful settlement in Illinois, called Nauvoo, flourished in the early 1840s. Smith, however, was assassinated, and his more determined followers migrated to Utah—then still technically Mexican territory—under the leadership of Brigham Young. Inspiration was believed to continue in the Mormon Church, concerned mainly with matters of doctrine and practice, polygamy being notoriously a controversial issue. The *Book of Mormon* remained, as it still remains, authoritative Scripture, together with the Bible. Mormons share a belief in the Second Coming with other denominations, but they add a prophecy that Christ will establish his rule in Utah, where Brigham Young said long ago, "This is the place."

Further Reading

Brodie, Fawn M. *No Man Knows My History: The Life of Joseph Smith*. London: Eyre and Spottiswood, 1963.

West, R. B. *The Kingdom of the Saints*. New York: Viking Press, 1957.

SOLOVYEV, VLADIMIR (1853–1900)

Russian author who made comparative studies of western and eastern philosophical thought and argued that Russia had a special contribution to make through its Orthodox Christian tradition, though, if fully understood, this would lead to a greater Christianity in communion with Rome.

The last of Solovyev's books, published in 1900, is entitled *War, Progress, and the End of History*. It is written in the form of imaginary conversations. Five Russians meet in France and discuss various current topics. One, called "the Prince," is more or less Tolstoy, and he expresses his conviction that Christianity means total pacifism and nonviolence. A General advances traditional points of view, a Politician is an ardent believer in progress as the solution to all problems. An elderly Lady does not voice a positive opinion but makes perceptive comments. The fifth member of the group, Mr. Z, is quiet for most of the time but speaks for the author when he does speak.

Mr. Z surprises the others by saying that "visible and accelerated progress" is "a symptom of the end." History will not run on smoothly into an indefinite future; it will boil up to a crisis involving an ultimate conflict of good and evil. This is foreshadowed in the Christian prophecy of Antichrist. However, the person to fear would not be an obvious tyrant or persecutor but an impostor posing as the "true" savior of humanity, a culmination of progress itself.

Mr. Z produces a manuscript said to have been written by a monk, Pansophius, entitled *A Short Story of the Antichrist*. This literary device forestalls any notion that Mr. Z, or Solovyev, is making serious predictions. The fictitious monk's story illustrates the possible danger in a guise of fantasy, with a future setting because the threat is hypothetical, not immediate.

Looking back from an imagined standpoint in the twenty-first century, the storyteller says by way of preface that the twentieth century saw the last major wars. An Asian coalition led by Japan conquered most of Europe and held it for fifty years. The continent recovered its independence, but its traditional cultures were blurred, and its political structures had crumbled. In the early twenty-first century, a United States of Europe was in being, prosperous but ideologically empty. Hardly anyone had positive ideas any more. A reduced Christianity still existed, divided, as ever, into Catholic, Orthodox, and Protestant branches. The remnant was of higher quality than before, but its influence was slight. The pope had been driven from Rome and lived in Saint Petersburg.

One man took Christianity seriously, after his own fashion. A handsome, charismatic writer and political theorist, aged thirty-three, he was widely adored as superior to common humanity. (Solovyev anticipated the adulation of Hitler, which would have been unthinkable to most of his contemporaries.) This "superman" regarded Christ as his predecessor: he was greater himself because he was later—in progressive terms, that was enough. He saw himself as destined to unite humanity by great benefactions, and he awaited a message from God confirming his mission.

What actually happened was a bizarre mystical experience. It dawned on him that his personal theology would not work. If he acknowledged Christ, even as a precursor, he could not subordinate him to his own monstrous ego.

> "If this Galilean came down to earth, would I not kneel down before him and ask, like every stupid Russian peasant, for his forgiveness?" Fear was born and grew in his heart, followed by a burning envy which consumed all his being. In his rage he left the house and stumbled to a deep precipice. He tried to leap from it, but was held by an invisible power. A luminous image with two eyes and an unearthly voice told him that he was the only begotten son, not that crucified mendicant: "Do thy work in *thine own* name, not in mine. . . . I demand from thee nothing . . . receive thou my spirit. . . . As before my spirit gave birth to thee in *beauty*, so now it gives birth to thee in *power.*"

Charged with demonic energy, the visionary produced another book, *The Open Way to Universal Peace and Well-Being.* It proclaimed a worldwide program and sold in millions, appearing in cheap editions with a picture of the author. He was hailed as the savior of the world and gained swiftly in wealth and influence. His family background was obscure—he was, in fact, very probably illegitimate—but with the end of the hereditary principle, nothing stood in his way, and his personal virtues impressed everybody. He was elected president of the United States of Europe and then emperor. His manifesto began, "Nations of the world! I give you my peace." Most countries outside Europe were drawn into his system, and his social reforms and welfare measures were put into effect everywhere.

While he was in Rome, a strange figure arrived from the remote east. Apollonius by name, he was several things in one—semi-Asian and semi-European, a magician and a bishop, a scientist and a mystic. The emperor made Apollonius his close companion and employed him to dazzle the populace with apparent miracles. For the first time, Christians became disquieted. The emperor responded by summoning all "true Christians" to a world congress in Jerusalem for the solution of religious problems. He and his entourage, in which Apollonius was prominent, came to the gathering with a band playing the "March of Unified Mankind."

The emperor's solution was an attempt to bring all three branches of Christianity under his control by massive patronage. He would restore the papacy to Rome, he would establish a great Orthodox center in Constantinople, and he would endow an institution for biblical studies to please the Protestants. All he wanted in return was the Christians' "inner heartfelt recognition of himself as their sole protector and patron." He won over most of the delegates but not Pope Peter II, not the principal Orthodox spokesman, Elder John, and not the Protestant leader, Professor Pauli.

Elder John realized what many did not. With all his talk of true Christianity, the emperor never spoke the name of Christ. John called on him to do so. The emperor's unearthly voice spoke to him again, telling him to keep silent. His face turned pale, and the sky darkened. John shouted, "It is the Antichrist!" and fell dead, struck by lightning. The emperor tried to treat John's death as a divine judgment and ordered his secretaries to record that all Christians now recognized him as their supreme leader and lord. But the pope also denounced him and also fell dead.

Pauli assembled the few dissenters and led them away into the wilderness.

The emperor ordered his Catholic collaborators to elect Apollonius as pope, induced other Christians to accept his supremacy, and announced the reunification of Christendom. (A genuine reunification among the dissenters, in the wilderness, passed unnoticed.) Apollonius bewitched the multitudes with "unheard-of forms of mystic lust and demonry, communion between living and dead [a glance at Spiritualism]," and many other pseudomiracles. Prompted once again by his mysterious voice, the emperor declared himself "the sole true incarnation of the supreme deity of the universe."

This ultimate blasphemy brought his downfall, at the hands of the Jews. Hitherto, many had believed that he was their Messiah. Now, they were disillusioned, and—a grotesque yet fatal discovery—it turned out that he was not circumcised. They revolted against him. Like the faithful Christians, they did not fit into his autocratic Utopia, and when the flaw appeared, his mask of universal benevolence was dropped. Thousands of Jews and Christians were executed. Jewish rebels got control of Jerusalem; the emperor, marching to recapture it with a "pagan" army, was destroyed by earthquakes and eruptions. Pansophius's story ends with a vision of Christ returning.

See also: Antichrist; Benson, Robert Hugh
Further Reading
Unzer, Egbert. *Solovyev.* London: Hollis and Carter, 1956.

SOUTHCOTT, JOANNA
(1750–1814)

English religious founder who claimed to fulfill a biblical prophecy and is associated with a mysterious box.

Joanna Southcott was the daughter of a farmer in Devon. She worked for a time as a domestic servant and was briefly a Methodist, but in 1792, she began to compose rhymed "prophecies" and announced that she was the woman in Revelation 12:1–2, 5:

> A great portent appeared in heaven, a woman clothed with the sun, with the moon under her feet, and on her head a crown of twelve stars; she was with child and she cried out in her pangs of birth, in anguish for delivery. . . . She brought forth a male child, one who is to rule all the nations with a rod of iron.

Joanna attracted disciples and moved to London, where she opened a chapel, and her congregation grew. William Blake was aware of her but was not one of her converts. In various writings, she taught that as Eve had led Adam astray and caused the Fall, so another woman—herself—would undo that catastrophe. Aiming to build up a following of 144,000, a total derived from Revelation 7, she "sealed" numerous people, for a fee. They received a certificate and were assured of salvation. Their leader expected them to keep many of the Old Testament laws usually regarded as binding on Jews only. In 1809, one of her sealed "elect" was convicted of murder, a disaster that cast doubt on her selection procedure. However, she went on producing books and pamphlets and sending letters about herself to prominent persons.

To fulfill the prophecy, she had to give birth to a messianic child, and she promised to do so on October 19, 1814: he would be "Shiloh," the "Prince of Peace." Doctors examined her, and some thought she actually was pregnant. A crowd of disciples gathered outside her house to await the birth, but nothing happened; it was hardly surprising, as she was sixty-four years old. Though not pregnant, she was mortally ill, and she sank into a coma and died of a brain tumour soon afterward.

The followers who remained faithful speculated that she would rise again, and some of them maintained that she had given birth to a "spiritual" child. At the middle of the nineteenth century, there were still at least 200 re-

Joanna Southcott, who claimed to fulfill biblical prophecies. She enrolled many followers who expected her to give birth to a miraculous child in 1814. (Ann Ronan Picture Library)

maining. Splinter groups broke away, however, and expanded into separate sects. Presently few Southcottians remained. Most of them were in Walsall, Staffordshire, where they held meetings under a railway arch. They had in their possession a curious legacy from the founder—a sealed box that would transform society when it was opened, perhaps at a time of national crisis. Supposedly, it had secret writings in it. The difficulty was that the opening had to be performed in the presence of an assemblage of bishops, and the bishops refused to cooperate.

Southcottism would doubtless have expired quietly if it had not been revived early in the twentieth century by Alice Seymour. She founded the Panacea Society, based in Bedford, and campaigned for the box to be opened. In 1927, it was, without the bishops, and was found to contain a lottery ticket and a nightcap. The Panacea Society made out that this was not the genuine box and continued for many years to put advertisements in the papers informing the public that crime, banditry, and other evils would increase until the real one was opened with the bishops present. This never happened. An alleged X-ray photograph of the second box has been published; the most conspicuous object inside is a pistol.

See also: Revelation

Further Reading

Dictionary of National Biography (British). Article "Southcott."

Folklore, Myths and Legends of Britain. London: Readers Digest Association, 1973.

Cavendish, Richard, ed. *Man, Myth and Magic.* London: BPC Publishing, 1970–1972. Article "Southcott."

SPHINX

This Egyptian monument near the Pyramids of Giza became a theme for prophetic speculation when Edgar Cayce, the American "Sleeping Prophet," claimed to know more about it than Egyptologists did. He had visions of ancient Egypt, which he assigned to a much earlier period than usually supposed. He also had visions of Atlantis, and he connected the two. One physical link, he said, was an underground chamber or hall of records near the Sphinx, containing Atlantis's history. It is still there with the documents in it, and some day it will be uncovered.

Cayce gave directions: "Walk due east of the Sphinx on the other side of the road leading to the Great Pyramid where there is a small sand-hill. If you tunnel down at this point, a small pyramid will be found that is located above the chamber of records. It is here that the records of Atlantis will be found."

Colin Amery, who developed Cayce's revelations and involved them with other "fringe" topics, claimed to have identified the spot. He thought the hall of records contained "a veritable library of the whole history of humanity, starting with the original records on which Genesis is based and working backwards from there, far beyond the story of the creation. . . . For what man must learn, if he is to survive into the future, is that he is little more than a piece of property belonging to the cosmic masters on a much higher plane of evolution." There is an echo here of Madame Blavatsky's Theosophy, which is at the root of a good deal of speculation about Atlantis and kindred topics. As a matter of fact, Amery quotes her as referring to "submerged temples and libraries": she may have given Cayce the original hint for the hall of records itself.

The purpose of the Sphinx is not fully explained, and its age is uncertain, but the various unorthodox notions about its nature and alignment, its relation to the Pyramids, and the Pyramids themselves may probably be dismissed, and there is no evidence for Cayce's chamber-to-be-revealed.

See also: Atlantis; Cayce, Edgar

Further Reading

Amery, Colin. *New Atlantis: The Secret of the Sphinx*. London and New York: Regency Press, 1976.

Bro, Harmon Hartzell. *Edgar Cayce*. Wellingborough, England: The Aquarian Press, 1990.

Collins, Andrew. *Gateway to Atlantis*. London: Headline, 2000.

SPURINNA (FL. 44 B.C.)

Soothsayer who warned Caesar of danger on the Ides of March—the day, as it turned out, of his assassination.

The Roman month was anchored calendrically on three days, the Kalends, Nones, and Ides. In March, the Ides fell on the fifteenth. Shakespeare brings Spurinna anonymously into *Julius Caesar*. His first appearance is in the crowd at a public ceremony in the year 44 B.C.:

Soothsayer: Beware the Ides of March.
Caesar: What man is that?

Brutus: A soothsayer bids you beware the Ides of March.
Caesar: Set him before me; let me see his face.
Cassius: Fellow, come from the throng; look upon Caesar.
Caesar: What say'st thou to me now? Speak once again.
Soothsayer: Beware the Ides of March.
Caesar: He is a dreamer; let us leave him:— pass.

In the ensuing days, the conspiracy builds up. On March 15, when Caesar is to attend a meeting of the Senate, he hesitates to leave his house because his wife has had a frightening dream, and the official augurs announce a bad omen. However, he is persuaded to go. As he approaches the Capitol, the soothsayer is nearby.

Caesar: The Ides of March are come.
Soothsayer: Ay, Caesar; but not gone.

Caesar enters the building and takes his seat. The assassins, led by Brutus and Cassius, gather round and stab him.

The Ides of March warning has been cited as the most successful prophecy ever. As a fact, it need not be disputed, but a careful scrutiny makes it less impressive. Spurinna, in reality, seems to have told Caesar that danger threatened him "not later than the Ides of March," not necessarily on that day. Also, the plot was known, complete with the zero hour for action, to many besides the actual assassins. More than sixty of the dictator's enemies are said to have been involved. Leaks surely occurred, and Shakespeare himself recognizes this. In his play, a well-wisher hands Caesar a written warning, which he unwisely ignores, and a senator, Popilius, tells the assassins that he hopes their "enterprise" may thrive. They realize that people know of it who are not supposed to. Shakespeare does not admit the inference that Spurinna might have been one of them, but as a matter of historical fact, it is obvious.

Caesar is warned by the soothsayer Spurinna to "Beware the Ides of March": A scene from Shakespeare's Julius Caesar. *(Ann Ronan Picture Library)*

See also: Dreams
Further Reading
Suetonius. *The Lives of the Twelve Caesars.* Translated by Joseph Gavorse. New York: Modern Library, 1931.

Wallechinsky, David, Amy Wallace, and Irving Wallace. *The Book of Predictions.* New York: William Morrow, 1980.

STAPLEDON, OLAF (1886–1950)

English writer on philosophical and political topics and author of *Last and First Men,* an established classic of science fiction that raises the issue of foreknowledge and offers an explanation for it.

Last and First Men, published in 1930, is an exploration of humanity's possibilities, extending an immense distance into the future. Stapledon never aspired to be a novelist, but he followed this success with further stories developing his ideas. The most ambitious is *Star Maker,* which leads up like Dante's *Divine Comedy* to a vision of the Supreme Being, who, however, is not called God and is conceived very differently. C. S. Lewis recoiled from this vision but paid generous tributes to the wealth of Stapledon's imagination. A small but striking instance is his description of an atomic explosion, fifteen years before the actual event, as forming a "gigantic mushroom."

He explores the possibilities to the limit by conjuring up a whole succession of human species over innumerable millions of years. When projecting the future of the First species—ourselves—he is concerned chiefly with political and cultural matters. Various conflicts lead to an Americanized world, with China as the main secondary factor. The World State flourishes for some centuries but sinks into a decline owing to energy depletion. Nuclear disaster (due not to war but to the misuse of atomic power) almost depopulates the globe. After a long dark age, the Second humans evolve. They are not radically different, though superior mentally and morally, but their lives are disrupted by a Martian invasion. The issue confronted here is alien contact. Stapledon makes a noteworthy effort to picture an intelligent life-form that is not even vaguely humanoid.

The Third humans, who emerge after another dark age lasting millions of years, are biologically inclined. They experiment with remolding humanity itself and produce the Fourth species—gigantic brains with only vestigial bodies. The brains' career exposes the barrenness of pure intellect. However, they construct the carefully planned Fifth humans, who are further advanced in most ways than any of their predecessors. Unhappily, they too encounter a crisis. Foreseeing that the Moon will break up and bombard Earth with fragments, they migrate to Venus (which was widely believed, when Stapledon wrote, to be capable of supporting life). Since most of Venus is covered with ocean, one result of the changed environment is an artificially created winged species. The "Flying Men" spend much of their time airborne, attaining new spiritual insight when aloft. At last, a flare-up of the Sun forces a migration of nonfliers to Neptune, followed by an almost total collapse into subhumanity. After a very long time indeed, several new species arise, culminating in the Eighteenth, whose world is a Utopia but a doomed Utopia, owing to another impending catastrophe to which there is no answer. They are the "Last Men" of the title.

Obviously, this vast panorama, stretching aeons ahead, ranges far beyond any normal notion of prophecy. Stapledon described it as an "essay in myth." Nevertheless, he gave the narrative a frame that invites reflection on prophecy in general. It starts with an introduction attributed to one of the Last Men, the climactic Eighteenth species. He begins:

This book has two authors, one contemporary with its readers, the other an inhabitant of an age which they would call the distant future. The brain that conceives and writes these sentences lives in the time of Einstein. Yet I, the true inspirer of this book, I who have begotten it upon that brain, I who influence that primitive being's conception, inhabit an age which, for Einstein, lies in the very remote future.

The actual writer thinks he is merely contriving a work of fiction. Though he seeks to tell a plausible story, he neither believes it himself, nor expects others to believe it. Yet the story is true. A being whom you would call a future man has seized the docile but scarcely adequate brain of your contemporary, and is trying to direct its familiar processes for an alien purpose. Thus a future epoch makes contact with your age.

So *Last and First Men,* which seems to consist of twentieth-century conjectures about the future, has really been transmitted back from the other end, by an informant for whom it is all past history.

The weakness of this device, as Stapledon uses it, is that the first chapter began to be falsified by events within a short time of publication and is not history from any point of view. Yet it does not matter much. His wrong guesses have been left behind and are not significant. As his vision extends through all the millions of years, it grows increasingly powerful, and the conception of back-communication by a future informant, inspiring prophecy (or, in Stapledon's words, a prophetic "essay in myth") remains interesting—perhaps more so than he realized himself.

In the course of the story, the informant has a good deal to say about transtemporal contact. He says the Fifth species made a momentous discovery—mental time travel. They found how to enter into long-ago minds and experience the past through them, directly. The technique was forgotten but rediscovered. The highly accomplished Last Men are experts and have explored the past in great detail. That is why the one who has ostensibly dictated the book knows so much about humanity's history, over a stretch of time that no physical records could have covered.

But what about the dictation? How could he have poured his knowledge into Stapledon, who, from his point of view, lived a very long time ago; and how could he have induced him to put it into writing? To do so would have meant intervening in a past mind, in other words affecting it, changing its inner processes; and the usual assumption is that changing anything in the past is impossible, because it is fixed forever, and any other supposition creates difficulties that look insurmountable, like the notorious "killing the grandfather" paradox. (If you traveled back in time in whatever way and killed your grandfather—or got some contemporary to do it—before your father was born, you wouldn't have been born yourself, therefore your grandfather wouldn't have been killed, therefore you *would* have been born, therefore . . . and so on, round and round.)

Stapledon faces the problem, at least as it concerns intervention in past minds. The member of the Eighteenth species who transmits the story tells how scientists in his own world have extended the scope of mental time travel beyond simple inspection of the past. The passage needs to be quoted fairly fully. Stapledon postulates, here and elsewhere, an "eternity" outside the temporal flow, but it could probably be redefined for readers dismissive of metaphysical terms.

We have long been able to enter into past minds and participate in their experience.

Hitherto we have been passive spectators merely, but recently we have acquired the power of influencing past minds. This seems an impossibility; for a past event is what it is, and how can it be altered at a subsequent date, even in the minutest respect?

Now it is true that past events are what they are, irrevocably; but in certain cases some feature of a past event may depend on an event in the far future. The past event would never have been as it actually was (and is, eternally) if there had not been going to be a certain future event, which, though not contemporaneous with the past event, influences it directly in the sphere of eternal being. . . . In certain rare cases mental events far separated in time determine one another directly by way of eternity.

Our own minds have often been profoundly influenced by direct inspection of past minds; and now we find that certain events of certain past minds are determined by present events in our own present minds. . . .

Our historians and psychologists, engaged on direct inspection of past minds, have often complained of certain "singular" points in past minds, where the ordinary laws of psychology fail to give a full explanation of the course of mental events; where, in fact, some wholly unknown influence seemed to be at work. Later it was found that, in some cases at least, this disturbance of the ordinary principles of psychology corresponded with certain thoughts or desires in the mind of the observer, living in our own age. . . . We now found ourselves in possession of an amazing power of communicating with the past, and contributing to its thought and action. . . .

Our first inexperienced efforts were disastrous. Many of the fatuities which primitive minds in all ages have been prone to attribute to the influence of disembodied spirits, whether deities, fiends, or the dead, are but the gibberish which resulted from our earliest experiments. And this book, so admirable in our conception, has issued from the brain of the writer, your contemporary, in such disorder as to be mostly rubbish.

A scientist of the Eighteenth species, infiltrating a past mind, could presumably im-

plant knowledge of happenings that are future for the past person concerned, enabling
that person to foretell them. That is what the
communicator in *Last and First Men* is supposed to have done with Stapledon, or tried
to do.

Did Stapledon put forward the notion seriously? In his own preface, before the voice
of the far-off communicator breaks in, he
says that it was more than a narrative convenience. "Only by some such radical and be-
wildering device could I embody the possibility that there may be more in time's nature
than is revealed to us."

Quite so. Backward-reaching intrusions
by scientists in the future may seem too far-
fetched. Yet it is a fact, however paradoxical,
that some cases of apparent prevision do suggest a process along these lines. In such cases,
it is certainly *as if* there were a rapport between the person who anticipates and a future informant on the far side (so to speak)
of what is anticipated—someone who knows
of it and conveys that knowledge to the
mind of the anticipator, against or outside
the normal time sequence.

This may be illustrated by a spatial analogy. Two drivers, Jim and Jane, are going
along a road in separate cars. Jim is some
distance ahead of Jane, who has to wait for
a passenger. He passes a place where driving is hazardous because of a rockfall.
Using his car phone, he warns Jane. She
takes her passenger on board and says,
"There's a rockfall three miles ahead."
When they come to it, her prior awareness
may seem mystifying or paranormal if the
passenger doesn't know about Jim. But
Jim, an informant farther along, together
with the means of communication, accounts for it.

See also: Dante Alighieri; Milton, John;
    Prophecy, Theories of

Further Reading

Crossley, Robert. *Olaf Stapledon: Speaking for
    the Future.* Liverpool: Liverpool University
    Press, 1994.

STEAD, W. T. (1849–1912)

William Thomas Stead, a famous English
journalist who foreshadowed the *Titanic* disaster and his own death in it.

In 1886, as editor of the *Pall Mall Gazette,*
he published an imaginary account of the
sinking of a great passenger liner, with heavy
loss of life. He appended an editorial note
singling out a hazard that deeply concerned
him—the shortage of lifeboats on big ships,
owing to the inadequacy of the laws for
safety at sea. "This," he wrote, referring to the
fictitious wreck, "is exactly what might take
place and what will take place if the liners are
set free short of boats."

Stead became a convert to Spiritualism. In
November 1893, he visited the United

*William T. Stead, a prominent English journalist who
predicted the* Titanic *disaster and died in it himself,
having defied a clairvoyant's warning and
premonitions of his own. (Ann Ronan Picture
Library)*

States, and the Chicago *Sunday Tribune* carried a long interview with him. The city's mayor, Carter Harrison, had been assassinated, and Stead observed: "He had, I am told, a premonition of his violent taking off. I have had a similar warning. I am to die a violent death." The interviewer asked about his interest in what would now be called the paranormal. He said: "I get communications from our living friends and also those which purport to come from friends who have quitted this earth. They are often more useful, because they often contain an element of prophecy." He mentioned a prediction of a change in his travel schedule, very much against expectation. Years afterward, he was still talking about his own fate. A friend recorded a conversation. "When my work is done," he said, "I shall die a violent death." "How do you know?" "I cannot tell, but I have had a vision, and I know that it will be true as surely as that I am talking to you."

In April 1912, Stead sailed aboard the *Titanic* on her maiden voyage. The society fortune-teller Cheiro had apparently advised him not to travel by water that month, but he ignored the warning and perished. The liner's collision with an iceberg doomed more than half her passengers and crew because she carried too few lifeboats. Stead's prediction was remembered. In June, a magazine reprinted the 1886 article with the comment, "After twenty-six years of 'progress,' the Board of Trade is responsible for the loss of 1,600 lives on the *Titanic*, because there were not enough boats!"

See also: Cheiro; Robertson, Morgan

Further Reading

Whyte, Frederick. *The Life of W. T. Stead.* 2 vols. London: Jonathan Cape, 1925.

Only the Fool has a counterpart in ordinary packs today, namely, the Joker. In that context, as an extra, he is the sole survivor of the Greater Arcana.

The twenty-two are as follows. They have similar Italian and French names that are earlier.

The Fool
I. The Magician
II. The Female Pope ("Papess")
III. The Empress
IV. The Emperor
V. The Pope
VI. The Lovers
VII. The Chariot
VIII. Justice
IX. The Hermit
X. The Wheel of Fortune
XI. Fortitude (or Strength)
XII. The Hanged Man
XIII. Death
XIV. Temperance
XV. The Devil
XVI. The Tower
XVII. The Star
XVIII. The Moon
XIX. The Sun
XX. Judgment
XXI. The World

TAROT

Name given to certain cards that are used for divinatory purposes, including prediction, and are said to symbolize esoteric and spiritual matters.

The derivation of the word *Tarot* is unknown. It has the French pronunciation, *taro,* but the cards seem to have originated in Italy, perhaps during the fourteenth century. Their adoption by gypsy fortune-tellers is later.

Card games may have been introduced into Europe from Asia. A German monk, Johannes of Brefeld, mentions them in 1377. He describes a four-suit pack resembling the present one. The Tarot pack, however, has twenty-two additional "major trumps," entirely different from the rest. They make their first indisputable appearance in 1415, when a set was painted for Filippo Maria Visconti, the duke of Milan. The pack, as generally known ever since, comprises these major trumps, called the Greater Arcana, and four suits of fourteen cards each, the Lesser Arcana. The suit denominators are Batons (or Wands), Cups, Swords, and Coins (or Pentacles), to which Clubs, Hearts, Spades, and Diamonds correspond. Each suit consists of ten cards numbered ace to ten, plus four court cards, the King, Queen, Knight, and Knave.

The Greater Arcana are separate. Each card has a title, with a picture purporting to illustrate it, though it is not always clear how. Twenty-one are numbered in roman numerals; the odd one, the Fool, has no number.

Some of these are strange. It would be interesting to know what a medieval person, such as the artist who painted the pictures for the duke of Milan, would have made of the Female Pope or, indeed, to know what suggested her in the first place. A hint may have come from the legend of Pope Joan (and there is an old card game so called) or from the sect founded by Guglielma of Milan, which was favored by the Visconti, the family of the Duke. Neither conjecture has any firm support. The Hanged Man, for some obscure reason, is upside down and suspended by a foot. The Tower has been struck by lightning; its top is shattered and

Two of the Greater Trumps or Arcana, the Empress from the most familiar version of the Tarot deck, the Fool from an older French one. (Dover Pictorial Series)

on fire. Judgment means the Last Judgment, but this is apparent only from the picture, which portrays an angel blowing a trumpet and the dead rising from their graves.

Occultists' interest in the Tarot during the nineteenth and twentieth centuries produced new packs. The one most familiar in English-speaking countries was devised by A. E. Waite in 1910 and reflects his ideas. It is substantially the same as ever, but the Papess has become the High Priestess, and the Pope, though still recognizably papal, has become the Hierophant. Artists with esoteric tastes have created further Tarots, some of them with pictures based on established

mythologies. There is, for instance, an Arthurian Tarot.

The full pack of seventy-eight (22 + 56) can be used for play. The game of "tarocco" combines the main principles of rummy and bridge: the players score by holding combinations of cards and also by winning tricks. However, the divinatory aspect is much more important. The person consulting a fortune-teller is sometimes called the querent. All seventy-eight cards have assigned meanings, and selections are dealt out in various arrangements called "spreads." Some of these are supposed to yield advice in the immediate situation. Others, especially the circular spread—twelve cards in a circle, with a thirteenth in the middle—are claimed to show the querent's future when suitably interpreted.

It is hard to see how the cards in themselves could do this, and the interpretation is evidently the part that matters. Some Tarot readers are undoubtedly successful: probably by developing information about the querent; perhaps, in rare cases, by insights that do elude rational explanation. Yet even in the latter case, it is questionable whether the images on the cards have much to do with the insights that emerge. They focus the mind and supply themes for discussion. But the predictions, if valid, are due to essentially the same process (whatever it is) that operates in any other fortune-telling technique, when it gives results that cannot be plausibly explained away. The technique is not the secret.

The following account of an actual case of Tarot reading, recorded by the querent, may serve as an illustration. Identifying details have been omitted.

In December I invited a Tarot expert to give me a reading for the ensuing four months. The expert was [C]. We went through a prescribed ritual of cutting the Tarot pack and dealing out cards. He told me that I had a plan for a long and important journey. In January there would be much doubt overhanging it. This would be resolved, and in March it would take place. A woman born under a Fire sign of the Zodiac would be concerned in it. Meanwhile, in January, a new archaeological project would have been brought to my attention, connected with a hill. Toward the end of the four-month period I would probably be moving into a fresh sphere of work and interest.

These were the main forecasts, and they were all fulfilled. The intended journey was to America. Factors beyond my control made it look uncertain in January, but I went in March. The chief purpose was to lecture at a university, under the sponsorship of a woman professor whose birthday was in July under Leo, one of the three Fire signs. The archaeo-

logical project was also delivered. A letter came in January from someone who had been trying to organize an excavation at a hill-fort which I had drawn attention to. The letter followed months of silence during which I had almost forgotten the project. It informed me, for the first time, that the dig was going ahead. As for the fresh sphere of work and interest, this could be fairly related to a book of mine which, in April, was on the verge of being published and had many consequences.

[C] could have picked up hints for some of this from conversation, but not for all of it. I had not, for example, told him the professor's birthday; I had not even mentioned her. Nor had I spoken of the excavation proposal. In fact I failed to recall it myself during the reading, and throughout December. It only came back to me when the letter arrived.

The sceptic will say: "Ah, but no doubt you've had your fortune told many times. You're just picking on the one time when it turned out well." Not so. I have not had my fortune told many times. To the best of my recollection, [C]'s Tarot reading was the only fortune-telling I have ever submitted to at the hands of a self-styled expert. It was a unique case, and it worked.

However, it did not dispose me to value the technique as such. I do not believe that the cards foretold anything, or even, strictly speaking, that [C] did. The cards gave him talking points and were doubtless well adapted to that purpose. His dealing and interpreting constituted a kind of patter suited to himself, which helped whatever-it-was-that-knew-what-was-shaping-up to slip in below the threshold of consciousness and cause events in his brain.

It is often asserted that there is more to these cards than meets the eye. The Greater Arcana have a special and understandable fascination. From the mid–nineteenth century on, interpreters were crediting them with a cryptographic aspect, encoding secret wisdom. A fact in favor of such a view was that there are twenty-two of them and twenty-two letters in the Hebrew alphabet. That correspondence opened the door to the Jewish esoteric system called the cabala. One factor in the cabala is the belief that Hebrew was the language of God. His creative fiats beginning "Let there be . . ." in Genesis were sentences actually uttered by him, and if he had spoken in any other language, the world would be other than it is. Consequently, the twenty-two letters of its alphabet, the basic sounds, were the matrices of Creation. Jewish sages were reputed to have performed magical feats by combining letters. If the Tarot trumps were matched to the letters, they might embody magic likewise, whatever its nature.

Thanks mainly to the Order of the Golden Dawn, a group founded in England about 1887, the trumps are alleged to have some kind of affinity with the Cabalistic Tree of Life, a diagram showing different aspects of divinity and humanity with lines or "paths" joining them. The twenty-two Hebrew letters are allotted to the paths and unfold the meaning of the Tree. It follows that the twenty-two trumps can be deployed similarly. But there has been a lack of agreement as to which letter corresponds to which card. While the cabala is a venerable and recognizable system, the Tarot connection seems very speculative.

In 1920, a medieval scholar, Jessie L. Weston, introduced another topic. She published *From Ritual to Romance,* in which she considered the four suits or Lesser Arcana instead of the trumps. She noted the occurrence in Grail legends of four sacred or magical objects called Hallows—the Cup itself, a Lance, a Sword, and a Dish—that resembled the Cups, Batons, Swords, and Coins of the Tarot pack. Claiming these images to be very ancient and involved with fertility magic, she wove them into a theory of a semipagan, semi-Christian cult that maintained an underground existence into the Middle Ages. Its ritual, she said, reappeared in certain mysterious episodes of the Grail Quest. T. S. Eliot's citation of this book in *The Waste Land* gave it a wider fame than it would otherwise have enjoyed. It has little academic standing, and despite its air of scholarship, it is not free from the occult notions that appear elsewhere.

To revert to the major trumps, attempts have been made to connect these too with some species of irregular Christianity, whether semipagan, Gnostic, or Cathar. Evidence is lacking. What is curious, however, is the fact that the images and themes are scattered through Dante's *Divine Comedy,* the greatest literary production of the Middle Ages, which is perfectly orthodox. They are distributed over its three parts, the *Inferno* (Hell), *Purgatorio* (Purgatory), and *Paradiso* (Heaven).

Several of the trumps are explicit in this context. A reader going through the *Inferno* encounters Lovers (in canto V:79–142, Paolo and Francesca); Fortune and her Wheel (VII:70–96); a Tower surmounted by flames (VIII:1–4); a Magician (XX:115–117, Michael Scott, with others); and the Devil (XXXIV:28 ff). *Purgatorio* has Temperance (XXII:130–154, images and instances) and a most impressive Chariot (XXIX:107–117 and later—Dante's word is *carro,* as in the Italian version of this trump). *Paradiso* has the Moon (II:49 ff); the Emperor (VI:10, Justinian); and Justice (XVIII:91, where the word is spelled out by living lights).

Ten thus far. The rest are not quite so clear-cut, but all or nearly all of the twenty-two can be found. The Star has a special interest. In English, it does not work because no single Star makes a convincing appearance in the *Divine Comedy.* But the Italian name of this trump is *Le Stelle,* a plural, and even the French and English pictures show several, though one is conspicuous. In *Purgatorio* I:22–24, the poet imagines four brilliant stars, *quattro stelle,* as visible in the Southern Hemisphere. The celestial symbolism of this canto accommodates the trump.

When the twenty-one numbered trumps are placed, they turn out to be evenly distributed. Seven are in the *Inferno,* seven in *Purgatorio,* and seven in *Paradiso.* No canto contains more than one. Some form sequences. Most of those in *Paradiso* occur at four-canto intervals, being in II, VI, X, XIV, XVIII, and XXII. It might be argued that in such a vast and wide-ranging work, the Tarot motifs could be expected to appear by chance. But even apart from the spacing and distribution of narrative images, the Greater Arcana sometimes seem to be hovering in the background, influencing the poet's thoughts. For instance, nothing in his narrative provides a Hanged Man, yet he practically forces one in—Haman—in *Purgatorio* XVII:25–30, by inventing a vision and bringing his Hanged Man into it. The Fool is the odd one, outside the numbered series, and the Fool alone has no satisfactory location in the text, as if Dante chose to leave him out or was uncertain where to put him.

It is futile to look for magical or heretical cryptograms in the work of an author who abhorred magic and heresy. The *Divine Comedy*, written early in the fourteenth century, is prior to any known appearance of the motifs in card form. If the hypothesis of prevision were to be admitted, the poet might be showing some kind of anticipatory awareness, as he seems to be doing in a much more important case; though prevision of anything so trivial, on the face of it, would suggest that the esoteric view is arguable after all and the cards do have some deeper significance.

See also: Dante Alighieri; Divination; Guglielma of Milan; Prophecy, Theories of

Further Reading

Cavendish, Richard, ed. *Man, Myth and Magic*. London: BPC Publications, 1970–1972. Article "Tarot."

Douglas, Alfred. *The Tarot*. London: Victor Gollancz, 1972.

TECUMSEH (1768–1813)

Shawnee chief, opponent of white encroachment. During the summer of 1810, William Henry Harrison, then governor of the Indiana Territory, sought his cooperation. He replied with an eloquent refusal, appealing to the "Great Spirit that rules this universe" as having allotted the Shawnee a living space that they would not surrender.

In the following year, he tried to enlist support for armed resistance. The most elaborate version of what he did says that he had slabs of wood carved with designs expressing his intentions and sent them to the chiefs of thirty major tribes. With each message slab, he sent a bundle of thirty sticks, carved and painted red. The recipients were to throw away twenty-nine of these at stated intervals and then watch for a sign in the sky. When this appeared, they were to cut the remaining stick into thirty pieces and burn a piece each night. The burning of the last piece would be followed by a greater sign.

Tecumseh's prophecies were fulfilled. The sign in the sky was a comet, and the greater sign was a widespread earthquake on a scale unusual in that part of the United States. But it was all wasted. Harrison had assembled a force to suppress the uprising, and Tecumseh, unfortunately for his plans, had a brother known as "The Prophet" who claimed supernatural powers and persuaded the Shawnee to attack Harrison's camp at Tippecanoe, near the present city of West Lafayette, Indiana. The move was premature, but he assured the warriors that his magic would paralyze the enemy, and watched from a rock still called the Prophet's Rock. This prediction failed, and Harrison won the battle, putting an end to the uprising. Tecumseh did not give up. In the War of 1812, still hoping to check the advance of the United States, he offered his services to the British while insisting on his people's right to their territory. He commanded a force of Native American allies and fell at a battle in Canada.

The comet and earthquake in 1811 were certainly recognized as signs foretold by Tecumseh. The story of the build-up with sticks has doubtless grown in the telling but may have a factual basis.

Further Reading
Dictionary of American Biography. Article "Tecumseh."
Sugden, John. *Tecumseh.* New York: Henry Holt, 1998.

TENNYSON, ALFRED (1809–1892)

English poet laureate who was created Lord Tennyson, and is sometimes credited with foretelling aerial transport and combat.

Tennyson wrote a great deal in various forms—lyric, narrative, and dramatic. He was one of the few poets to become a popular best-seller. His output includes several rehandlings of Arthurian legend, the most ambitious being the *Idylls of the King.* He touches on the theme of Arthur's return but very briefly. One curious poem describes an imaginary dream in which Arthur is reembodied as a "modern gentleman," apparently Prince Albert, Queen Victoria's husband. An Albert-Arthur parallel that appears elsewhere in Tennyson's work interested him more than the original prophecy.

Seekers of literary prevision have paid more attention to a passage in his long poem *Locksley Hall* (1842). This takes the form of a monologue. The speaker reminisces about his earlier life and hopes, when he reflected on the prospects for social and technological advances.

> For I dipt into the future, far as human
>   eye could see,
> Saw the Vision of the world, and all the
>   wonder that would be;
> Saw the heavens fill with commerce,
>   argosies of magic sails,
> Pilots of the purple twilight, dropping
>   down with costly bales;
> Heard the heavens fill with shouting, and
>   there rain'd a ghastly dew
> From the nations' airy navies grappling
>   in the central blue;
> Far along the world-wide whisper of the
>   south-wind rushing warm,

> With the standards of the peoples
>   plunging thro' the thunder-storm;
> Till the war-drum throbb'd no longer,
>   and the battle-flags were furl'd
> In the Parliament of man, the Federation
>   of the world.
> There the common sense of most shall
>   hold a fretful realm in awe,
> And the kindly earth shall slumber, lapt
>   in universal law.

In the early decades of the twentieth century, this passage was often recalled, especially when aerial warfare was in the news. However, it is fantasy, not anticipatory science fiction. No coherent images can be extracted from Tennyson's lines, even by extrapolation from his own time. Balloons, of course, were familiar, but, being at the mercy of air currents, they obviously could never be used on a large scale for regular commercial flights. A war fleet could not maintain formation or fight another fleet, and the "ghastly dew" of blood implies hand-to-hand combat between crews who could not, in practice, get at each other. "Magic sails" might suggest dirigibles resembling ships at sea, but this is no more than a phrase, and powered heavier-than-air flight was still far off.

What these lines are really about is the contemporary vision of progress, on which the poet, at the time of writing, agrees with the speaker in the poem. Humanity will advance to a triumph symbolized by the conquest of the air, in some way that Tennyson knows to be unforeseeable and does not attempt to picture realistically. This crowning achievement will lead through conflict to sanity asserting itself and bringing peace to the world.

See also: Arthur, King

THAXTER, CELIA

Author of a book of poetry published in 1887. One poem, "A Tryst," was singled out after the *Titanic* disaster in 1912 as an anticipation of it.

See also: *Titanic* and references under that heading

THEOSOPHY

A religious system of fairly recent origin that makes far-reaching projections of humanity's future.

The word *Theosophy,* meaning God-wisdom, goes back a long way as a term for mystical insight into matters divine. In its modern sense, it is applied to a specific movement that was built up during the late nineteenth and early twentieth centuries, expounding complex doctrines of spiritual evolution and reincarnation. Its founder was Helena Petrovna Blavatsky (1831–1891). Known to her followers as Madame Blavatsky or HPB, she was a Russian of somewhat mysterious an-

Madame Blavatsky, cofounder of the Theosophical Society, who invented a world time-scheme stretching far into the future. (Hulton Getty)

tecedents. Together with Henry Steel Olcott, a U.S. Spiritualist, she launched the Theosophical Society in New York in 1875. The immediate impulse came from a lecture on Pyramidology that they both attended.

HPB, who spent some time in India conferring with Hindu scholars, claimed that she was in contact with the Masters, or Mahatmas—exalted and elusive beings living in or beyond the Himalayas. Professedly under their guidance, she wrote *Isis Unveiled* and, in England, *The Secret Doctrine,* books that combine comparative religion, occultism, pseudoscience, and fantasy in a mélange that shows genuine if superficial research but is not free from unacknowledged borrowing and downright plagiarism. She followed these works with a shorter *Key to Theosophy.* It proclaims that there is no religion higher than Truth; that all religions embody the same Truth; and, not very consistently, that Christianity is a mass of lies.

The society flourished erratically for several decades, its maximum membership being about 40,000, scattered throughout Europe, the United States, India, and Australia; so one of its professed aims, the formation of an international fellowship, was to some extent achieved. Prominent though temporary sympathizers included W. B. Yeats, Gandhi, and Jawaharlal Nehru, the first prime minister of independent India. Another was the Austrian Rudolf Steiner, who headed the German section of the society but left to create a system of his own that had a noteworthy impact on education. Theosophy exerted influence that has not always been acknowledged—for instance, by reviving interest in astrology. Here Madame Blavatsky led the way herself, and a Theosophist writing under the name of Alan Leo was its first popularizer.

HPB's animus against Christianity may have helped to attract her most spectacular convert, Annie Besant, who, after a failed marriage to a clergyman, had spent several years preaching atheism. In 1907, with the two cofounders dead, she became president of the society. She moved Theosophy closer to Hinduism, though its more peculiar ramifications ruled it out for most serious Hindus. A center was established at Adyar, near Madras, as the society's headquarters. From 1909 onward, Besant was foretelling a new divine advent, in effect a new coming of Christ, and she was increasingly certain that the "World Teacher" would be manifested as an Indian. This conviction led to her grooming Jiddu Krishnamurti for the role and to his public refusal of it, with disastrous results.

She was not the only Theosophist to make unwise prophecies. However, the system's main element of prediction arose from its schema of human evolution, covering millions of years. It was meant to give substance to various prehistoric and mythical peoples and fit them together in a world history recognizing geologic changes (though not in a way that any geologist would approve). Central to HPB's design was one of her leading principles, that "the supreme number of the higher mysteries" is seven, which pervades all reality. Humanity has evolved and will continue to evolve through a succession of "root-races," and there will eventually have been seven of these. Thus far, there have been only five, so two more can be predicted. Each of them, after the first, has sprung from a portion of the one before, and each has been divided into seven subraces.

It appears that the members of the first root-race were not material beings. They lived in an "Imperishable Sacred Land" that cannot be pinned down on the map. Second came the Hyperboreans, their name known to Greek mythology, though still far from humanity as it now is; their home was an arctic continent that broke up, leaving Greenland and Spitzbergen as fragments. Third were the Lemurians, who inhabited the conjectured lost continent of Lemuria, now mostly submerged. Some of these were more or less human in the present sense, though with marked physical differences. Fourth

were the people of Atlantis, a more famous lost continent. Several of their subraces founded civilizations recorded in history, and many descendants survive. Fifth were the Aryans (the Indian word *Aryan,* discredited by Nazism, was respectable in Madame Blavatsky's time). Within this root-race, which is now dominant, five subraces have come into being—the Hindu, Arabian, Iranian, Celtic, and Teutonic.

The septenary plan requires two more subraces within the present Aryan root-race. Some Theosophists thought the sixth might emerge in Australia. Besant, however, decided in the 1920s that California was the place to watch, and she asserted that ethnologists were already finding physical and mental differences in the population along the Pacific Coast. After the sixth subrace, there would still have to be a seventh, as yet undefinable.

But even with the Aryan root-race completed, what about the next and the one after that? There was nowhere to put them but in a very remote future, with a geography that could only be justified by far-fetched conjecture or occult revelation. The outcome was a grandiose prophecy looking a long way ahead. The destined home of the sixth root-race might be Lemuria again, when a sufficient amount of the lost land had risen above the water. The process of formation would take hundreds of thousands of years. And the seventh and last root-race would be located far, far off in time, perhaps in South America.

This is prophecy with an arithmetical basis, which might seem to commend it, if the story could be believed. But it cannot, and in any case, the arithmetic is mystical, not mathematical. The whole series is a product of the mystique of seven, and the projected future is shaped to make up that number. Madame Blavatsky did not invent the seven mystique, which occurs widely, though not universally: it is prominent in the Bible—witness the last book of the New Testament, Revelation. In *The Secret Doctrine,* she attempted a study of it in different historical contexts and cultures, which could have been interesting, but, in her hands, is too fanciful and confused to have much value. Her panorama of ancient humanity and semihumanity has possibilities for fiction, and writers of fiction have taken ideas from it, but there is no way of relating even the less extravagant parts to recognized facts, and therefore, there is no reason to pay any attention to its extrapolations into the future.

It must be conceded that HPB was ahead of her time in spreading her humans and semihumans over such a long period. However, few except Theosophists ever accepted her "history" as a whole. Where she did have an appreciable if indirect impact, through her talk of Atlantis and Lemuria, was in encouraging twentieth-century fantasies about lost continents. It is also unfortunately possible that her account of the races and her pronouncements on their qualities and attributes supplied ammunition for racists of a more evil kind.

See also: Atlantis; Besant, Annie; Lemuria
Further Reading
Blavatsky, H. P. *Isis Unveiled.* 2 vols. Pasadena, CA: Theosophical University Press, 1972.
———. *The Secret Doctrine.* 2 vols. Pasadena, CA: Theosophical University Press, 1970.

THOMAS AQUINAS, SAINT (1225–1274)

Italian theologian and philosopher. His system, long favored by Catholic educators, has been influential in modern times as Thomism through the work of Jacques Maritain and others. It is treated with respect, though not with agreement, by agnostics such as Bertrand Russell.

In his *Summa Theologica,* Thomas Aquinas examines, among many other topics, the question of knowledge of the future. This issue is unavoidable because biblical characters make true predictions. The prophets of Israel are not the only ones: in Genesis, Joseph does it by interpreting other men's dreams. Such foreknowledge is held to be inspired by God. Joseph practices divination like the Egyptians around him, but that is not how he discovers what the dreams portend. In these crucial cases, the author draws a clear distinction. "Do not interpretations belong to God?" he has Joseph say.

Given the truth of the scriptural accounts, God must know the future, even when, as with Joseph and the prophets, this future depends on normally unpredictable behavior. Thomas Aquinas considers how such knowledge can be made intelligible. In his judgment, words like *foresee* are inaccurate. They imply that God exists as humans do in linear time and, so to speak, looks along it, as someone walking on a road might use binoculars to pick out an object far ahead that is invisible to other walkers. That, however, is not the case. God exists in eternity, outside time as human beings experience it, and knows it

Saint Thomas Aquinas, the Church's foremost philosopher in the Middle Ages, who discusses the problem of foreknowledge. The dove symbolizes the Holy Spirit teaching him. (Ann Ronan Picture Library)

as a whole. Thomas Aquinas's comparison is not to a person walking along a road with other walkers but to someone looking down on the road from a great height and surveying its entire length. God's standpoint in his "eternal Now" is different from ours. The future events that he knows are unknowable to us in the ordinary way because, from the human standpoint, they are still to come, but God communicates glimpses of them to prophets and seers.

Do any beings besides God have the same knowledge? Thomas Aquinas has much to say about angels, spiritual entities superior to ourselves. In his view, they are within time as we are and do not share God's eternity outside it. Therefore, they do not know the future as he does. If they give human beings information about it, they do so only as his messengers. Acting on their own initiative, they are better than humans at intelligent anticipation because they are more intelligent; that is all.

Thomas Aquinas is covering prophecy in the Judeo-Christian tradition, "good" prophecy, divinely ordained for divine purposes. A problem arises if we are to accept paranormal predictions of other kinds, as, for example, in the prophecies of Nostradamus. If they do not happen in the theologically approved way, how do they happen at all? God should surely not be imagined dictating cryptic verses to an astrologer, sometimes true, more often not, but in any case without spiritual significance.

Before Thomas Aquinas, Saint Augustine suggested that evil angels—demons—might have some knowledge of the future and use it to lead humans astray. This malicious forecasting, not discussed by Thomas Aquinas, was reinvented after his time as an accusation against alleged witches. A classic case is Shakespeare's *Macbeth,* with its three witches subject to diabolic "masters." Macbeth is lured by prophecies, which, though correct, are increasingly misleading, into murder and self-destruction.

Augustine's notion would be of no help with precognition that is nonreligious yet innocent. If it occurs, some explanation seems to be needed beyond any offered by either Augustine or Thomas Aquinas.

See also: Augustine, Saint; *Macbeth;* Prophecy, Theories of; Witchcraft

Further Reading

Pegis, Anton, ed. *Basic Writings of Saint Thomas Aquinas.* Vol. 1. New York: Random House, 1945.

THOMAS THE RHYMER (C. 1220–1297?)

Thomas Rymour of Erceldoune (now Earlston, near Melrose, in the Border country) was a Scottish poet and seer nicknamed "True Thomas." His name figures in legal documents that prove his reality, and he may or may not have been the author of an Arthurian romance, *Sir Tristrem.* A ruin in Earlston is associated with him. He is referred to also as Thomas Learmont.

Reputedly, he foretold the death of the Scottish king Alexander III in 1286, through an unexpected traveling accident. He also foretold Robert Bruce's victory over the English at Bannockburn in 1314. For these two predictions, some early evidence exists, and they and doubtless others gave him a reputation. From the fourteenth century to the sixteenth, various prophecies of his became current, some of them fabricated. A collection was published in 1603. He was credited with foretelling Henry VIII's victory over the Scots at Flodden, in 1513, and the accession of James VI of Scotland to the throne of England.

The second prediction is more interesting. At the village of Drumelzier in the Scottish Borders, a cairn by the Tweed River was supposed to mark the grave of Merlin. A creek called the Pausayl (Powsail or Willow) flows into the Tweed a short distance away. The prophecy was as follows:

When Tweed and Pausayl meet at
   Merlin's grave,
Scotland and England shall one monarch
   have.

In 1603, the creek temporarily changed course owing to flooding and joined the Tweed close beside the cairn. About that time, on the death of Elizabeth I, James VI of Scotland became also James I of England. Another prophecy concerns the Haig family:

Tyde what may, whate'er betide,
Haig shall be Haig of Bemersyde.

Bemersyde is a few miles south of Earlston. The family estates in that neighborhood were lost but recovered in 1921 by Field Marshal Douglas Haig, who took the title of Earl Haig of Bemersyde.

Thomas's reputation produced legends. A ballad composed in the early 1400s, possibly developed from a lost poem by Thomas himself, told how he met the Queen of Elfland, in green garb that was supposed to be ominous; she led him along a winding road to her mysterious domain. Thomas kissed her and was obliged to live with her for three years (or seven). His prophetic power was a gift of the queen. She also gave him a magic apple. As soon as he ate it, he had a "tongue that could never lie." Back in the mortal world, his consequent nickname "True Thomas" was confirmed by the accuracy of his predictions. In his old age, he was summoned to Elfland again by the queen, who sent a male and a female deer to guide him. He followed the two animals into a forest and was seen no more.

However, he was believed to have become immortal and to have reappeared occasionally. During seventeenth-century trials for witchcraft, several witches claimed to have had dealings with him. Stories of him hover around the Eildon Hills beside Melrose. In a version of the Arthurian cave legend, recorded by Sir Walter Scott, Thomas conducts a man through a secret entrance into a torch-lit cavern under the hills and shows him a great company of knights lying asleep.

He certainly seems to have had a prophetic gift of some kind, which accounts for the otherworldly traditions. But the shortage of hard evidence rules out any certainty as to how much he did foretell and how much may have been invented by others after the happenings that were allegedly foretold.

See also: Brahan Seer, The; Peden, Alexander

Further Reading

Cavendish, Richard, ed. *Man, Myth and Magic.* London: BPC Publishing, 1970–1972. Article "Scottish and Border Ballads."

Folklore, Myths and Legends of Britain. London: Readers Digest Association, 1973.

TITANIC

British oceangoing liner that struck an iceberg on her maiden voyage in April 1912 and sank with great loss of life because there were not enough lifeboats aboard.

This disaster was foreshadowed in various ways, even in a poem entitled "A Tryst" by Celia Thaxter. It was anticipated fictionally by Morgan Robertson, fourteen years earlier and in remarkable detail, and by Mayn Clew Garnett. Among the passengers who perished was W. T. Stead, a well-known journalist. He had warned of the danger of letting ships go to sea with too few lifeboats; he had predicted a violent death for himself; and, reputedly, he had been advised by the fortune-teller Cheiro not to travel by water in that month. Another who drowned was the financier John Jacob Astor. A Norwegian seer, Anton Johanson, had had a prevision of a ship sinking with an Astor aboard.

See also: Cheiro; Garnett, Mayn Clew; Johanson, Anton; Robertson, Morgan; Stead, W. T.; Thaxter, Celia

Further Reading

Wade, Wyn Craig. *The Titanic: End of a Dream.* New York: Penguin Books USA, 1986.

The collision of the world's largest passenger ship with an iceberg, a disaster foreshadowed by several authors and clairvoyants. (Ann Ronan Picture Library)

V

VIRGIL (70–19 B.C.)

Publius Vergilius Maro, the greatest poet of ancient Rome. The theme of his epic the *Aeneid* is Rome's legendary origin. It tells how Aeneas, a Trojan prince, escaped from the fall of Troy with a large party of followers and, after various adventures, arrived in Italy. Reputedly, the Romans were these Trojans' descendants. In Virgil's poem, when the migrants disembark in their new country, Aeneas consults the Sibyl at Cumae about their prospects. Virgil's account of her and her inspiration by Apollo sheds light on the way the Sibyls were imagined.

He acquired a prophetic reputation himself. In a poem written before the *Aeneid,* fourth in a series called *Eclogues,* he cites the Cumaean Sibyl as foreshadowing a new golden age, and he connects it with the approaching birth of a wonderful child. He addresses this imminent Messiah:

> "Enter on thy high honour—the hour
>   will soon be here—O thou dear
> offspring of the gods! . . . Behold the
>   world bowing with its massive
> dome—earth and expanse of sea and
>   heaven's depths! Behold, how all
> things exult in the age that is at hand! O
>   that then the last days of a long
> life may still linger for me, with
>   inspiration enough to tell of thy
>   deeds!
> . . . Begin, little boy, to know thy
>   mother with a smile."

Virgil's meaning is uncertain. He may be thinking of a son to be born to the wife of Octavian, later known as Augustus Caesar, or to the wife of Mark Antony, these two being the most powerful men in the Roman world, though it is hard to see how either birth could have had a messianic impact. In any case, as it turned out, both the wives gave birth to daughters. When Virgil came to compose the *Aeneid,* he said nothing further about his wonderful child and explained the golden age as the imperial peace brought by Augustus.

Later, however, the Fourth Eclogue was adopted by Christians. They noticed that it had likenesses to passages in the Bible, and

Ancient Rome's greatest poet, Virgil, was believed by many Christians to have had an unconscious prevision of Christ. (Ann Ronan Picture Library)

since it had not been fulfilled in the pagan world, they interpreted it as a prophecy of Christ. Virgil had been inspired, though unconsciously. This reading of the Eclogue continued to be familiar in the Middle Ages. Dante translates lines from it in his *Divine Comedy,* where another Roman poet, Statius, is introduced telling how it converted him to Christianity. This is almost certainly fiction, but fiction based on an established belief and perfectly plausible for a medieval reader. Several churches, notably one in Rouen, commemorated Virgil at Christmas as "Maro, Prophet of the Gentiles."

See also: Sibyls and Sibylline Texts

Further Reading

Ashe, Geoffrey. *The Book of Prophecy.* London: Blandford, 1999.

Grant, Michael. *Cleopatra.* London: Pantheon Books, 1974.

WANDERING JEW

An unwilling immortal who is the subject of a mythical prophecy by Christ.

The Wandering Jew, as such, is a fairly late arrival in Christian legend. However, he has antecedents far back, in the New Testament itself. The Gospels record certain sayings of Jesus that could be taken as predicting that someone would live to see his Second Coming. Hopes of this kind fastened on John, the "beloved disciple," concerning whom Jesus made a mysterious remark about his "remaining until I come" (John 21:20–23). John died, or ostensibly died, but a belief lingered for centuries that he was still living.

When the story surfaces next, it has undergone a strange transformation. It tells of an immortal called Cartaphilus. This name means "most beloved" and is obviously derived from the phrase that the gospel applies to John. But Cartaphilus, it seems, was not John. He had been a doorkeeper at Pilate's house at the time of the Crucifixion, and deathlessness was a penance and not a privilege. An Armenian prelate who visited England in 1228 claimed to have seen him and heard his history. As Jesus passed him bearing the cross, Cartaphilus shouted, "Go on faster!" Jesus replied, "I go, but you shall wait till I come." Cartaphilus witnessed the Crucifixion. He was converted, baptized, and given the Christian name Joseph. In the thirteenth century, he was still living in retirement, chiefly as a guest of religious communities. He would age until he appeared to be 100 and would then be miraculously restored to 30. Other Armenians corroborated the tale.

The actual name of the "beloved disciple" appears with a similar shift in a similar legend. Again, the protagonist is someone else: he is a different John dubbed Bottadio, meaning "God-smiter," identified with the official who struck Jesus before the High Priest (John 18:10, 22). He too is said to have lived on. Bottadio is mentioned by Guido Bonnati, an astrologer known to Dante. There are reports of his being seen at various times, notably in Italy early in the fifteenth century. The change from divine favor to divine punishment is the curious thing. A Buddhist legend tells of Pindola, an unworthy follower of Buddha, who was condemned to be unable to die, but no connection has been traced.

It is only in 1602 that the immortal becomes definitely a Jew and a wanderer, and the idea about John is finally left behind. The change is made in an anonymous German pamphlet that asserts that Paulus von Eizen, a Lutheran bishop, met a Jew in Hamburg in the 1540s who was more than fifteen centuries old. His name was Ahasuerus. He had been a cobbler in Jerusalem in the time of Christ, one of the crowd who clamored for his crucifixion. Jesus, carrying the cross, tried to rest on Ahasuerus's doorstep, but the cobbler pushed him away, saying, "Go where you belong." Jesus looked at him sternly and replied, "I will stand here and rest, but you shall go on till I return." Ever since, the bishop said, Ahasuerus had been wandering from country to country awaiting that event.

The story quickly became popular. The German pamphlet went through many editions, and versions of it appeared in French, Flemish, Dutch, Danish, and Swedish. There was also an English parody. One reason for

Ahasuerus, a Jewish cobbler in Christian legend, who spurned Christ and was condemned to live and wander until Christ's Second Coming. (Mary Evans Picture Archive)

its success may have been an outbreak of prophesying about the advent of Antichrist, with Jewish support; another reason might be the excitement of finding an eyewitness who confirmed the Christian narrative. The name given to the wanderer was usually Ahasuerus, as in the pamphlet. It was probably an echo of Jewish plays based on the book of Esther and performed at the feast of Purim, which made the biblical Ahasuerus a villain and laughingstock. In Belgium, however, the wanderer was called Isaac Laquedem, and in Spain he was Juan Espera-en-Dios (John Trust-in-God).

However fictitious the Wandering Jew may be, however like an adaptation of Cartaphilus and Bottadio, he is a more dramatic figure than these precursors, and he has been widely believed in. Reported sightings of him total about twenty, some of them said to have occurred before the pamphlet made him famous. Besides his meeting with the bishop in Hamburg, he was recognized in Spain in 1575, in Vienna in 1599, in Ypres in 1623, in Brussels in 1643, in Paris in 1644, and at various other places during the seventeenth century, mostly in central Europe. It may be, of course, that impostors with odd notions of humor impersonated him. Later on, the sightings were fewer. However, they included one in Newcastle, England, in 1790 and one in Salt Lake City in 1868, when a Mormon named O'Grady met him, an encounter reported in the *Deseret News.*

Several authors have taken up his legend, among them Goethe and Shelley. Sometimes, he becomes a sympathetic or tragic character, rebelling against his doom and longing vainly for death. A well-known French treatment is *Le Juif Errant* (1844) by the novelist Eugène Sue. Gustave Doré made the story the theme of a pictorial series. A Jewish dramatist, David Pinski, gives it a Jewish form, portraying the wanderer as searching for the Messiah. He also figures in an episode in Evelyn Waugh's historical novel *Helena* (1950).

See also: John, Saint

Further Reading

Cavendish, Richard, ed. *Man, Myth and Magic.* London: BPC Publishing, 1970–1972. Article "Wandering Jew."

WELLS, H. G. (1866–1946)

Prolific and versatile English author who was widely read during the first quarter of the twentieth century and whose story *The Time Machine* was a groundbreaking classic of science fiction.

This was his first important production. It appeared in 1895. He followed it with more works of science fiction and fantasy, several very good novels, and many brilliant short stories. He considered that he had an exceptional talent for perceiving "tendencies" in society, and, in the belief that he could see which way these were tending, he produced much fiction and nonfiction making prognostications. He invented a number of Utopias and Dystopias (the bad kind). At first somber in outlook, he became optimistic. In *The Outline of History* (1920), a best-selling survey of humanity's whole career, he tried to show that the long-term trend was onward and upward despite all disasters, stupidities, and crimes. *The Shape of Things to Come* (1933) was a detailed history of the future, moving through World War II—which Wells foresaw but was wildly wrong about—to various further crises and the creation of an enlightened, scientific world order by wiser inheritors. Wells's hopefulness went into a decline, but it permeated a large part of his output.

The Time Machine came before any of this and is very different, predating all of Wells's would-be rational guesswork about "tendencies." Its picture of humanity in a remote future is a wry comment on the England of his own day, rather than an attempt to assess where this might really be headed. The story originated, in part, from an article on time as a fourth dimension that Wells submitted to an editor who had previously encouraged him, but, in this case, did not. He adapted the rejected matter in conversational form as an introduction. When he came to the story, he sensibly did not try to make it specific or plausible. The Time Traveler—never named—is a scientist of high standing, but there is no hint as to what his specialty is, except for a cryptic reference to optics; nor is there anything to

The novelist Herbert George Wells, who, in The Time Machine, *criticized contemporary society by imagining how it might evolve in a distant future. (Ann Ronan Picture Library)*

indicate how his Time Machine works or even what it looks like, apart from a few uncoordinated details.

He is single and well-off, with servants (of course, in the 1890s) and a laboratory attached to his house. He has a lively circle of friends, mostly professional men in various lines, who often come to visit on Thursdays. At the beginning, he is talking to a group of them about time in general and the possibility of traveling in it. His attempts to explain the concept of a fourth dimension are met with polite skepticism. They lead up to an announcement that he has found a method of traveling in time and built a machine for that purpose. He demonstrates with a small model that disappears when activated. Then, he takes his guests to the laboratory to see the full-scale Time Machine that he has almost completed. It is a bizarre construction of nickel, ivory, and crystal, with four dials and a saddle for the operator. In spite of the demonstration, his friends are not convinced.

Next Thursday evening, another party assembles at his house. He has left a message telling his guests to go ahead with dinner if he is not there. He is not there, and they go ahead. Those who heard him the previous Thursday speculate, not very seriously, that their host may be away time-traveling. During the meal, he makes a surprising entrance. His clothes are filthy, he is disheveled and haggard, and he walks with a limp. He refuses to explain what has happened until he has washed, changed, and eaten. While he is out of the room, the talk of time travel becomes more insistent. He returns looking better and eats heartily—the meat seems especially welcome—and then invites his friends to move into another room, where they can listen in comfort.

The following is a summary of the story he tells.

When he had finished preparing his invention, he resolved to test it at once. About ten o'clock in the morning, he took his place on the saddle, started the mechanism, and quickly stopped it. Had anything happened? It had. The clock's hands were now close to three-thirty. Satisfied that the Time Machine worked, he paused for a few minutes' reflection and then set off into the future.

Day and night began alternating faster and faster until they were indistinguishable. After a while, the laboratory vanished—he assumed that the house had been pulled down. All changes in the sky blended, and the sun shot across so fast that it became an arch of light, swaying back and forth with the seasons. At ever shortening intervals, the green of spring and summer covered the hillside where his house had stood and then faded in winter. Other buildings appeared and disappeared, and the green became permanent, with no wintry intermission. He might reasonably have stopped, only he was apprehensive. What if some solid object were in the space that the Time Machine would occupy when it came to rest? While he pondered the question, its acceleration was driving it headlong through myriads of years. At last, he did bring it to a halt. It toppled over and had to be righted. He was in a violent hailstorm with low visibility and could see only grass underfoot and what looked like rhododendron bushes. The dials showed that the year was 802,701.

When the storm passed and the sun came out, he took stock of his surroundings. He was on a lawn in front of a colossal white statue of a winged sphinx. This had bronze doors in its base and presumably some sort of chamber inside, but the doors were shut. All around was an endless, beautiful garden. Great buildings stood among masses of unfamiliar flowers. Several humans approached along a path. They were hardly more than four feet tall. Both sexes—not easy to tell apart—were well proportioned, good-looking, and colorfully dressed, but they had an air of fragility. They did not speak English, and at first communication was minimal. The Time Traveler learned later that these people were called Eloi, a name that conveyed nothing.

So that he could leave the Time Machine with no risk of anyone else working it, he detached two small essential levers and put them in his pocket. With his retreat secured, he allowed the group to escort him into a nearby building. Many more Eloi were assembled in a hall, eating fruit. One thing that struck him almost at once was their lack of curiosity. He was much taller and obviously different, yet after a few minutes' inspection, most of them took no further interest in him. They all gave a general impression of mental nullity, and as time passed in their company, this did not change. With some difficulty, he explained his wish to talk. A few cooperated, teaching him their language, though they got bored quickly, and the lessons had to be short. The language was simple, and he picked up a fair number of words.

The Eloi lived in a gentle, easygoing style. They laughed and sang and danced, they decorated each other with flowers, they bathed in a river, they made love with no apparent intensity, and they never seemed to do much else. The buildings where they gathered had a sadly neglected look, and the great surrounding garden showed little sign of tending. They had no objection to the Time Traveler wandering among them, eating fruit as they did, and exploring the neighborhood; they asked him no questions. When he asked them questions himself, he failed to get enlightening answers.

He made one friend, of a sort—a little person called Weena whom he saved from drowning. Gender differentiation was so slight that he had his doubts, but he decided that Weena was female. Henceforth, she followed him everywhere, showing a childlike and sexless affection and alleviating his loneliness without being more informative than the others.

He supposed that this pretty and empty society was the result of a too-complete triumph of civilization. Long ago, every problem had been solved, every need had been met, every disease had been abolished. Most work had ceased to be necessary. Deprived of all challenges, humanity had sunk into a complacent decline. He was to learn that while this was part of the truth, it was only part. Quite early, in fact, he noticed something that seemed inconsistent. The Eloi were not totally carefree. They were afraid of the dark, slept together in large groups, and avoided going out at night.

Meanwhile, he was having to cope with a crisis. The Time Machine had vanished from the lawn below the White Sphinx. After a moment of panic, he investigated. Inspection of the turf showed that it had been dragged inside. The bronze doors must have been opened and closed again when it was safely in. He battered them without making much impression and saw that he would need something like a crowbar to force them. The feeble, incurious Eloi would never have done this. It was borne in upon him that he had other neighbors. Several times, he caught glimpses of white, apelike figures, and he began wondering about some shafts that went down into the earth; sounds drifted up them from below. When he tried to ask about them, the Eloi were not only uncommunicative but shocked, and the same happened when he asked about the White Sphinx. There was evidently some connection.

To Weena's horror, he climbed down one of the shafts to explore, using rungs attached to the side. At a considerable depth, he found his way into a tunnel that led to a cavern. Lighting a match, he saw repellent, pallid hominids with strange eyes—the apelike figures, in fact. He also glimpsed machines and a table with hunks of meat on it. The creatures could evidently see in the dark or whatever minimal light reached the cavern, but when some of them pressed close and threatened him, he found that he could hold them off by lighting more matches; their eyes were not equal to even that much extra illumination. He shook them off and climbed back to the surface, having used up most of his matches.

To judge from the number of shafts that dotted the landscape, these beings occupied a large network of subterranean spaces. He had no doubt that it was some of them who had come up inside the White Sphinx and hauled the Time Machine into it. However, he learned little more about them, except that they were called Morlocks. To account for them, he theorized further, revising his first notion drastically and inferring what had happened from the class structure of the society he lived in himself. On the one hand were the wealthy—the big property owners, the landed gentry, the capitalists. On the other were the millions of workers, many housed in slums and close to the poverty line. Reformers and Socialists had talked of closing the gap but (he guessed) unsuccessfully. The Haves and the Have-nots grew more different, not less. Over countless generations, the social classes diverged and evolved into two distinct species.

The Eloi were descendants of the Haves, leading a futile existence and living on the bounty of an improved Nature. Intelligence and initiative had long since withered. The Morlocks were descendants of the Have-nots, driven down out of the sunlight but surviving. They still had machinery. They were carnivorous. There were no domestic animals to supply meat, therefore . . . yes. On dark nights, they raided the upper world, carried off Eloi, and ate them. Perhaps they preserved them, even bred them. The Eloi yielded supinely to the situation. Now the Time Traveler knew why they were afraid of the dark. They would never have told him themselves. They blocked the Morlocks out mentally, as well as they could, and considered it bad form to mention them.

Aghast at the emerging reality, he needed to act. He had seen, several miles away, a palatial green building different from the others. This might be a refuge while he found a method of making fire to overawe the Morlocks and a suitable implement for breaking open the doors of the White Sphinx. Weena insisted on being with him, and they walked together to the green building. It was largely ruined but was recognizably a museum, with remains of extinct animals, mineral exhibits, ancient machines, and even decaying scraps of books. By a remarkable stroke of luck, he found a box of matches and a piece of camphor he could use as a candle. He disconnected a lever from one of the machines and kept it for his attack on the doors.

Abandoning the refuge idea, since there were traces of Morlocks in the museum, he headed for home territory through a wood. Weena was still with him. Night fell, and he lit a fire, which got out of control and set some of the trees ablaze. A crowd of Morlocks was gathering, and only their demoralization in the glare prevented a mass onslaught. As it was, he had to fight. They drew

back, but Weena was gone. Though they had probably not taken her for slaughtering, his grief was profound.

He returned to the White Sphinx with his iron bar ready and was surprised to find the doors open. Stepping inside he saw the Time Machine intact but with traces of tampering. The Morlocks had been trying to understand it. Now they obviously intended to trap him, and as he expected, the doors closed. The pale hominids were approaching and laying their hands on him. He escaped by starting the Time Machine and plunging off into an even more distant future.

His experience was not over. He could have stopped and returned, but the mystery of the world's fate lured him on. Advancing in ever-growing strides and pausing at intervals of thousands and eventually millions of years, he saw no revival of humanity; the last vestiges faded out. The sky darkened, and the sun became red and huge. He was on a desolate beach overlooking a dreary sea. The only visible creatures on it were giant crabs, and after further leaps ahead, these too were gone.

More than thirty million years into the future, he still saw no fundamental change. The red sun had grown enormous, the sky was darker, the air was colder, and the silence was terrible. Was he at least witnessing the end of life? Then, he looked at a sandbank across the water, and there was movement on it. A round black object with trailing tentacles was hopping fitfully about. Somehow, this alien Thing was beyond bearing. With his great questions unanswered, he put the Time Machine into reverse and came back. At last, buildings took shape again, his home materialized around him, and he was in his laboratory. Not quite at his starting point. Because the Morlocks had moved the Time Machine, it was now in another part of the room.

That is the substance of the Time Traveler's story. As his only evidence, he produces two white flowers that the playful Weena dropped into his pocket. Someone examines them and admits that they are botanically odd. He shows his guests the Time Machine, which certainly looks the worse for wear, but with one hesitant exception, they are incredulous. To support his claims, he sets out soon afterward on a fresh expedition, with a camera and other equipment. He indisputably vanishes, and so does the Time Machine, but they never reappear.

See also: Forster, E. M.; Prophecy, Theories of
Further Reading
Wells, H. G. *Experiment in Autobiography,* 2 vols. London: Victor Gollancz, 1934.

WITCHCRAFT

A collection of magical practices that came to inspire hostile views about prophecy, exemplified in two plays by Shakespeare.

Witches, meaning women credited with magical powers, have existed from time immemorial. In medieval Europe, most were individual practitioners, often old and solitary. Some, such as village wisewomen and healers, were more or less approved or at least tolerated. A reputed ability to see the future could give them status as fortune-tellers. With others, the popular image was sinister, owing to superstitions about the evil eye and malignant spell casting. But they were not seen as particularly important or as a threat to society. Dante, in his account of hell, imagines some as resident there, but he dismisses them in three lines, scornfully and anonymously. They are "wretched women" who have neglected ordinary household tasks to occupy themselves with wax images and potions. Stories of medieval witch-hunts are almost wholly fictitious; there was not the motivation.

However, the last part of the fifteenth century brought a change in beliefs and attitudes, leading to a paranoid witch mania and a persecution lasting for more than 200 years. One major factor was a papal pronouncement in 1484. Witchcraft was given a new diabolic meaning and extended to involve both sexes. Where the delusion flourished, the dominant opinion, both Catholic and Protestant, was that magical activities in general were elements in a vast conspiracy run by the devil and his minions, for the affliction of humanity and the ruin of souls. Now, a witch meant anyone supposedly taking part in this conspiracy. The conception could cover witchcraft in the old sense, including fortune-telling, but it covered a great deal more besides. Witches, once isolated, were now thought to conspire together by flying (on broomsticks or otherwise) to mass gatherings where they met the Evil One for unhallowed rites.

The first witch-hunters' handbook was a volume entitled *Malleus Maleficarum,* the Hammer of Witches, by two priests of the Dominican order. They described the ways in which Satan's host of demons could operate through consenting humans—usually women, but not necessarily—enabling them to work all manner of mischief. In that belief, as it would presently be developed, suspects were tortured until they confessed to satanic dealings and then put to death. Those who condemned them could cite the Bible, which contains such injunctions as "Thou shalt not suffer a witch to live." The overall total has often been wildly exaggerated, but it remains terrible. It was probably 40,000 or 50,000, perhaps 10,000 of them being male.

Despite this figure, it should not be thought that persecution was universal or continuous. Eastern Europe was free from it. England, with several hundred killed, suffered far less severely than Germany or Switzerland. Scotland was more witch-conscious, and its king James VI considered himself an expert on the subject, a notion that had literary consequences.

In that context, an opinion laid down by Saint Augustine in the fifth century, and now revived, affected ideas of prophecy. Among witches' unholy deeds in the *Malleus* survey

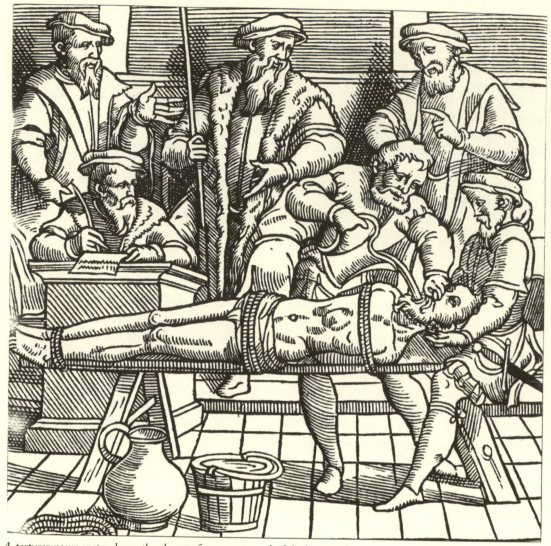

A torturer pours water down the throat of a man accused of dealings with Satan: one of various methods of extracting confessions. (Dover Pictorial Series)

is that they "show to others occult things and certain future events, by the information of devils." The authors recognize, as Augustine does, that foresight may have a natural cause and may be due simply to intelligent anticipation. But when witches, "by the information of devils," reveal the future, it will be to lead others astray and to do harm. If anyone relies on such forecasts, only misfortune can come of it. Though the authors of the Old Testament knew nothing of the devil or the diabolic view of witchcraft, it supplied at least one justification. When Saul tries to learn his future from the witch of Endor, it is made quite clear that his action is wrong.

Shakespeare twice illustrates these notions. He confronts the prophetic issue in a very early play, *Henry VI*, part 1. Much of the action takes place in France, where territory conquered by Henry V is being lost. The French recovery is inspired by La Pucelle, Joan of Arc, and since an Elizabethan audience would not have relished a presentation of English defeat, Shakespeare attributes

Joan's success to witchcraft in the contemporary sense. She makes a pretense of holiness but is, in fact, evil, with preternatural powers bestowed on her by fiends whom she addresses as

Ye choice spirits that admonish me
And give me signs of future accidents.

This is close to *Malleus Maleficarum*. When the fiends desert her, she comes to an ignominious end.

Shakespeare did not return to the subject until 1606 or thereabouts, when he wrote *Macbeth*. King James of Scotland had become king of England also, and his London establishment included a company of players. Shakespeare was one of them, and he probably wrote *Macbeth* for performance at court. It is about a Scottish monarch in the eleventh century whose story, or legend, involved prophecies. Dramatizing it, Shakespeare had to take account of his royal patron's interest in witchcraft. According to the chronicle that he used, before Macbeth was king his accession to the throne was foretold by a trio of mysterious women, possibly fairy-folk. The success of this prediction led him, long afterward, to trust promises by soothsayers that lured him to his downfall.

In Shakespeare's treatment, the three prophetesses become witches as pictured in his own time, with demonic "masters," and they have a continuing role using prophecy to ruin Macbeth. First, the promise of kingship impels him to fulfil it himself by murdering the present king and seizing the crown. His dreadful crime leads to others. He has no peace of mind, and when he suspects that enemies may act against him, he seeks out the witches, or "weird sisters" as Shakespeare calls them: he is "bent to know, by the worst means, the worst." At this second encounter their fiendish masters, speaking through apparitions, make predictions that apparently assure him of safety. Their words are ambiguous, but, believing that these beings "know all mortal consequences," Macbeth takes them at face value. Realizing the truth too late, he is overthrown and killed. In the play, the old story has acquired a theme of diabolic corruption and deception through prophecy, which belongs to the fantasies of witch-theorists like King James. Macbeth is the only Shakespearean tragic hero who ends in damnation and despair.

It need not be assumed that Shakespeare subscribed to the witch mania himself. His plays show no traces of it except in these two cases where the motif is functional. A later dramatist, Goethe, brings demonized witchcraft into his version of the story of Faust, with swarms of witches flying to meet their hellish masters on Walpurgis Night. Yet he lived long after the witch mania was over and certainly did not believe such things literally. Nevertheless, in defiance of all enlightenment, the sinister mythology still affects popular images of witches, even comic ones.

See also: Augustine, Saint; *Macbeth*

Further Reading

Cohn, Norman. *Europe's Inner Demons.* London: Paladin, 1976.

Sharpe, James. *Instruments of Darkness.* London: Hamish Hamilton, 1996.

Sprenger, Jacobus, and Heinrich Kramer. *Malleus Maleficarum.* Translated by Montague Summers and edited by Pennethorne Hughes. London: The Folio Society, 1968.

ZAMYATIN, YEVGENY (1884–1937)

Russian author of a dystopia, *We,* which influenced Aldous Huxley's *Brave New World* and George Orwell's *Nineteen Eighty-Four.*

By professional training, Zamyatin was a naval architect. During World War I, he spent some time in England supervising the construction of ten ice-breaking vessels for Russian use. Back in his homeland in 1917, he gave qualified support to the revolution that broke out that year but soon became disquieted by the course it was taking. He wrote stories, plays, and literary criticism, including studies of H. G. Wells, whom he translated, and gave courses in creative writing that fostered younger talents. However, he was one of the first Russian authors to get in trouble with the ruling Communist Party. In 1931, after enduring many attacks, he wrote a long letter of protest to Stalin himself, asking that he might at least be allowed to leave Russia. The novelist Maxim Gorky put in a word for him, and he went into voluntary exile, dying a few years later in Paris.

We, his fantasy of the future, was written as early as 1920 and refused publication in Russia. It appeared abroad in translation from 1924 onward. More truly prophetic than the novels by Huxley and Orwell, it foreshadowed the betrayal of the revolution by Stalin's dictatorship long before it happened.

The title refers to the total collectivism of a time when The One State, worldwide, has been developing for 1,000 years. Everything must now be thought of in terms of *we;* theoretically, no *I* exists except as a unit in the collective. The setting is the principal city of The One State. The inhabitants have numbers, not names, and all live by the same schedule, laid down by the Hourly Commandments. Buildings are transparent so that the State police, the Guardians, can keep the occupants under observation, and a surrounding wall shuts out the world of nature. Food is a chemical compound. State-controlled sexual promiscuity on fixed days, regulated by ticket, has replaced love and marriage. Everyone is sexually available to everyone else (Huxley adapts this phrase in *Brave New World*). Anyone judged to have infringed the State's rules is asphyxiated under a huge bell jar.

At the summit is an awe-inspiring dictator, The Benefactor. He stands regularly for reelection on a Day of Unanimity, but no one ever votes against him. He personally executes persons whom he chooses to execute by a machine that liquidates them—literally.

The ultimate inspiration of the system is stated to have come from Frederick Winslow Taylor, the U.S. engineer who invented "scientific management," including time study, motion study, and other techniques of efficiency. (In *Brave New World,* the counterpart is Taylor's younger contemporary Henry Ford.) The guiding principle is that humanity can have liberty *or* happiness but not both, and The One State has long since opted for happiness, or what is regarded as happiness.

Zamyatin's narrator is a mathematician, D-503, whose mathematical obsessions pervade his whole life. He is in charge of the building of a rocket-powered spaceship, the Integral. (Russians were ahead of the West in theorizing about rocket propulsion.) He is thrown off balance by a mysterious and alluring woman, E-330. She turns out to be a leader of a subversive group called the

Mephis. They make a breach in the city's surrounding wall, and D-503 discovers that there are humans in the wild country outside. The plotters have notions of capturing the Integral. D-503 protests at their "madness," and E-330 replies that madness is the key to salvation. When the Benefactor is re-elected, many of them are in the audience and actually express dissent. Their votes, of course, are disallowed without even being counted.

Meanwhile, The One State's scientists, aware that the citizens are still not completely mechanized, have found how to make them fully equal to machines by the surgical abolition of "fantasy"—more properly, imagination. The operation is made compulsory, and when D-503 undergoes it, he is freed from irrational misgivings: he betrays E-330 and her associates, "the enemies of happiness," and sits beside the Benefactor with equanimity as they are tortured. Orwell echoes this conclusion in the last sentence of *Nineteen Eighty-Four*, when Winston Smith "loves Big Brother." "Rationality," says D-503 in Zamyatin's last sentence, "must conquer."

See also: Huxley, Aldous; Orwell, George; Wells, H. G.

Further Reading

Carey, John, ed. *The Faber Book of Utopias*. London: Faber and Faber, 1999.

Zamyatin, Yevgeny. *We*. English translation by Bernard Guilbert Guerney, with Introduction and Bibliographical Note by Michael Glenny. London: Jonathan Cape, 1970.

ZEVI, SABBATAI

See Sabbatai Zevi

BIBLIOGRAPHY

Amery, Colin. *New Atlantis: The Secret of the Sphinx*. London and New York: Regency Press, 1976.

Ashe, Geoffrey. *Atlantis: Lost Lands, Ancient Wisdom*. London: Thames and Hudson, 1992.

———. *Avalonian Quest*. London: Methuen, 1982.

———. *The Book of Prophecy*. London: Blandford, 1999.

———. *Camelot and the Vision of Albion*. London: Heinemann, 1971, and New York: St. Martin's Press, 1971.

———. *Dawn behind the Dawn*. New York: Henry Holt, 1992.

———. *King Arthur: The Dream of a Golden Age*. London: Thames and Hudson, 1990.

———. *The Land and the Book*. London: Collins, 1965.

———. *Land to the West*. London: Collins, 1965, and New York: Viking, 1962.

———. *The Landscape of King Arthur*. Exeter, England: Webb and Bower, 1987.

———. *Mythology of the British Isles*. London: Methuen, 1990.

Augustine, Saint. *The City of God*. Translated by Henry Bettenson. Harmondsworth, England: Penguin Classics, 1984.

Bander, Peter. *The Prophecies of St. Malachy*. Rockford, IL: Tan Books, 1973.

Baring-Gould, S. *Antichrist and Pope Joan*. Caerfyrddin, Wales: Unicorn, 1975.

Barker, Ernest. *From Alexander to Constantine*. Oxford: Clarendon Press, 1956.

Bate, H. N. *The Sibylline Oracles, Books III–IV*. London: Society for the Promotion of Christian Knowledge, 1918.

Blavatsky, H. P. *Isis Unveiled*. 2 vols. Pasadena, CA: Theosophical University Press, 1972.

———. *The Secret Doctrine*. 2 vols. Pasadena, CA: Theosophical University Press, 1970.

Boorstin, Daniel J. *The Discoverers*. New York: Vintage Books, 1985.

Bowder, Diana. *The Age of Constantine and Julian*. London: Paul Elek, 1978.

Boyde, Patrick. *Dante: Philomythes and Philosopher*. Cambridge: Cambridge University Press, 1981.

Bramwell, James. *Lost Atlantis*. London: Cobden-Sanderson, 1937.

Bro, Harmon Hartzell. *Edgar Cayce*. Wellingborough, England: The Aquarian Press, 1990.

Brodie, Fawn M. *No Man Knows My History: The Life of Joseph Smith*. London: Eyre and Spottiswood, 1963.

Broughton, Richard. *Parapsychology*. New York: Ballantine, 1991.

Brown R. E., J. A. Fitzmyer, and R. E. Murphy, eds. *The New Jerome Biblical Commentary*. Englewood Cliffs, NJ: Prentice-Hall, 1990.

Burland, C. A. *The Ancient Maya*. London: Weidenfeld and Nicolson, 1967.

Campbell, Eileen, and J. H. Brennan. *The Aquarian Guide to the New Age*. Wellingborough, England: The Aquarian Press, 1990.

Campion, Nicholas, and Steve Eddy. *The New Astrology*. London: Bloomsbury, 1999.

Carey, John, ed. *The Faber Book of Utopias*. London: Faber and Faber, 1999.

Cavendish, Richard, ed. *Man, Myth and Magic*. London: BPC Publishing, 1970–1972.

Cazotte, Jacques. *The Devil in Love*. Translated by Stephen Sartarelli. New York: Marsilio, 1993.

Cervé, W. S. *Lemuria: The Lost Continent of the Pacific*. San Jose, CA: Rosicrucian Library, 1982.

Cheiro. *Cheiro's Language of the Hand*. London: Corgi, 1967.

Cohn, Norman. *Europe's Inner Demons*. London: Paladin, 1976.

———. *The Pursuit of the Millennium*. London: Paladin, 1970.

Collins, Andrew. *Gateway to Atlantis*. London: Headline, 2000.

Coren, Michael. *Gilbert: The Man Who Was G. K. Chesterton*. London: Jonathan Cape, 1989.

Crossley, Robert. *Olaf Stapledon: Speaking for the Future*. Liverpool University Press, 1994.

Décote, Georges. *L'Itinéraire de Jacques Cazotte*. Geneva: Librairie Droz, 1984.

Dick, Oliver Lawson. *Aubrey's Brief Lives*. London: Secker and Warburg, 1971.

Dictionary of American Biography.

Dictionary of National Biography (British).

Dixon, Jeane. *My Life and Prophecies*. London: Frederick Muller, 1971.

Dodds, E. R. *The Greeks and the Irrational*. Berkeley: University of California Press, 1951.

Douglas, Alfred. *The Tarot*. London: Victor Gollancz, 1972.

Dunne, J. W. *An Experiment with Time*. Revised and enlarged edition. London: Faber and Faber, 1938.

Early Irish Myths and Sagas. Translated by Jeffrey Gantz. Harmondsworth, England: Penguin Books, 1981.

Eliade, Mircea. *Shamanism*. Boston: Routledge and Kegan Paul, 1964.

Encyclopaedia Britannica. 15th edition. Chicago, 1998.

The Encyclopedia of Islam.

Folklore, Myths and Legends of Britain. London: Readers Digest Association, 1973.

Geoffrey of Monmouth. *The History of the Kings of Britain*. Translated by Lewis Thorpe. Harmondsworth, England: Penguin Books, 1966.

Gill, Anton. *A Dance between Flames*. London: John Murray, 1993.

Gould, Rupert T. *Oddities: A Book of Unexplained Facts*. London: Philip Allan, 1928.

Grabsky, Phil. *The Lost Temple of Java*. London: Orion, 1999.

Grant, Michael. *Cleopatra*. London: Pantheon Books, 1974.

———. *Nero*. New York: Dorset Press, 1989.

Graves, Robert. *The Greek Myths*. 2 vols. New York: Penguin Books, 1960.

Gribbin, John. *Time Warps*. London: J. M. Dent, 1979.

Guthrie, W. K. C. *The Greeks and Their Gods*. New York: Methuen, 1950.

The High Book of the Grail (i.e., *Perlesvaus*). Translated by Nigel Bryant. Cambridge: D. S. Brewer, and Totowa, NJ: Rowman & Littlefield, 1978.

Holroyd, Michael. *Bernard Shaw*. Vol. 3. New York: Random House, 1991.

Howe, Ellic. *Urania's Children*. London: William Kimber, 1967.

Hoyle, Peter. *Delphi*. London: Cassell, 1967.

Isserlin, B. S. J. *The Israelites*. London: Thames and Hudson, 1998.

Jacoff, Rachel, ed. *The Cambridge Companion to Dante*. Cambridge: Cambridge University Press, 1993.

Jewish Encyclopaedia. New York and London: Funk and Wagnalls, 1901–1906.

Kastein, Joseph. *The Messiah of Ismir: Sabbatai Zevi*. Translated by Huntley Paterson. New York: Viking Press, 1931.

Knox, Ronald Arbuthnott. *Enthusiasm; A Chapter in the History of Religion, with Special Reference to the XVII and XVIII Centuries*. New York: Oxford University Press, 1950.

Koestler, Arthur. *Arrow in the Blue.* London: Collins, with Hamish Hamilton, 1952.

Krauss, Lawrence M. *The Physics of* Star Trek. London: HarperCollins, 1996.

Lacy, Norris J., ed. *The New Arthurian Encyclopedia.* New York and London: Garland, 1991.

Leoni, Edgar. *Nostradamus and His Prophecies.* New York: Bell Publishing Company, 1982.

Lewis, C. S. *The Discarded Image.* Cambridge: Cambridge University Press, 1964.

Lindblom, J. *Prophecy in Ancient Israel.* Oxford: Basil Blackwell, 1962.

Loomis, Roger Sherman, ed. *Arthurian Literature in the Middle Ages.* Oxford: Clarendon Press, 1959.

The Mahabharata. Translated and edited by J. A. B. van Buitenen. Vol. 2. Chicago: University of Chicago Press, 1973–1978.

Manuel, Frank E. *A Portrait of Isaac Newton.* Cambridge, MA: Harvard University Press, 1968.

Martindale, C. C. *The Message of Fatima.* London: Burns Oates and Washbourne, 1950.

McGinn, Bernard. *Visions of the End: Apocalyptic Traditions in the Middle Ages.* New York: Columbia University Press, 1979.

Melville, John. *Crystal Gazing.* Reprint. New York: Weiser, 1970.

Milton, John. *Christian Doctrine.* Translated by John Carey. In *Complete Works of John Milton.* Vol. 6. New Haven, CT: Yale University Press, 1973.

Montgomery, Ruth. *A Gift of Prophecy.* New York: Bantam, 1967.

Mother Shipton. Reprint of anonymous booklet. Bath, England: West Country Editions, 1976.

Nethercot, Arthur H. *The Last Four Lives of Annie Besant.* London: Rupert Hart-Davis, 1963.

The New Catholic Encyclopedia. Washington, DC: Catholic University of America, 1969.

North, Christopher R. *The Second Isaiah.* Oxford: Oxford University Press, 1962.

Ossendowski, Ferdinand. *Beast, Men and Gods.* London: Edward Arnold, 1922.

Pegis, Anton, ed. *Basic Writings of Saint Thomas Aquinas.* Vol. 1. New York: Random House, 1945.

Piggott, Stuart. *The Druids.* London: Thames and Hudson, 1985.

Pile, Stephen. *The Return of Heroic Failures.* London: Penguin Books, 1989. Sequel to *The Book of Heroic Failures.*

Pritchard, James, B., ed. *Ancient Near Eastern Texts Relating to the Old Testament.* Princeton, NJ: Princeton University Press, 1955.

Rees, Alwyn, and Brinley Rees. *Celtic Heritage.* London: Thames and Hudson, 1961.

Reeves, Marjorie. *The Influence of Prophecy in the Later Middle Ages.* Notre Dame: University of Notre Dame Press, 1993.

———. *Joachim of Fiore and the Prophetic Future.* New York: Harper and Row, 1977.

Reeves, Marjorie, ed. *Prophetic Rome in the High Renaissance Period.* Oxford: Clarendon Press, 1992.

Roerich, Nicholas. *Altai-Himalaya.* London: Jarrolds, 1930.

Sargent, H. N. *The Marvels of Bible Prophecy.* London: Covenant Publishing Company, 1938.

Sayers, Dorothy L. *Introductory Papers on Dante.* London: Methuen, 1954.

Schom, Alan. *Napoleon Bonaparte.* New York: HarperCollins, 1997.

Sharpe, James. *Instruments of Darkness.* London: Hamish Hamilton, 1996.

Sprenger, Jacobus, and Heinrich Kramer. *Malleus Maleficarum.* Translated by Montague Summers and edited by Pennethorne Hughes. London: The Folio Society, 1968.

Stewart, Desmond. *Theodor Herzl.* London: Hamish Hamilton, 1974.

Suetonius. *The Lives of the Twelve Caesars.* Translated by Joseph Gavorse. New York: Modern Library, 1931.

Sugden, John. *Tecumseh*. New York: Henry Holt, 1998.

Swete, Henry Barclay. *The Apocalypse of St. John*. London: Macmillan, 1907.

The Tain. Translated by Thomas Kinsella. Oxford: Oxford University Press, 1969.

Taylor, Paul B., and W. H. Auden, eds. and trans. *The Elder Edda*. London: Faber and Faber, 1969.

Todd, Ruthven. *Tracks in the Snow*. London: The Grey Walls Press, 1946.

Toland, John. *Adolf Hitler*. 2 vols. New York: Doubleday, 1976.

Trevor-Roper, Hugh. *The Last Days of Hitler*. London: Macmillan, 1947.

Turville-Petre, E. O. G. *Myths and Religion of the North*. London: Weidenfeld and Nicolson, 1964.

Unzer, Egbert. *Solovyev*. London: Hollis and Carter, 1956.

Wade, Wyn Craig. *The Titanic: End of a Dream*. New York: Penguin Books USA, 1986.

Walker, Patrick. *Six Saints of the Covenant*. Edited by D. Hay Fleming and S. R. Crockett. Vol. 1. London: Hodder and Stoughton, 1901.

Wallechinsky, David, Amy Wallace, and Irving Wallace. *The Book of Predictions*. New York: William Morrow, 1980.

Ward, Maisie. *Gilbert Keith Chesterton*. London: Sheed and Ward, 1944.

Watt, Diana. *Secretaries of God: Women Prophets in Late Medieval and Early Modern England*. Cambridge: D. S. Brewer, 1997.

Wells, H. G. *Experiment in Autobiography*. 2 vols. London: Victor Gollancz, 1934.

West, R. B. *The Kingdom of the Saints*. New York: Viking Press, 1957.

Whyte, Frederick. *The Life of W. T. Stead*. 2 vols. London: Jonathan Cape, 1925.

Wilson, Colin. *The Occult*. London: Hodder and Stoughton, 1971.

Zamyatin, Yevgeny. *We*. English translation by Bernard Guilbert Guerney, with an introduction and bibliographical note by Michael Glenny. London: Jonathan Cape, 1970.

INDEX

ABOUT THE AUTHOR

Geoffrey Ashe is an author, lecturer, and independent scholar. Born in London, he was educated at the University of British Columbia (B.A.) and Cambridge University (B.A., M.A.). His twenty-six books include the recent *Book of Prophecy* (1999), the culmination of a lifelong interest in prophetic phenomena. Widely known as an authority on early British myth and history (*Mythology of the British Isles, Kings and Queens of Early Britain*), he was cofounder of the Camelot Research Committee, a turning point in dark-age archaeological discoveries, and has long been respected in international Arthurian circles. His books explore topics that range from the history of Glastonbury (his first major work, *King Arthur's Avalon*), to pre-Columbian explorations of North America (*Land to the West, the Quest for America,* coauthored with Thor Hyerdahl), to the life of Gandhi; from the lost Atlantis to the Hell-Fire Club of West Wycombe; from the Virgin Mary to myths and origins of the ancient goddess religions. His Arthurian books include *The Discovery of King Arthur* and *King Arthur: Dream of a Golden Age.* He is coauthor of *The Arthurian Encyclopedia* and *The Arthurian Handbook,* a standard reference work in American university courses. His career has included numerous visiting professorships at American and Canadian universities. He now resides in Glastonbury, England.